CONTRACT NEGOTIATION
HANDBOOK

Second edition

Contract Negotiation Handbook

Second edition

P. D. V. MARSH

A Gower Handbook

First published 1974 by Gower Press Limited, Epping, Essex.

Second edition published 1984 by
Gower Publishing Company Limited,
Gower House,
Croft Road,
Aldershot,
Hants GU11 3HR,
England

Reprinted 1987

British Library Cataloguing in Publication Data

Marsh, P. D. V.
    Contract negotiation hand book. – 2nd ed
1. Business 2. Contracts 3. Negotiation
I. Title
658   HF5353

ISBN 0-566-02403-9

Printed in Great Britain by
Redwood Burn Limited, Trowbridge, Wiltshire

CONTENTS

List of illustrations   ix

Introduction   1

PART ONE The background to planning

1   The planning process   11

2   Decision techniques   15
2.1   Choice under risk—the decision rules   15
2.2   Expected value   17
2.3   Utility under risk   21
2.4   The theory of games   26
2.5   Riskless utility   39

3   Establishment of the target objective   51
3.1   Statement of the target objective   52
3.2   Assessment by the negotiating team   52

4   Appraisal of the target objective and formulation of the negotiating objective   54
4.1   General   54
4.2   Bidding—competitive   55
4.3   Procurement   75
4.4   Contract dispute   86

5   Strategy selection   101
5.1   The first offer—bidding and procurement   101
5.2   Contract dispute   112

6   The level of the first offer   120
6.1   Bid submission   121
6.2   Procurement   173
6.3   Contract dispute   177

7   **The psychology of negotiation**   190
7.1   Personalistic objectives   190
7.2   Conflict and adjustment in the negotiator's motivation   205
7.3   The negotiator's belief pattern   206
7.4   Personality interaction between negotiators   210

PART TWO Organisation and administration

8   **The negotiating environment**   225
8.1   Identifying all issues which may be relevant   226
8.2   Selection of those issues relevant to the negotiation   230
8.3   Acquisition of detailed knowledge of relevant issues   232
8.4   Deciding on how strategic planning should take environmental issues into account   232
8.5   Selection of appropriate tactics and the negotiating team   233

9   **The negotiating team**   235
9.1   Character and composition of the team   235
9.2   Appointment and duties of the team leader   241
9.3   Visits by senior personnel   244

10   **Communication and security**   246
10.1   Communication   246
10.2   Security   250

11   **The negotiating brief**   254
11.1   The negotiating objective   255
11.2   Minimum acceptable terms   256
11.3   Time period for negotiations   256
11.4   The negotiating team   257
11.5   Communications and reporting   257

12   **The negotiating plan**   259
12.1   Definition of initial strategy   259
12.2   Supporting arguments   260
12.3   Supporting data   261
12.4   The location of the negotiations   261
12.5   Administrative arrangements   262

13   **Conducting the rehearsal**   264
13.1   Value of the rehearsal   264

PART THREE Structure and sequence of the negotiation

14	**The approach**	267
14.1	Stages of the negotiation	267
15	**The opening**	269
15.1	Written proposal/answer without discussion	269
15.2	Written poposal/answer supplemented by verbal discussion	271
15.3	Verbal proposals only	273
15.4	Conclusions	274
15.5	Exposing the negotiating area	274
16	**Review of the opening**	279
16.1	Bargain immediately identifiable	279
16.2	Bargain foreseeable	280
16.3	No bargain foreseeable	287
16.4	Supplementary notes	291
17	**The follow up**	296
17.1	Reappraisal of Opponent's concession factor	296
17.2	The influence of time	306
17.3	Threat strategy	308
17.4	The tactical effect of time	314
17.5	Modification of the negotiating objective	318
17.6	Making the next move	320
18	**Identifying the bargain**	328
18.1	Signalling to Opponent	328
18.2	Communication and coordination	331
18.3	Policy issues	337
19	**Concluding the bargain**	340
19.1	The final review	340
19.2	The final concession	340
19.3	Timing	341
19.4	Magnitude	341
19.5	Coupling	342
19.6	Ensuring agreement is genuine	342
19.7	Recording the bargain	343

PART FOUR Negotiating tactics

20	**Attitudinal tactics**	347

20.1   In the opening phase   348
20.2   In the later phases   353

21   Situation tactics   364
21.1   Offensive tactics   364
21.2   Defensive tactics   378

Epilogue   387

Appendix 1   Checklist of factors   388
Appendix 2   Resources required for bidding and contract   389
             execution
Appendix 3   Checklist: contract dispute   391
Appendix 4   Strategy choice reasoning   394
Appendix 5   Estimating succes probability in bidding,   397
             taking account of customer's non-price bias
Appendix 6   Data checklist   401

Index   405

ILLUSTRATIONS

1:1	The activity cycle	12
2:1	Expected value of an offer	18
2:2	Expected value of an offer may lead to a counter offer	19
2:3	Comparison of the expected value of two offers	23
2:4	Typical utility curves under risk	25
2:5	Example of self-replacing decision rule	27
2:6	Comparison of bid expected values	28
2:7	Comparison of two bid strategies	28
2:8	Strategy pay-off table	29
2:9	Example of zero-sum game with saddle point	30
2:10	Commercial example of zero-sum game	31
2:11	Example of zero-sum game, no saddle point	31
2:12	Example of non-zero-sum game	33
2:13	Commercial example of 'the prisoner's dilemma'	35
2:14	Example of non-zero-sum game–collaborative	36
2:15	The negotiating set	37
2:16	Commercial example of a game against nature	39
2:17	Example of preference ordering: riskless utility of price and delivery	41
2:18	Additive utility values for price and delivery	42
2:19	Revised additive utility values for price and delivery	44
4:1	Analysis of tendering costs, success ratio and return of sales for ABC plc, a mechanical engineering company	57
4:2	Bid desirability and success probability–independent and interdependent factors	60
4:3	Bid desirability questionnaire	62
4:4	Marked example using bid questionnaire	65
4:5	Point comparison between Party's bid and that of his competitors	67
4:6	Bid expected value	70
4:7	Table of actions to improve Party's success probability	71
4:8	Programme and time/resource chart	73
4:9	Network for procurement action	81
4:10	Cost/time evaluation table	82
4:11	Savings/cost trade-off graph	85

4:12   Activity/resource schedule   87
4:13   Decision tree: validity of contract and its   89
        enforceability
5:1   Strategy selection in relation to Party's state   102
        relative to Opponent
5:2   Comparison between offers of Party and Opponent   103
5:3   Strategy values—Party bidding in a state of   106
        uncertainty
5:4   Party's success probability for possible strategies   107
5:5   Expected value of Party's strategies   108
5:6   Purchaser's strategy choice   109
5:7   Matrix of supplier's and purchaser's strategy   111
        choice expected values
5:8   Pay off to purchaser of varying his strategy choice   112
        over a series of tenders
5:9   Expected value to Party of varying strategies in a situa- 118
        tion of contract dispute
6:1   Bidder's normal utility curve   125
6:2   Bidder's utility curve: poor order book   126
6:3   Outcomes between which Party is indifferent   127
6:4   Bidder's utility curves: full order book   128
6:5   Bidder's utility curve: poor order book and contractual   129
        risk
6:6   Graph of Party's success probability for a range of bids 131
6:7   Party's conditional success probability   132
6:8   Party's expected success probability   133
6:9   Expected utility to Party of a series of bids   135
6:10   Decision tree of possible outcomes to multiple bids   138
6:11   Utility curve: multiple bids   139
6:12   Expected utility value to party of a combination of two   140
        bids
6:13   Decision tree–Party's bid against competitor A   142
6:14   Utility curve for marketing manager   144
6:15   Expected utility values   144
6:16   Value to Party of possible outcomes to an initial offer, 159
        discounted to present value and taking time costs into
        account
6:17   Net and total gain curves   160
6:18   Additive utility values of price and time of agreement   163
6:19   Possible changes resulting from the presence of other   168
        competitors
6:20   Game theory matrix   169
6:21   Expected value of the lowest competitor's bid   170
6:22   Expected outcome to the purchaser arising from his   175
        initial response to the supplier's offer

6:23   Expected outcome to the purchaser of negotiating with   176
       more than one supplier
7:1   Approach-avoidance situation for the negotiator   205
10:1   Make up of selling price   248
15:1   Guide to negotiator's behaviour in the opening phase   275
16:1   The negotiating area: initial position   281
16:2   The negotiating area: after negotiation   282
16:3   Comparison of the value of concede and the expected   284
       value of not concede
16:4   Resistance points on price for Party and Opponent   285
17:1   Comparison between true and assumed concession   297
       factors
17:2   Decision problem: stay with present strategy or change   300
       to hard line
17:3   Decision tree–Opponent concedes less or slower than   304
       anticipated
17:4   Table of major items covered by the negotiation   320
17:5   Expected value of a series of possible strategies   321
18:1   Table of negotiating motives   332
20:1   The Nash solution   356
A:1   Bid price and utility values   395
A:2   Production comparison grid   397
A:3   Utility curves for the authority for each of Party's   399
       possible bids

INTRODUCTION

Negotiation is a dynamic process of adjustment by which two parties, each with their own objectives, confer together to reach a mutually satisfying agreement on a matter of common interest. This definition contains the essential themes which it is the purpose of this book to develop. The chosen field is that of commercial contracts whether for the sale or purchase of goods and services or the construction of engineering works. The area of labour relations is excluded although many of the concepts could be applied there, particularly the strategic and tactical bargaining moves as developed in Part Four.

A DYNAMIC PROCESS OF ADJUSTMENT

The process of negotiation takes place within a series of ascending time scales. First there is the short period during which the negotiator must prepare for, and execute, the initial approach. Then follows the period during which the parties must reach agreement for the common interest to be realised. During the third period the agreement itself operates and may give rise to the need for further negotiation. Finally there is the very extended period within which the parties contemplate a continuing commercial relationship and which, in certain instances, eg major equipment suppliers/contractors to the government and public utilities, can be regarded as infinite.

The first two short periods provide a discipline for the negotiators and significantly affect the value of the outcome. As Cross has stated 'If it did not matter when the parties agreed it would not matter whether or not they agreed at all'.[1]

The extended periods affect the attitudinal structure of the negotiation. Both parties know that the absolute value of any bargain reached is limited because of the opportunities provided in the subsequent administration of the contract or by other tenders to correct any serious out-of-balance. As a precedent, however, the bargain may be of significant value in the consequences which it possesses for the future, not only because of its actual terms, but also for the manner of its negotiation and its impact on human relationships. This point has been explicitly recognized as of major importance in labour negotiations, but is of equal significance in the field of commercial contracts in those instances where the element of a long-term continuing buyer/seller relationship is present.[2]

EACH PARTY'S OBJECTIVE

A party in setting the objective which he wishes to achieve from a negotiation will do so in relation to a level of aspiration which reflects the economic and social morality of the society within which he operates. 'Society' in this context may mean the particular business area with which the firm is concerned or the wider field of trade in general.

Society does not in general aim to ensure through regulation or religious teaching that commercial dealings are on 'fair terms' or at 'a just price' as was the case in England during the Middle Ages despite the passing of the somewhat mis-named 'unfair Contract Terms Act'.[3] Business firms are expected to be able to look after their own interests. However, the philosophical concept of 'fairness of trade', originated by the early Christian Church and stated so clearly by Thomas Aquinas, and the parallel teachings of the Qur'an,[4] remain and are of significance even today within many societies so that a criticism made by one negotiator that certain terms are 'unfair' will immediately provoke a response, even if it is only an indignant denial. The problem is that there is no objective definition of the term 'fair'. What is 'fair' to a client's evaluation committee may be considered as grossly 'unfair' by those whose bids are being evaluated. Within the negotiating situation no universal 'practice' exists to which reference can be made in deciding upon whether or not particular acts can be justified: there are no 'constitutive rules' of general application from which one can derive a moral 'ought', although such rules may exist in particular circumstances.[5]

Aside from morality the objective will take account of the economic structure within which the parties do business and the motivation of the individual negotiators. This latter will be directed internally within the party's own organization and externally towards the negotiators of the other side who, in many instances, they will know personally. Just because it is a microactivity, often resolving itself in the ultimate to bargaining between two persons, the process of contract negotiation is necessarily complex and there are three levels upon which the parties will interact.

The structural or economic level

For a particular negotiation this will generally be invariant although the structure itself may have been determined by the choice of one of the parties made in the prenegotiation state, eg by the buyer defining his requirements in such a manner that they can only be responded to by one supplier (see Section 4.3).

The corporate social level

The extent to which a firm as a matter of policy adopts aggressive maximizing behaviour, whether on sales or profits, will clearly affect the setting of the initial objective and of the minimum acceptable terms. This is an area in which the personality of the chief executive of the firm will have a decisive impact.

The personal social level of the negotiators

It would simplify our task if we could treat the firm and the individual negotiator as one and the same and ignore the role occupied by the negotiator within the on-going system of relationships between himself and other members of the firm, predominant among which is the dependent relationship between the negotiator and the dominant power group within the firm.[6] It is to this group which we are really referring when we speak of 'the firm' a point which must never be forgotten otherwise we shall commit the error of reification and assign to the firm as an entity personality characteristics which properly belong only to individuals. References to the 'firm' are only a convenient form of shorthand. The importance of recognizing these relationships is that the attractiveness of any particular bargain is likely to be different for the negotiator and for 'the firm' and it may be expected that the negotiators will bargain not only with each other but additionally with their own firms, even at times to the point of forming informal alliances between themselves, so as to frustrate what they regard as the 'the firm's' unreasonable behaviour.

The negotiators will also react to each other as personalities; they may be attracted or repelled. Personalistic objective setting is strongly influenced by the emotional feelings which Party has towards Opponent as a person, and this would appear to apply even when such feelings are derived solely from written evidence of Opponent's personality and the two negotiators have never met![7] Tactics by Party designed to minimize emotional antagonism or indifference, and to provide the environment for constructive problem solving are considered in Part Three.

MUTUALLY SATISFYING AGREEMENT ON A MATTER OF COMMON INTEREST

Where the interests of the parties directly conflict, eg in the price to be paid, so that the gain to one will result in less for the other, the bargaining will be referred to as *distributive*.[8] Each party will press for the attainment of its own goal. But some element of cooperation must be present otherwise there will be no agreement at all and the opportunity to take part in the activity will be lost. The dual elements of conflict and cooperation have been described by Siegel and Fouraker in the following terms. 'It is in the mutual interest of the participants to come to *some* agreement and this provides a cooperative aspect; however, given that an agreement will be achieved, the interests of the participants are opposed, and this is a basis for rivalry'.[9]

The negotiator is pulled in two directions at the same time; towards holding out for more with the risk of losing all; towards agreeing to his Opponent's demands, and securing the bargain, but in so doing possibly sacrificing the chance of a higher reward.

For each party there is an upper limit representing the bargain which he believes is the best he could possibly achieve, within the restrictions imposed by the bargaining structure, and a lower limit below which he would prefer not to participate. Provided that the upper limit of one of the parties lies between the upper and lower limits of the other, ie there is a degree of overlap between them, then a bargain is feasible. Whether it will be achieved or not, and if so at what point, are questions which will have to be considered (see Chapter 6). They involve the issues of how each party values a series of potential bargains and the process of anticipation and adjustment by which, over a span of time, the negotiators will tend to coordinate. Assuming that finally agreement is reached the result is compromise; neither is wholly satisfied but both recognize that it is more beneficial to them to agree than to disagree.

Negotiation, however, in the context with which we are concerned has as its end result the supply of goods/services or the construction of engineering works on a basis profitable to both parties. Merit exists therefore not just in making the bargain but in its proper fulfilment.

This should lead both parties to emphasize the cooperative nature of their relationship and to convert, as far as practicable, the issues dividing them into problems to be solved. By so doing the bargaining process is changed from distributive to integrative. This change completely alters the character of the bargaining process since it admits the possibility, which distributive bargaining does not, of introducing alternatives and of increasing the total benefits.[10]

An example would be negotiation over the period for delivery. The supplier offers say 12 months; the buyer wants the work completed in 10 months. Distributive bargaining would lead to a compromise, possibly 11 months, which might or might not be achieved. Integrative bargaining, however, would involve a joint examination of the problem by both parties to ascertain the holding factors, such as long lead items, special test and inspection procedures, etc, and a joint decision between them on these problems aimed at an optimum solution which was at the same time realistic. The finding and implementation of such a solution would be a 'superordinate' goal in Sherif's terminology. The following out of this concept can have fruitful consequences both for the immediate contract and for the future relationships between the parties, and will be reviewed later.[11]

SCOPE OF STUDY

It will be evident from this brief examination of the definition of negotiation that the subject encompasses more than one discipline in its total understanding. Economics can provide the basic framework; primarily through its treatment of bilateral monopoly. For the evaluation of a range of possible offers and the establishment of a formal structure for decision taking under risk, the related fields of operational analysis and game theory are examined. Finally because it is individuals who are involved, psychology is required to provide an insight into the personal motivational drives of the negotiators and the manner in which they will seek to satisfy these. To this is added a behavioural analysis, drawn from practical experience, of the strategies and tactics adopted in the field by negotiators.

Negotiation is treated not as an isolated event but as an integral part of the total business activity. Through the agreements negotiated the links are established in the chain by which goods are traded, services provided and facilities constructed. In this respect negotiation as a function is subservient to the general commercial interests of the parties involved and is directed towards the achievement of their overall objectives.

Success in negotiation is seen not to be measured therefore in points scored off one's opponent but in the contribution which the negotiation makes to the successful operation of the activity as a whole. This applies also within the negotiation itself. Each participating function must accept the need to modify its own demands as necessary to meet the requirements of the negotiating objective. There is shown to be no room in a negotiating team for the individual who insists on pursuing limited departmental interests to the detriment of his team's overall success.

PLAN OF STUDY

This study begins by emphasizing that success in negotiation depends primarily on the skill and care with which the negotiating plan is prepared. Part One describes the background to planning and introduces the theoretical concepts drawn from operations analysis and the theory of games. Utility values rather than monetary ones are used and the negotiator's objective is first stated in terms of limited maximization of subjective expected utility. Later it is shown how this is modified by the negotiator's own personal motivation.

Three negotiating situations are identified: bidding, procurement and contract dispute, and the factors relevant to the planning for each are worked out. The influence of time on the negotiation is analysed and a bargaining model developed for the initial demand which owes much to Cross.[1] It does not follow Cross completely in that it assumes a higher order of interaction between the bargainers and treats also the case where the negotiating time is bounded.

Part Two is severely practical. After examining the environment in which negotiation takes place it identifies the problems involved in the selection of the negotiating team and the duties which they are expected to perform. It considers the manner in which the negotiating team is first briefed by management and later how they prepare their own negotiating plan.

Parts Three and Four move to the negotiating table to review the stages through which the negotiations will pass, how the expectations of the parties will be adjusted and the tactics appropriate to each negotiating situation.

NOTES

1. J. G. Cross, *The Economics of Bargaining* (New York: Basic Books, 1969).
2. R. E. Walton and R. E. McKersie, *A Behavioural Theory of Labor Negotiations* (New York: McGraw Hill, 1965) p.3.
3. See, for example, the ancient offence of *forestalling,* the practice of buying up goods intended for the market with the object of putting up the price.
4. Thomas Aquinas, 'Summa theologica' in P. J. Glen, *A Tour of the Summa* (St. Louis: Herder Book Co., 1960), p.235. 'It is cheating to sell a thing at an exorbitant price... if a buyer takes advantage of a mistake or ignorance of a salesman to get superior goods for the price of inferior goods the buyer must make restitution... to make an unreasonably great profit by overcharging is cheating.'
5. Edward de Bono has pointed out that 'the Japanese businessman works on the principle that with two intelligent people negotiating one does not even try to deceive the other in contrast to the USA where sharp wheeling and dealing is a basic part of business'. *The Financial Times* (October 5 1971).
6. A. Coddington in his *Theory of the Bargaining Process* (London: George Allen and Unwin, 1968), p.6, assumes that the negotiators have as their objective the simple maximization of utility. He also implicitly draws no distinction between the negotiator as an individual and the firm. Thus 'If each party to the bargaining process is an organization rather than a single person we suppose that it acts in a perfectly coordinated way regarding its choice of a demand'.
7. See L. E. Siegel and S. Fouraker, *Bargaining Behaviour* (New York: McGraw Hill, 1963), pp. 65 and 66 for examples of such behaviour.
8. R. E. Walton and R. E. McKersie, op. cit., pp. 4 and 13.
9. L. E. Siegel and S. Fouraker, *Bargaining Behaviour* (New York: McGraw Hill, 1963) p.7.
10. R. E. Walton and R. E. McKersie, op. cit., pp. 127-28.

11. M. Sherif, *Group Conflict and Cooperation* (London: Routledge and Kegan Paul, 1968) p. 88 ff.

PART ONE
The background to planning

1

THE PLANNING PROCESS

The process of negotiation is one of progressive commitment. Depending on the tactics which Party adopts he will increase his commitment as the negotiation proceeds by one of the following two ways:

1   Continuing to repeat his initial offer, each repetition making it that much more difficult for the negotiator to concede without losing his reputation for firmness.
2   Moving towards Opponent so that with each move made the area remaining for further movement is automatically reduced. Only exceptionally will a negotiator be able to increase his area of movement by returning to, or withdrawing from, a position previously conceded whilst at the same time retaining his integrity.

Planning for negotiation is necessary therefore in order to ensure that:

1   The initial offer and the timing and extent of subsequent changes are in accordance with the degree to which the management of the company are willing to be committed.
2   At all stages the moves have been fully prepared for in advance, the facts established and the strategy selected.

In this activity, planning and action are partners not opposites; they are successive stages of a single process, the third stage of which, monitoring and review, completes the total cycle. This is illustrated in the activity cycle, Figure 1:1.

During a single negotiation this cycle will be repeated many times. The review and planning stages may be the subject of a formal review meeting held away from the negotiating arena, or a quick ten-minute adjournment part way through a negotiating session. Whatever their form the purpose of such meetings must be to satisfy the two requirements stated above. If these are not met then the negotiators should not continue or they will be drawn inevitably into the position of making unscheduled concessions or establishing unwanted precedents, from neither of which will it be possible for them later to withdraw. When afterwards called on to justify their actions the

11

negotiators may well recall the lines of W. H. Auden:

> Look in your heart for there lies the answer
> Though the heart like a clever conjuror or dancer
> Deceives you oft into many a curious sleight
> And motives like stowaways are found too late[1].

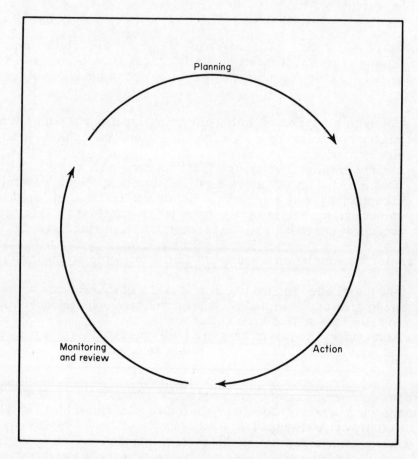

Figure 1:1 The activity cycle

The steps in the planning sequence are identified as follows:

1 Establishment of the target objective.
2 Appraisal of the target objective and validation of its acceptability as the objective for the negotiation.
3 Selection of the negotiating strategy for the first offer.

4 Choice of the level for the first offer.
5 Reconsideration of the first offer, following opponent's reaction, and decision on any adjustment either to level or negotiating strategy.

For any negotiation, steps 1–4 will be carried out only once and completed prior to entering into the phase of definitive commitment which is characterized by the submission of the first offer. Step 5, however, will be repeated at each stage in the negotiation until either agreement is reached or the negotiations are finally broken off.

A distinction is drawn between the target objective, which is that initially proposed by management, and represents the desired outcome, and the negotiating objective, which is that agreed to by management following the negotiating team's assessment of the feasibility of the target in relation to the factors affecting its achievement.

Realistically this assessment can be made only after exploratory and informal discussions have been held with Opponent, since Party's level of aspiration when setting his negotiating objective will be directly influenced by the amount of information, relevant to the parameters of the negotiation, which he possesses regarding Opponent. Experimental evidence in support of this proposition has come from Siegel and Fouraker and from Liebert, Smith, Hill and Keifer. Both found that the initial bid of Party was adjusted according to the information available to him regarding Opponent's pay off.[2]

In contract negotiations it is essential for Party to identify Opponent's technical, contractual, commercial and financial norms and so be in a position to determine the extent to which he finds them unattractive. Also he needs to establish the extent to which Opponent feels committed to such norms and the reasons for such commitment; for example, is it a matter of conforming to government regulations or to an internal standard? Therefore, the preliminary and informal talks will be directed towards identifying the degree of resistance which Opponent is likely to show to any suggestions of modifying such norms, and the extent to which Opponent would at least not dismiss out of hand Party's own proposal, eg because they would be beyond Opponent's budget.

Before proceeding with the review of each of these steps in the planning process it is useful to discuss briefly some of the ideas and techniques which will be used to assist in the development of a quantitative approach to decision making and the selection of the optimum expected course of action. This discussion is intended only as an elementary guide to those features of decision and game theory which can usefully be applied to contract negotiations. The treatment is largely conventional and no originality is claimed other than for the application of:

1 The additive theory of riskless utility to the comparison of competitive offers.
2 'The prisoner's dilemma' game to the selection of negotiating strategy.

Since these applications are considered further in the examples in Section 5.1 the reader who is familiar with these subjects may pass on to Chapter 3. The reader who is interested to learn more is referred to the further reading below.[3]

NOTES
1. W. H. Auden, *The Dog Beneath the Skin* (London: Faber & Faber, 1938).
2. L. E. Siegel and S. Fouraker, *Bargaining and Group Decision Making* (New York: McGraw Hill, 1960) reported on the adjustment made by Party downwards, ie nearer to the final settling point, in his initial bid when provided with knowledge as to Opponent's pay off.
    Liebert showed that given information as to the profit arising to Opponent from the level of Party's bid, Party will set his aspirations accordingly, and will not be influenced by the actual initial offer made by Opponent. In the absence of information, however, Party will set his aspiration level on the basis of Opponent's first bid. R. M. Liebert, W. P. Smith, J. H. Hill and M. Keifer, 'The effect of information and magnitude of initial offer on interpersonal negotiation', *Journal of Experimental Social Psychology,* vol. 4 (1968), pp. 431–441.
3. The following books are suggested for further reading in decision and game theory. R. G. Coyle, *Decision Analysis* (London: Nelson, 1972). W. Edwards and A. Tversky (editors), *Decision Making* (Harmondsworth: Penguin, 1967). W. Lee, *Decision Theory and Human Behaviour* (New York: Wiley, 1971). J. Forester, *Statistical Selection of Business Strategies* (Homewood, Illinois: Irwin, 1968). R. D. Luce and H. Raiffa, *Games and Decisions* (New York: Wiley, 1967).

2

DECISION TECHNIQUES

2.1 CHOICE UNDER RISK[1]—THE DECISION RULES

One basic problem in contract negotiation is that of choosing between two or more alternative courses of action under circumstances in which:

1 It cannot be predicted with certainty whether the choice will lead to the desired outcome or not and, therefore, in making the choice one defined combination of value and risk must be preferred to another.
2 Generally the probability of reaching agreement can only be increased by selecting a course of action which is of lower value, and conversely by selecting a course of action of higher value that probability will be reduced.

In order to make the selection the following are required:

1 To define the objective in such terms that a value judgement can be placed on each alternative course of action.
2 A method whereby such value judgements can be made consistently, to weight them according to assessment of success or failure and finally to select that course which optimizes the achievement of the objective.

Consider this problem in relation to the submission of any offer. Traditional economic theory asserts that the rational decision maker will act so as to maximize some value, usually profit. It will be seen later (Section 6.1) that in most instances the value to Party of any offer cannot properly be expressed solely in monetary terms and certainly not in terms of profit which, in any event, has a different meaning to the economist and the businessman.[2] The value to Party will be his assessment of the worth of a mixture of the immediate financial gains and other less tangible benefits, to be derived from the acceptance of his offer, with the contractual risks and asset utilization involved. The whole being expressed in relation to Party's needs at that time and his attitude towards risk taking. For the moment reference is made to the

15

worth of the offer to Party, the objective being to maximize this worth function.

The concept of the rational decision maker as a 'maximizer' has been challenged on the grounds that it does not accord with how people in business behave in practice, and it assumes a degree of knowledge and capacity for immediate calculation which no businessman, even when supported by a computer, can hope to possess.

As an alternative it has been proposed, primarily by Simon, that the businessman is a 'satisficer', that is to say he limits himself to selecting some course of action which satisfies one or more minimum criteria and once he has done this he searches no further for any improvement.[3]

As a description of how many people and firms behave, the 'satisficing' theory is clearly correct. Observe how often a manager asked to approve the submission of a capital goods tender will simply ask whether or not the bid meets the profit contribution or other target set by his budget or business plan. If it does then his approval is assured; if it does not, then he will require significant justification before giving his agreement, or else require that the bid is adjusted to comply with the target. He does not ask how far the price could be increased so as to provide a contribution in excess of the target without at the same time making a bid unacceptable to the recipient.

Also it is agreed that maximizing in its complete sense is in most circumstances impracticable; there is not time or knowledge to identify and evaluate every possible alternative.

However, as a normative theory, satisficing is conceptually unacceptable. Psychologically it provides no framework which allows for the exercise of that restless ambition which goads man ever forward; the need of the individual for what Maslow referred to as 'self-actualisation' – 'the doing well of the thing one wants to do' so that one never stops short of the fullest possible realization of one's potentialities.

Economically the theory is equally unattractive. Any target established by a profit plan will be an average. Unless the manager is motivated to aim to exceed that average on every possible occasion the final result of the year's trading will be a below-target performance. Compare the case of the motorist who wishes to drive at an average of 40 mph. Unless he takes every chance of a clear road to travel at the legal maximum he is most unlikely to reach his target, taking into account delays due to speed restrictions, traffic lights, roundabouts and road congestion. All businesses have their counterparts to these restrictions: factors which operate to depress the contribution actually earned on certain individual contracts well below those anticipated at tender stage. It is to compensate for this that the manager should never be content with any satisficing level but should always be aiming to maximize profit contribution on each and every occasion.

But the satisficing theory has brought out two valuable points; the existence of target levels, which it will be the first objective of the manager to achieve, and the need to limit the practice of maximizing by reference both to the state of knowledge and the cost/opportunity of improving it within the time scale and computational facilities which are available. However, the latter are imposed operational restraints, the severity of which will vary according to circumstances, and not self-imposed norms limiting ambition.

Combining these features of satisficing with the basic concept of maximization of worth the following two rules emerge; these will be the objective for decision taking in relation to the submission of any offer.

1 The submission of an offer is preferred to no submission, provided only that the expected value of its worth satifies some predetermined minimum requirement and no more favourable opportunity for the use of the assets involved can be identified within the limits of existing knowledge, computational ability and time available.
2 Subject to satisfying rule 1, the worth of the offer selected will have the maximum expected value determinable within the limits of existing knowledge and such further data as it may be decided to acquire, the time available and the capability for computation.

Expressed in operational terms it is proposed therefore to maximize the expected value of the worth of the offer subject to:

1 Satisfying the minimum requirement.
2 The limits of the existing state of knowledge and any further data it may be decided to acquire.
3 The time scale within which the offer must be submitted.
4 The ability for computation and comparison.

This defines the objective. The method for evaluating and comparing each course of action to be considered is now needed. The techniques for determining expected value and for assessing the worth of any given offer under conditions of risk are required for this purpose.

2.2 EXPECTED VALUE

The beginning of Section 2.1 referred to the proposition that the more valuable the offer is then in general the lower the probability that it will be accepted by the person to whom it is made. Since the value which the offer has is realized only if it is accepted, and its rejection may cause a positive loss in expenses and unrecoverable overheads, for the purpose of comparison a single value is need for the offer which will take account of:

1 The value if the offer is accepted
2 The probability of acceptance
3 The loss suffered by rejection
4 The probability of rejection

The standard procedure for arriving at such a value, known as the *expected value* of the offer is as follows:

1 Ascertain the value of the offer if it is accepted. This is referred to as the *conditional value* of the offer since it is conditional on the event 'offer accepted' occurring.
2 Estimate the probability that the other party will accept the offer.
3 Multiply the conditional value of the offer by the probability that it will be accepted.
4 Ascertain the loss to be suffered by the offer's rejection which becomes the conditional value of rejection.
5 Multiply the conditional value of the offer if rejected by the probability of its rejection. If no possibility of a counter offer exists, and it will be assumed for the moment that it does not, then the two events 'offer accepted' and 'offer rejected' are mutually exclusive and collectively exhaustive. In accordance with the rules of the probability calculus the probability of rejection must therefore be equal to one minus the probability of acceptance.
6 Add the two values so obtained together, their sum being the expected value for the offer.

A simple example is given in Figure 2:1.

Event	Conditional value £	Probability	Expected value £
Offer accepted	10 000	0.6	6 000
Offer rejected	—1 000	0.4	—400
		Expected value of the offer	5 600

Figure 2:1 Expected value of an offer

In calculating the expected value of an act it is essential to ensure that *all* possible events have been included. It was assumed in the example in Figure 2:1 that a 'go' – 'no-go' situation existed and that the offer would be either accepted or rejected. If, however, there was reason to believe that the recipient would make a counter offer then that event must be included in the example which might then become Figure 2:2.

Event	Conditional value £	Probability	Expected value £
Offer accepted	10 000	0.3	3 000
Counter offer	8 000	0.5	4 000
Offer rejected	—1 000	0.2	—200
		Expected value of the offer	6 800

Figure 2:2 Expected value of an offer may lead to a counter offer

The procedure outlined above is based on the ability to measure two independent variables: the probability of the offer being accepted and the value of that offer conditional on either its acceptance or rejection. How this is to be done will be considered in the next two sections. First comment is necessary on the independence condition of these two functions.

If consistency in making comparisons between the expected values of any two or more offers is to be maintained, then the conditional value placed on the acceptance or rejection of any offer A_1 must not be influenced by the assessment of the probability of that offer being accepted. Equally the estimate of the probability of offer A_1 being accepted must not be affected by that conditional value. Similarly for any other offer A_2.

Normatively the independence requirement is clear, but it is less clear whether it is satisfied by actual human behaviour to an extent which justifies the use of expected values as a guide for decision making.

Some evidence suggests that people put a higher estimate of success probability on gambles on which at worst they stand to break even than they do on gambles on which they could actually lose.[4] From this and other experiments it has been deduced that optimism in probability assessments tends to be associated with desirable outcomes and pessimism with undesirable ones.[5] (See also p. 198 for a discussion of this problem in relation to the negotiator's level of aspiration.) This is also supported by the observation that a manager whose objective is sales maximization will be more inclined to assign a lower success probability to a higher-priced bid than will a manager whose primary objective is the maximization of profit.

In practice, therefore, some interaction between conditional value and subjective probability appears likely. However, provided that the danger is recognized and positive action taken to minimize it by, for example, a cross-check of the manager's assessment by someone with a different motivation, it is not considered that such interaction is sufficient to invalidate the use of EV (expected value) techniques.

Probability assessments

The objective probability of a future event occurring is that which any rational man would assign to that event if he had complete data available to him and perfect capability for assessment of such data. In all but the simplest cases it is an abstraction. Subjective probability is that which would be assessed by a rational man on the basis of the data available to him, at the time of such assessment, and his own personal judgement and experience.

By definition there can only be one objective probability for any given event but there can be more than one subjective probability according to the different data available to, and the judgement/experience of, the individual assessing the event's probability. In Laplace's well-known example of three urns, one containing black balls and the other two containing white balls, a rational man would assess the probability that the third urn contains black balls as one third, with no other knowledge available. If, however, it is known by another person that the second urn contains white balls then his subjective probability of the third urn containing black balls would be one-half.

The probabilities under consideration are those of the managers involved in any particular negotiation. They are subjective probabilities based on the judgement and experience of the managers concerned and of the information which they possess. It is permitted to use these probabilities for the purpose of decision making, and to assume that they comply with the normal mathematical laws relating to probabilities, provided only that:

1   When assigning a probability assessment to a given event the manager acts rationally, having regard to his experience and the evidence before him; specifically he does not act arbitrarily.
2   So far as is practical, probabilities are assigned to those events of which the manager has the most experience, and the theory of probability is then used to compute the probabilities of events of which he has lesser experience.
3   The manager is consistent in his assignment of probabilities.

It is the last requirement of consistency which causes the most problems. An individual's consistency of judgement would appear to be a function of:

1   His maturity—children have been shown to exhibit far more inconsistencies in the assessment of probabilities than adults.[6]
2   The degree of his business training and experience—the skilled negotiator will develop a 'feel' for the probability that his opponent will accept or reject an offer.

3 A built-in bias which is partly due to his intrinsic personality characteristics and partly derived from his own previous experiences. The ever-optimistic salesman is an example.

Factors 1 and 2 will clearly respond to training and experience; factor 3 is more difficult. If, however, over a period of time the manager's bias remains more or less constant, ie he continually overestimates his changes of success by, say, 10 per cent, then provided this can be established by comparing his past forecasts with what actually happened, the bias can be allowed for and the appropriate correction factor applied. The need to do this in relation to estimating costs is amusingly if somewhat cynically described by Lock but experience would certainly support his general conclusions of wildly optimistic estimating by engineers.[7] He also refers to the bane of any manager's existence—the inconsistent estimator whose only reliably displayed characteristic is his inconsistency! Unfortunately Lock does not suggest a means of dealing with such individuals.

2.3 UTILITY UNDER RISK

So far in referring to the value of the offer, whether positive or negative, such value has been expressed in monetary terms. The purpose, however, is to compare the expected outcome of what is in effect a gamble, and for this purpose, where any significant sums of money are involved, monetary values themselves are not adequate.

Supposing that I am offered a choice between a certain gain of £1 000 and a 30 per cent chance of winning £10 000 and a 70 per cent chance of nothing. I would take the £1 000 certain and so would very many other people. Some, for a variety of reasons, would prefer the gamble. Yet on an expected monetary basis the gamble is the mathematically 'correct' choice since the expected value of the gamble is £3 000.

Clearly in my judgement, and that of others who would act similarly, a certainty of £1 000 possesses a greater 'worth' than a gamble of securing £10 000 which has a 30 per cent chance of success. If, however, I already had £100 000 then I might decide to take the gamble; I would definitely want more than an offer of £1 000 certain to persuade me not to take the gamble.

What is true of individuals in their private lives is true of the same individuals as company managers and is followed, therefore, in the behaviour of their companies, or should be if the company's judgement is properly to reflect the worth to that company of an offer under conditions of risk. This worth function will clearly vary from one situation to another and is not linear with money. Factors which contribute to this variability and non-linearity are as follows.

1   The potential loss involved in the rejection of the offer in relation to the company's resources. If this is significant then the company will value each pound they stand to lose more highly than those which they might gain. An example would be a small company with low liquid assets which would not be able to afford the risk of high legal costs and an award of damages against them if they lost an action for breach of contract. To such a company, the negative value of losing say £5 000 would be higher than the positive value of a gain of a similar amount and a break-even point could be positive. This implies that our worth function takes into account what Pruitt has described as the *risk level* of the gamble and distinguishes between our preference for gambles of high and low risk.[8]

2   The setting of budget of planned targets of profitability which managers are expected to achieve. Alternatively the acceptance within a firm that certain contribution rate is 'normal'. Due to satisficing behavioural tendencies of the type already discussed there will be an increasing lack of interest at any point above the profit norm and at some point even a certain anxiety that the profit is perhaps unreasonable or may create a precedent which the manager would find embarassing in the future.[9] Accordingly the marginal rate of increase in worth of each additional pound of contribution above the norm will progressively decline.[10]

3   The manager's attitude as a person towards risk taking. As previously suggested it seems probable that the manager carries with him into business the same attitudinal behavioural pattern towards risk taking as he has in his private life. The fact that if he is only a salaried employee without equity participation in the business the money is in no sense his own, does not appear to be sufficient to alter what is a very deep-rooted personal characteristic.[11]

4   The manager's need at any particular time to obtain business in order to fulfil other targets, eg maintenance of shop output, retention of key staff or conversely the lack of any such need.

It follows that where the monetary values are significant, for the purpose of comparing the expected value of one offer with another, or indeed of making any strategy comparison, a system of worth assessment which will take into account all the factors concerned is required:[12]

1   The actual cash gain or loss involved.
2   Other benefits to be derived or lost.
3   The strength of the ambition to secure the cash gain/other benefits and to avoid suffering loss.

4 The risks involved in the venture.
5 The attitude towards risk taking.

Any such assessment will be subjective to the individual who makes it and peculiar to the particular circumstances under which it is made. It will reflect at that time, and under those conditions, the individual's attitude towards the factors listed.

The construction of an index of preference, or scale of utility values as it is usually called, is carried out as follows:

1 Decide on the best and worst possible outcomes of the risk decision which has to be made. Assume, for example, that these are gain £1 000 and gain £0.
2 Assign to each of these two possible outcomes an arbitrary value. Any values may be selected provided only that the value assigned to the best is greater than that assigned to the worst. Conveniently for the best outcome in the example gain £1 000, the value 1 will be selected, and for the worst outcome 'gain £0', the value 0. These then are the two end points of our utility scale.
3 Assume that there is the choice between the receipt of a stated sum of some value between £1 000 and £0 and participating in the risk venture. On that basis decide for what probability of success in the risk venture 'gain £1 000–gain £0' the choice would be exactly balanced between receiving for certain the particular sum or taking the risk. For example, if the sum offered was £300 the choice might be balanced between that amount or a 50/50 chance of winning £1 000 or £0.
4 Because the choice is balanced between these two events they can be said to possess the same utility. By substituting in the equation for expected value the two fixed reference points and the probabilities assessed, it is now possible to determine the utility of gain £300 as being $U(£300) = (1 \times 0.5) + (0 \times 0.5) = 0.5$.
5 By repeating this process for a number of possible values a scale can be built up and a curve of the utility values plotted on a graph. This scale can then be used to predict the conditional utility values of differing gains without any further calculation. By applying the estimates of the probabilities of their being accepted to such

Offer	Value £	Utility if accepted	Probability of acceptance	Utility if rejected	Probability of rejection
A	80 000	0.7	0.7	0	0.3
B	100 000	0.8	0.6	0	0.4

Figure 2:3 Comparison of the expected value of two offers

conditional values, the offer, which on this occasion and under the defined risks possesses the maximum utility, can then be selected.

An example is set out in Figure 2:3.
The expected values of the two offers are:

$$A \quad (0.7 \times 0.7) + (0 \times 0.3) = 0.49$$
$$B \quad (0.8 \times 0.6) + (0 \times 0.4) = 0.48$$

Offer A should therefore be selected. It will be noted that had the expected value of money been used the decision would have been different since the expected value of offer B in monetary terms (£60) is greater than (£56) the monetary expected value of offer B.

The reason is that the utility scale has taken into account the preference for a lesser degree of risk taking and also the diminishing marginal value of money. To this extent it accords with the observed practice of managers and the intuitive feel for the correct solution.[13]

The validity, however, of the above calculation depends on the persons making it possessing certain basic attributes of rationality of which the most significant are:

1 Transitivity. If A is preferred to B and B to C then A must be preferred to C.
2 Continuity of preference. If there is a preference to participate in the risk venture rather than to receive a sum certain when the probability of sucess is 1, and equally prefer the sum certain to participating in the risk venture when the probability of success is 0, then at some probability value, p, we will be indifferent between the risk venture and the receipt of the sum certain.
3 Preference for success probability. If a choice has to be made between two outcomes of the risk venture which are of equal value then the one which has a higher probability of success should be chosen. It is interesting to note that this means the challenge of overcoming the greater risk or the excitement of winning against the odds cannot be taken into account. At this point it is suspected that being rational also carries the penalty of being dull!

Utility values on the scale described represent a precise ordering of preferences over the length of the scale. Therefore it is possible to additionally interpret the results when shown graphically as indicating:

1 Through the shape of the curve the general attitude towards risk taking under the conditions defined for the particular exercise for which the curve was drawn. The three curves shown in Figure 2.4 illustrate three differing attitudes for the same risk venture. Curve X is typical of that of a cautious man more concerned with the near

certainty of a low profit than the lesser chance of a high one. Curve *Z* is that of the gambler who eschews low profits. Curve *Y* may be said to be that of the 'middle of the road' manager.

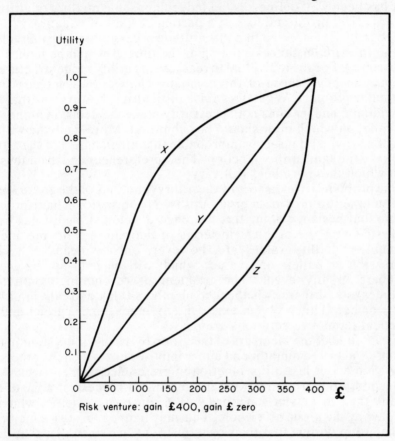

Figure 2:4 Typical utility curves under risk

2   By a comparison between the slope of the curve at different points how the attitude varies as the level of the offer changes. This will enable a comparison to be made of the relative strength of feelings for particular changes and a decision to be taken on the lines of resistance as part of the negotiating plan.

Before leaving the subject of utility under risk, of which the above is necessarily only a brief outline, a word of caution is necessary. The units of utility have been defined in terms of ordinary numbers which, although convenient, is also dangerous, since it may lead to the belief that they can be treated mathematically in all respects, as if they were ordinary numbers. But they cannot, since each unit of utility represents a separate value/risk assessment; the utility of gain £500 in the example is not twice that of gain £250.[14] The true nature of the utility unit has been well defined as 'an indecomposable mixture of attitude towards risk, profit and loss in a particular kind of situation'.[15]

Secondly it is stressed that this attitude is personal to the individual and to the circumstances existing at the time at which he makes his assessment. For the individual to reassess his utility value structure as circumstances or those of the company change does not pose any particular problem. What does raise difficulties, however, is that the individual manager does not necessarily make the decision alone, for example, on which offer should be submitted. More likely he will be one of a group and it seems improbable that all members of the group will have the same utility function. Their preferences and the intensity with which these are held will vary.

The problem arises as to how the utility functions of the group are to be combined to provide a group utility. No formal mechanism on a theoretical basis for doing this has been developed, and it has been suggested that the problem in terms of defining a 'fair' method is insoluble.[16] Utility values are, however, only a means of giving expression to beliefs and values which will be held by the group members in any event. The problem of reconciling conflicting attitudes is still there, whether the members think and talk in utility terms or not. This problem exists in any management group and in practical terms two solutions are possible.

Firstly one of the members of the group by virtue of his standing or authority acts as a dictator and either imposes his will on the others or they each adopt his utility function in preference to their own.

Secondly the group interact and through a process of adjustment modify their own value functions until a concensus emerges which is adopted by the group as a whole. This may happen through a majority of the group finding that their own functions are so similar that they can act as one and the minority accepting their view. Alternatively the group may be led by one or more of its members to coordinate one particular function where this is recognized as having some particular aptness to the decision in question.

2.4 THE THEORY OF GAMES

In selecting a decision rule which he believes will optimize the value to him of any strategy Party must necessarily make assumptions as to the decision rule which will be chosen by opponent and the same is true for Opponent in relation to Party. Both firms will therefore make their decisions according to their beliefs as to how the other will behave.

Coddington has drawn a useful distinction between two types of decision rule:[17]

1   A 'self-generating' decision rule. One which satisfies the condition that if Party expects Opponent to follow rule A then this also leads Party to adopting rule A. If the negotiation concerned the division of £100, and Party expected Opponent to follow the rule split 50/50 this could lead Party to follow suit.

2   A 'self-replacing' decision rule. One which satisfies the condition that if Party expects Opponent to follow one rule then this leads Party to adopt some different rule. In the above example of dividing £100, if Party believes that Opponent will adopt decision rule B: ask for 60/40 this will lead Party to choose some other decision rule, say, ask for 75/25.

It has been shown by Coddington that in relation to self-replacing rules one or both of the bargainers will be wrong in their judgement as to the other's expectations.[18] Party's judgement will only be correct if Opponent has made an error in assessing how Party will behave and conversely if Opponent is right in assessing Party's intended behaviour then his judgement of how Opponent will behave must be wrong. In rule 2 if Party was correct in his assessment of Opponent's demand then Opponent was wrong in his judgement of Party, since his choice of decision rule B could only have been based on an expectation that Party would choose some other decision rule A, say '55/45'.[19]

As an illustration of how this problem arises in regard to the submission of any offer, assume that Party is intending to quote at a price level of 96 based on his belief that Opponent will tender > 98. The position looked at from Opponent's viewpoint is shown in the first three columns of figure 2:5, and, to complete the picture, column four shows the correctness of Party's judgement on Opponent.

Opponent's belief as to Party's action	Opponent's reaction	Opponent's view of Party	Party's view of Opponent
1 Party will bid <96	bid 94	wrong	wrong
2 Party will bid ⩾96<99	bid 95	correct	wrong
3 Party will bid ⩾99	bid 98	wrong	correct

Figure 2:5 Example of self-replacing decision rule

It will be seen that in no case are both parties right. In 2 when Opponent is correct in his judgement as to Party's action, Party is wrong, since his decision to bid at 96 was based on his belief that Opponent would tender at least 98.

This result is quite general and confirms the theory that in any instance where Party adopts a self-replacing decision rule then either he or Opponent or both will be mistaken in his expectations regarding the decision rule adopted by the other.[20]

Unfortunately for Party's marketing manager he has still to decide on the actual level at which to submit his bid, despite the uncertainty he feels as to Opponent's intentions. To assist him he prepares a bid pay-off table on the lines set out in Figure 2:6.

Price level	Probability (p) of bid being successful	Conditional utility of an award at that price	$p \times u$	Probability $(1-p)$ of bid being unsuccessful	Utility of losing the bid	$(1-p) \times u$	Bid EV
99	0.05	10	0.5	0.95	−1	−0.95	−0.45
98	0.25	9	2.25	0.75	−1	−0.75	1.50
97	0.60	8	4.80	0.40	−1	−0.40	4.40
96	0.80	7	5.60	0.20	−1	−0.20	5.40
95	0.95	5	4.75	0.05	−1	−0.05	4.70

Figure 2:6 Comparison of bid expected values

The strategy having the maximum expected value is bid at price level 96 and this is clearly best in the sense that it provides the optimum expected return against the manager's assumed probability distribution for Opponent. However, such a strategy is clearly not as safe as that of bid at price level 95. This is shown by Figure 2:7 which, using the same probabilities, compares the expected values of the two strategies conditional upon whether Opponent tenders above or below Party.

	Expected value to Party	
Price level	Opponent tenders above Party	Opponent tenders below Party
96	5.6	−0.2
95	4.75	−0.05

Figure 2:7 Comparison of two bid strategies

If, therefore, Party's marketing manager prefers to minimize risk, rather than maximize profit opportunity, he will prefer the strategy bid at price level 95 for which his expected loss is only 0.05.

The concept of a strategy choice which maximizes one's security against the worst which one's adversary can do is central to that branch of decision theory known as *the theory of games.*

This theory was first developed comprehensively by Neuman and Morgenstern in 1944 and has since been the subject of considerable study and elaboration.[21,22] For present purposes the account of the theory is limited to its simplest form and attention is concentrated on that part which has the most relevance to a two party bargaining position.

The theory describes a conflict of interest situation referred at as a *game* in which strictly:

1   Each player has a finite number of possible courses of action referred to as his strategies for the game.
2   Each player has complete information as to his own and his opponents' possible strategies, and the resulting pay-off values, depending on the strategies selected by each.
3   The players make their strategy choices simultaneously, ie neither knows the other's choice until he has made his own.
4   The pay-off values for each player are expressed in terms of utilities as described in Section 2.3 and represent, therefore, a strict ordering of preferences such that the player will always prefer the higher to the lower value. The player's objective is the maximization of utility and it is assumed that he will act at all times in the manner best calculated to achieve this, ie each player assumes that his opponent's choice will be optimal.

It will be appreciated that these conditions, if applied strictly, would severely limit the application of the theory to real life situations. The extent to which they can be relaxed without destroying the essential spirit of the theory will now be considered.

Since two-party bargaining is the main interest the games will be restricted to those with two players which conventionally are divided into two types. *Zero-sum games,* in which the gains of one party are the losses of the other. For this reason such games are strictly competitive and collusion between the parties would not bring them jointly any advantage. *Non-zero-sum games,* in which, as might be expected, the gains of one party are not necessarily the losses of the other and very often it is only through collusion that the players can optimize their joint strategies.

The set of strategies for Party in any game is donoted by $a_1.. a_2.. a_i.. a_m$ and those for Opponent by $b_1.. b_2.. b_j.. b_n$. To the strategy choice $a_i b_j$ there is an outcome O_{ij}. The presentation of this is given in the form of a pay-off table as in Figure 2:8.

		Opponent			
		b_1	b_2	b_j	b_n
	a_1	O_{11}	O_{12}	O_{1j}	O_{1n}
Party	a_2	O_{21}	O_{22}	O_{2j}	O_{2n}
	a_i	O_{i1}	O_{i2}	O_{ij}	O_{in}
	a_m	O_{m1}	O_{m2}	O_{mj}	O_{mn}

Figure 2:8 Strategy pay-off table

Zero-sum games

The usual convention in zero-sum games is to draw only the pay-off function for Party since it is known that the pay-off function for Opponent is the negative of this. Considering the pay-off matrix given in Figure 2:9 which strategy should each party adopt, assuming that Party wishes to gain as much as possible and Opponent to lose as little as possible?

		Opponent		
		b_1	b_2	b_3
	a_1	5	4	8
Party	a_2	12	3	2
	a_3	0	2	20

Figure 2:9 Example of zero-sum game with saddle point

Consistent with rule 4 for the game, 'assume that your opponent's choice will be optimal for him', the greatest gain of which Party can be certain, *irrespective of Opponent's strategy choice,* is equal to the maximum of the minimum value in each row. It will be remembered that Opponent's losses are the reverse of Party's gains and therefore it must be expected that Opponent will select that strategy which minimizes Party's gains. The three minima values are 4,2 and 0, so that the strategy which maximizes Party's certain return, in game-theory terms *his security level,* is a_1 which gives Party an assurance of a gain of at least 4. This strategy is known as Party's *maximin strategy.*

Similarly Opponent can guarantee his smallest loss by selecting that strategy which contains the minimum of the column maxima. Since these are 12, 4 and 20, Opponent's *minimax strategy* is b_2 which restricts his loss to 4.

The unique pair a_1b_2, sometimes referred to as a *saddle-point,* is in equilibrium in the sense that neither party has any incentive to change his strategy provided that the other does not change his. Stated more formally a strategy pair a_{io}, b_{jo} is in equilibrium if:

1   No outcome O_{ijo} is more preferred by Party than O_{iojo}.
2   No outcome O_{jio} is more preferred by Opponent than O_{iojo}.

It follows that the entry O_{iojo} wil be the maximum of its column j_o and the minimum of its row i_o.

Do zero-sum games with equilibrium pairs exist in the real world or are they only theoretical abstractions? Luce and Raiffa suggest there could be an application in military decision making, and quote an example from Haywood drawn from World War II.[23,24] Other writers are more doubtful, the principal stumbling block being the requirement that the gains of one player are the losses of the other.[25]

One commercial situation which approximates to a zero-sum game with an equilibrium pair is that of a duopoly market in which the brand loyalty of each firm's products is low, the elasticity of demand relative to price is high, and the market is just saturated. For each vendor, his present price maximizes total revenue, given that the other does not change his price. The choice facing the duopolists is whether to raise the price 5 per cent, or leave it as it stands, and may be represented by the matrix given in Figure 2:10.

		Vendor B	
		b_1 Raise price	b_2 Maintain price
Vendor A	a_1 Raise price	0	—1
	a_2 Maintain price	1	0

Figure 2:10 Commercial example of zero-sum game

The strategy pair a_2b_2 (maintain the price as its current level) is the unique equilibrium pair.[26]

Zero-sum games—no saddle point
Not all zero-sum games have an equilibrium pair. Which strategy, for example, should Party adopt in order to maximize his security in the game shown in Figure 2:11?

		Opponent	
		b_1	b_2
Party	a_1	5	3
	a_2	4	6

Figure 2:11 Example of zero-sum game, no saddle point

His reasoning when trying to make up his mind could go something like this

> If I choose a_2, I guarantee myself at least 4. But if Opponent believes I will choose a_2 then he will take b_1, and if he is going to do that, then I would be better off with a_1. I must, however, regard Opponent as being clever enough to work that one out and if he does then he is bound to select b_2. In that event I am better off with a_2 which is where I started.[27]

Is there any way out of this circular reasoning? It can be shown that Party maximizes his security by playing $^1/_2a_1$ and $^1/_2a_2$ and similarly that Opponent maximizes his security by playing $^3/_4b_1$ and $^1/_4b_2$.[28] If the game were to be played only once it would be interpreted as saying that Party should make his choice by the use of some device which would select a_1 with a probability of 50 per cent and a^2 with the probability of 50 per cent. Party's strategy of $^1/_2a_1$ and $^1/_2a_2$ is described as a maximum mixed strategy and the two mixed strategies $(^1/_2a_1:^1/_2a_2)$ and $(^3/_4B_1:^1/_4b_2)$ are an equilibrium pair. It can further be shown that every two-person zero-sum game has an equilibrium pair when mixed strategies are permitted.[29]

Whilst mathematically elegant does the concept of a mixed strategy have any relevance to real life? Clearly it is not suggested that a negotiator should select his strategy by tossing a coin or selecting a card!

The use of randomized strategy can be seen as a form of hedging, bluffing and concealment of intentions. For example, over the period of a long-term bargaining relationship one negotiator will start to learn the type of strategy the other is likely to adopt.[30] To prevent this happening one bargainer may at irregular intervals delegate the strategy choice to a colleague of known different views, having first bound himself to accept his colleague's decision. Schelling suggests something similar when he points out that by randomizing his choice of strategy, Party defeats any attempt by Opponent to coordinate their strategy choices based on deductive reasoning as to Party's probable intentions.[31] The act of randomization itself ensures that Opponent can have no better chance of being right than the odds involved in the random selection.

This is not theoretical. Firms manufacturing a standard product or providing a standard service with a limited number of known competitors, e.g. motorway construction, do maintain long term records of their competitors' bidding behaviour from which they seek to predict what will be their competitors' price level on the next bid opportunity. If for example firm X is believed never to have bid at less than say total cost plus a margin of around 7 per cent then given that Party can reasonably estimate X's construction costs for the job in question he can arrive very closely at X's most likely lowest bid price. If however, X now decides to bid without addition for profit not only will Party's predictions for that tender be upset but more importantly he can no longer be so certain as to how X will behave on *any* future occasion, which will make it that much more difficult for Party to assess his own success probability – see further p.133.

Non-zero-sum games
Most bargaining situations can only be represented by a theory which permits the respective gains and losses of the parties for any outcome to be different. This means that both parties can gain from a given

outcome and therefore allows for the case in which the maximum joint gain is achieved by collusion between the parties as to the strategy each will adopt.

In the analysis of this type of game a distinction is made between those which permit collaboration and those which do not.

Non-collaborative non-zero games

Both players have a preferred strategy which would maximize their expected gain, but only if the other player is obliging enough to use his inferior strategy. If both players adopt their preferred strategies then both will lose.[32]

A suitable illustration of this game is a situation in which two bargainers have a single major issue, the contract price, to settle before an agreement can be concluded. Each has a preferred price level and each knows what he believes the other party might accept as a compromise. Therefore, each bargainer is aware generally of the value to himself and to his adversary of concluding a bargain at either the preferred or compromise level and of the value of no bargain. The time available for negotiation has almost expired and so the choices open to the parties are restricted to sticking to their present offer, which is the preferred level, or offering a compromise. The problem can be represented by a game matrix in the form shown in Figure 2:12.

		Opponent	
		b_1 stick	b_2 compromise
Party	a_1 stick	0,0	6,1
	a_2 compromise	1,6	3,3

Figure 2:12 Example of non-zero-sum game

The parties are assumed to make their strategy choices simultaneously and to be committed to them, ie they cannot change their minds after hearing the other's choice. The higher value shown for the strategy choice compromise in a_2b_2 is based on the idea that the original concessions may not bring final agreement, but would bring it so close that the parties would then bridge the remaining gap between them by each making a further minor concession. If, on the other hand, Opponent has chosen to stick and Party to concede then Party will be compelled to continue to concede to the point of matching Opponent's preferred level, which must represent a worse bargain for Party, although one which he presumably prefers to no bargain.

Party's maximum strategy is clearly a_2 concede since this would guarantee him at least 1. If Opponent is also a maximiner and reasons in the same way then Party would gain 3. It is at this point that Party is tempted to argue that if Opponent is a maximiner and is going to concede then why does he, Party, not stick out and so gain 6? On an expected value basis, at any probability > 25 per cent that Opponent will concede, strategy a_1 stick has a greater expected value (1.5) than strategy a_2. But it is not a guaranteed value and if Opponent adopts the same line of reasoning then both will finish up with gaining nothing. At this point Party settles for a_2 concede, only again to think perhaps that his decision was cowardly and that he should have taken a chance.

Party is left still making up his mind because there is no one answer. The game has two equilibrium pairs a_1b_2 and a_2b_1 but these are neither equivalent nor interchangeable and the game has therefore no solution.[33] Party can only judge on the importance to him of some bargain rather than no bargain and on his experience of Opponent. How will he reason? Leaving the realm of 'pure' game theory, that of judgement and psychology is now examined.

If a solution has to be suggested, then on the utility values given in the matrix, if experience of Opponent showed that the chance of his conceding was greater than 25 per cent, strategy a_1 stick would be adopted. Alter the utility value for Party of no bargain to, say, -3 and for any subjective probability of Opponent adopting b_1 stick greater than, say, 20 per cent, a_2 concede would now be selected. This is so even though, on an expected value basis, a_1 would remain the apparent optimum choice up to a 40 per cent probability of Opponent choosing b_1 stick. The consequences of no bargain are now too serious; more formally the risk level of the gamble select a_1 has increased sharply to a point at which it would be regarded as unacceptable.[34] This argument is reinforced by the fact that, in accordance with game-theory convention, Opponent would be aware of the change in the utility to Party of no bargain, and this would strengthen his view that Party would not dare to choose a_1; therefore, Opponent was safe in choosing b_1 stick which would provide him with his maximum return.

It should be clear from the above analysis that the theory in relation to non-zero-sum games is far less developed than it is for zero-sum games and can offer much less precise guidance to the course of action to be adopted. The trouble is that the maximin strategies need not form an equilbrium pair and there is always therefore the temptation to defect. For further discussion see Luce and Raiffa.[35]

Even when there is only one equilibrium pair troubles still persist. In the classic non-zero-sum non-cooperative game, the prisoner's dilemma, the outcome represented by the single equilibrium pair is one which both parties would prefer to avoid, if only they could find a rational way of doing so![36]

The game is of the form shown in Figure 2:13.

Opponent

		b_1	b_2
	a_1	(4, 4)	(—3, 6)
Party			
	a_2	(6, —3)	(—1, —1)

Figure 2:13 Commercial example of 'the prisoner's dilemma'

In terms of contract negotiations it would seem more appropriate to regard this game as representing the situation facing two duopolists who are submitting a tender to a monopoly buyer in a market in which demand for their product is declining, the product is homogenous, and the cost is highly volume conscious.[37] The problem facing the two bidders is whether to maintain the current price level, their first strategy in Figure 2:13, or to reduce prices in an effort to obtain increased volume and maximize profit: strategy two.

Strictly their second strategy in each case dominates the first and the outcome a_2b_2 is the unique equilibrium pair. That pair would be selected therefore as the solution to the game, provided there was no opportunity for the parties to cooperate either openly or tacitly.

Open cooperation, to stand even a chance of being effective, would need to be supported by a binding agreement between the parties, the penalty for breach of which would be more severe than any likely gain.[38] This is so because neither a_1b_2 nor a_2b_1 are in equilibrium and so either party will always be tempted to defect if he believes that the other will not follow suit. The existence of an agreement, if it is loose or informally expressed, will support such belief despite the apparent irrationality in one player believing that the other will act differently from the way in which he intends to act himself.

Tacit coordination could arise simply from the competitive bidding being repeated a number of times. The suggestion made by Luce and Raiffa is outlined as follows:

> In most cases it is felt that an unarticulated collusion between the players will develop, much in the same way as a mature economic market often exhibits a marked degree of collusion without any communication among the participants. This arises from the knowledge that the situation will be repeated and that reprisals are possible.

The experimental results referred to by Lee and the bidding experiments carried out by Siegel and Fouraker do not appear to support this proposition.[39,40] Both found that the competitive choice a_2b_2 predominated over the collaborative choice a_1b_1.

The explanation may lie in the motivation of the players. Lee has suggested that the subjects playing the games to which he refers were largely motivated by the desire to 'outscore their opponents'.[41] Siegel and Fouraker identified simple profit maximization as the primary motive of the subjects. Significantly, however, although the games in these experiments were repeated a number of times, the bargaining relationship between the parties was essentially short term and little or no opportunity existed for the development of personal relationships between the players.[42] Conditions were therefore weighted against the parties establishing a maturity of understanding or of learning to control their aggressive tendencies in the interests of long-term stability.

It is also of significance that when Siegel and Fouraker increased the amount of data available to the bargainers at the end of each game, thus more accurately simulating real-life conditions, there was far more support for the collaborative choice.[43] In certain bargaining pairs, one player by continually repeating the bid which maximized joint profit 'taught' his opponent that he was prepared to coordinate on this choice. (Siegel and Fouraker allowed no communication between the bidders who did not even see each other, so that this can only be regarded as pure tacit coordination.)

The urge to win, even if the victory is pyrrhic, is a deep-rooted human emotion often originating in a basic feeling of insecurity. This theme will be reconsidered in Chapter 7 when ways of satisfying a negotiator's personal motivational drive are discussed.

Collaborative non-zero-sum game

It has already been indicated several times that the difficulties facing the players in making their strategy choices would be eased if they were allowed to communicate with each other before doing so and to enter into collaborative agreements. Certainly it would enable them to agree on the outcome which maximizes joint profits, which otherwise they are unlikely to do.

In a static situation where the choices are limited, and once made irrevocable, prior communication and the ability to make binding agreements may enable the parties to identify and agree on their joint pareto-optimal choice.[44]

In a dynamic situation, however, problems still remain which may be illustrated with the aid of the matrix given in Figure 2:14.

		Opponent	
		b_1	b_1
Party	a_1	(u_1, u_5)	(u_i, u_j)
	a_2	$(0, 0)$	(u_5, u_1)

Figure 2:14 Example of non-zero sum game—collaborative

Diagramatically this is shown in Figure 2:15, in which the line between the two maximin strategy outcomes u_{51} and u_{15} is known as the *negotiation set* and represents all undominated outcomes of the game. Since the players know each other's utility pay offs, it is assumed that they will not accept an outcome less than optimal and will therefore select some bargain on this line. It is inferred that the outcome u_{ij} is the choice of both parties, ie given that Opponent will select b_1 with a probability p_1, and b_2 with a probability p_2, $(p_1 + p_2 = 1)$, then for Party $U (p_1u_1 + p_2u_1 > U (p_2) + p_2O + p_2u_5)$.

However, what is the value for u_{ij}? Is it feasible to predict a single solution for this game?

Normatively it has been proposed by Nash that having set the utility functions for both players of no bargain at zero pay off, the solution is that point which maximizes the product of the player's utilities: in

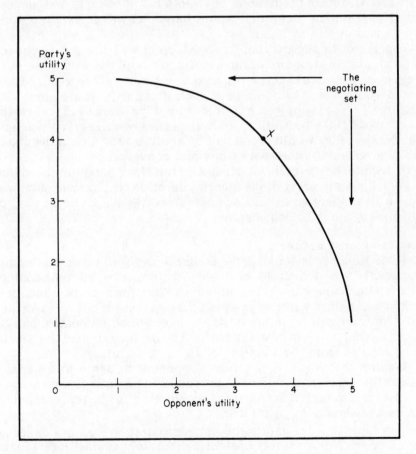

Figure 2:15 The negotiating set

Figure 2:15 the point marked X.[45] Other suggestions have been made, based primarily on the principle that a bargainer will concede if his loss would be smaller than that of his opponent.[46] Mathematically this proposal will lead to the same answer as Nash. These solutions have been reviewed by both Cross and Coddington.[47]

The difficulty with all these theories is that they are static; the outcome can be predicted without the players even being present. The static nature of game theory was no problem when dealing with the competitive bidding decision which is in itself static given that post-tender negotiations are excluded. Each party has a single opportunity with no possibility of later adjustment.

Bargaining, however, is dynamic. There are a series of decisions to be made over a time scale, each dependent on what has already occurred and on the bargainer's future expectations. According to past events, future predictions as to both his opponents and his own behaviour, and the factor of time, the bargainer will adjust his present offer accordingly.

This is not to suggest that the Nash point will never describe the outcome. If the structure of the negotiations and the anticipations of the parties are such that the Nash point is intuitively recognized as a landmark on which to coordinate, then it can be expected to be the outcome[48]. The simplest example would be bargaining over the division of £100 where utility for both parties was linear with money. The Nash theory would predict a 50/50 division as would the above theories, given no other points of equal convergence.

In dispute, however, is the claim that the Nash point or indeed that predicted by any other of the theories describes the *unique* outcome. That is dependent on a multitude of factors which it is the purpose of our present study to consider.

Games against nature
So far in this discussion of game theory it has been assumed that the Opponent is a deliberate adversary who will at all times adopt maximizing behaviour. Many situations can, however, be character-ized in game-theory format in which the opponent is not an adversary but a state of nature; a circumstance over which no control can be exercised but the form of which will determine the extent of the benefit to be derived from the adoption of any given strategy.

Assume that Party is asked by Opponent to agree to a penalty clause for delay and believes that should he refuse Opponent will insist on a discount of 5 per cent. The situation can be represented by the matrix shown in Figure 2:16.

In a game against nature the maximin strategy can no longer be relied upon. Nature's acts are not deliberately against individuals. (For example, it will not rain tomorrow just because a picnic has been

| | | State of nature (delay) | |
		Delay does not occur	Delay does occur
Party	Agree to penalty	0	− 1% up to 10% dependent on period of delay
	Do not agree to penalty	− 5%	− 5%

Figure 2:16 Commercial example of a game against nature

planned.) Equally performance of the contract will not be delayed just because it has been decided to accept the penalty. Indeed the reverse can be argued; by accepting the penalty the danger will be minimized by taking all steps possible to ensure that the work is not delayed.

Clearly the maximin strategy would be too pessimistic to provide a realistic guide to action since, for any possibility of the penalty causing a loss in excess of 5 per cent, it would propose that the discount should be offered.

Given that the situation can be treated as being one of risk, the probabilities of the two events no delay and delay can be assessed and the strategy with the most favourable expected value selected.[49]

Assuming the utility is linear with money, in the above example for any probability p of delay occurring for which $p \times$ (delay penalty) < 5 per cent of the contract price the decision should be to accept the penalty clause.

It must, however, be recognized that adopting this approach of selecting the strategy which has the maximum expected value for all possible states of nature involves a certain gamble. The assessments of probability being subjective may be wrong; the outcome most disliked may occur. This is a chance which must be taken willingly, the alternative being to play safe and follow the conservative maximin rule.

2.5 RISKLESS UTILITY
The previous discussion of utility theory was concerned with the situation of risk. The decision maker may also be faced with the problem of choosing between two or more alternatives under conditions of certainty in which the choices open to him are multidimensional and the same choice is not best on all dimensions. The theory of riskless utility seeks to establish a method by which to explain and predict how that choice will be made. For this purpose it is necessary to construct an index for the decision maker which will accurately reflect his ordering of preferences.

It has been proposed that riskless utility can be measured only over an ordinal scale, ie the scale represents only a pure ordering of preferences and says nothing about the strength of one preference as compared with another.[50] Clearly such a scale could not be used to predict behaviour or to compare movements in relative worth. The difficulty is recognized of composing other than an ordinal scale when dealing with an individual's preferences for such items as books and pictures. In contract negotiations, however, provided the assumption is made that the decision maker is behaving rationally, then it is proposed that the choices open can be compared and evaluated in terms of their worth to the negotiator and that an index of cardinal utility can be constucted.

However, it will still not be a pure cardinal index in the sense that it will not be possible to subtract one utility value in the index from another and say that the difference between them represents the difference between the monetary values to which they relate. Referring to Figure 2:19 the utility of £120 000 cannot be subtracted from £100 000 (0.7–0.5) to give the utility of – £20 000 equals 0.2, but it can be said that under the conditions for which the scale was constructed, and for that particular decision maker, a change in the value of the offer from £100 000 to £120 000 represents a reduction in utility to the buyer of 0.2.

Further, this change can be compared with that which occurs between £120 000 and £140 000 and the conclusion drawn that the reduction in utility is 2.5 times greater over £120 000 than it is below £120 000.

Rate of change prior to £120 000 $= \dfrac{1 - 0.8}{1} = 0.2$

Rate of change over £120 000 $= \dfrac{0.8 - 0.4}{0.8} = 0.5$

Construction of the index[51]

The basic assumption behind the construction of any such index is that riskless utility is additive, ie the utility of an offer is the sum of the utilities of its component parts: price, quality, delivery, etc. The particular case of riskless utility to be considered is a comparison of the strength of an individual's preferences for a defined combination of two or more factors with another combination of the same factors under conditions in which the best and worst possible factor combinations can be established in advance. Specifically this will be required (see p. 103) in order to:

1 Know the order in which a buyer would rank, say, three tenders each offering him different price/delivery combinations.

2 Predict if the buyer were to be presented with a fourth tender how he would prefer this in relation to the other three.

The two components in each tender are regarded as ordered pairs where x_1 represents price and x_2 represents delivery. The first component x_1 will be a member of a set K_1 in which $x_1 > y_1 > z_1$ and the second component x_2 will be a member of a set K_2 in which $x_2 > y_2 > x_2$.

The utility of any pair of components to the buyer, U, represents the strength of the buyer's preference for that combination over any other. The value 1 is arbitrarily assigned to the combination $U(x_1x_2)$ which, by definition, is the most favourable to the buyer and which he believes he will receive, and the value 0 to any combination in which either component has a value below the minimum which is acceptable to the buyer. This is justified on the basis that the buyer would automatically reject any offer in which one of the components failed to meet a mandatory requirement, eg price in excess of his budget, *irrespective of the value of the other component.*[52]

The value U of any ordered pair of components is then equal to the utility of the one component added to the utility of the other, ie for all x_1 in K_1 and for all x_2 in K_2 $U(x_1x_2) = u(x_1) + u(x_2)$ provided that both components have a value above zero.

It is then crucial to decide the proportion of $U(x_1x_2)$, to which the value 1 has been given, to be assigned to $u(x_1)$ and the proportion to $u(x_2)$. This can only be done by asking the buyer how valuable he regards price relative to delivery. Having done this, through the additive assumption, a complete matrix of preference ordering can be determined for all tenders which the buyer anticipates he will receive by:

1 Establishing from the buyer his preference strength for y_1 compared to x_1 and z_1 compared to y_1. Note that this preference ordering takes no account of the member of the set K_2 with which the component is paired; the two sets are ordered independently.

Component	Price in £	Utility
x_1	100 000	0.7
y_1	120 000	0.5
z_1	140 000	0.1

Component	Delivery in months	Utility
x_2	12	0.3
y_2	13	0.25
z_2	14	0.1

Figure 2:17 Example of preference ordering: riskless utility of price and delivery

2   Similarly establishing from the buyer the strength of his preference for y_2 compared to x_2 and for z_2 compared to y_2, again ignoring the member of the other set.
3   Adding together the values so obtained for each combination.[53]

A simple matrix to illustrate the above formulation is given in Figure 2:18 based on the table of preference orderings (Figure 2:17).

			Delivery		
			x_2 12 months	y_2 13 months	z_2 14 months
	x_1	£100 000	1.0	0.95	0.8
Price	y_1	£120 000	0.8	0.75	0.6
	z_1	£140 000	0.4	0.35	0.2

Figure 2:18 Additive utility values for price and delivery

Assumptions
The additive model set out in Figure 2:18 is based on the following assumptions.

1   The ordering of preferences is transitive, ie if $x_1 > y_1$ and $y_1 > z_1$ then $x_1 > z_1$.
2   x_1 is only preferred to y_1 if $u(x_1)$ is greater than $u(y_1)$.
3   Each of the sets K_1 and K_2 can be ordered independently of the other. This means that since x_1 is preferred to y_1 then $(x_1x_2) > (y_1x_2)$ and similarly for any other values in set K_2. In the example the buyer will always prefer the lower price if the deliveries quoted are the same and equally he will always prefer the shorter delivery if the prices quoted are the same.
4   The strength of the buyer's preference for any component is not affected by the component in the other set with which it is paired. Thus the buyer's preference for x_2 over y_2 does not change as the price level alters. The value of one month saved is the same at a price of £100 000 as at £140 000.[54]

This can be inferred from assumption 3 but does not necessarily follow. Intuitively, however, there seems no reason why the worth of either price, quality or delivery taken on its own should be affected by the value of any two of the other three factors. Preference for, say, quality alone will not diminish as the price increases. The worth of the price/quality combination will diminish, relative to other offers, as the accelerated marginal reduction in the utility of the price component at the higher price levels takes effect.[55]

It must again be stressed that if the value of either component falls below that which is acceptable to the buyer then he must automatically assign to that combination the value zero, *regardless of the value of the other component.* Thus, if in the example in Figure 2:18 a delivery period exceeding 14 months was longer than the buyer could tolerate then an offer of £100 000/15 months must have the value zero.

Domination and conflict

A pair in which both components are preferred to the other components in the alternative pair may be said to dominate that pair and creates no problem in the analysis of the buyer's preferences. If both price and delivery in offer A are better than those in offer B then the buyer will obviously prefer offer A. Of more difficulty are the pairs in which one component is preferred from the first pair and the other component is preferred from the second pair, eg the pairs (x_1y_2) and (y_1x_2). How will the buyer resolve the conflict and will his answer stay constant over a range of offers?

It is proposed that:

1 The buyer will resolve the conflict by comparing the utility intervals between x_1 and y_1 and between y_2 and x_2 and choosing that offer with the maximum utility. Thus he will prefer the lower-priced longer delivery offer to the higher-priced shorter delivery offer, provided that the advantage in price outweighs the loss in utility due to extended delivery. In the above example the buyer would have no hesitation in choosing x_1y_2 from the two pairs since $0.95 > 0.8$.

2 His preference will not necessarily stay constant. If in any matrix, as shown in Figure 2:18, at utility values of either component which approach the maximum, he consistently prefers any combination with the higher-valued price component then it is predicted that, as the value of the delivery component moves towards its limits of acceptability, at some point his preference will change. At that point he will prefer (or be indifferent to) a combination with a lower-valued price component, but higher-valued delivery to at least one combination with a higher-valued price but lower-valued delivery.

Whether or not such a point exists within the range of practical possibilities, and if it does at what point it will occur, depends on:

1 The weighting of the price to the delivery component in the combination x_1x_2. The greater the value of x_2 to x_1, ie delivery to price, the sooner the preference change point will occur.

2 The rate of change of the price component relative to the delivery component in all values lower than x_1x_2. The slower the rate of change of the price component relative to delivery then again the sooner the change point will occur.

This is illustrated by redrawing the matrix shown in Figure 2:18 with the value of the delivery component relative to the price component increased, and the rate of the delivery component relative to that of the price component also increased. The revised values and the amended matrix of combined utilities are set out in Figure 2:19.

	x_2 (0.4)	y_2 (0.3)	z_2 (0.1)
x_1 (0.6)	1.0	0.9	0.7
y_1 (0.5)	0.9	0.8	0.6
z_1 (0.3)	0.7	0.6	0.4

Figure 2:19 Revised additive utility values for price and delivery

It will be seen that the following preference changes occur where the higher-priced shorter-delivery offer is preferred to the lower-priced longer-delivery offer:

y_1x_2 and y_1y_2 are preferred to x_1z_2

z_1x_2 is preferred to y_1z_2

With the revised matrix it is most unlikely that an offer with a delivery of 14 months will be accepted even though it is at a lower price.

Supposing now that the buyer were offered a fourth tender at a price of £110 000 and a delivery of 13 months. It can be predicted from the matrix in Figure 2:19 that the utility value of such an offer would be:

$$u(x) + u(y) = 0.55 + 0.3 = 0.85$$

(It is recognized that this makes the assumption that the utility interval between £100 000 and £120 000 is linear.)

The buyer could therefore be expected to prefer such an offer to any except x_1x_2, y_1x_2 and x_1y_2.

NOTES

1.   Risk is used here in Knight's sense of a situation in which the outcome is not certain but the probabilities of the alternative outcomes are either known or can be estimated. From the practical viewpoint it is considered that the decision maker in contract negotiations will always have some evidence on which to construct a subjective probability distribution. S. H. Knight, *Risk Uncertainty and Profit* (Boston: Houghton Mifflin, 1921); reprinted by The London School of Economics in *Scarce Tracts in Economics,* No. 16, 1933.

2.   For the nature of this distinction, see W. J. Baumol, *Economic Theory and Operations Analysis* (New Jersey: Prentice-Hall, 1965), pp. 315–16.

3.   H. A. Simon, *Models of Man* (New York: Wiley, 1957) p. 204.

4.   W. Edwards, 'The prediction of decisions amongst bets', *Journal*

of Experimental Psychology, vol. 51 (1955), pp. 201–14.

5.   W. Lee, *Decision Theory and Human Behaviour* (New York: Wiley, 1971), pp. 123–26.

6.   W. Lee, op. cit., p. 65.

7.   D. Lock, *Project Management* (Aldershot: Gower, 3rd edition, 1984), pp.43–45.

8.   D. G. Pruitt, 'Pattern and level of risk in gambling decisions', *Psychological Review,* vol. 69 (no. 3, 1962), pp. 187–201.

9.   Walton and McKersie in discussing the utility function of a labour negotiator suggest that the value to him of a high wage settlement could be negative in that it would make life difficult for him in the future. Having achieved so much that time he would be expected to achieve even more in the future. Some practical experience suggests that this could apply also to commercial negotiators. R. E. Walton and R. E. McKersie, *A Behavioural Theory of Labour Negotiations* (New York: McGraw Hill, 1965), p. 26.

10.   The converse is equally true. Most company control systems are based on punishing managers for any deviations below the control level. A manager is likely to react strongly against any suggestion for risk taking which could lead him to being exposed in terms of achieving his performance 'norm'. See also R. O. Swalm, 'Utility theory—insights into risk taking', *Harvard Business Review* (November/December 1966) quoted in J. S. Hammond, 'Better decisions with preference theory', *Harvard Business Review* (November/December 1967).

11.   It is recognized that others have come to a different conclusion. R. O. Swalm and J. S. Hammond (see note 10) have suggested that because of the system by which managers are punished or rewarded, the manager in a large corporation will have a more conservative attitude towards risk taking than the corporation would consider desirable. Others have felt the opposite, that the manager will tend to take greater risks with the company's money then he would do with his own. Hence the slogan printed and distributed to all managers in one company: 'Would you do it if it were your own money?'

12.   J. Forester, *Statistical Selection of Business Strategies* (Homewood, Illinois: Irwin, 1968), p. 71, suggests the following tests for determining whether or not there is a need to use utility values:

1   Is the proposition merely one of many for which the possible losses and profits are similar?

2   If a loss resulted would this materially affect the company's working capital?

3   If a loss resulted would it affect the ownership of the company?

4   If successful would the proposition enable the company to expand into new fields?

These tests have been thought of in relation to a small business. In a large corporation they should be applied to the division or other unit concerned.

13. R. O. Swalm, 'Utility theory–insights into risk taking', *Harvard Business Review* (November/December 1966), p. 123.

14. In the theory of utility under risk as developed here, there is no such thing as the 'utility of £100'. All that can be said is that for a particular individual, at a particular time and under stated conditions of risk, his preference for an offer of £100, as compared to his preference for any other offer, can be represented by a utility value. Utility values are only a representation of preferences. Offer X is preferred to offer Y; therefore a higher utility value is assigned to X than to Y and never the other way round.

15. R. Schlaifer, *Probability and Statistics for Business Decisions* (New York: McGraw-Hill, 1959), p. 42.

16. K. J. Arrow, *Social Choice and Individual Values* (New York: Wiley, 1951). See also the discussion on pp. 327–68 in R. D. Luce and H. Raiffa, *Games and Decisions* (New York: Wiley, 1957).

17. A. Coddington, *Theories of the Bargaining Process* (London: George Allen and Unwin, 1968), p. 60.

18. A. Coddington, op. cit., p. 62.

19. In choosing a decision rule Party selects that demand which is optimum against Opponent's anticipated choice. For the factors contributing to such optimality, particularly the effect of time, see Chapter 6.

20. There would seem to be one partial exception to this rule, in which although both parties are correctly aware of the other's intentions neither alters his decision rule. Thus, in the example, assume the parties were duopolists dealing with a monopoly buyer. Party could decide that although he believed Opponent would bid, say, 95, which was correct, he would not alter his decision of bidding at 96, and reduce the price to 94, since this would lower the market price level. Party's strategy would then be based on securing the next order at a more favourable price and at a time when he anticipated Opponent's capacity would be taken up with the first order. His decision rule would then be to bid at 96 to maintain that as his price level on the basis that Opponent will secure the order at 95 but he will have a better chance of securing the next order at 96.

Opponent could also be correct in assessing that Party would bid at 96, and might even be shrewd enough to work out the remainder of Party's strategy. However, this would not cause him to change his decision rule to bid at 95 since he believes this will be a winning price and he needs the order.

Coddington has not dealt with this case which involves a difference in motivation between the parties, leading them both to retain their original decision rules even though they correctly recognized their limitations. It cannot be suggested that either party has acted in a manner inconsistent with the maximization of subjective expected utility but only that they differ in identifying the utility to them of an immediate order.

21. J. Neuman and O. Morgenstern *Theory of Games and Economic Behaviour* (Princeton: Princeton University Press, 1947).

22. R. D. Luce and H. Raiffa, *Games and Decisions* (New York: Wiley, 1957). R. Shubik, *Game Theory and Related Approaches to Social Behaviour* (New York: Wiley, 1964).

23. R. D. Luce and H. Raiffa, *Games and Decisions* (New York: Wiley, 1957).

24. O. G. Haywood, 'Military decision and game theory', *Journal of the Operations Research Society of America*, vol. 2 (1954), pp. 365–85.

25. See W. Lee, *Decision Theory and Human Behaviour* (New York: Wiley, 1971), p. 286. 'The zero-sum game does not appear to model real-life interactions very well.' See also J. Forester, *Statistical Selection of Business Strategies* (Homewood, Illinois: Irwin, 1968), p. 35, and W. J. Baumol, *Economic Theory and Operations Analysis* (New Jersey: Prentice-Hall, 1965), p. 542.

26. An interpretation of this game could be two ice cream vendors at a fair on a cool evening. If either raises his price and the other follows suit the revenue of each will stay constant, the increase in price being offset by a reduction in demand (the balance of demand being absorbed on other products). If either does not follow the other's lead then he increases his total revenue by gaining the other's customers, total demand in this case remaining static.

27. If the differences are regarded as too trivial to make a choice worth considering, then think of the numbers as representing an equivalent amount of pounds thousand.

28. If Opponent chooses the pure strategy b_1, then Party's expected return from playing a_1 with a probability of x and a_2 with a probability of y, would be given by $5x + 4y$, and similarly if Opponent selects b_2, Party's return would be $3x + 6y$. The security level is given by the values for x and y for which these two expected return functions are equal; $x + y = 1$. This is 5/2 and $x = \frac{1}{2}$, $y = \frac{1}{2}$.

The same concepts apply for Opponent whose security level is given by $5p + 3Q = 4p + 6q$ where he selects b_1 with probability p, b_2 with probability q and $p + q = 1$. His expected return against either a_1 or a_2 is 5/2; $p = 3/4$, $q = 1/4$.

29. R. D. Luce and H. Raiffa, op. cit., Appendix 2.

30. The following comment from a negotiator in an experimental negotiation is illustrative: 'One thing I noticed with certain strategy groups was you could begin to detect after a while what their strategy was. They would concede the smaller issue and skip over the most

important wages and then hopefully come back later and use the argument "oh since we gave you that, how about . . ." '. B. M. Bass, 'Effects on the subsequent performance of negotiators of studying issues or planning strategies alone or in groups', *Psychological Monographs General and Applied* (no. 614, 1966), p.20.

31. T. C. Schelling, *The Strategy of Conflict* (London: Oxford University Press, 1963).

32. A pay-off matrix similar to that given in figure 2:12 has been used by Samuelson to illustrate the classical price-cutting war between two departmental stores. In the absence of a collusive agreement the two firms will end up with the pay off a_1b_1, since the solution at a_2b_2 is not stable in the sense that both firms could gain more if only the other would adopt his weaker strategy. Samuelson also points out that the 'safeguard' against collusion is the existence of more than two competitors.

33. For a non-cooperative game to be soluble in any sense the equilibrium pairs must be interchangeable; to be soluble in a strict sense the pairs must be both interchangeable and equivalent.

The pairs (a_1b_2) and (a_2b_1) are equivalent if $v_1(a_1b_2) = v_1(a_2b_1)$ and $v_2(a_1b_2) = v_2(a_2b_1)$, where v_1 and v_2 are the pay offs to players 1 and 2 respectively. The pairs are interchangeable if (a_1b_1) and (a_2b_2) are also in equilibrium.

34. *Risk level* as defined by D. G. Pruitt (see p.22 and note 8) is the sum of the negative outcomes of a gamble multiplied by the respective probabilities of their occurrence. Pruitt's suggestion is followed that as the risk level of a gamble increases so will the conflict between that function and the expectation of gain. At some point, no matter how favourable the anticipated gain may be, the risk involved will not be willingly accepted.

35. R. D. Luce and H. Raiffa, op. cit., Chapter 5.

36. The interpretation which gave the game its name is that two prisoners interrogated separately have the alternative of confessing or not confessing. If neither confesses they will each receive a light sentence; if either confesses and the other does not, he receives a nominal sentence but the other is punished severely; if they both confess they will receive less than the maximum sentence. The first strategy is not confess and the second confess.

37. A similar formulation was suggested by L. E. Siegel and S. Fouraker in *Bargaining Behaviour* (New York: McGraw-Hill, 1963), p. 104, Table 7.2.

38. Any such agreement between firms carrying on business in the UK would be registrable under the 1956 Restrictive Trade Practices Act unless it related exclusively to export.

39. W. Lee, *Decision Theory and Human Behaviour* (New York: Wiley, 1971), pp. 293–97.

40. L. E. Siegel and S. Fouraker, *Bargaining Behaviour* (New York: McGraw-Hill, 1963), Chapter 10.

41. See W. Lee, op. cit., p. 297: 'Perhaps subjects are largely motivated by a desire to outscore the opponent regardless of the absolute levels of the pay off.'

42. L. E. Siegel and S. Fouraker expressly disallowed any contact between the bargainers. W. Lee, *Decision Theory and Human Behaviour* (New York: Wiley, 1971), reports that in experiments by McLintock, Nuttin and McNeel (1970) friendship, or to a lesser degree prior acquaintanceship, decreased the percentage of competitive choice. The personal relationship between the marketing managers of the duopolists could therefore be of significance in this context. If both prefer to live on friendly terms, neither is likely to opt for the competitive choice; in simpler terms 'dog does not eat dog'.

43. See L. E. Siegel and S. Fouraker, *Bargaining Behaviour* (New York: McGraw-Hill, 1963), p. 188, Table 10.11, which shows that under conditions of complete information 13.4% of all transactions were negotiated at the pareto-optimal price as compared with 0.4% under conditions of incomplete information.

44. A situation is described as *pareto-optimal* when it is impossible to effect a change which benefits one party without adversely affecting the other.

45. J. F. Nash, 'The bargaining problem', *Econometrica,* vol. 18 (April 1950), pp. 155–62.

46. J. C. Harsanyi, 'Approaches to the Bargaining Problem', *Econometrica,* vol. 24 (April 1965), pp. 144–57.

47. A. Coddington, *Theories of the Bargaining Process* (London: George Allen and Unwin, 1968), Chapter II. J. G. Cross, *The Economics of Bargaining* (New York: Basic Books, 1969).

48. See the discussion in T. C. Schelling, *The Strategy of Conflict* (London: Oxford University Press), Appendix B.

49. Risk is used here in S. H. Knight's sense of a situation in which the outcome is not certain but the probabilities of the alternative outcomes are either known or can be estimated. See note 1.

50. R. D. Luce and H. Raiffa, op. cit., p. 15.

51. The index proposed here is derived from the model described by E. W. Adams and R. Fagot in 'A model of riskless choice', *Behavioural Science,* vol. 4 (1959), pp. 1–10, but I devised the actual detail of the means of construction.

52. This is the equivalent of personnel selection decisions based on multiple criteria. As Stagner has pointed out these should be based on minimum cutting scores on a number of variables rather than a single regression equation. 'The personnel manager will want to hire workers who will have good absentee records, will accept supervision and will produce at a high level of quality and quantity. There is a point on each

of these beyond which the employee is unacceptable regardless of how good he is on other aspects of performance.' R. Stagner, 'Corporate decision making', *Journal of Applied Psychology,* vol. 53 (February 1969), Part 1.

53. Latane in his paper 'The rationality model in organizational decision making' delivered to the first seminar in the Social Science of Organization, Pittsburgh, June 1962, and published in *The Social Science of Organization* (New Jersey: Prentice-Hall, 1963) has described a similar model for selecting a secretary. I noted this paper after completion of my own model. The only difference of approach is that Latane initially valued the factors personality and efficiency on the same 0–1 scale and then applied a weighting factor when combining the two, which leads arithmetically to the same result as that given by method of construction used here. For interest of comparison, and in case the reader might find the method suggested by Latane easier, his secretary example is set out below:

Possible Actions	Value Measures		
	Personality	Efficiency	Combined
Ms C	0.9	0.5	0.8
Ms D	0.5	0.8	0.6
Combining weight	0.7	0.3	1.0

Value measure rating on a scale from 0–1.0 for each characteristic. *Combining weight.* The weighted average of the two measures reflects the opinion of the decision maker as to their relative importance.
Decision Rule. Choose that strategy with the maximum combined value measure.
Choice. Ms C.
Note that it is complete coincidence that both Latane and I chose the same combining ratio!

54. The same assumption is made by K. Simmonds in 'Competitive bidding, non-price features', *Operational Research Quarterly* (March 1968), pp. 5–14.

55. Again, the same conclusion is reached by K. Simmonds in 'Competitive bidding, non-price features', *Operational Research Quarterly* (March 1968), pp. 5–14.

3

ESTABLISHMENT OF THE TARGET OBJECTIVE

Planning must be positive and demands that management identifies at the outset the optimum target which they would wish to attain. In so doing they should not allow themselves to be held down by imagined technical or commercial restraints. The initial thinking must be bold or all that follows will suffer.

Compare these two statements:

Company X: 'Our aim is to secure a 25% market share with a pretax net income of 25%.'

Company Y: 'Because of competition we cannot expect to aim for more than a 15% market share with a pretax net income of 10%.'

The approach of company Y is unfortunately only too typical of the type of thinking which pervades a significant area of British management. Its exponents would characterize it as 'realistic'; in truth it is negative and half defeatist from the start.

Company X, however, starts off by stating quite simply the target it wants to reach. From that point the company's negotiators can develop their strategies and identify the problems which will be encountered along the way. In so doing they may find that their products are not sufficiently competitive because designs or manufacturing techniques are obsolete, to achieve the desired rate of growth would make too heavy a demand on liquid resources or their sales force is inadequately trained. While each of these problems may appear to be restraints on their attaining the goal which management have set, they only become actual restraints to the extent to which they are allowed to be. Problems should be regarded as a challenge to action and not an excuse for inaction.

This does not imply that all such problems can be solved at once; some will clearly require longer-term action which will extend beyond the period available for the particular negotiation. The immediate target objective will accordingly have to be modified to take account of this, while at the same time other plans will be developed in parallel to ensure that on the next occasion the necessary resources are at the company's disposal. It would be as wrong to pursue the target objective regardless of resource availabiltity as it would be to accept such lack of resources as a permanent restraint.

3.1 STATEMENT OF THE TARGET OBJECTIVE

The starting point for the preparation of any negotiating plan should be an explicit statement by management of their target objective. Vague generalizations will not do. There must be no phrases like 'we must obtain the maximum profit we can', or 'we must buy at the lowest price consistent with quality'.

Both these statements are meaningless because they are not quantitative. They could not be used in conjunction with any of the decision-making techniques described in Chapter 2 and provide no definitive base from which to compare the worth of alternative strategies. To be of any value they need restating in such terms as:

> Our gross margin after an allowance of 5 per cent for contingencies and based on recovery of full shop costs and overheads should be not less than 30 per cent.
>
> For quantities of 1 000 per week we need to purchase at a price not in excess of £1.50 per article and using our sampling plan B the rejection rate must not exceed 3 per cent.

Even statements such as these would obviously need amplification before they became sufficiently comprehensive to provide the negotiators with a proper understanding of their intended task. Acceptable provisions for such items as delivery period, specification, penalty risk, warranty liability, terms of payment, etc, will all need to be defined since they all have an effect on price (see p. 123 and Chapter 11).

3.2 ASSESSMENT BY THE NEGOTIATING TEAM

Once the definition of the target objective has been accomplished, either for the individual opportunity or for a range of opportunities through the medium of a business plan, the negotiating team should have a definitive and quantified expression of the outcome which management want to achieve. Whether this becomes the final negotiating objective, or has to be modified, will depend on the outcome of its assessment by the negotiating team in relation to the factors which will affect its achievability, including the results of any exploratory discussions with Opponent.

Preparation of a negotiating plan is therefore a three-stage process:

1 Establishment by management of the target objective.
2 Assessment by the negotiating team of the feasibility of achieving the target objective.
3 Agreement between the negotiating team and management on any modifications to the target objective which then becomes the negotiating objective.

Described in this way the process may appear tortuous. In practice, however, depending on the scale of the negotiations, the whole sequence may be covered by one meeting, with the unit manager starting the proceedings by stating what he wants to achieve, the negotiating team leader pointing out the problems, and the meeting ending with an agreed definition of the negotiating objective. The essential requirement of recording the negotiating objective in writing may be the only formality involved.

In a more complex case an intial meeting may be followed by exploratory talks with Opponent and the negotiating objective only settled by further discussion after that feedback has been obtained.

The advantages of going through this process (listed below) strongly outweigh the time which may be involved. Indeed it could be argued that if the company cannot spare the time for this preparatory work then they have no right to be negotiating at all.

1   The desired outcome is expressed boldly without the pessimism of past precedent being applied.
2   The negotiating objective is nevertheless set at a level which is not unrealistically optimistic.
3   Management accepts the commitments necessarily associated with achieving the negotiating objective. In this it is assumed that the negotiating team leader will bring these specifically to management's attention and obtain their agreement, for example, to such items as the allocation of key personnel and advance ordering of long lead items, to support an improved delivery promise.
4   The negotiating team are personally committed to the negotiating objective since they have played a part in its formulation.
5   The negotiating team have a clear understanding of their precise terms of reference and so do management. Provided that the negotiating team act in accordance with these there should be no need for 'inquests'.

4

APPRAISAL OF THE TARGET OBJECTIVE AND FORMULATION OF THE NEGOTIATING OBJECTIVE

4.1 GENERAL

The appraisal of the target objective and subsequent formulation of the negotiating objective must be carried out within the context of the total business activity. Negotiation should never be considered, or allowed to become, an isolated act. It has to be integrated within the marketing or purchasing function of the company concerned and subordinated to that company's overall business strategy. Success in negotiating is measured only in terms of the positive contribution which that negotiation has made to the attainment of the corporate strategic goal.

It follows that the initial approach to the appraisal should be broadly based and related to the three critical factors which will affect the viability of the target objective concerned:

1   Strength of negotiating position
2   Competing objectives
3   Resource requirement and availability

Within the time scale for an individual negotiation these three factors have a single total value so that an increase in the value of one can be secured only at the expense of a decrease in the value of one or both of the others. Negotiating strength can be increased if all competing objectives are abandoned or reduced in scale so that the available resources are wholly or largely concentrated on one project. For example, the sales manager could himself spend, say, three months negotiating personally one major contract, on which his own skills were of particular significance, provided it was accepted that his assistants could handle the remaining orders and inquiries. If this could not be accepted, then a consequent reduction in negotiating efficiency and in the probability of obtaining the order on the most advantageous basis must follow. At the extreme end of the scale the company should decline to participate in the major project rather than try to manage with the part-time efforts of their sales manager, since the end result would either be the loss of the contract, and perhaps other business as well, or the securing of the contract on unfavourable terms because of the lack of concentrated attention. Either way the company would lose.

Generalizing from this example, if the resources are greater than those which can be made available without interfering with other projects, then either a reduction in negotiating strength must be accepted or one or more competing objectives abandoned. Although it should never be allowed to happen, all too frequently the available resources are spread across so wide a range of objectives that the negotiating strength on each is reduced to the point at which real success is achieved on none.

The appraisal of the target objective will now be considered in relation to the three identified negotiating situations:

1 Bidding
2 Procurement
3 Contract dispute

Before doing so, one point should be clarified. Although there is a need to define the target and negotiating objectives in a manner as precise and quantified as possible this does not mean that they are necessarily single points. Particularly in the planning stages the negotiating objective would be expected to be a range of values, from the maximum which the negotiating team and management have agreed is feasible to the minimum which they have agreed would be acceptable. This range will cover not only the price level but also all other factors which would significantly affect price or risk, eg in a bid situation, penalty clauses and warranty liabilities (see Chapter 11).

Only if Party's first offer will also be his final one, so that there will be no subsequent opportunity to modify its terms, must Party select a single negotiating objective from within the range of possibilities (see p. 105).[1]

4.2 BIDDING—COMPETITIVE

For certain industries, eg major process plant design, the target objective may be established separately for individual bid opportunities; more commonly in manufacturing industry an operating unit is required to achieve an average return on sales or assets over the budgeted period. This return may be a single figure across the unit's activities, or more properly differentiated by product line and/or market, eg home and export, sales to public authorities and commercial customers, catalogue products as opposed to those requiring customer application engineering.

Whichever way the target is set its achievement for any particular bid or series of bids is dependent on the response which is obtained from an analysis of the bidding opportunity or opportunities in relation to both:

1　Bid desirability
2　Success probability

This analysis is carried out in two stages:

Stage 1. A preliminary analysis made rapidly in order to reach the bid/no bid decision.
Stage 2. A more detailed analysis for the purpose of determining the optimum level at which to submit the offer and the terms against which such submission should be made.

This section is concerned only with stage 1; stage 2 is considered in Chapter 6.

The bid/no bid decision
Every company has limited resources both physically and financially. Equally every company has a number of potentially desirable activities over which those resources could be employed. The scale of resources required at any one time to satisfy *all* those activities will be greater than those which the company possesses. A business's ability to make profits depends very largely on how effectively it utilizes its resources by concentrating them on those activities which will provide the maximum return for effort expended, over the time scale for which the business is being planned.

The distinguishing feature of resources used at bidding stage is that they are only profitably employed if the bid is successful.[2] If the award is lost then the resources have been wasted in the sense that they have made no contribution to income.

In the short term the major proportion of the costs involved in tendering are largely fixed since they consist of the salaries and related on-costs of the marketing, engineering and other staff involved.[3] They are related directly to the bidding effort required to achieve the budgeted sales volume and net income. One way of increasing profitability, therefore, is by keeping these costs to a minimum whilst maximizing the success ratio. This is illustrated by Figure 4:1.

The direction and control of bidding effort is therefore a vital management function and as a first step towards achieving this a defined routine is required for reaching a quick bid/no bid decision using the two criteria previously referred to: bid desirability and success probability.

These factors are to some degree interdependent and to some degree independent. The price level at which the offer is made is clearly interdependent; by increasing the level the bid becomes more desirable but conversely the chances of success are reduced. While the

1	Sales target for the year	£10 000 000
2	Success ratio anticipated	1 in 20
3	Volume of business to be tendered therefore	£200 000 000
4	Average value of each tender	£5 000 000
5	Number of tenders to be submitted therefore	40
6	Sales department annual tendering costs	£2 000 000
7	Proportion of annual costs incurred by other departments, eg engineering, estimating, accounts, expended in direct support of sales	£2 000 000
8	Total average costs of submitting each tender therefore	£100 000
9	Average level of net income on sales	10%
10	Total net income per annum	£1 000 000

If the success ratio could be improved to 1 in 4 *without any increase in effort per tender or the incurring of any other additional selling costs,* then the position would be:

11	Volume of business to be tendered	£150 000 000
12	Number of tenders to be submitted therefore	30
13	Total cost of tendering*	£3 000 000
14	Reduction in tendering costs*	£1 000 000
15	Percentage increase in nett income (line 14 as a percentage of line 10)	100%

*Costs are assumed to be directly proportional to tendering effort. In practice this is more likely to be a step function but the general result at any particular level of effort will be the same. It is also recognized that since many of the tendering costs are semifixed, eg staff salaries, it would take time to achieve any such increase in profitability through the reallocation of staff to other duties or a reduction in headcount due to natural wastage.

Figure 4:1 Analysis of tendering costs, success ratio and return of sales for ABC plc, a mechanical engineering company

desirability of a bid will be affected by the extent to which the manufacturing shops are already loaded, this is a factor which has no impact on either the customer or competitors, and has, therefore, no direct relevance to success probability.[4] Accordingly it is classified as independent.

The position is illustrated in Figure 4:2 in which column 1 shows the independent factors relating to bid desirability and column 2 those which are interdependent with success probability. Similarly column 3 shows the interdependent factors for success probability and column 4 those which are independent. Although in Figure 4:2 'Bidders political connections' is shown as independent under the heading 'Success probability' there are circumstances in which there is a relationship between political connections and bid desirability. The case of total independence is where the political relationship between the UK government and that of the territory concerned is such that no action on the part of the bidder is likely to change it.

At the time of writing Malaysia is a case in point. Given, however, that the political connections between the two governments are at least neutral and the project is of such a nature and size that it attracts governmental attention – eg steelworks, aircraft for the state airline, major infrastructure projects such as hydro-electric schemes and large-scale processing and mineral extraction plant – then it is open to the bidder to act politically in a manner which will improve his success possibility but such action can also affect bid desirability. If he can persuade his own government to assist with securing the project, normally through extraordinary financial support, then the bid desirability may actually be improved. Alternatively, if the bidder has to secure political support from within the territory through the appointment of particular agents and the payment of exceptional commissions or promising to share the work with a prominent local contractor on either a sub-contract or joint venture basis, then the bid desirability can be reduced. See further the author's *Business Ethics* at pp 225 and 226.[5]

As regards political factors generally their importance must never be overlooked even if the World Bank, ADB or similar institution is providing the project funding, and the project is therefore under the aegis of international consultants. Tender appraisal can often be the art of deciding on the reasons why a particular bid should be preferred to all others once the need for such behaviour has been identified.[6]

The treatment of financing terms on export contracts is complex. To an extent the terms which can be offered are outside the contractor's control being a function of ECGD and the Department of Trade's policy in relation to the country in question within the framework of the consensus agreements of the export credit insurers union. Equally the availability of a soft loan or aid for a portion of the costs so as to reduce the total overall interest rate and perhaps provide support for the financing of local costs, is again a matter of government policy towards the country concerned. In these respects the credit terms which can be offered are independent of bid desirability although they will have a major effect on success probability. Further the terms which the contractor manages to secure will, to a degree, depend on his own efforts, the way in which he manages to present his case to the government and not taking no for an answer. He may be able, for instance, to secure better terms by making out a national interest case based on the additional employment opportunities which would exist within the UK if the contract were secured, especially if these were located within areas of high unemployment.

Bid desirability will however be affected by the financing terms for the portion of the contract not covered by ECGD supported credit ie the 'front-end' finance which is either paid for by the buyer in cash or covered by a Euro-dollar loan and the payment terms for the local costs. Bid desirability will be increased to the extent that:

1   The 'front-end' finance, 15 per cent on a buyer credit, is provided under a Euro-dollar loan which is under the control of the contractor's bank, ie is specifically designated for the particular contract involved and not made available generally to the customer or to the central bank of the country in question. Ideally, the loan should be located off-shore and never enter the buyer's country. In any other case there is a risk of the loan being used for other purposes and the buyer defaulting in payment.
2   The amount of the down payment is sufficient to ensure a positive cash flow when taken in conjunction with any other mobilization payments which the contractor is entitled to receive.[7]
3   Local costs are forward funded so that the contractor is again always in a positive cash flow situation and ideally has enough in hand to meet the costs he would incur in terminating should the buyer default in payment.

The routine for determining the bid/no bid decision is then as follows:

1   Look at the independent factors. If any one of these is strongly negative, eg inability to meet a significant mandatory specification requirement, then the decision should be no bid. It will be noted that in Figure 4:2 the marketing importance of the bid is identified as an *independent* factor. We take the position therefore that if the bid is right outside the company's marketing plans then the decision should be *no* bid, irrespective of success probability.[8]
2   Prepare an analysis of the bid desirability on a points scale using the method described below and the questionnaire given in Figure 4:3.
3   Estimate the success probability utilizing the method described on p. 66 and illustrated in Figure 4:5.
4   Multiply the bid desirability function by the factor for success probability and compare the product with a predetermined norm.

Because of the interdependence of a number of the factors as shown in Figure 4:2, eg price level and contribution, delivery and penalty risk, it may be necessary to carry out the exercise several times, varying the input factors. (A simple computer program would both simplify the task and speed up production of the answers.)[9] Assuming that one or

1 Bid desirability independent factors	2 Bid desirability interdependent factors	3 Success probability interdependent factors	4 Success probability independent factors
Marketing importance of the bid:	Profit contribution expected	Price level	
(a) Territorially	Delivery required by customer	Delivery to be offered	
(b) For the particular customer			
	Risk of paying delay penalty		
(c) For the product to be offered	Extent to which product is responsive to customer specification or could be made so	Reservations to be included in the offer on items where product non-responsive	Ability to meet mandatory specification requirement
(d) Relative to the competition			
Production importance of the bid in relation to (a) possibility of securing another order within same time scale, (b) existing order book and (c) inventory	Favourable or adverse terms of payment and cash flow	Financing terms to be offered	
	Currency risk and availability of ECGD cover on export contracts	Financing terms to be offered	
	Warranty risk	Response to be made to customer's commercial terms	'Bidders record of performance on past contracts
	Any other contract clause having a significant risk element		Bidders political connection
	Local production element on export contract	Willingness to offer local investment	Bidders local image and nationality

Figure 4:2 Bid desirability and success probability–independent and interdependent factors

more factor combinations result in an outcome which is favourable to bidding then the decision to tender would be conditional on the bid being structured in that manner, eg in relation to the acceptance of contractual risks.

Bid desirability analysis

Figure 4:3 sets out a list of questions. From the answers to these questions a bid desirability table can be prepared which may be divided into four main sections:

1 Marketing
2 Production
3 Financial
4 Contractual

Suggested marking scheme

A *Marketing*

   1 Does the tender fall within the main stream of the
      company's activities or is it only peripheral?   10

   2 How does the tender fit in with the company's plans
      for market development or retention in relation
      to the following factors:
      (a) territory
      (b) the particular customer
      (c) the product(s) to be offered   10
      (d) the company's competitors

   3 What is the company's existing order book for the
      product(s) concerned and what percentage of
      the sales budget is covered by firm orders?   10

   4 What alternative opportunities exist now or will do so
      within the period covered by the tender for the
      use of the same capacity?   10

   5 Of the balance of the sales budget uncovered by firm
      orders what are the chances of obtaining other
      business on no less favourable terms?   10
                                        — 50

B *Production*

   6 Would the contract if secured require any special facilities,
      eg special tooling, or involve the production of special
      parts or the use of non-standard components?   10

Figure 4:3 Bid desirability questionnaire

7   Would securing the contract impose any significant strain on production resources in terms of machines, labour, inspection and test facilities, etc?   10

8   What would be the effect of *not* securing the contract on:
    (a)   Retention of staff/labour
    (b)   Unrecovered overheads or adverse shop variances }   10

9   Has the product been manufactured before? If so, is it responsive to customer's specification or are there risks in meeting mandatory requirements? If not, what degree of confidence exists in the ability of the product to meet such requirements?   20
                                                                    —   50

C   *Financial*

10   Is the anticipated cash flow positive or negative?   10

11   Are there any risks foreseen in relation to:
    (a)   Cost escalation
    (b)   Currency exchange rates   }   15
    (c)   Customer's financial stability

12   Is the anticipated profit contribution as a minimum in line with the unit's planned target either overall or for that product line/market?   25
                                                                    —   50

D   *Contractual*

13   Will any contract be based on the company's terms or customer's?   —

14   Are there any contractual risks forseen in relation to:
    (a)   Penalty for delay
    (b)   Warranty
    (c)   Consequential damages
    (d)   Inspection and testing requirements   }   50
    (e)   Inability to obtain truly independent decisions on any disputes
    (f)   Termination either for default or customer convenience
    (g)   Performance guarantees
                                                                    50
                                                                    ——
                                                                    200
                                                                    ——

Figure 4:3 (concluded)

The marking scheme suggested in Figure 4:3 while to some extent arbitrary has been designed to:

1   Avoid any undue bias or weighting in favour of any one particular factor. Depending on his function in the company an individual will tend to concentrate on the matters peculiar to that function. By limiting the marks both for functions, and for items within functions, correction of or allowance for any such behaviour is being made.
2   Ensure that all relevant factors make a proper contribution to the final answer. It is easy to emphasize out of all proportion any one factor which is wholly favourable or wholly unfavourable; a balanced approach is required.

Both the marking scheme and indeed the table format (Figure 4:13) may be varied to suit any individual type of business. If, for example, contractual risks were negligible, since the firm only accepted orders on their own standard form and for standard products, then the contractual section could be downgraded. Equally, the form has been designed bearing in mind primarily the needs of the manufacturing industry and mechancial/electrical contracting. For building and civil engineering the section on production would need some amendment.[10]

It will be understood that in awarding points a higher mark denotes either a greater need for the business or lower risk, whilst conversely a lower mark denotes either a lesser need for the business or a higher risk. It follows that:

1   The more *strongly affirmative* the answers to questions 1, 2, 9, 10 and 12 the *higher* the mark.
2   The more *strongly affirmative* the answers to questions 3, 4, 5, 6, 7, 8, 11, 14 the *lower* the mark.

An example of the use of the bid desirability table with commentary on the marking is set out in Figure 4:4.

One question which arises in connection with the bid desirability table is how and by whom it should be completed in practice. It is suggested that one department is made responsible for each section, although they would probably have to call on others to provide some of the inputs and the whole exercise would be coordinated by marketing. Thus responsibility would be allocated as follows:

Section A Marketing
         B Production supported by Engineering and Quality Assurance
         C Finance supported by Marketing on the price level
         D Contracts[11]

Each section to be complete would contain not just the quantified assessment but also a brief statement of the reasons which lead to that figure being selected. As before the degree to which it is necessary to go into detail will depend upon the bidding situation. If the tender is of a routine nature the answers can be extremely short. If it is a major project then the sections when put together will form a comprehensive memorandum descriptive of the opportunity and of the risks involved.

Looking now at the bidding proposition described in Figure 4:4 this appears to be at best a borderline case. Neither marketing nor production indicate any essential need to obtain the order and the profitability level envisaged is not encouraging. However, before taking a final decision, and so allocating tendering resources, it is necessary to examine the chances of winning the order and to bring the two factors of bid desirability and success probability together.

Success probability
As indicated by Figure 4:2 success probability is in many respects interdependent with factors other than price. At the bid/no bid stage, and assuming the decision is in favour of bidding, these other factors need to be treated as variables and develop strategies which will strengthen areas of competitive weakness. Therefore, the objectives in estimating success probability at this point are:

1   To assist in making the bid/no bid decision.
2   If the decision is bid, then to enable us to plan means of improving our chances of success.

For this reason the approach will differ from that which will be adopted later when the sole objective in estimating success probability will be to decide on the optimum bid price, and the non-price factors will be treated as parameters of this decision.

In developing the technique for estimating success probability three cases may be distinguished:

1   Buying decision made on price only with a single decision maker.
2   Buying decision made on multifactors but with a single decision maker.
3   Buying decision made on a multifactor choice with multiple decision makers.

Case 1
This is the simplest position, an example of which would be bidding to a strict public authority against their standard specification, where it is known that at least one other competitor can meet the authority's

Question reference number	Mark		Comment
A 1	8	}	Bid fits in well with the company's marketing programme
2	8		
3	4	}	Order book is already largely covered and further promising opportunities have been identified
4	4		
5	4	28	
B 6	8	}	Product is part of company's standard range and within existing resource capabilities
7	8		
8	2		No adverse effect foreseen
9	16	34	Although product is standard the customer's specification is tighter than normal on inspection limits
C 10	8		Customer has reputation for paying some 30 days later than company's normal terms
11	12		To maintain a competitive price a complete allowance for cost escalation cannot be included
12	13	33	Severe competition is expected for the order and it is anticipated that to be successful the company would have to reduce to about 70% of planned target
D 14	30	30	Because of the need to meet competition the delivery will be tight and, therefore, there is some risk of penalty which cannot be allowed for in the price; again due to competitive considerations. There could also be a problem on testing and inspection on which the customer is known to take a hard line
	125	(62.5%)	

Figure 4:4 Marked example using bid questionnaire

requirements and no possibility exists of the use of 'influence' to direct the award either in or against Party's favour. That is the assumption is made that the sole decision maker will act both rationally and objectively considering only the authority's best interests. In such circumstances Party can only use his judgement based on past experience of competitors' prices, trade gossip and market 'feel' to judge his chances.

Case 2

In this instance Party must first identify those factors which the buying decision maker will use for assessing tenders and the relative importance he will attach to each. Then Party must decide how he compares with his competitors in respect of each such factor when looked at through the eyes of the buying decision maker. For this purpose it is suggested that Party makes use of the format given in Figure 4:5 but the weighting function would reflect only the valuation of that factor to the decision maker relative to the other factors.

Case 3

This is the most complex case and one which represents the norm for capital goods' tenders for process plant, mechanical, electrical or electronic engineering, and some commercial building and civil engineering projects. The buying decision in these fields is widely diffused over a number of functional departments and management levels, each of which has differing interests and powers of influence.[12] Indeed those involved in the decision making process on the customer's side may well extend beyond the limits of the customer's own organization to include Ministers or even Heads of State where the Project is that of a public authority and of major economic importance to the country concerned. This situation, therefore, must be represented in such a way that Party's chances can be evaluated and identification can be made of both the factors and the points of contact in the customer's organization and outside on which Party should concentrate his efforts in order to improve his competitive position.

Method for estimating success probability and identifying marketing action

A tabular comparison is made between Party and each assumed competitor, utilizing numbers on a points scale. The list of possible factors to be included in such tabulation will clearly vary widely between industries and even between bids within the same industry. A comprehensive checklist from which the relevant factors may be selected is given in Appendix 1.

An example of such a comparison is given in Figure 4:5 and the steps leading to its formulation are set out below.

Step 1. Party selects from the checklist (Appendix 1) the factors relevant to the particular bid.
Step 2. Each factor is allocated the same number of points and Party ranks himself against his competitors so that the total for each factor adds up to 100, the higher the number in the row the more attractive the bidder appears to the customer on that dimension. To achieve objectivity this ranking should be done by more than one function whose interests do not coincide. Note that it must be done, so far as Party has the ability to do so, from the viewpoint of the customer since it is customer's preference which matters.
Step 3. Party identifies the functions within the customer's organization which will contribute significantly to the buying decision.
Step 4. The value of each factor assessed under step 2 is weighted by the combination of Party's estimate of:

(a) The value which each function in customer's organization will give to that factor.
(b) The influence level which that function possesses in the making of the buying decision.

It must be stressed here that, as in other examples, sophistication of method does nothing to improve imperfect data. If the original estimates have a substantial margin of error, so too will the final answer. For this reason some 'practical' managers have doubted the value of such exercises. It has also been suggested at seminars that the figures will tend to be adjusted by the person doing the exercise to provide the answer he wishes to obtain.

Factor	Allocation of points			Weighting function[13]	Allocation of points after weighting function		
	Party	Firm A	Firm B		Party	Firm A	Firm B
Price	25	40	35	0.3	7.5	12.0	10.5
Delivery	40	30	30	0.25	10.0	7.5	7.5
Technical merit	45	30	25	0.20	9.0	6.0	5.0
Influence	35	35	30	0.25	8.75	8.75	7.5
Total points after applying the weighting function					35.25	34.25	30.5

Therefore success probability:
Party   35%
Firm A   34%
Firm B   31%

Figure 4:5 Point comparison between Party's bid and that of his competitors

The reply to both these criticisms is that the simple requirement of making people give consistent, quantitative answers to questions imposes its own discipline. They apply more thought to the process than they would if merely asked to estimate their chances of success. It is agreed, however, that the results so obtained must be treated broadly and although the first place of decimals is used in the calculations this certainly does not mean that the answer possesses that degree of validity. Thus the results of Figure 4:5 in relation to success probability would be interpreted as showing an even position between Party and firm A with both having some lead over firm B.

As an additional safeguard it is again suggested that the assessment be carried out separately by more than one department, and the results compared so as to guard against either excessive optimism or pessimism of the individuals concerned.

Determination of bid expected value and the bid/no bid decision
The figures used in Figure 4:5 are based on the same assumptions as those behind the estimation of the bid desirability given in Figure 4:4. It is now possible to move to item 4 in the routine for making the bid/no bid decision given on p. 63, and by multiplying the two factors of bid desirability and success probability together to arrive at an expected value function for the bid. This becomes 22 (62.5×0.35). If this is above the minimum level established by the company for bidding, and no better opportunity exists, then Party should tender.

The acceptable minimum bid expected value function is a matter for each firm to decide either generally or in relation to particular product lines and the minimum could itself be varied according to the business position in which the company finds itself. If trade is buoyant then the minimum could be raised so as to restrict still further the volume of tenders submitted and ensure concentration on the most favourable opportunities.

As a general guide line, preference would be for a minimum of not less than 25. In Figure 4:6 the solid line has an expected value of 25 and the shaded area to the left represents those inquiries for which the decision should be no bid.[14] By selecting a single expected value function it is required that the lower the bid desirability the higher must be the success probability and the converse equally applies. This seems consistent with how firms behave in practice even though they may not develop their approach to the problem by the use of a formal technique.

Objection may be raised to the proposition implicit in Figure 4:6 that if the bid desirability is less than 50 per cent the decision should be no bid, *irrespective of the success probability*. It is certainly true that many firms do not operate in this way and that in order to maximize order intake they will tender for work just because it is believed they have a high probability of success.

If, however, the bid desirability is less than 50 per cent then at least two of the following considerations must apply.[15]

1   The Bid does not fit in with the company's marketing plans.
2   The company already has its sales budget largely covered.
3   The contribution value is low.
4   There are significant technical or commercial risks involved.

On this basis either the firm should be concentrating its resources on the orders already on hand, while developing its main-line marketing effort on a more forward basis, or it should be looking for ways in which it can utilize its assets more profitably and with less risk.

Improving success probability

The impression may have been gained that the estimation of bid desirability and success probability is a 'one-time' operation. This is not so. The need to treat success probability as a variable throughout the whole bid preparation process has already been noted. In this the approach differs from that adopted in the papers which describe models for determining the optimum bidding price through the use of expected value techniques.[16] These models are static; they react to a series of single inputs derived from costing data, assumed competitor price levels and customer bias.[17] If all are favourable to Party, as in the case described by Edelman, no problem arises.

Too often, however, all factors at first sight are not favourable and this possibility is increased as more factors are considered. Since the analysis is extended to include factors of contractual, technical and financial risk, together with assumed levels of influence, which the bidding price models apparently do not, then it is much more likely that a conflict of interest situation will arise.[18] However, the opportunity may still exist during the bidding period to overcome the unfavourable points, provided that these are immediately identified and specific corrective strategies developed.

The secondary objective, therefore, of the bid desirability table is to identify those areas in which it may be possible for Party to do one of the following:

1   Improve his success probability directly through accentuating customer's existing bias in favour, or reducing any bias which he has against Party.
2   Indirectly minimize or eliminate risks associated with the bid which would otherwise influence management to add contingency factors to the price so reducing the competitiveness of the bid.

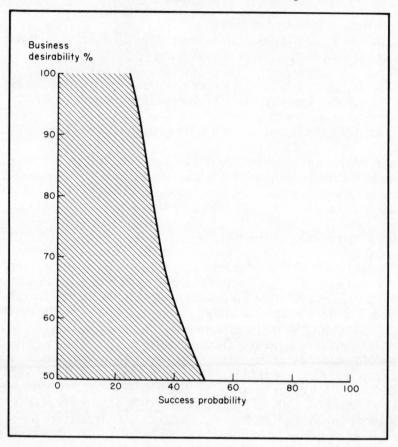

Figure 4:6 Bid expected value

Referring again to Figures 4:4 and 4:5 and assuming the decision were to consider a bid, provided that its expected value could be increased to a level acceptable to management, then the problem areas would be defined and action responsibilities assigned as described in Figure 4:7.

In following out these strategies Party will be acting offensively to improve his rating relative to that of his competitors and defensively to protect himself against the effects of their actions. As noted in the discussion on game theory (p. 30) Party must allow for Opponent's strategy choice being optimal. Thus he must assume for instance that firm B will bring pressure to bear on customer to try and ensure that the award is made to the lowest bidder. This in turn will lead Party to emphasize even more strongly to customer the dangers of buying cheap and nasty.

Reference	Problem	Action assignment
B9	Higher than normal inspection/test standards	Marketing, with engineering and Q.A. support, to visit customer, stress the technical excellence of the product and proven nature and ask for some relaxation down to Party's normal standards. The extra time and cost of the higher inspection/test to be given as the reason
C 10	Late payment	Marketing to examine cash flow with finance and consider suggesting to customer discount for prompt payment
C 11/12	Price level	Marketing to lobby all three customer departments concerned with the buying decision with a two-pronged attack: 1 Stressing the role of price as an indicator of quality[16] 2 Asking that any price comparison should be made not on initial price only but on total cost over the whole product life. This would bring engineering more into the price comparison which on the evidence of Figure 4 : 5 should be helpful to Party
D 14	Delivery and penalty	Marketing to establish just how important delivery really is to customer. If its apparent importance is confirmed, then as this is a standard product management could be asked to approve a stock order for long lead items. (As marketing have already identified other favourable bidding opportunities the inventory risk is low)

Figure 4:7 Table of actions to improve Party's success probability

Resource employment

The interdependence between success probability and bid desirability has already been recognized in Figure 4:2. Equally both of these can be affected in turn by the extent to which resources are allocated both to bidding and contract execution. By devoting greater effort to bidding in the form of extensive customer preconditioning, or in the development of alternative solutions to technical problems, the chances of success can be increased. Bid desirability can be improved also through more careful examination of problem areas leading to minimization of technical/commercial risks, eg on-site investigation of local conditions, careful vetting of proposed subcontractors.

But it may only be possible to employ these resources once during a given time period—there may be only one man with the right contacts to obtain access to customer at board level. The same man may also be valuable in other directions so that the task to be given priority must be chosen. Therefore, before proceeding with the type of strategy action described in Figure 4:7 it is necessary to review *all* the resources which will be required both at bidding and contract stages, and to be assured that the employment of these resources on this particular opportunity represents an optimal decision within the limits of data and computational facilities. To assist in this review a complete checklist of resource requirements is given in Appendix 2.

Resource employment at contract stage

In using the checklist in Appendix 2 to review the resources which will be required by Party for the execution of the contract, it is necessary to consider both absolute quantity of the resource and the time at which it must be available. The method of doing this will vary with the nature of Party's business.

If this is repetitive with the product already engineered and relatively standardized, so that control on an individual contract basis is not required, then the programme controller would simply be expected to put a dummy forward load on his overall production schedule. If, however, the business is non-routine, eg jobbing engineering, civil construction, process plant design, then it will be necessary to prepare an individual time/resource chart. This will utilize data derived from the resource check list, Appendix 2, and preliminary contract programme, and identify those activities which lie on the critical path. An example is given in Figure 4:8.

Which ever method is used the results should be referred to the individual departmental managers who would be concerned with the contract's execution and a commitment obtained from them that the requirements can be met. Any doubts or potential bottlenecks, eg a single machine already heavily loaded, must be brought out for management decision on the allocation of priorities and if necessary for increasing plant capacity.

If resources are not adequate then early action is essential if future problems are to be avoided. Simply because they are in the future, and there is always the chance that they may in fact not materilize, the tendency is for action to be postponed, particularly if capital spending is involved. Resource development must, however, be maintained in

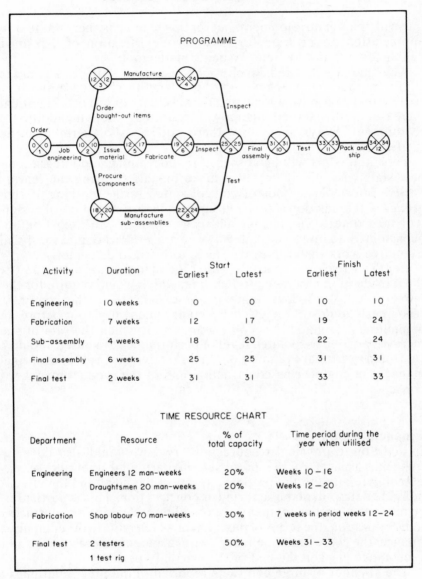

PROGRAMME

Activity	Duration	Start		Finish	
		Earliest	Latest	Earliest	Latest
Engineering	10 weeks	0	0	10	10
Fabrication	7 weeks	12	17	19	24
Sub-assembly	4 weeks	18	20	22	24
Final assembly	6 weeks	25	25	31	31
Final test	2 weeks	31	31	33	33

TIME RESOURCE CHART

Department	Resource	% of total capacity	Time period during the year when utilised
Engineering	Engineers 12 man-weeks	20%	Weeks 10 – 16
	Draughtsmen 20 man-weeks	20%	Weeks 12 – 20
Fabrication	Shop labour 70 man-weeks	30%	7 weeks in period weeks 12–24
Final test	2 testers	50%	Weeks 31 – 33
	1 test rig		

Figure 4:8 programme and time/resource chart. Note that:

1   The critical path runs through the engineering to prepare the specification for the bought out items and their subsequent procurement. If the initial engineering could be done before order date the delivery period could be reduced by 3 weeks.

2   Although machine operation A is scheduled for weeks 11 to 15, it could take place any time between weeks 11 and 22. Similarly there is a 3-week flexibility in scheduling machines B and C.

3   However, there is no flexibility on preliminary engineering, procurement, assembly and test. Any delays here will result in the contract running late.

line with market development; but for this to happen there has to be an appreciation of the time lag between identification of a resource deficiency and that deficiency being made good.

Any increase needed in physical resources will need company capital authorization which may be a lengthy procedure and items such as test gear have a long lead time. If there has to be a significant increase in the skilled manpower resources then in addition to recruitment delays inevitably there will be short-term operating inefficiencies.

Time and effort will be absorbed in the training and integration of new staff who will themselves make mistakes during the learning period; informal methods of control suited to the working of small groups will break down as the groups get larger; new control systems will take time to implement and cause friction with existing staff accustomed to more casual ways; managers who previously did executive work themselves will have to learn to delegate.

For these reasons proposals, either for an individual opportunity or the introduction of a new product line, which would require for their implementation an immediate major expansion in the company's resources should be reviewed by management in depth before any commitment is made. Every assumption on which the rate of such increase and the associated level of performance are based should be subjected to critical examination. In this activity the role of the project manager in engineering construction and of the product manager in consumer-based industries will be vital.

Financial resources

In addition to physical resources the review should also cover the financial aspects of the proposal, in particular the rate of cash outgoing relative to the proposed terms of payment and the effect of possible delays in manufacturing or construction. This is particularly significant when the company is expanding and taking on contracts of longer duration, the terms of payment of which require the company to finance the work until delivery, with a percentage retention until acceptance or even the end of the warranty period.

The glamour of large contracts reported in the press continues to attract some sales managers who see in them reflected glory, but the lesson for managements who are concerned with profitability is clear: such contracts are only worth the strain they impose on the company's resources, and the additional risks they involve, if the margin is sufficient to absorb such risks and costs and still return a net contribution which properly reflects the use made of the company's assets.[20]

Summary of Section 4.2
Methods have been described for preparing quantified estimates of:

1 Success probability
2 Bid desirability
3 Resource requirement/availability

In making these assessments it has been assumed that the customer's behaviour is rational and to that extent the approach has been normative rather than behavioural.[21] The interdependence of these three factors has been stressed and similarly that the examination of them must be both broad and thorough. In comparing the results of the analysis with the target objective set by management, either generally in the businessplan or specifically for this bid opportunity, the following guidelines have been proposed for decision making:

1   If the bid opportunity meets the target objective without requiring abnormal resource utilization or any departure from the company's normal commercial/technical standards then marketing can go ahead with the development of the bid without further reference to management.
2   If the bid expected value is below management's target then the decision should be no bid unless management are prepared to authorize bid preparation on the basis that action will be taken during the bidding period to improve the bid expected value. Submission of the bid would then be subject to confirmation that such action had been successful.
3   If to achieve the target would require abnormal resource utilization, eg design engineering effort, then specific management authority to proceed must be obtained.
4   If any factor, say success probability, is dependent on departing from normal company standards, eg acceptance of unlimited consequential damages, then again the issue must be referred back to management for their approval.
5   Finally if the bid desirability is less than 50% then irrespective of the other factors the decision should be *no bid*.

It has been stated that if an engineering company cannot spare the time for preparatory work in negotiation they have no right to be negotiating. This may now be paraphrased to suggest that if such a company does not have disciplined operating procedures along the above lines they have no right to be in business at all.[22]

4.3   PROCUREMENT
The governing issues in determining the ability of the buyer to meet

any target objective are the nature of the competitive market existing for the product in question and the manner in which the buyer exploits that market.[23] The term market is used here not in any physical or geographical sense but as descriptive of the supply–demand relationship through which buyer and seller interact.

The nature of the market at any time is determined by:

1   Total demand.
2   Composition of the demand and the extent to which it is dominated by a single buyer.
3   Nature of the product and the degree of substitutability between the product and any other item/service.
4   Total supply available from existing capacity.
5   Composition of the supplying industry and the extent to which it is dominated by a single supplier or a small number of major suppliers.
6   Costs and time needed to create new capacity; costs, time scale and other barriers to the entry of new firms into the market, eg technical knowledge required, patent rights.
7   Ease with which information relating to price levels becomes generally available within the market.

It is assumed that the buyer's preference would be for the market to approximate as closely as possible to one of perfect competition. In such a market there would be a tendency towards a single equilibrium price established by the supply–demand mechanism, which would not be affected by the actions of a single buyer or seller since each would be too small in relation to the total market size. This price would be just sufficient to maintain in the market a supply capacity just adequate to meet current demand, and each firm would produce that quantity which satisfied for their cost function the expression; price = marginal cost (MC).[24]

The revenue conditions for all firms in the market would approximate to the same; only their cost conditions would differ. At any level of demand, therefore, the only firms in the market would be the lowest cost producers whose total capacity was capable of meeting that demand. Higher cost producers would be excluded unless demand increased and the price rose to a point at which it became attractive enough for them to enter. In the same way, as soon as demand dropped and subsequently the price, they would be the first firms to leave.

The extent to which the market in which he buys is competitive or not depends very largely on the buyer. It is well known that 'pure' competition, apart possibly from some commodity markets, is an abstraction. Nevertheless, it is possible for the buyer to increase significantly the degree of competition in any market through:

1   The manner in which he specifies his requirements.
2   His selection of potential vendors.

How this can be accomplished is now considered in relation to the following factors which tend to make a market competitive.

1   Total demand adequate to sustain a number of suppliers.
2   Demand spread amongst a number of buyers.
3   High degree of substitutability for the product by others.
4   Supplying industry divided into a large number of firms none of which is predominant.
5   Ability for capacity to be easily expanded and low entry barriers for new firms.
6   Ease of communication of prices, but no collusion between suppliers.

Many of the comments to be made are common to more than one factor and have been grouped broadly under the two headings of factors relating to supply and factors relating to demand. It must be made clear at this point that the sole concern here is with the issue of increasing the buyer's ability to meet his target objective through strengthening his negotiating position by improved competition. There may be other and legitimate reasons, eg national security, balance of payments, local unemployment which would in certain instances pull in opposite directions. This possibility is recognised but the resolution of any such conflict is a political rather than a commercial issue.

It follows from this that normatively the purchasing agent should ignore such considerations and concentrate his efforts on the professional performance of his function. Behaviourally however it would be less than realistic not to recognize that the greater his awareness of the political factors involved and the less secure he feels in resisting them, the more probable it is that he will 'bend' his commercial judgement in favour of the preferred political answer or at least that he will not oppose it. Only if he is secure within his own function, and that function is secure within the organization, can he be expected to withstand political pressure either from outside or from his own Board and whether it is legitimate or derived from particular interest.

Demand
The buyer should always aim to buy in the widest possible market. Specifically:

1   He should avoid insisting on a 'special' so that the market becomes

the market for that special, the demand for which may be so small that the buyer has of his own accord created a sole source supply situation. His objectives should be to use a standard readily-available industrial item, if necessary redesigning his own product to do so. If this is wholly impractical then he should think in terms of make rather than buy.

2   By maximum standardization of common user items, eg ball and roller bearings and bulking his orders, the buyer will make his business that much more attractive to supply firms and again widen the market.

3   If the buyer is a home-market monopoly purchaser, so that he is in a position to set his own specifications to which industry must respond, then he should ensure that such specifications and standards are prepared so that:
    (a)   They can be responded to by the maximum number of suppliers.
    (b)   The supplying companies can make the same articles for export. In practice this means under rather than over design.
    (c)   The technical and commercial conditions imposed are no higher than those which are essential and engineering 'frills' are avoided.

4   By defining his requirement in appropriate cases in terms of the performance required, rather than restricting the supplier to a defined means of achieving that performance, the buyer will again widen the competitive field. Consider the simple domestic example of a person wishing to purchase a central-heating installation. If he specifies the method of heating then he is at once restricted to virtually a monopolistic supplier with only minimum competition on the installation itself. If, however, he defines his requirements in terms of performance under specified conditions then he can invite competitive bids from gas, oil and coal.

Supply

There is no competitive problem when the buyer's demands, together with all those of others in the market, are less than the capacity of the industry to supply. The buyer can then be certain of obtaining at least some genuinely competing bids since, even if the suppliers did attempt to enter into a price fixing agreement, the attractions would be such that on any individual inquiry it could be assumed that at least one firm would defect (This is the equivalent of the game-theory discussion of the prisoner's dilemma–see p. 35 and the matrix in Figure 2:13.)

Under such conditions the buyer has two additional objectives:

1   In the short term to encourage the more efficient producers to stay

in the business. He does this through careful selection of the firms invited to tender and his responsibility is obviously greater the nearer he approaches to being a monopoly buyer.

2 In the long term, if he can see the reduction in demand being maintained, to encourage the survival of the most efficient producers. This would also cover in certain instances the retention of important research and development facilities. Again the responsibility of the monopoly buyer is that much heavier since their's is a mutual dependency relationship.

It is likely that at some stage the objective of obtaining the lowest price now will conflict with one or both of the two objectives stated above. In resolving that conflict it seems that the buyer should give greater weight to the long-term stability of his purchasing relationships with the industry concerned rather than to the achievement of an immediate minor financial gain.

The competitive situation is more difficult for the buyer, particularly if he is 'tied' to the product or service in question, when the industry's capacity is less than the buyer, either alone or with others, is demanding. Classical economic theory of supply/demand would state under these conditions that in the short run existing firms would expand capacity and in the long run new firms would enter the market, attracted by the higher price levels.

Whether either of these events happens in practice will depend on:

1 The costs involved in expanding existing capacity.
2 The costs of entry in the market.
3 Restrictions on entry, eg patent rights.
4 The supplying firm's estimates of the period over which the buyer's demand will exceed existing capacity, relative to the costs of increasing capacity or new entry, and the time that would take.

Clearly the answers to the above questions will vary widely according to the nature of the industry concerned, the capital required for investment and the timescale of bringing the new capacity into operation. Increasing the number of coffee bars in town with a rapidly expanding teenage population is perhaps near one end of the scale. Investment costs are relatively low and the new coffee bar can be opened in a matter of weeks. At the other end of the scale is heavy engineering, and there are several examples here of where capacity was increased with very significant capital expenditure but by the time the new capacity became fully effective, the buyer's demand was already declining.[25]

Conditions will arise in which firms will not expand capacity to meet demand and the buyer will be unable to pursuade new firms to enter the market. The buyer will be compelled to accept longer delivery periods and higher prices until the time is reached when the anticipated decline in demand occurs. Until then each firm will know that it is bound to obtain a proportion of the business and has therefore no incentive to reduce prices. In fact a price equilibrium would be expected to develop between suppliers.

The tender submarket

The moment the buyer invites tenders for the supply of particular goods/services he creates a submarket limited to the firms from whom he has requested offers. To that extent he has reduced competition; there may be firms whom he has not invited who would be willing to meet his requirements at a lower price than any of the firms listed but who have not been given the opportunity.

It might be suggested from this that the buyer would gain from longer rather than shorter tender lists, and even possibly from open tendering by advertisement. These practices have been strongly argued against elsewhere and the arguments have lost none of their validity with time.[26] Indeed the arguments may be reinforced by pointing out that if a supplier believes there is a 75 per cent chance that his bid will be lower than a single random competitor, if the number of competitors increases to five, this probability reduces to 25 per cent and it seems likely that the tenderer's interest in the bid opportunity would follow suit. The profitability of one large construction company in America was increased sharply following their acceptance of a consultant's recommendation never to submit a bid for any project for which there were more than five firms tendering.

The buyer should maximize competition within the tender submarket by ensuring that, consistent with his requirements for quality, service delivery and reliability, he has selected a short list of firms most likely to submit low-price bids. This ought to be achievable through the professional purchasing officer's up to date knowledge of his supply industry and the operation of a proper vendor rating scheme.

Ultimate use

In the preoccupation with the achievement of the target objective in terms of price, delivery, etc, it must not be forgotten that purchasing action is only taken to enable the purchaser to fulfil some further objective: in the commercial world to make a profit. No matter how well the purchase has been negotiated in other directions—how tight the terms of contract have been drawn or how low the price reduced—if the purchase fails to meet the end-use requirement then the operation has been a failure. Purchasing is never an end in itself.

For example, in establishing the specification for the product if this

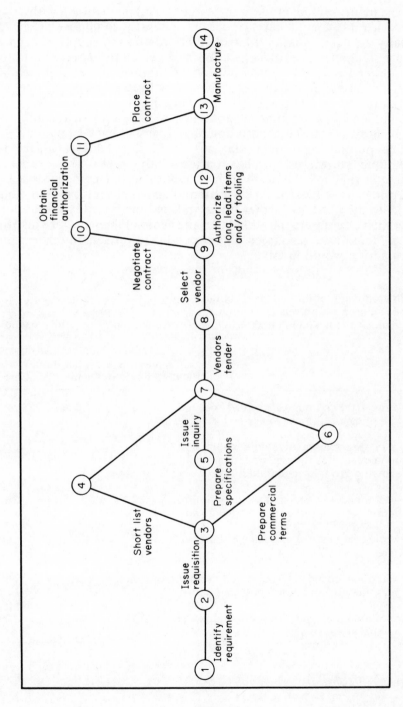

Figure 4:9 Network for procurement action

is to be incorporated into an item which it is intended to sell with a five-year warranty then, clearly, it will be necessary to impose more than usually stringent quality control standards on the supplier, coupled with extended rights of inspection and rejection. This will almost certainly go against the intentions of widening the market, since it will limit the number of suppliers able or willing to respond, and will certainly put up the price. If, however, the five-year period passes without a warranty claim, so earning customer goodwill and minimizing support costs, the negotiating objective will have been achieved.

The purchasing officer may also find it helpful to utilize the technique known as purchase price analysis (PPA) in order to estimate what he believes the price ought to be, and compare this with the prices as tendered. Any substantial gap between the two would indicate the need for further investigation, and possibly a search for alternative suppliers, provided that the scale of the purchase justified the allocation of resources and expenditure on search costs which such action would involve.

Estimated value of the tender: £100000
Time required for normal competitive tendering: 12 weeks
Time required for a negotiated bid allowing 2 weeks negotiating time: 8 weeks

Item	Estimated saving in time (weeks)	Estimated saving/cost in money	
		Saving (£)	Cost (£)
1 Value to the company of each.week saved to a maximum of six weeks.	6	9000	
2 Estimated excess of single negotiated price over price for a competitive tender allowing 2 weeks negotiating time.	4		5000
3 Additional excess if the negotiating period were reduced, per week 1.25%.	2		2500
4 Additional cost/risk of issue of letter of intent.	2		1000
5 Additional cost/risk through early ordering of tooling and other long lead items.	2		500
6 Additional cost/risk through eliminating purchaser's inspection.	1		2000

Figure 4:10 Cost/time evaluation table

By far the most common circumstance which leads to a modification of the target objective, as expressed in pure purchasing terms, is the necessity of having the purchase completed within a time scale which, from the purchasing viewpoint, is less than optimal. For every activity there is a natural time which can be improved upon only by either spending more money or allocating more resources. A simple network analysis of a standard procurement action is given in Figure 4:9. This network represents the activity/time norm which should enable the purchase to be made at the most economic price and in accordance with the company's purchasing standards. If, however, when the times allotted to each activity (including the estimated manufacturing period) are added together it is found that the total exceeds the time which can be permitted (because, for example, the purchase is tied in with the company's seasonal marketing programme) then something less than the norm must be adopted for this particular procurement.

Thus the decision could be taken to negotiate with a single vendor which would eliminate activities 7 to 9 in Figure 4:9. The period allowed for negotiation could be reduced or a letter of intent issued in advance of the formal order so that some manufacture could commence before contract details were finalized. Long lead items or tooling could be committed as soon as the necessary specifications had been established. The company could rely on the vendor's final inspection and eliminate their own.

Each of the steps referred to would clearly involve the company in some additional cost or risk of extra cost. The possible time savings should therefore be evaluated in terms of the benefits which would be derived in comparison with the risks which would have to be accepted, and the optimum course selected. A convenient way of doing this is by the use of the cost/time evaluation table, an example of which is set out in Figure 4:10.

Comment on Figure 4:10
Item 1 represents the value to the company of the time saved. This could be an earlier start to revenue earning through quicker introduction of new plant capacity, securing a reduction in the waiting time of installation personnel on site by shortening the delivery period for materials or test gear or making an earlier start to, and so catching a greater proportion of, a seasonal trade such as heating.

Items 2 and 3 can only be subjective estimates. My own experience would tend to suggest a figure of around 5 per cent for item 2; item 3 can only be judged in relation to the complexity of the transaction and the points at issue but as a guide a figure of 2½ per cent is suggested.

Items 4 and 5 will be dependent on the value of the commitments being made and the costs which would be incurred should the transaction have to be cancelled. In practice for short periods cancellation costs are usually very low since it is largely a matter of getting the order booked with the vendor and into his production schedule.

Item 6 is more difficult since it is dependent on the buyer's judgement, supported by his quality assurance manager, of the chance that a unit which will pass the supplier's inspection will be rejected by buyer's inspection, and the consequences which would follow from this.

It will be appreciated that care must be taken to ensure the time savings shown are cumulative and not overlapping and in case of doubt reference should be made to the network analysis.

Where, as in Figure 4:10 the total of possible time savings exceeds that which is of genuine value to the company, eg any earlier delivery would merely create an inventory problem, then the time savings should be selected so as to minimize cost. This is illustrated in the graph shown in Figure 4:11; the dotted line shows the minimum expected cost at which a time saving of six weeks could be achieved utilizing:

Item 2	Negotiation with a single vendor	4 weeks
Item 5	Early ordering of tooling	2 weeks
		6 weeks

Competing objectives and resource requirement/availability
In marketing the company always has the alternative of bid/no bid. If for a particular inquiry the bid expected value analysis gives an unfavourable result then, unless political considerations are involved, the company will decide not to proceed but to employ its resources on some preferred opportunity. In procurement, however, once a demand has been established, as a result of a prior commitment into which the company has already entered, then no matter how unfavourable the negotiating position the purchasing department must meet this commitment, and at the same time make the best possible bargain.

The necessity for determining first the nature of the competitive situation and then considering resource requirement/availability lies in the need to:

1 Advise management as to the probability of the target objective in terms of price, delivery, quality being achieved.
2 Select those procurement activities on which the negotiating effort of the department should be expended.

Resources for procurement are basically skilled effort and time. The

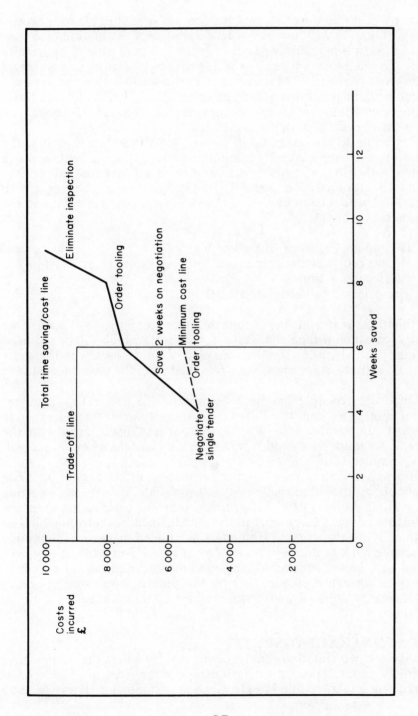

Figure 4:11 Savings/cost trade-off graph

ultimate cost of a purchase and the time/effort available for negotiation will tend to vary inversely. In the cost/time evaluation table one week's negotiating effort was equivalent to 1¼ per cent of the purchase price. Given the parameters of the negotiating situation, and the target objective as defined by Management, particularly in so far as it relates to end use, the purchasing manager must plan his activities and those of the other people involved and compare the resources he needs, and for what period, with those available.

Returning to the example in Figure 4:10 it is assumed that the decision has been taken by management to negotiate with a single vendor rather than go to competition on the basis that this will result in a time saving of four weeks and will not increase the cost by more than £5 000. This decision has placed three operational restraints on the purchasing manager:

1 He can only go to a single vendor.
2 He has only a limited time, say four weeks, in which to complete purchasing action.
3 The price must not exceed £105 000.

Within these restraints the purchasing manager must now identify the activities which will be involved, the resources which will be required and the time which can be allocated. A convenient means of doing this is by an activity/resource allocation schedule of the type illustrated in Figure 4:12.

Once the schedule has been completed the purchasing manager should obtain a commitment from the other departments concerned to support him in the plan, and in the earliest discussions with the potential vendor he should similarly make clear the effort which will be demanded from him.

If it appears at any time that the resources either cannot be made available at all within the proposed time scale, or only by diverting them from projects of equal priority, then the purchasing manager must immediately refer back to the management level from which he obtained his directions. Emphasis is placed here on immediate reference back to the right management level. Too often this type of problem is kicked around so long at a junior level, at which no clear-cut decision can be made, that by the time it is referred to senior management it is already too late for maximum benefits to be achieved.

4.4 CONTRACT DISPUTE
Unlike the two situations analysed previously where the parties have been only contemplating a relationship, in the situation to be considered now a relationship has already been established. However, as a

Activity	Elapsed time (weeks)	Man-weeks Purchasing	Engineering	Legal
1 Engineering				
1.1 Prepare specifications			3	
1.2 Evaluation and selection of vendor			3	
1.3 Answering queries from vendor			1	
1.4 Negotiation with vendor			1	
2 Purchasing				
2.1 Evaluation and selection of vendor		2		
2.2 Preparation of terms of contract		2		
2.3 Answering vendor's queries		1		
2.4 Negotiation with vendor		}2		
2.5 Finalization of contract				
3 Legal				
3.1 Advice on terms of contract				1
3.1 Assistance in finalizing contract				1
4 Vendor				
4.1 Answer evaluation inquiries				
4.2 Review specification and terms of contract				
4.3 Prepare quotation				
4.4 Negotiate contract				
4.5 Finalize contract				
Total man-weeks effort		7	5	2

Figure 4:12 Activity/resource schedule

result of the acts of one or both of the parties, or the occurrence of some event outside their control, either the terms of that relationship are no longer mutually acceptable or their interpretation is a matter of debate.

The relationship between the parties found its expression in the contract they signed which is itself a part of, and subject to, the system of law by which it is governed.[27] That system of law is in turn subordinate to the particular country's political and social ideology which may differ widely in substance, although not in form, from that of our own. When the proper law of the contract is foreign it is important not to be misled into believing that both parties to the contract necessarily mean the same even when the same terminology is used. Whether the terminology used means the same or not is a matter not of law but of political and social intent. As Friedman has pointed out:

> Legal technique is always subordinate to social ideals. The technically more divergent legal systems can attain similar social ends if inspired by similar purposes; on the other hand the closest affinity of legal technique gives no basis for harmony and cooperation where the purposes differ.

Given certain conditions therefore, although there is a contract in form, its enforceability in practice may be doubtful if not impossible, and if this is so then it must be assumed that the knowledge is shared equally by the opponent. Whilst through negotiation legal proceedings would hopefully be avoided the potential or otherwise for taking effective legal action will be a significant factor in determining both Party's and Opponent's attitude towards any proposals for settlement. The smaller the real capability of Party for obtaining and enforcing any judgement against Opponent, the harder he can afford to be in resisting Party's demands or pressing his own case.[28]

It follows that the analysis of any contract dispute situation must commence by examining the realities of the legal framework within which the contract exists, followed by a consideration of the factors of legal, financial and commercial power as they are balanced between the parties. A full checklist covering all questions which may need to be answered in making the total assessment is given in Appendix 3.

The legal framework
The three main problem areas which exist in relation to the legal framework are:

1   Which legal system governs the contract?

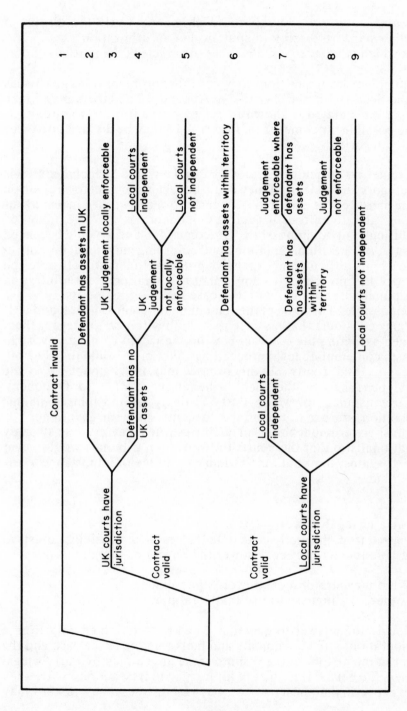

Figure 4:13 *Decision tree: validity of contract and its enforceability*

2   Which court or tribunal would ultimately settle the dispute if either party referred to dispute to law or arbitration?
3   In which country or countries are the assets of the parties situate?

The complete set of questions to which these problem areas give rise is given in Section 1 of the checklist in Appendix 3 and the way in which they are interrelated is shown in decision-tree form in Figure 4:13.

The possible outcomes from Figure 4:13 may be divided into three broad categories:

1   Creates no difficulty. Outcomes 2 and 3 would be included in this category since clearly Party could expect judgement to be given on the merits of the case and if judgement were awarded in his favour to be able to enforce it against Opponent.
2   Difficult but not impossible. Outcomes 4, 6 and 7 would be placed under this heading. Obtaining and enforcing judgement is going to be a long, difficult and expensive process but it is still feasible and Party has no reason to doubt that the local court or arbitration tribunal will not deal with the case again on its merits.
3   Impossible. This covers the remaining outcomes: 1, 5, 8 and 9. If Party considers that his case would fall within this category then, even assuming the contract is valid, he would be most unwise to even contemplate legal proceedings. Not only would they be both lengthy and costly but he is now in serious doubt as to the independence of the local tribunal in relation to Opponent. Circumstances in which Party is likely to find himself in this position are usually confined to contracts with government or quasi-government bodies in countries whose regime is so strongly nationalistic that the courts or arbitration tribunals would never find against their authorities in a case of major importance to the regime.

Exercise of legal power

Given that from the analysis to date the practical possibility exists of being able to exercise legal power the questions remain:

1   What measure of legal power is possessed?
2   Is there willingness to use that legal power?

Obviously the answer to question 1 can be determined only from a consideration of the documents and facts relating to the case and the earlier in the history of the dispute these are studied by Party's legal advisers the better. It is so easy for laymen to take actions which they believe to be in their best interests but which, however useful they may be from a practical viewpoint, may seriously weaken their legal rights. The simplest example is that of urging a seller who is late in completing his contract to make delivery by a new date. Unless the buyer expressly reserves his contractual rights such action could be construed as constituting a waiver of his right to claim damages for delay.[29]

Question 2 raises the interesting issue as to whether, even if legal power is possessed, it would be exercised.

There is certainly a tendency in the UK and apparently also in the United States of America, not only to attempt to settle the dispute without the involvement of lawyers but also to negotiate a settlement without reference to the legal rights of the parties under the original agreement.[30] [31] The parties may not even refer to the contract document.[32]

This conclusion seems more applicable to the private than to the public sector. Within the latter where there is less opportunity for commercial give-and-take and the authority's negotiators may be constrained by the doctrine of public accountability, it is more likely that legal power will be threatened, even if not exercised, and the authority will be guided in its actions by the legal advice which it receives.

The reasons for this appear to be:

1 The belief of Party's commercial negotiator that he will be able to settle things on a person-to-person basis with his opposite number and on terms which both will accept as reasonable. If, however, Party brings in his lawyer then Opponent will do likewise and immediately the negotiations will become rigid and formal.
2 Following on from 1, fear by the commercial negotiator that he will lose control of the negotiation to the lawyer who will make things difficult by sticking to the strict legalities of the case and not compromising.
3 The wish by Party not to be thought of as legalistically minded which Opponent might hold against him on a future occasion. Macauley quotes one businessman as saying: 'Any dispute can be settled if lawyers and accountants are kept out of it. They just do not understand the give and take needed in business.' The judgement seems a little harsh; but certainly the view is widespread in the UK within my own experience.

Following on from the comment made above all these reasons apply far more strongly to the private than to the public sector if only because the commercial negotiators in the private industry, particularly if at Board level, possess a far greater freedom of action than their counterparts, for their interest is in the bottom line figure on the contract profit and loss account.

In general business practice, therefore, certainly within the UK and often within other territories, legal powers and lawyers remain in the background, to be used as weapons of last resort and therefore probably at a stage when the parties no longer contemplate future business with each other so that personal relationships and goodwill no longer matter.[33]

Financial power

The most potent form of power, because the impact is both immediate and direct, is the ability of Party to act in one of the following two ways:

1 Withhold payment from Opponent for goods already delivered or services rendered.
2 Make deductions from monies or security belonging to Opponent which Party holds in his possession.

Any appraisal of the balance of negotiating power in a contract dispute situation must take particular note of:

1 Amounts unpaid and owing to the supplier.
2 Retention monies held by the purchaser.
3 Performance bonds or bank guarantees held by the purchaser.

The first two items are straightforward issues of fact; the third may involve problems of law. Generally two types of bond are distinguished:

1 A cash bond which, as its name implies, the purchaser can take to the bank at which it is payable and demand the value of the bond *without the need for giving any proof of the supplier's default.*
2 A guarantee bond issued normally by an insurance company, guaranteeing performance of the contract by the supplier, but which the purchaser cannot cash without satisfying the insurance company that there has been substantial default by the supplier in the performance of his contractual obligations. As part of their general clauses such bonds may include provisions for arbitration if the supplier disputes the allegations. On bonds and their enforcement generally see the author's *Contracting for Engineering and Construction Projects* 2nd edition at pp. 104-8.

The importance of the distinction is obvious as is the difference in risk to the supplier should the bond be in the hands of an unscrupulous purchaser. If the bond has been issued overseas in connection with an export contract it is essential for the supplier to have the local laws relating to the enforceability of bonds checked, since in my own experience there are wide variations between one territory and another.

Commercial power

In practice the threat, open or implied, of the application of commercial sanctions is the most widely used means of coercing settlement of a dispute. The appraisal must show, therefore, the means that both parties have of bringing commercial pressure to bear on each other. These means may be organizational or personal.

Under organizational the following would be included.

By the purchaser against the supplier

1 Removing a supplier from the approved list.
2 Downgrading the supplier's vendor rating.
3 Withholding the placing of an order about to be awarded to the supplier.

By the supplier against the purchaser

4 Threat by the supplier to cease reciprocal trading with the purchaser.
5 Threat by the supplier in a monopolistic position, or where demand substantially exceeds industrial capacity, to give lower priority to future orders from the purchaser.

The personal means refer to the web of complex personal relationships which exists between the executives of one company and another. These may arise through common membership of professional institutions, industry committees or social clubs or simply through a long period of people dealing with each other regularly and getting to know each other personally. This is the power to which Party's commercial negotiator was referring when stating his belief that he would be able to settle things on a person-to-person basis with his opposite number.

At their highest level such personal relationships are founded upon the mutual respect of one professional manager for another which neither will wish to lose. So a complaint by the purchasing director for Party to the production director of Opponent, both being members of the same golf club relating to late delivery will be taken by the latter as a personal challenge which he must resolve if he is to retain his standing in the other's eyes. Equally the purchasing director would not make such a complaint unless he had already investigated the matter and assured himself that it was genuine, for fear again of losing face, and this would be known to Opponent's production director. These are the tacit rules of understanding by which such games are played.

At the lowest level unfortunately such relationships degenerate into a kind of mutual 'back-scratching' of the type in which favours are bought by other favours: sometimes by presents and occasionally by outright bribery.

Conclusions of the appraisal
At any stage in a contract dispute there will be four possible courses of action open to Party which, in order of 'hardness', are:

1   Accept Opponent's current offer
2   Propose a compromise solution
3   Stay with Party's current offer
4   Refer the dispute to law/arbitration

From the appraisal of the three power factors and with the aid of the checklist in Appendix 3 it should now be possible to set against each course of action the estimate of the consequences which would flow from its adoption, expressed in financial or even preferably utility terms, and the probability of these consequences being realized.[34]

The appraisal may be concluded, therefore, with a situation analysis in decision-tree form with a recommended next step.

Resources and competing objectives
The conclusions arrived at so far have been based entirely on an assessment of the probabilities of success, and have assumed that whatever resources are required, either for negotiation or legal proceedings, will be made available. With a very large company this assumption may well be true, and the question of resource availability can on this occasion safely be ignored. However this may not be so for the smaller company. The larger company will have its own legal department, the costs of which form part of the overheads; the smaller company must employ outside solicitors whose costs will form an additional expense. The larger company can hire technical experts; the smaller must rely on its own engineering staff and suffer the opportunity costs of so doing. The larger company can afford financially to wait for the outcome of the negotiations or litigation; the smaller company has the problem of finding the money to pay its wages bill. If the larger company has a cash-flow difficulty, the bank manager is likely to be sympathetic for fear of losing the account; the smaller company will be politely requested to put its accounts in order and have attention drawn to its overdraft limit.

For the smaller company, therefore, the issue of resources, and the need to use these in the most cost-effective manner to generate new income, can raise real problems. Can they afford the effort and costs which will need to be expended on protracted negotiations or litigation and the waiting time for results? Often the answer is no, and is a prime reason why the smaller company is so vulnerable to the type of commercial pressure which is based simply on the possession of greater resources, legal, technical and financial, and the ability to wait.

In terms of the approach to negotiation, this vulnerability will be reflected in the preference of the smaller company for lower-risk gambles, which in turn will mean that their utility function will show that much more strongly the risk-aversion characteristic typical even of managers in large companies.

NOTES
1.   For example, in bidding to a strict public authority which does not engage in post-tender negotiations. Even then Party may try to leave a little flexibility within his offer.
2.   This ignores the case where the bid is made for 'political' reasons, or simply to keep Party's name in front of the customer and so avoid being passed over when the next invitation to tender is issued.
3.   Expenditure on advertising is an exception. Other than for prestige purposes the better the success ratio the less we need to spend.
4.   Indirectly it may do so by altering the attitude towards the risks Party is willing to take. For example, normally only a 12-month warranty limited to free replacement defective parts may be accepted. If, however, work is short, and chances of success for a major order would be greatly reduced unless a 24-month full repairing warranty were agreed to, Party may be willing to accept the more onerous obligation, but would not do so were the economic pressures for obtaining the order less.
5.   P.D.V. Marsh, *Business Ethics* Associated Business Press, 1980.
6.   See the article 'Who sets the rules? Evaluating contractor bids on Third World Projects in Worldwide Projects' (February/March 1980) *Intercontinental Publications,* USA.
7.   See further the author's *Contracting for Engineering and Construction Projects.*
8.   This may appear harsh and it is admitted that it might have to be tempered by the order-book position. However, the pursuit of business outside the company's marketing plans must lead to a diversion of resources. If the long-term opportunity is good then perhaps the marketing plans should be changed, if this can be done without interfering with other preferred objectives.
9.   Computer programmes already exist for estimation of the optimum bidding price. See S. Edelman, 'Art and science of competi-

tive bidding', *Harvard Business Review* (July/August 1965).

10.   Suggested revision of Section B for constructional or building contracts.

B Construction	Suggested marketing scheme

6   Would securing the contract impose any significant strain on construction resources in terms of plant, labour or supervision?   10

7   What would be the effect of *not* securing the contract on retention of staff and skilled labour and unrecovered overheads?   10

8   Has work of a similar nature been executed before? Are the standards indicated in the customer's specification those to which the firm is accustomed to working?   10

9   Does the construction site impose significant difficulties relative to facilities, ground conditions, weather, location and construction programme?   20

11.   It is appreciated that a separate contracts department is usually only found in larger companies. In others this section would be the responsibility of the commercial department or possibly of the company secretary where he was responsible for contractual terms and conditions, otherwise the legal adviser where the company maintained its own legal department.

12.   H. Buckner *How British Industry Buys* (London: Hutchinson, 1967).

13.   To illustrate the method used, the calculation of the weighting function for price is shown below. It is emphasized that the degrees of influence possessed by the customer's departments and the values given by them to the function, are the subjective estimates of Party. Obviously the better the knowledge of customer and of the real part played by the various departments in the buying decision the more accurate these estimates will be.

Customer department	Estimated degree of influence (%)	Estimated value given by that department to price	Weighting to be applied
Purchasing	30	5	0.15
Engineering	30	1	0.03
Line management	40	3	0.12
Total weighting to be applied in respect of price			0.3

The scheme suggested here assumes that each customer department has the same number of points, namely 10, to be divided amongst the factors relevant to the bid. Thus purchasing, having been assumed to allocate 6 to price, has now 4 points left to be divided between delivery and technical merit. Similarly engineering has 8 points remaining, of which, in the example shown in Figure 4:5 5 were allocated to technical merit and 3 to delivery.

14. In making this statement bids which are submitted on political grounds and also the practice of 'cover' prices have been disregarded. However, the case of the company which may be temporarily short of work is being allowed for, since the flexibility of the bid desirability table will enable this to be taken fully into account. Any such position would reflect in high marks for Sections A and B and, by considering 'contribution' rather than margin, and probably for Section C, since it can be assumed that there is already an under-recovery of fixed costs and that any 'contribution' target would be based as a priority on their liquidation. As Edelman has rather cynically pointed out 'margin' is only an overliquidation of fixed costs! S. Edelman, 'Art and science of competitive bidding,' *Harvard Business Review* (July/August 1965).

15. The proposal which was reviewed in Figure 4:4, for which it will be remembered the score was 62.5%, qualified for 2, 3 and 4 and was only saved from immediate rejection because the product was a standard one which fitted in well with the company's marketing plans. As it was, the bid expected value function of 22 would mean by our standard of judgement a no bid decision, unless some other factor intervened such as the need to bid to maintain customer goodwill.

16. S. Edelman, 'Art and science of competitive bidding', *Harvard Business Review* (July/August 1965). R. M. S. Wilson, 'Competitive bidding theory and practice, *Management Decision* (Summer 1970); P. Brigham, 'Pricing strategy', *Building Technology and Management* (October 1969). J. H. Willenbrock, 'A comparative study of expected monetary value and expected utility value bidding strategy models', Thesis, College of Engineering, Pennsylvania State University (March 1972).

17. S. Edelman makes this clear in describing the operation of the model.

18. Factors related to the contract to be fed into the model are limited to contract quantity, time span, unit standard cost and variable cost content per unit. S. Edelman, Exhibit V (table), 'Art and science of competitive bidding', *Harvard Business Review* (July/August 1965).

19. A. Gabor and C. W. J. Granger, 'Price as an indicator of quality', *Econometrica,* vol. 33 (1966) pp. 43–70.

20. In arriving at the assessment of the value of the company's assets which will be employed, the fact must not be overlooked that such contracts normally occupy a disproportionate amount of senior management time, with consequential adverse effects on the remainder of the business.

21. It has been suggested that those involved in the industrial buying decision only do act rationally and that therefore the distinction which

is sought is one without a difference. However, the alternative view is supported that the industrial buyer and plant engineer, and indeed all involved in the buying decision, act from mixed motives: part organizational and part personal. This point is returned to in Section 7.1 when the modification of the approach to take account of personal motivational factors is considered. See P. Kotler, 'Behavioural models for analysing buyers', *Journal of Marketing,* vol. 29 (1965) pp. 37–45, and sources quoted therein.

22. Objection may be taken to this statement on the grounds that the company is too small, its contracts of too low a value or that there is just not enough time. From the way in which the analyses have been presented, it should be clear that they are sufficiently flexible to be prepared for a simple tender almost in a matter of minutes and for a complex bid over a period of days. However, no time is 'lost' since the data needed to complete the analyses is precisely that data which is required to prepare the bid and develop bidding strategies. Experience in operating a somewhat similar system has shown no difficulty in preparing the analyses for even very major tenders within 7–10 days of receipt of the bidding documents. It has also led to the very much earlier identification of the 'non-runner' and enabled a no-bid decision to be defended against internal pressures.

It is recognized that many businessmen do not like discipline; they feel it deprives them of flexibility. They prefer not to plan their contracts in detail but to sort out problems as they arise. For an account of this attitude see S. Macauley, 'Non-contractual relations in business', *American Sociological Review*, vol. 28 (1963), pp. 55–66, to which reference will be made again in discussing contract disputes.

There is also the marketing man, more artist than analyst at heart, who hates written plans and enjoys 'flying by the seat of his pants', described by L. Adler in 'Systems approach to marketing', *Harvard Business Review,* vol. 45 (no. 3 1967), pp. 105–18. No pretence is made that he will welcome the system, but if he can only learn to live with it then his artistic contribution can be channelled into areas where it can be used to maximum effect.

23. In this section the term 'buyer' will be used to refer to those participating directly in the buying decision and is not limited to members of the purchasing department.

24. Average revenue (AR) = $\frac{e}{e+1}$ × Marginal revenue (MR) where e is the price elasticity of demand (negative) and is greater than unity.

At the most profitable output MR = MC.

Therefore price = $\frac{e}{e+1}$ × MC.

Under perfect competition e equals infinity and therefore
$$\text{price} = \text{MC}.$$

Marginal cost is used here in the economist's sense and so includes the costs of providing finance, including the charges which must be paid to the firm's owners. Therefore it covers 'normal' profit.

25. Capacity was increased in the mining machinery industry to meet anticipated NCB demands but only came into operation coincident with with the large reduction in ordering, following the drop in demand for coal. The heavy electrical engineering industry expanded to meet the demands of the CEGB and the Area Boards, only again to find that the demand for electricity had fallen below estimates so that the industry was left with substantial over capacity.

26. P. D. V. Marsh, *Contracting for Engineering and Construction Projects* (Gower, 2nd edition, 1981), pp. 30-1.

27. A contract is governed by what lawyers term 'the proper law of the contract'. Generally this will be the law stated in the contract, or if no law is stated, then an English court will apply a number of presumptions as to which law the parties intended should apply, of which the two most common are the place where the contract is to be performed and the law of the Arbitration Tribunal or Court named in the contract for settling disputes. For a full statement of the position see C. M. Schmitthof, *The Export Trade* (London: Stevens and Sons, 1980), p. 127 ff.

28. 'The legal position of the parties can influence negotiations even though legal rights or litigation are never mentioned in their discussions; it makes a difference if one is demanding what both concede to be a right or begging for a favour.' S. Macauley, 'Non-contractual relations in business', *American Sociological Review*, vol. 28 (1963) pp. 55–66.

29. If one party to a contract has voluntarily agreed not to insist on its strict performance then he cannot arbitrarily set aside that agreement. If he wishes to reintroduce the strict terms again then he must give the other party reasonable notice of his intention of doing so. If, however, the party granting the indulgence has obtained some consideration for the favour, eg the supplier in return for the concession of the revised date for delivery agrees to undertake some additional service, then there is an agreement to amend the terms of the original contract and this new agreement is binding on both parties. See C. M. Schmitthof, *The Export Trade* (London: Stevens and Sons, 1980), p. 101.

30. See the opinions and statistics quoted by S. Macauley in 'Noncontractual relations in business', *American sociological Review,* vol. 28 (1963), pp. 55–66.

31. In 10 years experience of the negotiation, letting and administration of major engineering contracts with a large number and variety of contractors of varying sizes I can only remember coming into personal contact with the legal department of one firm yet my administration experience covered the handling of a number of large claims.

32. A purchasing agent quoted by Macauley: 'If something comes up, you get the other man on the telephone and deal with the problem. You do not read legalistic clauses at each other if you ever want to do business again.' S. Macauley, 'Non-contractual relations in business', *American Sociological Review,* vol. 28. (1963), pp. 55–66.

33. In South Korea there is a saying: 'You never need a lawyer for a marriage, only for a divorce.' Certainly in the negotiations for the multimillion pound project with which I was associated, the customer's organization never employed a lawyer; and it was not revealed to them that I was a lawyer by profession although not employed as such at that time.

34. This is assuming the consequences are serious enough for money not to be a realistic guide to action. See Section 2.3.

5

STRATEGY SELECTION

5.1 THE FIRST OFFER–BIDDING AND PROCUREMENT

In relation to the level and terms on which any offer is submitted or accepted there are only two basic negotiating strategies which can be employed. These may be conveniently described as:

1 'Quick kill' (sometimes referred to as 'final-offer-first')
2 'Hold back'

Quick kill is the strategy of selecting an offer which it is anticipated the recipient will accept without further negotiation, or of responding to an offer by accepting it at the level and in the terms in which it was made.

Hold back is the strategy of selecting an offer which is sufficiently attractive to the recipient not to be rejected out of hand, but at the same time contains a margin for negotiation which is considered adequate:

1 To enable the party submitting the offer to meet the recipient's demands.
2 To ensure that at the end of the negotiations the party submitting the offer obtains a bargain which at the least satisfies his minimum Negotiating Objective.

Alternatively, to the recipient it is the strategy of bargaining with the party of parties submitting offers until terms are secured which meet at least the recipient's minimum negotiating objective, and which he considers are the most advantageous he can obtain taking into account the time factor for negotiation.

It is important to note that the concern here is only with strategies which are aimed directly at securing a bargain, so enabling the venture which is the subject of the bargain to proceed. Obviously if a party were indifferent to the result he could make any proposal he chose, regardless of whether it would be acceptable to the recipient or not, ie he could submit a tender at a price level which, if accepted, would meet his own negotiating objective, without considering the bids likely to be made by his competitors or the price level at which the purchaser was likely to place the order.

Relationship of Party and Opponent

The correct strategy for Party to select is determined by his state of domination/subordination or uncertainty relative to Opponent in accordance with Figure 5:1.

State of party relative to opponent	Correct strategy to select
(a) Domination	Quick kill
(b) Subordination	Quick kill or hold back depending on strategy assumed to have been selected by Opponent
(c) Uncertainty	Hold back

Figure 5:1 Strategy selection in relation to Party's state relative to Opponent

Domination by Party as a supplier

1   If Party knows he is a single-source supply for the purchaser then Party will be in a dominant position provided that:
   (a)   The worth of Party's offer to the purchaser is marginally greater than the minimum which the purchaser would accept.
   (b)   The worth of such an offer to Party would at least meet Party's minimum negotiating objective.
2   If in a competitive situation the worth of Party's offer to the purchaser taken as a whole is marginally greater than the worth of any competitive offer, and this is known to Party, then Party will be in a dominant position within the limitations that:
   (a)   The worth of the offer to the purchaser is just greater than that any of competitors and at the same time meets the purchaser's minimum acceptable level.
   (b)   The worth of such an offer to Party would at least meet Party's minimum negotiating objective.

To Party as a supplier, the significance of the domination relationship is that, within its limits as described above, Party is free to set his offer at a level which maximizes its value to Party and having done so is in a position to resist departing from that level. His strategy is therefore quick kill.

The second case of domination may not be immediately recognized as such and an example may help to clarify the concept.

It is assumed that the purchaser will value the factors comprised in the subject offer, and in the most favourable competing offer, by comparing their utility values and selecting the offer which has the highest utility in the manner described in Section 2.5. Three such factors are identified: price, delivery and technical merit. Using the same notation as before the components in each tender will be regarded as ordered pairs, where x_1 represents price, x_2 represents delivery and x_3 technical merit. The first component x_1 is a member of set K_1 in which $x_1 > y_1 > z_1$ and similarly for sets K_2 and K_3.

The comparison between Party's offer and the competitive order is given in Figure 5:2.

Factor	Maximum utility value	Party's offer	Competitive offer
Price	3	y_1 (1.5)	x_1 (3)
Delivery	2	y_2 (1)	x_2 (2)
Technical merit	5	x_3 (5)	y_3 (2)
	10	7.5	7

Domination exists since $U(x_3 - y_3) > U(x_1 - y_1) + (x_2 - y_2)$
$(5-2) > (3-1.5) + (3-2)$

Figure 5:2 Comparison between offers of Party and Opponent

Because of his technical superiority Party is able to increase the price and extend his delivery to the point at which the bid is just preferable to the competitive offer. Knowing this, Party could resist any request by the purchaser to reduce his price based on comparisons between Party's price and that of the competitive offer.

Domination by Party as a purchaser
Party will be dominant if he knows for certain that he will receive at least two genuinely competing offers from bidders who satisfy the following conditions:

1 The bidders know that each of them will meet the purchaser's minimum requirements for acceptance of a tender in respect of all relevant factors, eg price, delivery, etc. Obviously if a bidder knew that one competitor did not meet, say, a particular mandatory specification, then he need no longer consider the price level which that firm would submit, and the bidder would move into a position of at least partial domination under the previous analysis of Party as a supplier.
2 Neither bidder possesses any non-price advantage which would enable him significantly to raise his price level above that which would satisfy that bidder's minimum negotiating objective. Again possession of any such advantage would move the bidder into a position of some domination as illustrated in the example given in Figure 5:2.

3   The bidders are confident that Party will award the contract to the most economic offer submitted, without post-tender negotiation directed towards securing discounts or other reductions. If the bidders do not have this confidence then the case is treated as one of uncertainty, unless the opposite applies and they know Party will expect to bargain. In that event Party is in a quasi-dominant position, in that he can compel the bidders in their own interests to adopt a hold-back strategy. He is not strictly dominant, however, since all bidders can now be expected to have included a negotiating margin.

Again Party's strategy is that of quick kill, and this should enable him to buy at the most economic level related to the conditions under which, and the firms from whom, he has invited tenders.

Subordination by Party as a purchaser
If Party as a purchaser is subordinate to Opponent as a supplier, ie the converse of the situation illustrated in Figure 5:2, then it is presumed at the start that Party's strategy should be hold back. Opponent's bid is most likely to be at a level well above the minimum which would be preferred by him to no bargain. Through negotiation Party would hope to reduce that level. However, this presumption would be reversed by the existence of any factor which would lead Party to believe that he would lose rather than gain from any such negotiation. Such factors could be:

1   A feeling of mutual confidence between Party and Opponent developed through a long-term and continuing business relationship. Party is satisfied that Opponent will not have sought to take unfair advantage and does not wish to encourage Opponent into adopting a hold-back strategy in the future and adding negotiating margins.
2   Delay which would be caused by the negotiation in award of the contract and as a result of this probably also in the final completion of the project (see p. 173).
3   Party's recognition of the basic weakness of his negotiating position and his unwillingness to lose face by starting a negotiation which would most likely prove to be abortive. This would again apply most strongly to the situation in which there was a long-term relationship between the parties.

It would be expected in practice, therefore, that Party would only adopt a hold-back strategy if:

1   His buying in that particular market was random and so no long-

term relationship was to be considered.

2   He was in a position to develop a genuine 'threat' strategy, for example, by threatening not to place the contract at all or to adopt a different solution which would reopen the whole tendering on a basis less favourable to Opponent, eg reducing the technical standards or eliminating particular specification requirements which had given Opponent his advantage.

Subordination by Party as a supplier

When Party is in a strictly competitive position bidding to an authority known not to indulge in post-tender negotiations then Party has no alternative. He *must* basically adopt a quick-kill strategy; he has only one chance open to him. However, depending on circumstances and the degree of strictness of the authority concerned in applying their rules, he may employ a partial hold-back strategy by making non-specific reservations on the terms and conditions of contract or the specification such a way that Customer must call him in for discussions before being in able to complete his tender appraisal or place a contract. Party would then adopt a negotiating strategy related to the knowledge he had been able to glean of his competitive position. If within certain limits this was favourable then his position within those limits would be one of quasi-domination, and so he could afford to take a hard line up to the point at which the domination equation was no longer true. If his position was unfavourable he could relax the reservations or discard them altogether, in the hope that this would compensate for the factors in which his offer was otherwise inferior.

However, when Party knows that whatever offer he submits Opponent will expect to bargain, then equally Party *must* select a hold-back strategy and submit his first offer at a level which includes a defined negotiating margin. It is a common delusion of firms dealing with a known bargainer for the first time to believe that if they submit a truly competitive or 'fair' offer then the recipient will recognize the fact and be prepared to accept it without bargaining. Such firms fail to realize that to a bargainer the willingness of the other side to negotiate and to have concessions extracted from him forms a significant part of the emotional worth of the offer. Depending on the motivation of the bargainer, a refusal to negotiate will create suspicion, anger or even contempt and may lead to a rejection of an offer even in circumstances when objectively it would be in Opponent's interests to accept.[1]

Uncertainty

So far in discussing domination and subordination it has been assumed that both parties know with reasonable certainty the facts of the negotiating situation. In practice the reverse will often be the case; the supplier will be uncertain as to the degree of domination (if any) which he enjoys or the price level above which the purchaser will not place the order. The purchaser will not know the realities of the competitive situation nor the minimum price level or other terms which the supplier would be willing to accept.

Because of these uncertainties neither party may feel inclined to risk all on a single throw. The purchaser may find the lowest price too high for his budget; the supplier may find that he could have obtained more for his goods and services. Both have some incentive to employ a hold-back strategy but are reluctant to lose the possible advantages of quick kill. Neither can be certain of each other's intentions. Suppose one of them, perhaps through a misjudgement does decide to use quick kill, what would be the position of the other? In a state of uncertainty what should be the strategy of each party?

| Strategy choice | | Description | Conditional |
Party	Opponent		utility value
HB	QK	Contribution value of an award which would result from Opponent's acceptance of an offer which contained a margin for negotiation over the level of Party's minimum negotiating objective.	6
HB	HB	Contribution which Party considers would result from a successful negotiation with Opponent, following submission by Party of a bid which contained a margin for negotiation. Party has allowed for a proportion (but not all) of the negotiating margin to be conceded.	5
QK	QK	Contribution value of an award to Party at the level which just meets his minimum negotiating objective.	4
HB/QK		Loss which would result to party from failure to secure an award.	—1

Figure 5:3 Strategy values–Party bidding in a state of uncertainty

Strategy choice for the supplier–The situation will be looked at first from the viewpoint of Party as a supplier. Using the method outlined in Section 2.3, it will be assumed that Party is able to establish a scale of the utility values of the possible outcomes of submitting the bid, dependent on the strategy choices of Opponent and himself. These are set out in order of preference in Figures 5:3. The values shown in the figure are themselves quite arbitary and selected only for the purpose of providing a numerical example. The format of the table and the order of preference, however, are of general application.

It will be noted that no reference has been made to the fourth possible strategy combination of Party selecting quick kill and Opponent seeking to negotiate. It is considered that having selected a bid which just satisfies his minimum negotiating objective Party would prefer to lose the award rather than secure it at a level below that objective.

In order to arrive at the expected utility values for each outcome Party must now estimate his subjective probabilities of achieving success and these are as shown in Figure 5:4.

Strategy choice		Probability		Notes
Party	Opponent	Success	Failure	
QK	QK	0.7	0.3	Party's estimate of his chances on a straight competitive bid.
QK	HB	0.1	0.9	The low chance of success reflects Party's refusal to reduce below his minimum negotiating objective.
HB	QK	0.3	0.7	Reduced chance of success on a straight competitive bid due to addition of negotiating margin.
HB	HB	0.6	0.4	The slightly lower chance of success than for QK/QK reflects the risk of a competitor cutting his price.

Figure 5:4 Party's success probability for possible strategies

Using the technique described in Section 2.2 the expected value can now be computed for each outcome, as shown in Figure 5:5.

Finally in order to select which strategy he should adopt Party must choose the decision rule which he wishes to use. In Chapter 2 two such rules were identified:

1 The maximin criterion which would lead Party to select the strategy row which is the maximum of the row minima (see p. 30).

2 The Bayes procedure of assigning subjective probabilities to

Opponent's strategy choice and choosing that strategy for Party which is optimal against that assumed probability distribution (see pp. 27 and 28).

Opponent's strategies

		QK	HB
	QK	$(0.7 \times 4) + (0.3 \times -1) = 2.5$	$(0.1 \times 4) + (0.9 \times -1) = -0.5$
Party's strategies			
	HB	$(0.3 \times 6) + (0.7 \times -1) = 1.1$	$(0.6 \times 5) + (0.4 \times -1) = 2.6$

Figure 5:5 Expected value of Party's strategies

So far in the discussions all situations have been treated as situations of risk and, therefore, it has been considered realistic to assume that Party is able to make some meaningful assessment of the probability that Opponent will prefer one strategy to another. Since this situation has been identified as one of uncertainty it is important to include now the case in which Party has no 'feel' for the situation and cannot, therefore, make any such assessment.

This does not mean that the Bayes procedure must be abandoned. Under such circumstances Party would be justified in adopting the Laplace criterion which states that if absolutely no information is available about the relative probabilities of Opponent's strategies then each should be judged equiprobable. This principle (also known as that of insufficient reason) is older than any other but has often been criticized on the grounds that it is not always easy to identify which events should be considered equally probable and that by changing the number of events the probabilities are automatically changed.[2,3] However, its use can be justified in a simple case where the alternatives can be strictly limited to two or three.

Also it is recognized that it is usual to apply the Laplace criterion only to games against nature and not to games against an opponent in which Party is expected to act on the basis of his knowledge of Opponent's pay-off function and the assumption that Opponent's strategy will be optimal. But because this situation is one of uncertainty Party will have no knowledge of that function, and that being so the game becomes analogous to one against nature.

If the assumption of equal probability is applied to Opponent's strategy choice then the utility value to Party of his two strategies becomes:

Quick kill $(0.5 \times 2.5) + (0.5 \times -0.5) = 1$
Hold back $(0.5 \times 1.1) + (0.5 \times 2.6) = 1.85$

Party's strategy choice would therefore be hold back. It is also interesting to note from Figure 5:5 that the same result would be reached if Party adopted the maximum criterion.

Although this result has been obtained with particular figures it is maintained that in a state of uncertainty, in which Party cannot make a rational subjective probability assessment of Opponent's strategy choice, the result is quite general and Party's strategy choice should always be hold-back. The reasons for reaching this conclusion are set out in Appendix 4.

Strategy choice for the purchaser–It is assumed that Party as the purchaser is free to select whichever negotiating strategy he prefers, ie he is not restricted by public tendering rules which forbid him from negotiating with the lowest, or indeed any other bidder, after receipt of the tenders.

The case in which Party will receive at least three competitive tenders may be considered as typical. This means that there are four possible ways, from a bidding strategy viewpoint, in which the bidders could act:

1   All bidders select quick kill
2   The majority of bidders select quick kill
3   All bidders select hold back
4   The majority of bidders select hold back

Party is unable to assess the subjective probabilities of each course of action occurring but using the method outlined in Section 2.5, he is able to estimate his preference for the outcome associated with each possibility. The results of this are shown in Figure 5:6.

		Party's strategies	
		QK	HB
	All QK	8	9
	Majority QK	7	8.5
Bidder's strategies			
	All HB	1	5
	Majority HB	4.5	6

Figure 5:6 Purchaser's strategy choice

Notes on Figure 5:6–Party adopts a quick-kill strategy:
1   If all the bidders adopt QK then the result will be favourable to Party since all bidders will by definition of the QK strategy have

put forward a price which just satisfies their minimum negotiating objective.

2　If only a majority select QK there is some reduction in Party's expected utility since there is now a chance that the bidder who was previously lowest will have added a negotiating margin which would put his bid above that of the next lowest bidder. Party would therefore be obliged, having decided to adopt a QK strategy himself, to accept the tender from the bidder who was previously next to lowest.

3　If all bidders adopt HB and therefore add a negotiating margin the result is extremely unfavourable to Party. Such a margin would be likely to be around 10 per cent and this is the extra which Party would have to pay. The Matrix assumes that the outcome is still just above Party's minimum acceptable level; if it was not then Party would have to retender.

4　If one bidder adopts QK then there is a marked improvement since there is a chance that this will be either the original lowest or next to lowest bidder.

Party adopts hold-back strategy:

5　If the bidders have all adopted a QK strategy it is assumed that either the lowest or the next to lowest will, under pressure, be willing to grant a small discount.[4]

6　In the straight bargaining situation where all bidders have adopted hold back the outcome is based on Party being able to secure a concession of approximately half the negotiating margin.

7　If one bidder has adopted QK then Party's expectations improve slightly on the chance that this could be either the original lowest or the next to lowest bidder, so that his bargaining would start from a lower base. It is still assumed that Party will seek to bargain on the grounds that his decision is based on personal motivational drives as much as rational thinking.

The above reasoning is quite general and does not depend on the particular values selected. (The complete working out on which the matrix in Figure 5:6 is based is given in Appendix 4.) Therefore in any case of uncertainty Party as the Purchaser would select hold back as his negotiating strategy since this is clearly dominant over quick kill *particularly if Opponent were himself to select hold back* which is the supplier's preferred strategy in a situation of uncertainty.

General conclusions

Bringing the respective utility values for the supplier and the purchaser together in one game-theory type matrix produces the pay-off position illustrated in Figure 5:7.[4] It must be stressed that no comparison can be made between the utility values of the events for the two parties since the utility scales are personal to each and have no relationship with one another.

		Purchaser's strategies	
		b_1 QK	b_2 HB
	a_1 QK	(2.5) (7.5)	(−0.5) (8.75)
Supplier's strategies			
	a_2 HB	(1.1) (2.75)	(2.6) (5.5)

Figure 5:7 Matrix of supplier's and purchaser's strategy choice expected values

The supplier will not select a_1 for fear that the purchaser will choose b_2. The purchaser will equally not select b_1 for fear that the supplier will select a_2. Therefore the strategy choice a_2b_2 represents the 'solution' in the game-theory sense, ie both parties will adopt hold-back strategies.

The outcome a_1b_1 will *not* be reached by both parties acting independently of one another. There must be cooperation between them to the extent that both have complete confidence in the strategy which will be selected by the other, ie the situation is no longer one of uncertainty.

Purchasing conclusions–From the purchasing viewpoint four important conclusions can be drawn from this analysis:

1   If the buyer is continually in the market he should seek to gain the confidence of genuinely competing suppliers and *always* adopt quick kill. He will thereby maximize the gain to himself.

2   If the buyer is only occasionally in the market so that suppliers have no opportunity to obtain such confidence, the buyer should adopt hold back since this will maximize the gain to himself *irrespective of the strategy selected by the suppliers.*

3   The buyer who is continually in the market will lose rather than gain by mixing his strategies. Assuming he goes out of tender five times with the strategies set out in column 2 of Figure 5:8 then the strategies likely to be adopted by the suppliers (assuming they start with confidence) are set out in column 3 and the pay off to the buyer is given in column 4. All suppliers are regarded as knowledgeable and will therefore use the same strategy. It will be seen that the total pay off to the buyer is 28 compared with 40 for adopting quick kill every time.

The crucial tender is number four. It is believed that having been caught once the suppliers would select hold back. Having then been proved to be correct, in that the buyer tried it again, they would adopt hold back next time and from then onwards.

4   Provided there is genuine competition the buyer who is regularly in the market and who adopts hold back as a strategy will lose, as compared with quick kill, once confidence has been established in the suppliers so that they too adopt quick kill as a strategy.

The values shown in the matrix are the end worth of the strategy to the purchaser in present value terms. They do not take into account the time and trouble in which he would be involved by continual negotiation.

Tender number	Buyer's strategy	Supplier's strategy	Pay off to the buyer
1	QK	QK	8
2	HB	QK	9
3	QK	HB	1
4	HB	HB	5
5	HB	HB	5
			28

Figure 5:8 Pay off to purchaser of varying his strategy choice over a series of tenders

5.2   CONTRACT DISPUTE

The distinguishing feature of contract dispute negotiations is that the two sides are already in a contractual relationship. Each has therefore at any time four alternative options open to it:

1   Accept the contract situation as it is and the actions, proposals or interpretations of the other.
2   Maintain the contract in being and accept its validity, but object to and seek to negotiate further within the contractual framework, the actions, proposals or interpretations of the other.
3   Terminate the contract.
4   Act outside the contract provisions recognizing that this could lead to an action for breach of contract by the other. That is the assumption is made that either party may decide to act knowingly in breach of contract if it perceives such a course to be to its advantage.

In deciding as between alternatives one and two, Party, as the recipient of proposals from customer, must always weigh-up the benefit to be gained from showing resistance and establishing a reputation for firmness, as compared to the ill-feeling he may engender in customer's staff which may have unfortunate repercussions at a later date. Even if Party is right on a minor issue, it may not pay him in the long run to prove this to customer, particularly if such action would bring public discredit on a member of customer's staff. It is easy to be right and dead.

Party as the initiator of proposals which he considers are based entirely on a proper interpretation of the contract and factual matters capable of proof which he has provided may reasonably expect Opponent to accept. However, at this point emotion may take over from reason and this is a reaction which Party should anticipate.

By preventing Opponent from developing any counter proposals Party has deprived Opponent's negotiators of the opportunity to be seen to be carrying out their function. They may therefore react violently and substitute abuse for rational argument or become bitter and wait their chance to even the score. An example from the field of labour relations, in which abuse was used in reply to the company's policy of proposing a package which they intended should be accepted by the unions without substantial modification, is given by the following exchange between the chief negotiators for General Electric of America and the IUE, quoted by Walton and McKersie.[5]

> Moore (GE's chief negotiator): 'Your items are inflexible.' Carey (for the IUE): 'Yes, they are inflexible. We have an inflexible position on them. You can mess with the small items but not with the principles. All of our items in this proposal are important. Mr Moore we are going to get all of them even if we have to walk over your face. Understand that? Even if we have to walk over your face, Mr Moore.'

Party should anticipate the possibility of this reaction in putting forward his case and be at pains to show that he has taken note of Opponent's views in developing his own position. In this way he will enable the negotiators for Opponent, when reporting to their own management, to achieve credit for having been responsible for moderating Party's claims, or improving his offer, from that which he first intended to submit. If this is not sufficient then Party must consider modifying his strategy and adopting a limited form of hold-back which will be adequate to satisfy the personal motivation of Opponent's negotiators. Again it is stressed that situations of contract dispute are the most difficult to treat normatively. The degree of personal and emotional involvement is too great.

Intangible situation
Here Party's case is based to a significant extent on matters which are

resistant to absolute proof and depend on factors of subjective judgement. In arriving at Party's strategy a distinction is made between intangible issues which are related to circumstances genuinely outside the control of either side and intangibles which arise from Opponent's default including that of an agent from whom he is responsible, eg a consulting engineer. A further distinction is necessary between the acceptance of a claim in principle and agreement to its quantification. We arrive therefore at four possible combinations and these are listed below together with Party's suggested strategy.

Case No.	Circumstance	Issue	Strategy
1	Happening outside control of either side	Agreement to claim in principle	QK
2	Happening outside control of either side	Quantification of claim	HB
3	Happening due to Opponent's default	Agreement to claim in principle	QK
4	Happening due to Opponent's default	Quantification of claim	HB

Although in Case 2 the strategy proposed is Holdback it is considered that the negotiation to be added by Party should be minimal in the absence of any prior knowledge as to Opponent's bargaining behaviour which would lead Party to make a different assessment, eg Opponent is known always to cut any claim in half. The reason is that Opponent will also under such circumstances have suffered a loss himself through no fault of his own and he is likely therefore to regard any demand by Party, which he considers to be excessive, as unjust and an attack upon his status. His response will accordingly be both emotional and antagonistic. If however Party goes out of his way to express understanding of Opponent's position and presents his claim as modestly and deferentially as possible he is much more likely to be treated sympathetically. At the same time Party must not appear to be so weak that Opponent treats him with contempt. 'Fair but firm' should be taken by Party as his guideline.

The problem arises in an even more acute form with Cases 3 and 4. Here what is significant is not Opponent's loss as such, but the certain loss of esteem and possibly even the disciplinary action which would be suffered by the members of the Opponent's staff involved, if Party's claim were to be accepted. Additionally, it must be expected that those same members of Opponent's staff will be amongst those detailed to investigate and advise on the validity of Party's claim. An example of such a situation would be a contractor's claim for additional costs of site working due to loss of productivity caused by the employer's frequent design changes, the Engineer under the contract responsible for adjudicating on the claim, being the employer's Chief Engineer in charge of his design department.

As regards acceptance of the claim in principle it is contended that the strategy here should be quick kill on the basis that Party should submit his claim strictly in accordance with the facts and the contract documents without exaggeration so that should the claim be rejected he has an irrefutable claim to present either to Opponent's directors or whichever tribunal has jurisdiction under the terms of the contract. On the quantum of the claim, Party must expect that Opponent will bargain, since it is the only means by which he has objectively minimized what he pays, and subjectively, from the viewpoint of the negotiator, the only way in which they can secure their objective of protecting themselves against loss of esteem if not actual security. Party must be willing to explore with them ways in which the claim can be structured, by for example introducing a scapegoat such as the R & D Department on whom the necessity for the design changes can be blamed, so protecting them whilst allowing Party to achieve his objective. Party's negotiating margin should represent his belief as to the concessions which Opponent's negotiators will need to be able to demonstrate to their own management they have secured so that they are protected and management's approval to the settlement will be forthcoming.

In all claim negotiations it will be to Party's advantage if he can support his statements with factual evidence so removing them from the arena of 'pure' bargaining and providing Opponent's negotiators with justification for their acceptance. No problems are foreseen with this where the factual evidence relates to events outside the control of either side, eg usually severe weather conditons. There can however be a problem when the facts are concerned directly with the conduct of one or more of Opponent's staff. Any public reference to this by Party can only lead to the negotiators for Opponent closing ranks, much as any criticism by an outsider of any member of a family will be bitterly contested by the other members, however much they might agree with the criticism in private amongst themselves. If possible the facts should be stated without reference being made to the individual concerned either by name or title. If this is not possible then the reference should be made in such a way as to imply that anyone might have done the same and that no personal criticism of the individual is intended. Obviously, there are difficulties with this type of approach if the basis of Party's claim is negligence and he wishes to preserve his legal rights. In the event that Party has decided – along the lines indicated earlier (see p. 90) that he both possesses legal power and is willing to use it – then his approach will necessarily be that much harder.

Because of this Party must expect Opponent to bargain; it is the only means which he has for ensuring that he pays the minimum which Party will accept. It follows that Party's strategy must be hold back and also, by way of corollary, the better the factual evidence he can present to support particular items in his claim, the more he will remove such items from the pure bargaining arena and so give Opponent's negotiators justification for their acceptance. For example, a claim for extension of time and extra costs due to exceptionally inclement weather, supported by local Meteorological Office figures showing rainfall 50 per cent above average for the period in question.

Consultants
Party's strategy may also be affected by whether Opponent's negotiators are members of Opponent's own staff or are a professional firm of consulting engineers or quantity surveyors engaged by Opponent to undertake the task of contract administration. If the latter, relevant points to be considered are:

1   If Opponent's team are professionals of the same discipline as those of Party then this may make it easier for Party to present his case factually and gain Opponent's consent. It can also lead to the establishment of informal alliances between members of Party's team and those of Opponent even to the point at which formal meetings are held only to record agreements reached the evening before during a social drinks session.
2   Party must recognize Opponent's need to justify himself to his client and the fees he is charging. This applies particularly overseas where the concept of the consultant acting in an independent role between contractor and employer is virtually unknown and the consultant is regarded quite simply as the agent of the client employed to protect his interests – see further the author's *Contracting for Engineering and Construction Projects,* Chapter 19.

Action outside the contract
In not every situation will either Party or Opponent follow the contractual route in the resolution of their differences, nor will they be willing to allow that the existence of rights under the contract, uncontestable on any proper interpretation, shall be decisive of the matter. Examples of the type of situation in which this can happen are alleged excessive profits being made by a firm working on a government fixed price contract, contracts made under one government which its successor alleges were obtained by corruption and projects for which a government agency finds it cannot pay or no longer wants

because of changed economic or political conditions.

Under any of these circumstances not only is the employer's action likely to be arbitrary as regards the main contractor's contractual rights, but the main contractor himself is likely to follow a similar course with his sub-contractors. Equally a main contractor working overseas faced with a payment default which he believes will not be remedied, may decide that immediate stoppage of work and withdrawal of his staff will minimize his losses as compared with the cost of carrying on working and shipping equipment, whilst he follows the often tortuous route of giving the proper notices required under the contract and waits for the employer's response.

There is a strong temptation for the side against whom arbitrary action has been taken to act emotionally in the presentation of claims and issue threats which cannot in reality be sustained. It is however a temptation which should be resisted. What it is feasible for Party to do and to demand will depend on his rational assessment of the strength of his bargaining position considering all the factors referred to earlier on pp. 88. It is indeed on these factors that the decision in favour of arbitrary action itself should be taken in the first instance. The success of arbitrary action in either an offensive or defensive situation depends on the possession of real power and the willingness to use it. Power here is the ability to hurt in the sense of depriving the other side of what they most want and which they cannot, at least easily, obtain in any other way. Willingness to use it means being tough and not departing from the selected course even when subject to abuse or threats. It usually means the end of any possibility of future business relationships but then this is a factor taken into account before the action is started. It falls clearly under the heading of a quick kill strategy.

Sensitive issues

Apart from the two cases stated above Party must also consider separately his strategy on any issue on which he is vulnerable and to which he knows that Opponent is sensitive. Party's strategy on such an issue should be quick kill in order to avoid further bargaining. Specifically his offer should be made at a level which he believes will be recognized by Opponent as acceptable. If in doubt Party should offer more rather than less. Since the issue is sensitive, and emotions may well run high, Opponent is likely to regard any offer which does not satisfy him as insulting and either terminate the bargaining or insist on the acceptance by Party of a much higher offer. Whichever way Opponent reacts Party stands to lose and will suffer the additional disadvantage of having antagonized Opponent and so created further problems for the future.

An example, based on my own experience, will illustrate the type of situation under discussion.

Party had failed to comply with a contractual obligation which would not affect the performance or operation of the equipment concerned. Opponent, however, regarded the contractual non-compliance as insulting. To remedy the problem by modifying the equipment would cost Party 25% of the contract value. Party ascertained that Opponent would be willing to consider the offer of a discount in settlement of the issue. The problem then arose as to how much discount should be offered.

Party considered that 5% would be the lowest offer acceptable to Opponent, and the highest likely to be asked for would be 10%. The danger of an offer at 5% was that Opponent would not consider it sufficient to eradicate the insult in view of his known feelings on the subject and the consequences of being made to perform the contract were disastrous. Party drew the matrix in Figure 5:9 as an aid to making his decision.

	Opponent's strategies		
	Quick kill	Hold back	Strategy EV to Party
Quick kill	7.5×0.8	10×0.2	= 8%
Party's strategies			
Hold back	5.0×0.1	10×0.9	= 9.5%

Figure 5:9 Expected value to Party of varying strategies in a situation of contract dispute

Party's assessment was that an offer at 7.5% had an 80% chance of being accepted. It was high enough to reflect Party's contrition and could not possibly be regarded as insulting. An offer at 5% was not considered likely to be accepted and any bargaining would be likely to finish at around 10% since Opponent would act in one of two ways:

1   Offer 10% on a take-it or leave-it basis.
2   Start the bargaining at 15% which would mean a final deal at around 10%.

Although the matrix shows a very low probability of the 5% offer being accepted in fact the two strategies do not have an equal value until the probability rises to 40%.

In fact the offer was made at 7.5% and accepted. I will never know whether I could have got away with any less.

NOTES

1.   Interesting experimental support for this proposition was obtained by Komorita and Brenner. In one of their bargaining experiments one side made an initial offer at what could be considered a 'fair' price and thereafter remained firm. Their comment on the result of this experiment was that 'this strategy was not an effective way of reaching agreement'. The reason, they concluded, was that both sides knew this was a bargaining session and therefore both expected to bargain and to extract concessions from the other. In the present analysis failure by the seller to make any concession from the 'fair' price did not induce the buyer to raise his offer to that level, although objectively he recognized its fairness, because of the emotional resentment directed at a seller who refused to 'play the bargaining game'. S. S. Komorita and A. R. Brenner, 'Bargaining and concession making under bilateral monopoly', *Journal of Personality and Social Psychology,* vol. 9 (no. 1, 1968), pp. 15–20.

2.   It was first formulated by Jacob Bernouilli (1654–1705).

3.   N. J. Baumol, *Economic Theory and Operations Analysis* (New Jersey: Prentice-Hall, 1965), p. 554.

4.   It is recognized that this could be considered as contradicting the statement made on p. 107, that having submitted a quick-kill bid, Party will not be willing to grant a discount. However, the values shown in the matrix represent the purchaser's assessment of how he believes that the bidders will behave and, in practice, it is thought that a purchaser would consider that he would be able to secure a small discount from at least one of the bidders.

5.   R. E. Walton and R. E. McKersie, *A Behavioural Theory of Labor Negotiations* (New York: McGraw-Hill, 1965), pp. 362–63.

6

THE LEVEL OF THE FIRST OFFER

The planning carried out so far has established for the particular negotiation the objective which Party has chosen to achieve and the basic strategy which he intends initially to employ. The next stage in the planning activity is to decide on the level at which to submit the first offer. Once that offer has been made then the negotiation enters into its definitive phrase and the process of commitment begins, since the original offer will establish one of the following:

1   The level at which the bargain will be made.
2   The level below which the bargain will be made.
3   That no bargain can be made.

The possibility is excluded that the bargain will be made at a level higher than that of the original offer. It is appreciated that in non-psychological bargaining theory either party can increase their demand as the negotiation proceeds; the bargaining model developed by Cross, which will be considered in detail later (p. 151) explicitly permits this.[1] At the same time Cross himself recognizes that such behaviour may cause an unfavourable impact on Opponent and for this reason is unlikely to occur in practice.[2] By choosing the level of his first offer Party determines therefore the maximum benefit which he will gain directly from the negotiation.

Objection may be made to the generality of this proposition on the grounds that occasions do arise when a contract price is finally settled at a level higher than that of the original tender. When this happens it will invariably be found that the technical content, delivery or some other factor has been changed or that customer has failed to accept the offer within its validity period. Even then the contractor will usually be pressed to extend such validity against the implied threat of his offer no longer being considered should he fail to do so. If no factors are changed then the price level of the first offer will be that at which, or below which, the bargain will be concluded. The decision on that level is crucial therefore to the success of the whole negotiation; a wrong move at this point will be virtually impossible to correct.

6.1 BID SUBMISSION

In choosing the decision rule by which Party should select the level at which to submit his first offer, six cases may be distinguished:

1   Competitive bidding, single opportunity, purchaser's strategy quick kill.
2   Competitive bidding, multiple opportunities, purchaser's strategy quick kill.
3   Competitive bidding, single opportunity, purchaser's strategy either hold back or Party uncertain as to purchaser's strategy.
4   Competitive bidding, multiple opportunities, purchaser's strategy either hold back or Party uncertain as to purchaser's strategy.
5   Non-competitive bidding, Party's position dominant.
6   Non-competitive bidding, Party's position subordinate.

The expression *single opportunity* refers to the situation in which Party's sales forecast shows this opportunity as the only chance of utilizing the same resources within the same time scale. Similarly the expression *multiple opportunities* refers to the case in which Party's sales forecast has predicted that there will be other such opportunities within the same time scale.

The confidence which Party can possess in making any such forecast of other opportunities will depend largely on the flexibility with which he can use the resources concerned. In general building work, for example, it is possible to use the resources of men and plant over a wide variety of projects and customers and it would be exceptional for Party to have to treat any bid as a single opportunity. In manufacturing, however, particular machines and operator skills, or even whole manufacturing shops, may be tied to particular products which are themselves tied to particular customers. In the short term, and in the absence of any clearly identified alternative inquiry for that product, Party must treat the bid as a single opportunity.

In engineering designer–contractor type business, eg petrochemical plant or oil-refinery design and construction, the number of major bid opportunities is small and each one is usually significant in terms of the use which any resultant contract would make of Party's assets. Again Party would normally classify any such bid as a single opportunity.

Competitive bidding, single opportunity, purchaser's strategy quick kill

This is the classic case of bidding to a public authority or other corporation which follows the rules of strict competitive tendering, in circumstances in which Party cannot clearly identify any other opportunity for the use of the resources involved within the time period concerned. It is the only one which appears to have been treated extensively in the literature on the developing of bidding models.[3]

The essential feature of this situation is that Party has only one chance both in terms of winning the award and also of utilizing the resources. His decision rule should therefore be: *submit the bid at a level which will maximize its subjective expected utility value.*

The formula for determining expected value (see Section 2.2) requires Party to establish the following inputs:

1   The conditional utility value of the bid is successful.
2   The conditional utility value of the contribution loss and variable marketing expense which would be incurred were the bid to be unsuccessful.
3   The subjective probability of the bid being successful, taking into account any non-price bias for or against Party's bid.

Conditional utility value of the bid
Party is expected to have some idea from market research of the general level of prices ruling in the market in question. If the product or service is new then it is assumed that Party has already decided on his general pricing policy: whether he is aiming to skim the higher price segment of the market or to penetrate the market as a whole as deeply as possible.[4] He knows, therefore, the possible range of price levels which can be considered.

The first influence on Party in determining the conditional utility value to him of a bid at any given price level will be the profit contribution given by that price level, taking into account as profit any over-recovery of fixed overheads which would result from the award of the contract.[5] Unless, however, the assumption is made that Party's utility of money is linear with money and no other worth factor is involved, such profit contribution is only one factor in building up the bid utility value. Remembering the discussion on utility in Section 2.3, such an assumption is justified only in the very simplest case in which:

1   The award or loss of the bid would have no significant affect either on Party's business or the manager's achievement of any sales or profit target.
2   None of the factors referred to below regarding the effect of the bid on further marketing opportunities, contractual risks or asset utilization are present to any appreciable extent.
3   The manager has no positive bias for or against risk taking.

In any other case the view is taken that the use of the expected value criterion is only appropriate if utility rather than monetary values are used. The factors apart from profit contribution which will be of significance in establishing the manager's preference for one bid rather than another, and, therefore, in determining his utility value for a bid at that price level, are as follows:

1 The relationship of the profit contribution to any target level which the manager concerned has been set to achieve.

2 Party's immediate need to obtain income to meet the fixed expenses of running the business.

3 Party's need to obtain work in order to retain key staff.

4 Party's need to obtain a sufficient volume of production to support the engineering, marketing and other expenses incurred in maintaining a viable business for the product concerned.

5 The creation of a particular market price level or the disturbance of an existing market price level.

6 Longer term marketing benefits which Party might derive from an award of the contract. These could include:

   (a) Weakening a competitor's ability to stay in the market through depriving him of business or denying him the chance to enter the market.

   (b) Having the opportunity to obtain follow-on business on a negotiated basis, eg extensions to a plant or system.

   (c) Increased success probability on other business with the same customer because of the advantages of standardization or the compatability of other products with those being supplied under this contract.

   (d) Acquiring a base in the market from which to launch other bids. This may be particularly important if the market is overseas and the contracts concerned involve installation work.

   (e) Maintaining a presence in the market or with the particular customer in anticipation of more favourable opportunities in the future.

   (f) Obtaining entry to a new market in which there is judged to be the chance of securing future profitable business.

   (g) Securing recognition of Party as a competent contractor in the particular market through the prestige value of the contract and the reputation of the customer.

7 Contractual risks involved, particularly those relating to:

   (a) Risk on non-payment or late payment.

   (b) Currency devaluation.

   (c) Escalation of costs over the contract period.

   (d) Abnormal warranty liabilities, eg for consequential damages.

   (e) Risk of incurring delay penalty.

   (f) Any clause allowing customer to terminate for convenience.

   (g) Standards of technical performance required in relation to Party's normal standards.

   (h) State of the development of the product.

   (i) Subcontract work for which Party is contractually responsible but in which he has no expertise.

   (j) Non-recovery of extra costs incurred through *force majeure* or

customer default.

(k) Disputes not referable to truly independent arbitration or court of law.

(l) On-demand tender, advance payment and performance bonds.

*(m)*Adverse cash flow.

8   Any capital expenditure which would be involved to the extent that it would not be recoverable within the minimum quantity of the product to which the customer would be committed.

9   High tendering costs.

10 Resources which would be required for contract implementation in relation to those available.

11 The manager's attitude towards risk taking.

Possible form of the bid utility value

The utility value which Party will place on any given bid is an intimate blend of the monetary value of the profit contribution itself and each of the factors 1–10, to the extent of their relevance to the particular bid opportunity concerned. As stressed earlier (see p. 26) it is an assessment peculiar to the individual who makes it and to the time at which it is made. Further it should always be remembered that the utility value is an expression only of a preference for one bid as against another; bid A is preferred to bid B and therefore bid A is assigned a higher utility value, not the other way round. It is important to avoid the trap of saying that A is preferred to B because bid A has the higher utility.

To attempt a generalization of the form to be expected of the bid utility function is difficult since circumstances, and therefore preferences, will vary so widely. However, three general guide lines are suggested.

1   It will be assumed that the upper limit of the utility scale (the most favourable bid Party could contemplate) is taken as 10 and the bottom of the scale (the loss which Party would suffer from a rejection of the bid) as 0. Then the suggestion would be that a bid at the manager's target profit level would have a value of approximately 8, provided that all other factors which could affect his preferences for or against bidding were neutral, ie no serious contractual risks, no significant marketing benefit, no urgent need to obain the order.

2   On the same assumptions a bid at 75 per cent of the manager's target level would have a value of around 6. Thereafter any further reductions would cause the utility value to drop sharply so that a bid at 50 per cent might have a value of 2 and one at 25 per cent of the target level a value of 0.5.

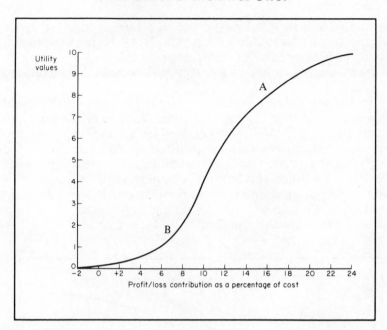

Figure 6:1   Bidder's normal utility curve

The general form of Party's utility function under the conditions stated in 1 and 2 is given in Figure 6:1 in which utility is plotted against profit contribution/loss expressed as a percentage of cost.

From the brief note on utility theory in Section 2.3 it will be remembered that the points on the curve represent indifference to the receipt of a sum certain and the taking of a gamble. If it is assumed that the costs are £100 000 then point *A* on the curve is based on being indifferent to a certainty of receiving a profit contribution of £16 000 and taking part in the risk venture with an 80 per cent chance of receiving a profit contribution of £24 000 and a 20 per cent chance of incurring a loss of £2 000.[6] Similarly point *B* expresses indifference between the certain receipt of a profit contribution of £8 000 and a 20 per cent chance of £24 000 and an 80 per cent chance of losing £2 000.

At point *A*, which represents the manager's target level, the expected value of the gamble in monetary terms of £18 800 is slightly higher than the target profit contribution of £16 000, which reflects the manager's somewhat cautious approach to bidding when the profit contribution satisfies his aspiration level.[7] However at point *B* the expected value in monetary terms of £3 200 is well below the profit contribution of £8 000. This is clearly the result of not being interested in bids at this level of profit, a lack of interest, however, which the graph shows diminishes rapidly as the profit contribution climbs up to 12 per cent. Thereafter the rate of increase is much slower up to the manager's target level and even slower still as the target level is passed.

Under the neutral conditions assumed so far it is believed that these results and the form of the curve derived from them are quite general and that their applicability would not be affected by the absolute values of either the costs or the profit contribution/loss. (It will be appreciated that under neutral conditions the loss can never be appreciable. If it were, then either Party must really need the business in order to avoid an unrecovery of fixed overheads or the tendering costs are high both in absolute terms and relative to the anticipated profit, and therefore the situation is no longer neutral.[8]

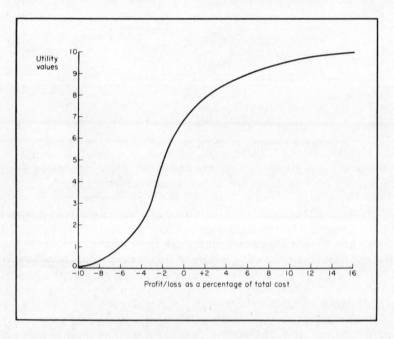

Figure 6:2 Bidder's utility curve: poor order book

3   The inclusion of any of the factors previously referred to as having an influence on Party's utility function would not significantly affect the general shape of the curve but would displace it along the horizontal axis. Two out of the many possibilities will be considered and in order to illustrate the general proposition one at each end of the range will be selected.

In the first possibility Party's order intake situation is such that he has a significant negative operating variance. Unless the position can be improved he will be compelled to discharge staff and close down a section of the business. An improvement in sales and margins is forecast longer term and Party is anxious therefore both to avoid losing key personnel and also to stay in the market. The bid being considered represents the one opportunity presently foreseen of bringing actual overhead recovery back in line with current expense. There are no significant contractual risks.

A suggested utility curve for Party under these conditions is shown in Figure 6:2. Assuming again costs of £100 000 Party's attitude is clearly shown by the table of Figure 6:3 which shows selected outcomes between which he is indifferent.

	Probability of	
Certainty	gain £16000	lose £10000
£'000s	%	%
6	90	10
2	80	20
Break even	70	30
—2	50	50

Figure 6:3 Outcomes between which Party is indifferent

This is obviously an extreme case but unfortunately it does happen and, when it does, it is not difficult to imagine a rather unruly exchange of views between the marketing manager and the line manager. The marketing manager will state that, from what is known of the competition, the company have a 50/50 chance at a 10 per cent margin, and probably about a 70 per cent chance at a margin of 5 per cent; the line manager will retort that he is not at all interested in probabilities and margins but just the business, as long as money will not be lost.[9]

In the second possibility Party's situation is happily the reverse of that just examined. Orders on hand are slightly ahead of budget; sales prospects are buoyant. The bid opportunity being considered is for export and there are certain contractual risks on delay penalty and abnormal warranty costs.

The suggested utility curve is shown in Figure 6:4. In comparison with that of the 'neutral' position shown in Figure 6:1, the worth to Party of a bid at a profit contribution of 16 per cent has declined from a utility value of 8 to one of 7. Party's preference under the changed circumstances is for the bid with the higher contribution. The loss should the bid be unsuccessful represents the variable marketing expense which would be incurred in overseas sales visits, etc.

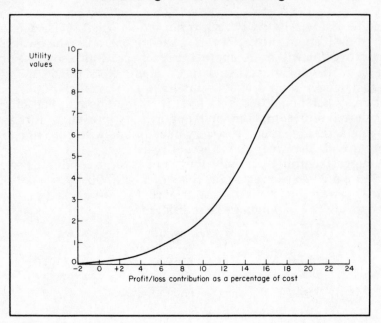

Figure 6:4 Bidder's utility curves: full order book

So far matters have been made easy by pointing all factors in the same direction. Unfortunately real life is not so simple; the bid opportunity which Party desperately needs to win in order to ensure full overhead recovery and maintenance of his position in the market, is likely to be just the one which involves a substantial measure of contractual risk. How will Party react to this? It is suggested that Party will be acutely sensitive to the issue of contractual risk at the break-even point, and just either side of it, but that this sensitivity will decrease as the profit margin rises. The likely effect is shown in Figure 6:5 where the solid line reproduces the curve shown in Figure 6:3 in which Party was most anxious to secure the award but there was no serious contractual risk. The dotted line shows the effect on this curve of importing into the situation issues of contractual risk.

Success probability
Party's assessment of his chances of success is a compound of:

1   Customer bias for or against Party's bid at any given price level due to non-price factors.
2   Party's subjective estimate of the probability distribution of competitor's prices.

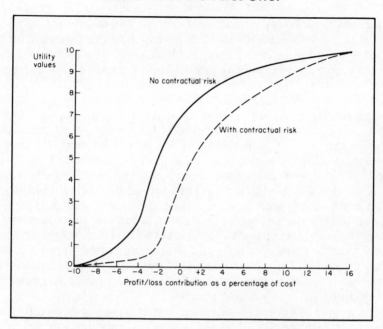

Figure 6:5 Bidder's utility curve: poor order book and contractual risk

Customer bias–In the discussion on riskless utility in Section 2.5 the following points were noted regarding the manner in which customer will value any offer:

1 That in determining the worth to him of any bid, customer will take into account non-price factors, eg delivery, supplier's reputation, etc.
2 That the worth to customer of each such factor and also the factor of price is determined independently of the other features of the bid, ie the worth to customer of a month's earlier delivery remains constant and does not vary with the price level.
3 That if any factor is below customer's minimum requirements he will reject the bid irrespective of the worth to him of the other factors.[10]
4 That any factor will be subject to decreasing marginal utility as it approaches its optimum value to customer, ie the value to customer of the sixth week saved will be less than that of the third week saved and at some point any further time saved would be of no value to customer at all. Conversely as any factor approaches its level of minimum acceptability to customer the marginal reduction in utility will increase rapidly, ie if the maximum

acceptable delivery period is 14 months and the minimum which is of interest to customer is 12 months, then the rate at which the utility value of delivery changes between 13 and 14 months will be much more rapid than between 13 and 12 months. This can be seen from Figure 2:18.

By preparing a product-comparison grid using the method outlined on pp. 41-2, but excluding the factor of price, it is possible to compare the non-price features of Party's offer with those of his competitors. This comparison must then be converted into a bias factor for or against Party which can be used to adjust the value to customer and, therefore, the success probability of any bid price.

The method adopted is to estimate the worth that customer will place on the non-price factors in Party's bid in comparison with those of his principal competitor(s). It is essential that this valuation is made strictly from customer's viewpoint. Party may justifiably be proud of the high quality of his products but if customer is only interested in whether or not they meet specification, Party cannot give himself any bonus points for being above specification.

For the unit of comparison either monetary or utility values could be used. Preference would be for utility values since this will enable the utility value of the non-price factor to be combined with price, and to give effect to the diminishing marginal utility of both as they approach their respective limits of acceptability. This is an important difference between the use of utility and monetary values.

If monetary values are used the effect of the bias factor would be a constant over the contemplated range of bid prices. If the worth to customer of, say, two months saved were to be estimated at £20 000 as in the example shown in Figure 2:18, and it was believed that Party had a two-month delivery advantage over his principal competitor, then it could be said that a bid at £120 000 by Party was equal to a competitor's bid of £100 000. Equally a bid at £140 000 by Party would be equivalent in worth to the customer of a competitor's bid at £120 000.

Using utility values, however, it will be seen from Figure 2:18 that whilst the bids at £100 000/14 months and £120 000/12 months are equivalent, the bids at £120 000/14 months and £140 000/12 months are not. In the latter the lower-priced longer-delivery bid is strongly preferred, as shown by the sharp reduction in worth to the buyer of the higher-priced bid as the price level moves towards the maximum which he is willing to accept. Experience indicates that this represents far more realistically the way in which bids are valued in practice. The sensitivity of the buyer to the same absolute differential in price will increase sharply as the price level rises.

The method used will therefore be that described in Section 2.5 and it is suggested that the reader should refer again to that section. Briefly the proposed method is to first identify the non-price features which will be of significance to customer and then rate these relative to the estimate of the worth to customer of the anticipated minimum bid price. A scale representative of the assumed preference of customer for each such factor is then prepared, together with that of the factor of price, over the estimate of the range of possible factor values derived from the product comparison grid. This scale will take account of judgement of the variable diminution in customer preference for each such factor as it moves towards the limit which it is believed customer would accept.

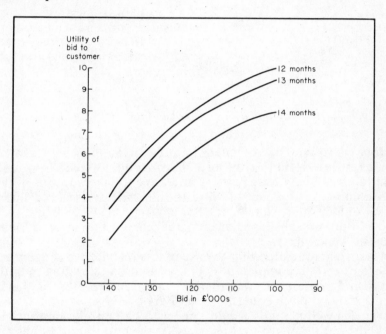

Figure 6:6 Graph of Party's success probability for a range of bids

These estimates can most conveniently be represented by a graph in the form illustrated in Figure 6:6 which is based on the same figures as those used in Figure 2:18. Reading the graph horizontally it is possible to determine the bids which are judged to possess the same value for customer and can therefore be regarded as equivalent in terms of success probability. By comparing the utility intervals between bids, Party's success probability can be estimated for any bid within the possible price range when combined with the bid of his principal competitor. Using the assumption that Party will bid with a delivery of

12 months and his principal competitor will offer a delivery of 14 months this comparison expressed in terms of Party's success probability is shown in Figure 6:7. It will be seen that the effect of the non-price bias in Party's favour diminishes rapidly at the higher price level but declines much more slowly at the lower level, again reflecting the customer's preference at the higher price levels for the lower price/longer delivery bid.[11]

		Competitor's bid (14 months delivery)									
		140	135	130	125	120	115	110	105	100	
	140	1	0.7	0.4	0						
	135	1	1	0.8	0.5	0.3	0				
Party's	130	1	1	1	0.9	0.7	0.4	0.2	0		Party's
bid	125	1	1	1	1	0.95	0.7	0.5	0.4	0.2	success
(12	120	1	1	1	1	1	0.95	0.8	0.7	0.5	probability
months	115	1	1	1	1	1	1	0.95	0.9	0.8	
delivery)	110	1	1	1	1	1	1	1	1	0.95	
	105	1									
	100	1									

Figure 6:7 Party's conditional success probability

Obviously this is a very much simplified example which is intended only as a description of the principles to be applied. In a real-life situation it is likely that Party would have to take account of two or more competitors for each of whom the non-price bias would differ and there would be more than one factor contributing to such bias. A fully worked-out example based on an actual case within my experience is given in Appendix 5.

It is also appreciated that the use of this technique is dependent on the accuracy and completeness of the input data relating to both the customer's preference and to the non-price features of the competitor's bids relative to those of Party. However, the following statement by Simmonds would appear to be entirely appropriate:[12]

> . . . the difficulties in finding out what the customer's values are for different features is no argument for not attempting to find out. And again the need is paramount to plan the acquisition and flow of information so that what is wanted from those making customer contact is known by them and the data efficiently transmitted to the decision-making point.

This issue of the acquisition and transmission of data will be further considered in Part Two.

Subjective estimate of success probability—Figure 6:7 gives Party's estimate of his success probability for any selected bid price, conditional on the price level quoted by his principal competitor. Since in practice Party cannot be certain of the price which his competitor will quote, his expected success probability for any bid will be the sum of each of these conditional values mutiplied by Party's estimate of the chance that his competitor will in fact bid at the level.

	Competitive bid £'000s								
Party's bid at £125 000	140	135	130	125	120	115	110	105	100
Line 1 Party's estimate of conditional probability taken from Figure 6:7	1	1	1	1	0.95	0.7	0.5	0.4	0.2
Line 2 Party's estimate of the probability distribution of the competitive bid	0	0	0	0	0.15	0.50	0.25	0.1	0
Line 3 Party's expected success probability line 1 × line 2	0	0	0	0	0.14	0.35	0.125	0.014	0

Figure 6:8 Party's expected success probability

Let us assume that party wishes to determine his chance of success at a bid price of £125 000. Line 1 in Figure 6:8 shows Party's conditional success probabilities for a bid at this level taken from Figure 6:7. Putting himself in his competitor's position, and knowing he has a disadvantage on delivery, Party now estimates that his competitor is likely to go in at a lower price. However, on past experience of his compeititor's pricing Party does not believe that he will drop below £105 000 and that his most likely bid will be between £120 000 and £110 000. Line 2 in Figure 6:8 gives Party's estimate of the probability distribution for his competitor's bid. Line 3 is simply line 1 × line 2.

In round figure Party's subjective estimate of his success probability at a bid of £125 000 is 65 per cent.

Repeating the process for the other possible bids given in Figure 6:7 the following values emerge:

Bid price	Party's subjective success probability
(£'000s)	(%)
140	0
135	5
130	30
125	65
120	90
115	95
110	100

So far only the case of one competitor has been considered. In practice Party will normally have more than one firm competing against him and in these circumstances it is suggested that the following procedure is adopted:

1   If the facts relating to the non-price bias and likely pricing policies of the other competitors are sufficiently similar they may be treated as an average competitor and the analysis, therefore, can be the same as if there were only one competitor.
2   If the facts are marked dissimilar, and each firm represents a competitive threat, then the analysis must be completed separately for each firm to the point of arriving at a subjective estimate of Party's success probability against each considered individually. Party's success probability for any bid price against all the competitors taken together is then the product of these; so if the individual probabilities are 0.7 and 0.5 and 0.8, then Party's success probability for the bid is 0.7 × 0.5 × 0.8 = 29%.[13]

One problem here is that of the competitor whose behaviour is not predictable in the sense that sometimes he will submit an extremely low bid, at which he would be certain to obtain the contract award, and sometimes bid normally. Party could simply ignore the possibility of a very low bid on the grounds that having taken the decision to tender knowing this risk exists, and not being prepared to match, there is no point in trying to bring the problem into the analysis since it will have no affect on Party's actions. In terms of the calculations given in figures 6.7, 6.8 and 6.9 if it is assumed that there is a 50/50 chance of competitor making a low bid ie of £105 000 or below then it can be shown that the effect will be to reinforce Party's bid of £125 000 as maximizing Party's SEU. This is because of the reduction in Party's expected success probability at both the lower and higher bid values and the non-linear relationship of Party's utility function to money. The results would of course be totally different were Party using money values and seeking to maximize expected contribution.

Alternatively Party could amend his assumptions regarding competitor's behaviour to allow for this possibility.

Computation of bid expected value
The necessary input data is now available to quantify the expected value for Party of a series of possible bid prices and to select that which maximizes his subjective expected utility function.

To provide a simplified example the utility function for Party given in Figure 6:1 which represents a 'normal' bidding position will be used and applied to the estimates of his success probability given on p.121. For this purpose costs will be taken as £110 000, ie the bid price at which party has a 100 per cent chance of success. The result is set out in Figure 6:9.

The bid at £125 000 should be Party's choice if he wishes to maximize his SEU function. The manager's target profit level of 15 per cent on cost which equates to a bid of approximately £126.5

should now be considered. Using the same method of calculation this would produce a bid expected utility value of 3.8 and it would not be surprising if in the end the manager was tempted to relax his perfect rationality and bid at this level. The calculations made have, however, given him a compelling alternative and the reasoned choice would certainly be for a bid at £125 000.

It is interesting to note that the same calculation if repeated for the other two situations where Party was anxious for business and where he was less so, would indicate in the first instance a bid of £120 000 as maximizing SEU and in the second case a bid of £130 000.

1	2	3	4	5
Bid price £'000s	Profit as % of cost	Conditional utility from Figure 6:1	Success probability from page 132 %	Expected utility col 3 × col 4
140	27	10	0	0
135	23	9.8	0.05	0.49
130	18	8.7	0.30	2.6
125	13.5	6.8	0.65	4.4
120	9	3.2	0.9	2.9
115	5	0.7	0.95	0.67
110	0	0.1	1	0.1

Figure 6:9 Expected utility to Party of a series of bids

It is hoped that the principles of the method suggested have been clearly established but to conclude this section the steps needed in carrying out the calculation are set out in sequential order.

1 Determine Party's utility function over the range of possible profit and loss values for the particular tender.
2 Estimate the conditional success probability for Party against each anticipated competitive bid taking into account any bias for or against Party.
3 Estimate the probability distribution of the competitive bids.
4 Multiply the results of steps 2 and 3 together to obtain the expected success probability for Party of any bid.
5 Determine the subjective expected utility for Party for each bid by multiplying step 1 by step 4.

Competitive bidding—multiple opportunities
Party's objective in this instance is to maximize his subjective

expected utility over a series of bids in the knowledge that he can take the longer-term view. In arriving at the method for achieving this two cases need to be distinguished:

Success probability remains constant—This implies two features in the bidding situation. Firstly that Party's own success or failure on the first bid will not affect his conditional success probability on the second or subsequent bids. Secondly that the competitive bid probability distribution also remains constant, ie that the competition will also not alter their bidding tactics depending upon whether their initial bid is successful or not. It will be assumed for the present that Party's conditional utility function is also not affected. Given these assumptions the task is simple. All that is necessary is to bid at a level which will maximize the expected utility value per award. If it is assumed that the probability of any one award is p, at a bid level of x, with a conditional utility value of U, then the expected value of the utility of any one award is given by the expression:

$$1 - (1 - p)^{n} U_{x}$$

where n is the number of bids under consideration. This is now applied to the significant bids in Figure 6:9 on the assumption that the number of bids in the series is three. It can be shown that the bid which now maximizes SEU over the three bids is that at £130 000, and this is the level at which the first bid should be submitted.[14]

Success probability does not remain constant—This is the more likely case. If the first bid is awarded to competitor X then Party must assume that competitor Y will be that much more eager to secure bid number two, and so the probability distribution of his bids will change. Party can expect, therefore, that the competition will be more severe on the second bid than the first. Equally it seems likely that Party's utility function will change. Not having secured the first award his anxiety for success on the second opportunity will be that much increased. The really interesting situation is reached on the third bid, if Party has again not been successful. On the one hand it can be assumed that his utility function has now changed dramatically to that of the contractor who desperately needs business as depicted in Figure 6:3; on the other hand he knows that both his competitors have secured orders and are therefore less likely to submit low bids so that his success probability for any given price level has increased.

The suggested strategy in these circumstances, given that the results of one bid are known before the next has to be submitted, would be:

1   Submit the first bid as if success probability was not going to change over the series, ie follow the rule just described.

2   If the first bid fails, submit the second bid as if it were an individual opportunity, adjusting as appropriate the probability distribution of the competitors' bids.
3   If the second bid also fails then the third bid must obviously be treated as an individual opportunity but with both the probability distribution and Party's utility function adjusted accordingly.

Multiple opportunities which are interdependent
So far it has been assumed that having secured one order in the series Party will have no great incentive, because of capacity limitations, to secure the second. That assumption will now be reversed to consider the case in which, not only would Party like to secure a further order, but success on the first would favourably influence his chances of success on the second. This could arise from standardization benefits to customer, contact between Party's and customer's engineers during execution of the first contract, etc.

    If acceptance or rejection of the initial offer would have an impact on Party's future business opportunities, particularly if the potential profit contribution from the second bid would be higher because of Party's preferred position in the eyes of customer, then this is clearly a factor which Party must take into account in deciding which intitial offer level would possess the maximum expected utility. The suggested method of doing this is as follows:

1   Party estimates the total maximum profit contribution which he anticipates could be earned by the two bids taken together. He then establishes a new utility scale on which the upper limit is represented by this combined maximum total profit contribution.
2   The conditional utility values of the two bids taken together are assessed by Party in the same way as he arrived at the value for the initial offer taken on its own.[15]
3   Party estimates the joint probabilities of the ultimate outcome. For each pair of bids taken together there are four posible outcomes.
    (a)   Win first bid, win second bid
    (b)   Win first bid, lose second bid
    (c)   Lose first bid, win second bid
    (d)   Lose first bid, lose second bid
    The joint probability of event *(a)* is the probability of the first bid being won multiplied by the probability of winning the second bid *given that the first bid has been won.*
4   The conditional utility values for the combined outcome of each event are then converted into expected values by multiplying by the joint probability of that event occurring.
5   The expcted ultimate value of the intitial bid is then the sum of these four amounts.

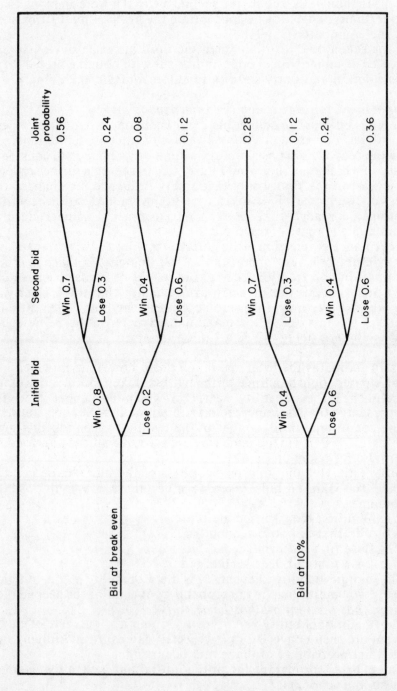

Figure 6:10 Decision tree of possible outcomes to multiple bids

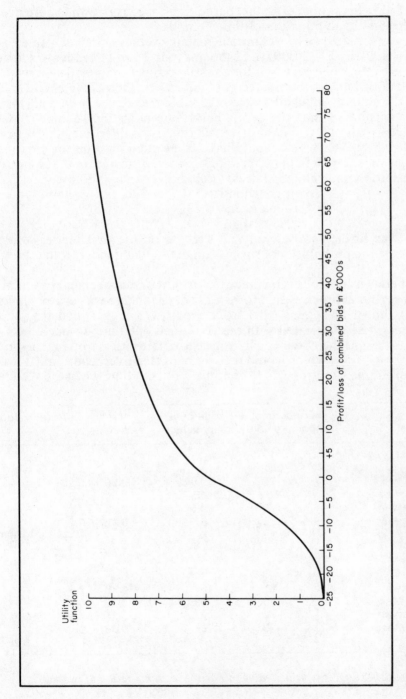

Figure 6:11 Utility curve: multiple bids

The following simple example, based on a case in my own experience, illustrates the application of this method.

A tender was to be submitted for an overseas project valued at approximately £100 000. In 12 months time a second tender would be issued by the same customer for a similar project estimated to be worth £500 000. Due to anticipated cost reductions then being engineered into the equipment which formed the subject matter of both tenders, it was considered that the profit contribution on the second tender could be about 15% and the price still remain competitive. On the first tender, however, which would have to be submitted on the existing design of equipment, market intelligence suggested that the profit contribition and related success probability were as follows:

Profit contribution	Success probability
Break even	80%
10% margin	40%

It was further considered that success on the first tender would increase the probability of success on the second tender from 40% to 70%.

There was obvious reluctance on the part of management to submit the first bid at break even. However, a decision tree was drawn on the lines shown in Figure 6:10 from which was determined the joint probabilities associated with the combined outcome for each bid.

At that time there was a definite need to obtain orders to maintain shop output at a level which would recover budgeted overheads, and it was believed this situation would continue until the time when the second

Event	Conditional monetary value	Conditional utility value	Joint probability	Expected value
Bid at break even				
	£'000s			
Win:win	75	9.8	0.56	5.5
Win:lose	—20	0.2	0.24	0.048
Lose:win	70	9.5	0.08	0.76
Lose:lose	—25	0	0.12	0
				—— 6.308
Bid at 10%				
Win:win	85	10	0.28	2.8
Win:lose	—10	1.5	0.12	0.18
Lose:win	70	9.5	0.24	2.28
Lose:lose	—25	0	0.36	0
				—— 5.26

Figure 6:12 Expected utility value to Party of a combination of two bids

tender was due to be submitted. No contractual risks were forseen on either bid. The profit contribution/utility function curve was, therefore, of the form indicated in Figure 6:11. Failure to obtain the first award would lead to a loss of £5 000 and failure to obtain the second award to a loss of £20 000.

Using the data provided by Figures 6:10 and 6:11 the expected utility values for the alternative bids, taken together, were calculated as shown in Figure 6:12. Based on this the decision was made to submit the initial bid at the break-even level.

A comment on the use of utility scales in competitive bidding
In arriving at his own scale of utility values for differing profit contribution levels for any one bid in a particular risk situation, a manager is indicating:

1   His own personal approach to risk taking.
2   His own degree of preference for one margin level as compared to another.

Such a scale does not represent for him the value of money although, obviously, the worth which he places on defined amounts of money under stated risk conditions is one of the factors which enters his assessment of utility values. Rather, the scale depicts his attitude in that particular situation towards a mixture of risk, profit and loss, from which it follows, as emphasized throughout, that his utility function will change as the factors relevant to his assessment change. It has also been noted that the manager when exercising his judgement to arrive at the 'mixture' will be applying many of the points which were listed in the bid desirability table (Figure 4:4). Thus the extent to which he has assets under or over employed, and the availability or otherwise of other opportunities, will both influence him in the degree of risk which he is willing to accept.

It may be objected, however, that in practice business managers do not calculate utility values in this way and that the whole exercise though interesting is entirely theoretical. This objection seems unsustained as there is significant evidence that the observed conduct of managers responsible for profit centres is explicable only on the basis that they do use expected utility values, rather than expected monetary values, in arriving at bidding decisions, even though they may not be familiar with the term utility value as such.

The following example, again taken from my own experience, is typical of such conduct.

Party was submitting a tender against known competitors A and B. Other firms might bid but their actions were classified as random and as such ignored. Firm A had a low cost structure and normally could

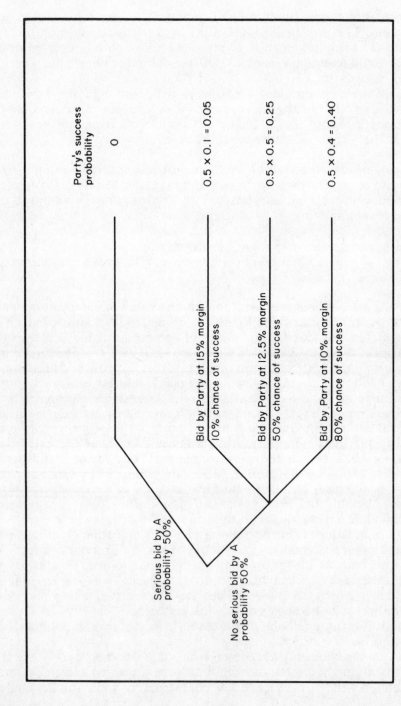

Party's success
probability

0

0.5 × 0.1 = 0.05

0.5 × 0.5 = 0.25

0.5 × 0.4 = 0.40

Serious bid by A
probability 50%

No serious bid by A
probability 50%

Bid by Party at 15% margin
10% chance of success

Bid by Party at 12.5% margin
50% chance of success

Bid by Party at 10% margin
80% chance of success

Figure 6:13 Decision tree—Party's bid against competitor A

142

be expected to under-bid Party by about 20%. Firm B's cost structure was similar to that of Party's. In this particular case, because of the use of a certain component which Party manufactured himself, Party has an off-setting cost advantage of 5% over firm A which reduced his overall deficit to around 15%. As against firm B Party had an advantage, which was difficult to quantify, of a far better performance record.

If therefore firm A were to bid seriously then Party knew he was wasting his time. However, Party considered that due to capacity problems there was at least a 50% probability that firm A would either not bid at all or would deliberately bid in such a manner as not to be competitive.

On the basis of the above facts and estimates Party's marketing manager drew up the following appraisal of the situation in the form of the decision tree shown in Figure 6:13.

Using the maximization of the expected value of money as the criterion by which to select the profit contribution then Party should submit the bid at a level of 10% since 40% of 10% > 25% of 12.5%. In fact the marketing manager selected the bid with the 12.5% margin. The total value of the bid was approximately £400 000 so that the difference in profit contribution was £10 000.

When questioned on his decision the manager justified his choice on the following grounds:

1 He did not need the order to sustain volume and he preferred to maintain his price level up, even although he was taking a serious risk of not securing the order.
2 He could forsee other business opportunities materializing in the near future with prospects at least as good.
3 His planned margin for that product line was 15% and he had therefore already made a reduction.

Clearly in the judgement of that manager the existence of other prospects, the lack of any pressing need to obtain orders, and the benefit to be gained from the additional £10 000 margin, if the gamble came off, were worth more than the extra 15% probability of securing £40 000 profit contribution. Assuming he was behaving rationally, and seeking to maximize expected value, this could only mean that he was using, even if unknowingly, utility values rather than money, and that his utility curve as against profit contribution in that particular situation was of the general form shown in Figure 6:14 from which the expected utility values for the two margin levels in question are as shown in Figure 6:15.[16]

When the above analysis was discussed with him the manager's actual words were as follows:

The existence of other prospects affected the degree of risk I was willing to accept at that time. I know that if the tender discussed was the sole and last chance of filling a production gap the importance of getting it would have been much different and so would therefore the acceptance of risk.

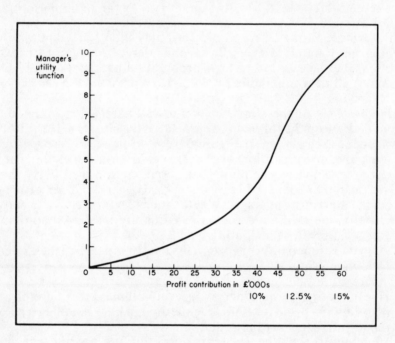

Figure 6:14 Utility curve for marketing manager

Profit contribution	Conditional utility	Success probability	Expected utility
10%	4	0.4	1.6
12.5%	8	0.25	2.0

Figure 6:15 Expected utility values

The manager accepted the analysis without reservation.

His comments, however, emphasize the point made already that an individual manager's utility function is not constant and is subject to significant change as business circumstances alter.

Competitive and non-competitive bidding—purchaser's strategy hold back or Party uncertain as to purchaser's strategy
For the purpose of first discussing the general principles by which Party should be guided in his choice of the level at which to submit his initial offer, when he cannot be certain that customer will adopt quick kill, the four cases listed separately on p. 121 can be treated as one. The more detailed points peculiar to each individual case will then be considered separately.

In submitting an offer which he believes customer may use as a basis for subsequent negotiations, Party's objectives are to:

1 Prevent outright rejection of his bid.
2 Avoid bidding below the level at which customer would be willing to place an order.
3 Ensure that at least Party's minimum negotiating objective is secured by the time that agreement is finally reached.

The bargaining zone
Separate consideration has already been given to how each side will value the worth of a particular offer. At either end of the range of theoretically possible bargains these valuations will vary widely. The area between the two sides is described as the bargaining zone and the correct identification of this is important both in deciding on the level at which to submit the initital offer and in the development of future negotiating strategy.

Limits of the bargaining zone
Before submission of the first offer by Party the upper limit of the bargaining zone is formed by the level at which customer would in the ultimate just prefer to accept an offer as opposed to no bargain. It is a value derived solely from customer's preferences and is not directly influenced by Party. If customer is willing, for his own reasons, to pay a high price for the goods/services concerned, then Party, consistent with his role as a maximizer, is assumed to take advantage of this. Indirectly, of course, Party may have influenced this upper limit by preconditioning customer to accept that he should be prepared to pay a certain price or agree to particular terms and conditions. This upper limit is not a function of time; it is the break-off point or minimum negotiating objective beyond which customer is not expected to concede no matter how long the negotiations last.

After submission of the first offer by Party the upper limit will be formed by the higher in value to customer (and therefore the lower in monetary terms) of:

1 The previous limit

2 Party's first offer
3 Any other competing offer

The lower limit of the bargaining zone prior to the submission of Party's initial offer is the higher in value to Party of:

1 The level at which Party would just prefer to accept a contract to no bargain.
2 The lowest level in real terms, at which customer expects to be able to place the contract.

If after submission of the offer by Party customer finds that 2 is lower than 1, ie if customer had expected as a minimum to have to pay more for the goods/services than Party's bid, then customer can be expected to revise his 'lowest' level to be the same as Party's offer. This is provided that customer does not consider the bid to be so low that it does not constitute a viable offer ie its acceptance could result in customer being landed with a 'losing' contractor with all the problems this creates in terms of delays to the project, poor workmanship and general unreliability. Some public authorities have actually instituted rules on this issue. For example in the Philippines any bid which is 30 per cent lower than the government's estimate is automatically rejected by the bidding committees of government agencies.

The minimum offer value which any competitor would accept does not affect the lower limit of the bargaining zone. Having decided as part of his negotiating plan on the offer which possesses for him the minimum acceptable utility value, Party is not expected to change from this unless there is a change in his own circumstances. Moreover, the change must be one which affects directly the preference assessment which led to the formulation of Party's utility function, eg sudden cancellation of an important existing order which causes Party to reappraise his need for work. A bid by a competitor below Party would not normally be such a change since the chance of this occurring was not part of the original preference assessment.[17] The lower limit is dictated solely by Party's preference function in the same way as the upper limit was by customer's preference function.

It is recognized, however, that emotionally the effect of a competitor's lower bid on Party's negotiators may be to encourage them to place a higher subjective value than before on securing the business. This reaction is only to be expected; no one likes to lose and the closer Party is to obtaining the contract award the stronger this reaction. Further it must be remembered that in business competitions there are no prizes for coming second.

Whilst, behaviourally, this reaction is anticipated, normatively it is not allowed for in the description of the bargaining zone, since it is a reaction which should be resisted. The worth or bid desirability of an award at any particular offer level is not affected by whether a competitor bids above or below Party, and it is only a change in that worth valuation which should lead Party to reconsider his bidding level.

The effect of time on the initial offer level

When customer's strategy was quick kill, and Party responded accordingly by putting forward his final offer first, Party's influence on the time which would elapse before contract award was minimal. The period was determined solely by the time taken by customer to adjudicate the bids and obtain any financial or other authority necessary for contract signature. If that period was likely to be extended then Party would, of course, have taken that into account in fixing his costs. However, there was no co-relation between Party's actions and customer's time scale so that in deciding on the offer he would make, Party did not need to allow for the effect of that decision on the time which would be taken by customer to finalize the contract.[18]

In the case under consideration Party has decided to adopt hold back either because he knows that customer has himself selected that strategy or because Party is uncertain as to which strategy customer will select.[19] As a result Party will now have a direct influence on the time which will elapse between bid submission and contract signature (unless Party is eliminated from further participation because his bid so far exceeds that of his competitor(s) or the amount customer is willing to pay).

Party's influence on the time scale for contract award arises first from the level at which he submits his initial offer. In general the higher Party's original demand, provided that it is not so high as to be summarily rejected, or recognized as pure 'padding', the longer the negotiations will take.[20] The second way in which Party will influence the negotiating time is through his decisions on the rate at which he will concede and the minimum bargain which he is willing to accept. Again it would be expected that the more favourable the bargain required by Party the longer will be the negotiating period.

Both these propositions which are intuitively appealing have received support from bargaining experiments. Pruitt and Drew found that when the negotiations were conducted under mild rather than acute time pressure there was both a higher initial demand and a higher minimal goal.[21] As they surmised, a tough negotiating strategy aimed at securing a highly favourable outcome takes time to produce the desired effect. Other experiments by Pruitt and Johnson found that Party's concessions were both greater and more frequent under extremes of time pressure.[22] One explanation could be that Opponent will regard any concessions by Party as less of a sign of weakness when he knows that Party is under severe time pressure than when he knows he is not, and because of this Party will be less concerned with appearing firm and saving his face by avoiding making concessions.

However, as Cross has pointed out: 'the more distant the agreement the less its present value'.[23] Since there are no benefits to be gained until final agreement is reached it is necessary to:

1 Discount the worth of any bargain, as valued at the time of agreement, back to its present value.
2 Deduct from that value the costs incurred directly in achieving that bargain.

The extent to which it is necessary to be conscious of time costs will obviously depend on the period involved since, in general, such costs may be expected to be linear with time. However, in an age of serious inflation even short periods of time can give rise to costs being incurred which will significantly erode the expected gains from further negotiation. These costs may be listed in five groups.

1 Negotiating costs. For example hotel bills, air fares for the negotiators.
2 Resource costs. The negotiators if not involved on this bid could be employed on other activities.
3 Escalation costs. The longer it takes to finalize the contract the later in calender time will be the period within which the work will be executed and therefore in times of inflation the higher the costs. Unless these are recoverable under a price escalation clause they must represent a straight reduction in margin.
4 Dislocation costs. The bid will have been made on the assumption that the work will be carried out within a certain period, during which the total activity has been forecast to be at a particular level. Any serious delay which places the contract work in a different calendar period, to which other conditions apply, may cause an increase in costs, eg the need to work overtime.
5 Discounting costs. The later receipt of funds which will be generated by the contract as a contribution to margin means that these must be discounted to bring them to present values.

In deciding on the level of his initial demand Party must balance the gain to be derived from demanding more with the loss which he will suffer from delaying agreement. The offer which maximizes worth to Party is that for which any increase in utility value, because of a higher demand, would be exactly offset by the reduction in utility due to the greater time costs necessarily associated with the achievement of such demand.

> Marginal increase in demand utility =
> marginal reduction in utility due to time costs

This will be recognized as the bargaining equivalent of the optimal output of a profit maximizing firm at which marginal revenue equals marginal cost.

It is not suggested that in practice Party will have available input data of sufficient reliability to justify the use of sophisticated equations for ascertaining the level of demand which would exactly satisfy the above requirement. The study of the appropriate mathematical expression is, however, justified on the grounds that it will identify the factors which are relevant in determining such demand, and the manner in which they are interrelated. From the understanding so gained the negotiator can formulate his own initial demand which will be optimal in relation to the information available to him and the degree of reliability which he can attach to it.

Model of the bargaining process in relation to the selection of the initial demand

Party's initial demand will be represented by q_1 and customer's initial offer by p_1 such that $q_1 - p_1 = M; M > 0$.

Party does not in general expect that he will be able to secure acceptance of his initial demand. His expectation is that at the end of the negotiating period he will have been able to secure a maximum concession from customer, at the price of having made some related minimum concession himself, and that these concessions when taken together will establish a bargain at some point $<q_1 :> p_1$, which customer would accept. Note that such a bargain would not necessarily be acceptable to Party. It represents only the optimal outcome to Party of the two initial demands, the related bargaining period, Party's expectation of customer's maximum concessions, and Party's expectation of his own minimum concessions necessary to produce those he expects to obtain from customer.

If formally the concession factor is represented by F, then in relation to the initial offers $(q_1 : p_1)$, Party expects that:

1. The maximum concession he can hope to secure from customer will be:
   $$F(p_1) \;_{\text{limit } (q_1 F(q_1) T_{11})}$$
2. In order to persuade customer into making that concession Party as a minimum will have to concede:
   $$F(q_1) \;_{\text{max } (F(p_1))}$$
3. It will take time T_{11} to achieve the above concessions
4. $F(p_1) \;_{\text{limit } (q_1 F(q_1) \, T_{11})} + F(q_1) \;_{\text{max } (F(p_1))} = M$

The notation is intended to express the idea that the concession factor $F(p_1)$ represents the maximum concession which customer would ever be willing to make, given his initial offer p_1, ie $p_1 - F(p_1)$ equals the level at which customer would just prefer a bargain to no bargain. In practice customer would first formulate his minimum settling figure and then add the negotiating margin, some or all of which he would hope to be able to retain, depending on how strongly Party presses his demands and the other pressures on customer to reach an agreement, which would be reflected in the form of his concession factor. This accords with the definition of hold-back strategy (see p. 101).

The true form of Customer's concession factor $F(p_1)$ will be unknown to Party. He can only make his own subjective assessment of what form the factor will take and in practice he will probably tend to underestimate. The subscript $(q_1 F(q_1) \ T_{11})$ represents the variance effect on customer's true concession factor of Party's negotiating plan, based on Party's subjective assessment of what he believes Customer's concession factor to be, expressed in terms of:

1   Party's initial demand.
2   The intransigence Party plans to show and the concessions he intends to make in terms both of timing and amount, ie Party's own concession factor.
3   The time scale over which Party plans the bargaining to take place.

The expression 'limit' indicates that each of Party's factors has a limiting value in terms of the maximum concessions which Party can secure from customer. If Party does manage to select all three factors at their optimal limit then his plan will be based on extracting the maximum concessions which customer is willing to make. If he selects a plan for which any one or more factors has a less than optimal value, ie he plans to concede more than customer would demand, then his ultimate return from that plan will be less than the maximum customer is willing to concede.

Equally, however, if Party goes beyond the limiting value of any one factor, eg by increasing his initial demand, then this will not increase customer's concession factor. Indeed any such action could have the reverse effect.

Associated with time T_{11} there are time costs C_1 which will be incurred by Party. Finally it is necessary to discount the value of any bargain reached by a discounting factor, r, which will convert it from the value at time T_{11} back to its present value.

The discounted outcome which Party anticipates from the above factors is represented by O_{11}.

In general form we can then state:

$$O_{ij} = [\, q_i - F \, q_{1 \max Fpj)} \,] \, (1 - r \, T_{ij}) - C \, T_{ij}$$

This expression is interpreted in the following way. For each initial demand which Party chooses to make $q_1, q_2 \ldots q_i$, related to the offer made by customer $p_1, p_2 \ldots p_j$, Party expects to be able to obtain a maximum concession from customer by offering some minimum concession $Fq_{1,2} \ldots {}_{j(\max Fp_{1,2} \ldots j)}$ and that agreement will only be reached at time T_{ij}. Associated with time T_{ij} there are time costs $T_{ij}C$ and the value of the agreement reached at time T_{ij} must be discounted back to its present value.

Relationship of the above model to that proposed by Cross
In deriving this model of the bargaining process, in so far as it relates to Party's choice of his initial demand, much credit is due to Cross and Coddington for their pioneering work in this field. However, it is believed that Cross's apparent wish to establish a theory which owed nothing to the behavioural aspects of bargaining has unduly restricted its further development. In particular three of his major assumptions are disagreed with:

1 The demands of the parties are independent, ie in making his initial demand party does not consider the absolute level of customer's offer and Party's expectation of customer's concession factor is not affected by the level of Party's initial offer.
2 Party expects to remain totally intransigent and that all concessions will be made by customer. It is true that through Cross's adjustment process Party would eventually concede if he found that customer was not conceding in the manner in which he had anticipated. However, this is made the only justification for Party making concessions. If customer does concede as expected by Party then Party remains intransigent and the same applies for customer. As Cross has stated: 'in terms of this model concessions are always a sign of weakness'.[24]
3 Customer's concession rate will be linear.

In the approach to negotiation Party plans a strategy designed to achieve an end result. In making those plans he allows for what he anticipates is going to happen and he will realistically plan for making some concessions and also, at times, for being intransigent, although it is stressed that Party's concessions are made solely in order to achieve larger concessions from customer. Party's concession factor is therefore a total strategy plan for the whole bargaining period, whilst as Coddington has pointed out: 'a Cross-type bargainer is involved only with tactics and concerned with immediate expectations.'[25]

In the description of the initial expectations which Party has of the mutual concessions factors of both customer and himself the F factor is allowed to take a wide form, the only restriction being that in relation to any pair of demands $q_i : p_j$ the factor from Party's viewpoint is optimal, ie it represents the minimum concession which Party anticipates having to make in order to secure the maximum concessions from customer.

Specifically, and again departing from Cross, it is maintained that these expectations which the two sides have of each other's concession factors are themselves, in part, a function of their initial demands. There exists therefore in this model, unlike that of Cross, a direct relationship between the F factor and the initial demands such that a change in either q_i or p_j may lead to a change in any or all of:

1 Party's own concession factor
2 Party's expectation of customer's concession factor
3 Party's expectation of the time of agreement

As regards the assumption of linearity of the rate of concession by customer (in Cross's model Party never expects to have to concede himself) Cross admits that this is only a convenient assumption made for the purpose of simplification. However, given the concept of the concession factor as representing Party's own plan and his expectation of Customer's plan over the negotiating period, it is an assumption which cannot be accepted. Rather a varying pattern of concessions would be expected, differing in amounts, with periods of intransigence in between, varying in length. In general it is proposed that:

1 The greater the total concession expected of customer the lower will be his average concession rate.
2 Customer's rate of concession will decrease the nearer the bargaining moves to his minimum acceptable level.

These propositions are based on the assumption of the increasing marginal utility of money the closer the negotiations approach to the limit at which customer would prefer 'no bargain'.

Cross recognizes this possibility but does not allow for it in his model, apparently on the grounds that Party cannot be expected to know customer's utility function. However, it is maintained that Party must attempt to assess this function and that it should be a primary objective of market intelligence activity to provide him with the necessary data to do so.

The less Party knows regarding customer's utility function the greater will be the gap between his belief as to the form of customer's concession function and the reality. Further, the interacting mechanism between Party's estimate of the worth to customer of the goods/services concerned, Party's behaviour and customer's concession factor, will operate to reinforce the effect of any such gap.

If Party underestimates customer's valuation of the goods/services then Party will demand less, and the less Party demands, the less customer will believe he needs to concede. He will regard Party's initial offer as a sign of weakness and behave accordingly.[26]

Alternatively if Party overestimates customer's valuation then Party will submit an initial demand well above the upper level of the bargaining zone. Since customer as a rational bargainer knows that Party's demand is related to Party's expectations regarding customer's behaviour, he will recognize that Party has made a mistake and in consequence will not increase his own concession factor.[27] Eventually, when as a result of customer standing firm Party is taught to understand his error, he will be compelled either to reduce his demands substantially and lose his reputation for firmness, or break off the negotiations.

This is the variance effect of Party's negotiating plan on customer's concession factor, and indicates how critical it is for Party to gain the maximum understanding of customer's utility function and hence of his concession factor. A list of the principal factors likely to be involved in any such assessment is given on pp. 156 and 157.

Selection of the optimal demand
Although the outcome has been defined in terms of Party's initial demand and his concession factor, together with the time at which Party expects agreement could be reached, it should be evident that both Party's demand and his concession factor are only a response to his expectations regarding customer's behaviour. If it is assumed that customer's initial offer is known with sufficient certainty by Party that it may be treated as a parameter, then Party's concern is with his judgement as to customer's maximum likely concessions from this offer, and the time which it would take to achieve these, for any given demand/concession factor which Party might select. Based on his judgement Party can then derive a series of possible outcomes using the equation on p. 151 and select that demand which is optimal.

In exercising that judgement the following are suggested as guide lines to the way in which the factors would be expected to interact:

1   When Party puts forward a demand intitially he should do so with the expectation of a pattern of responsive concessions occurring over the bargaining period. In union-management negotiations alternative moves have become almost a convention so that failure to make some response, even if it is only minimal, will lead to an accusation of lack of good faith.[28] The alternating of the frequency of concessions (although Party's concessions may be smaller than those of Opponent) has also

been reported in the experimental work referred to by Baron and Liebert.[29] My own negotiating experience in various parts of the world, covering Latin America, Europe and the Middle and Far East, has again been that to obtain a concession from Opponent one is expected at some stage to offer him something in return. Moreover, the timing must be such that he will recognize your concession as a response to his. To behave otherwise would be regarded by him as an insult. Further, because he expects you to behave in this manner, Opponent will artificially create bargaining counters to be given away to you in return for a concession which he wishes to secure.

2　The rate at which concessions will be made will be dependent on the intial gap between the parties and whether or not
    (a) Some particular bargain appeals as the unique outcome due to the manner in which the demands have been structured.[30]
    (b) The negotiators are concerned with their reputation and possible loss of face.

3　If the gap between the two initial demands is small, unless the marginal loss in utility of any concession would be significant, a high concession rate would be expected. With a small gap it should be easy for the two sides to identify a bargain with which both could be satisfied. Neither will wish to incur the time costs associated with a prolonged period of bargaining which could rapidly off-set any advantage gained by holding out for better terms. In practice the most likely bargain would be a 50/50 split.

Only if the identifiable bargain is at the outer limit at which both sides would only just prefer a bargain to no bargain, ie the marginal reduction in utility from any concession would be high, will the concession rate be low and the negotiations extended. This will most often happen when the outcome of the bargaining will establish a significant precedent for the future, even though its immediate impact may be small, and covers the case of bargaining on so-called 'points of principle'.

4　If Party increases his demands so that the gap widens then no final bargain is likely to be immediately identifiable and customer cannot be expected to make any early concessions. Rather he will seek to test the strength of Party's resistance, establish trade-off factors and so formulate his ideas about the level and shape of the final agreement.

Equally Party is in no position to encourage customer into conceding by making any early concessions himself, since to do so too soon and at a stage remote from the final bargaining area would only be taken by customer as a sign of weakness. He too will wish to explore and test whether his expectations of customer's concession factor are likely to be justified.

By increasing his demand Party will therefore have altered his expectations of the timing and the size of the concessions to be expected from customer, and so also the shape of his own concession factor. He must now balance the need to communicate with customer (to invite a reciprocal response) with the need to show firmness. He may have to plan to move first immediately he senses that to do so will lead to a response. The position has been well stated by Peters in this quotation from advice given by a mediator to a union official in America:

> You have offered the employer no inducement, none whatever, to take another step. The employer has made it clear. He is not tipping his hand any further. Not until you show him where you are going. When you are up at 30 cents you are telling him nothing. When you come down to a point where he can guess roughly where you are going then he will reciprocate. It is possible to come out on the short end by dropping down too fast but you are so far away from the real bargaining area yet you have not even come to grips with the employer. The time to get cagey is when the dentist's drill is near the nerve. Then there is some advantage in forcing the other side to move before you do.

Having increased his demand Party must either accept a long drawn-out negotiation and retain his reputation for firmness, or concede more rapidly so reducing the negotiating time but lose face to customer by appearing weak.

This latter point will be of particular importance where the parties contemplate a long-term continuing relationship and the negotiators can expect to meet on numerous future occasions.

A high initial demand, if a reputation for firmness is to be retained, carries with it therefore the penalty of extending the negotiating period so that the delicate process of exploration and adjustment can be given time to work itself out in the manner suggested by Peters.[31]

5   By way of corollary to the last point if the negotiating time is restricted by some factor which is external to the bargaining process, eg customer has a prior commitment to place the order by a definite date, then there is a limit on the intitial demand for which Party should ask, unless his position is one of total dominance, and he can genuinely expect that customer will do all the conceding. In any other instance if he exceeds this limit then Party will find that he can only make a bargain if he concedes at a rate which would seriously prejudice his reputation for firmness. He will then be compelled to choose between the lesser of two evils: loss of face or failure to reach a bargain.

Assessment of the concession factor

So far no attempt has been made to define how Party should assess customer's concession factor, although in the model such assessment is crucial to Party's choice of his own concession factor and his optimal demand. The following points are suggested as having the most relevance in making such assessment:

1   Party's knowledge of customer's budget and of the worth to customer of the contract. Is customer already committed to purchase? If not what are the alternatives open to him?

2   Past precedents which Party has established with customer, and Party's previous experience in dealing with the individual negotiators for customer and equally their experience of dealing with Party. The personality of the individual negotiators for each side and their knowledge of, and respect for, each other's skill and determination will have a significant effect on the expectations each side will form of each other's concession factor.

3   The manner in which the demand(s) are structured. An offer which is between round numbers usually implies that the person making it is willing to concede to the lower. Equally an offer in round numbers which has no obvious line of movement away from it may indicate a strong determination not to concede further.

4   The way in which customer will view his long-term relationship with Party and his expectation of Party's willingness to respect customer's viewpoint taking into account the prospects of future business.

5   The rationality of the concessions relative to the other factors in the total bargain and to customer's business. In relation to the conditions of contract and the associated risks the argument in favour of the concession is stronger, and therefore customer's acceptance of it more likely, if it can be shown to be fair and reasonable, and if the terms of the final contract as amended by the concession would form a logical whole.

6   Party's ability to involve a third party whose wishes customer must respect, eg mandatory requirements of a bank or credit insurer if customer requires credit to finance the contract.

7   Precedents as to price level or terms of contract ruling generally in the industry.

8   The extent to which Party believes that customer has either studied the problem or developed a firm negotiating strategy. Problem study by customer but without definite commitment to a negotiating strategy is likely to lead to greater flexibility and therefore a higher concession factor. Development of a firm negotiating strategy, to which Customer's negotiating team are committed to their own management, is likely to lead to a lower concession

factor and possibly to deadlock unless the negotiating objectives of Party and Customer substantially overlap, ie there is a wide bargaining zone.[32]

9 The effect which the granting of concessions would have on customer's business with other firms, and the ratio which Party's business with customer bears to customer's business as a whole in this particular field. Customer is more likely to grant concessions if these can be isolated from the remainder of his business and if the proportion of his total business affected by such concessions is small.

10 Mandatory requirements imposed on customer either from the existence if rules internal to his organization, national laws or regulations with which he is obliged to comply or restrictions imposed by an external organization such as the World Bank. This factor applies most strongly to contracts placed by governments or government controlled agencies.

11 Adverse criticism which customer as an overseas government or government agency might face either from political opponents, international bodies such as the International Monetary Fund or local interests at the award of a contract to a foreign firm on what appear to be favourable terms. This possibility which can, in particular countries, be only too real, may lead customer to adopt an apparent low concession factor and behave accordingly, while in reality be prepared to concede more if the concessions can be structured in such a way that any external criticism can be minimized.

The same situation can arise if there is a middle level of 'young Turks' in the authority's organization who either for personal advancement or more probably on the grounds of nationalistic idealism, wish to discredit their own top management. The author was involved in a case in a Latin American country where just this occurred and the local college of Engineers formally protested the contract award and its terms to the National Assembly.

In any such case it is essential for Party either directly or through his local agent or company to have established the right contracts at all appropriate levels in the customer's genuine concession factor and the means necessary to defend the bargain so arrived at against criticism. It is often a case of helping those who hold the ultimate decision making authority so that they can safely exercise that in one's favour and under these circumstances presentation becomes all important. Although the expression $F(p_1)$ $_{\text{limit } (q_1 F(q_1) T_{11})}$ has been referred to as Party's assessment of the *maximum* concessions he would expect to obtain from customer, clearly it is anticipated that in exercising his judgement Party will be realistic. In most situations it would be expected that Party's experience and judgement would enable him to arrive at a single point assessment with a sufficient degree of accuracy to make any attempt at further refinement not worthwhile, or even positively dangerous if it persuaded Party to believe that the final result possessed a greater degree of accuracy than was justified by the reliability of the input data.

However, there will be circumstances, particularly in relation to price level, in which it will be advantageous for Party to assess a range of possible concessions by customer, assign to each his estimate of the subjective probability of its occurring, and add the product of these together to arrive at an expected value using the technique described on pp. 18 and 19. Again it is suggested that these estimates should be made separately by more than one person, perhaps by all the members of the negotiating team, and the results compared in order to neutralize as far as possible individual bias.

A numerical example
In selecting his initial demand Party is concerned to balance the gains to be derived from increasing his demand with the time costs and discounting effect necessarily associated with the bargaining period, within the limitations of:

1   The concessions he can expect from customer.
2   The concessions he would have to make himself.
3   The period of bargaining which would be required.

A numerical example illustrates the way in which Party could approach this problem of choosing an optimum demand. For simplicity the example is expressed only in terms of price although it is recognized that in practice there would be other factors to be taken into account, such as terms of contract, delivery, etc. The principles enumerated are just as applicable to these other factors as they are to the price and, therefore, the same technique should be used for determining the optimum demand.

Assume that Party is aware that customer's initial offer will be £140 000 and believes that the maximum which customer would ever be willing to pay is £180 000. The costs to Party of carrying out the negotiation are £1 500 per month and the discount rate, which takes into account escalation in costs and the reduction in profitability due to the later receipt of the profit contribution, is 6% per annum.

Party wishes to establish the level at which to submit his initial offer so as to maximize the outcome. For the present it will be assumed that Party attaches no special significance to securing the order earlier rather than later, other than the effect of the discount factor.

For each demand which Party considers feasible he estimates:

Party's initial demand £'000s	Party's expectations of time which would elapse before agreement month	Concession allowed by party, up to time of agreement £'000s	Contract value at time of agreement £'000s	Discount factor 0.005 per month	Discounted value of agreement £'000s	Cost per month £'000s	Cost to time of agreement £'000s	Value of outcomes at present value less time costs £'000s
200	12	20	180	0.06	169	1.5	18.0	151
190	7	20	170	0.035	164	1.5	10.5	153.5
180	4	15	165	0.02	162	1.5	6.0	156
170	2	15	155	0.01	153.5	1.5	3.0	150.5
160	1	10	150	0.005	149.25	1.5	1.5	147.75
150	0.5	5	145	0.0025	144.5	1.5	0.75	143.75
140	nil	nil	nil	nil	140	—	nil	140

Figure 6:16 Value to Party of possible outcomes to an initial offer, discounted to present value and taking time costs into account

1   The maximum concession which he believes customer would make relative to customer's intitial offer of £140 000 and the minimum concession which Party would have to make in order to obtain that maximum concession from customer.
2   The minimum time which he would expect to elapse before agreement was reached. In this example no constraint is placed on the time available for negotiation, ie it is regarded purely as a function of the bargaining process.

Party then prepares a table in the form shown in Figure 6:16. It will readily be seen that his optimal demand is £180 000 with an anticipated negotiating period of four months. This can also be represented in graphical form, Figure 6:17, in which the total gain derived from any demand and the time costs involved have been plotted against time. The net gain is the difference between these two and is at a maximum at the point at which the marginal net gain from increasing the demand would be zero. It will be appreciated that this is the point at which using the differential calculus the first order derivative of the net gain curve is equal to zero.

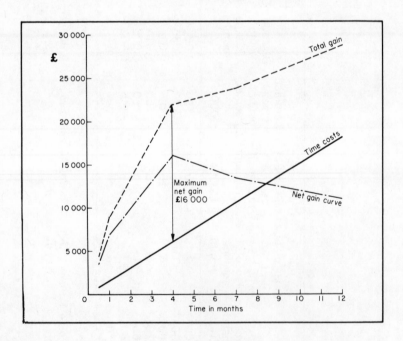

Figure 6:17 Net and total gain curves

Therefore it is proposed that Party should demand £180 000, with the expectation that the bargain will be made at £165 000, provided that this bargain would satisfy at least his minimum negotiating objective and that he is willing to allocate four months' effort to the negotiation.

If the assumption that the bargaining period is a function only of the bargaining process is amended by imposing an external restriction on the time available for negotiation, then Party must limit his demand to that which will result in the most favourable outcome within that period. Thus from Figure 6:16 if only one month is available within which to settle the bargain then Party in that example should not demand more than £160 000.

At that level and over the period the initial demands of the two sides and their expectations of each other's concession factors would be in balance so that by the end of one month both would recognize £150 000 as an acceptable solution. If Party demands more than £160 000 then that balance is disturbed and could only be restored by extending the negotiating period. This would permit Party to slow down the rate at which he made concessions and to become more intransigent. This would in turn cause customer to revise his own expectations of the bargain which Party would accept. During the extended negotiating period balance is once again restored through the operation of the adjustment process. Whether the final outcome at the end of the longer period is more favourable to Party or not depends on the form of the respective concession factors, the manner in which these are adjusted, and the discount rate/time–cost factor. In Figure 6:16 an increase in demand to £170 000, which would absorb an additional month of negotiating time, would in fact result in an additional £2 500 discounted benefit to Party.

Supposing, however, that Party increases his demand to say £170 000 and the restriction assumed on the available period for negotiation remains. He must now bring pressure to bear on customer to concede at a rate which, taken in conjunction with Party's own concession factor, will bring the two demands close enough together, before the end of the month, for both sides to identify an acceptable bargain. Unless this is done, neither side at the final bargaining session will be willing to concede enough to bridge the gap between them, since to do so would constitute an unacceptable loss of face unless accompanied by a similar concession from the other side. However, for such an exchange of mutual concessions to take place each must have already given the other an appropriate and recognizable signal by their previous pattern of intransigence/concession behaviour.

It is again stressed that, provided a bargain at the upper limit of the bargaining zone would at least satisfy Party's minimum negotiating objective, the level of Party's first offer will not be related to that which would be acceptable to Party but to the minimum Party believes would be acceptable to customer. Given a reasonable width to the bargaining zone this will lead Party to adopt a hard rather than a soft approach; to pitch the intitial demand at an extreme rather than a moderate level. Certainly the question of fairness will not enter into Party's calculations.

This approach is consistent with that of the rational bargainer of Harsanyi and with the experimental results obtained by Bartos, Cagguila, Siegal and Fouraker, and Chertkoff and Conley, all of which have shown that the hard-line negotiator who has made an extreme offer and conceded little, slowly, has obtained the best of the bargain.[33, 34]

One word of caution, however; neither the time costs nor the cost of failing to reach agreement have been significant in these bargaining experiments. The participants have not been concerned with long-term bargaining relationships and the emotional disturbance to such a relationship which the adoption of a hard-line strategy may create. Later a study will be made of how consideration of these psychological factors within the context of a continuing relationship between the negotiators may lead to a softening of approach. In commerce as in military matters it is the winning of the war, not the battle, which counts.

Utility value of price/time of agreement
So far the example has been simplified by assuming that neither Party nor customer has any special interest in reaching agreement at an early date apart from the effect of the time costs and discount rate. The time at which agreement is reached may, however, have a special significance to either side which would affect their preference for one combination of bargain/time of agreement as against another. The most obvious example is that of the supplier who needs the work urgently because he has men and machines idle or at least not working to capacity. If that is so then the worth of any bargain may only properly be represented by a utility function which takes account of both the profit contribution and the need for an early settlement, and also allows for the decreasing marginal utility of each such factor as it approaches its optimal value.

If it is assumed that the bargain with the higher profit contribution will take longer to obtain then the negotiator for Party will be concerned to choose the initial demand which he expects will result in the combination of contribution margin/time of agreement having for Party the maximum utility value. This is identical to the problem of comparing two competing offers considered on p 42 and the same means of solution may be adopted.

First it is necessary to determine the weighting to be given to time of agreement relative to profit contribution in the total utility value. Taking 10 as representing the utility value of the most preferred outcome, time to profit contribution may be weighted in the ratio of 6:4. The minimum acceptable price level and maximum acceptable time period must then be decided. £145 000 and eight weeks are selected. Any price below £145 000 and any time beyond eight weeks is therefore assigned the utility value zero and this means that combination including either of those is also assigned the utility value zero (see also p. 41).

Finally it is necessary to decide on the utility values for each factor, recognizing as before that each is ordered separately from the other (see p. 42). For the range of possible values taken from Figure 6:16 the worth of each factor may be assessed as set out in Figure 6:18.

Price level	Utility value	Time of agreement	Utility value
140	0	0	6
145	0.5	2	5.5
150	1.5	4	4.0
155	3.5	8	1.5
160	4.0	8	0.5
		8	0

Figure 6:18 Additive utility values of price and time of agreement

From the Figure 6:18 and the data in Figure 6:16 the only feasible combinations of price level and time of agreement and their additive utility values are:

Combination of price level/time	Utility value
145/2 weeks	6.0
150/4 weeks	5.5
155/8 weeks	4.0

An initial demand of £150 000 would therefore be selected with the expectation of achieving an outcome of £145 000 in two weeks. It is interesting to note that the reduction in utility by dropping from £150 000 to £145 000 is twice as much as the loss in utility by extending the negotiating time from now for two weeks. The plan would therefore be to remain intransigent for most of the negotiating period in the hope that it might be possible to improve on the 50/50 split.

Time and the limits of the bargaining zone
It has been previously established that the upper limit of the bargain-

ing zone, prior to the submission of Party's initial offer, is the level at which customer would ultimately just prefer a bargain to no bargain. After submission of the initial offer the upper limit of the bargaining zone is represented by the lower of Party's offer and the previous level (assuming there is no competitor).

Subsequently it has been shown that Party will expect customer, over varying negotiating periods to be willing to reach agreement at some maximum level which is in part a function of the elapsed negotiating period. Further, there is some level beyond which customer would never concede, no matter how long the negotiations were to last. Does this mean that customer's preference function and therefore the upper limit of the bargaining zone will change over the negotiating period?

The answer in the model constructed is no; customer's preference for a bargain as opposed to no bargain does not change over time. However, as a result of Party's bargaining behaviour, there is a change in Customer's belief as to the money which he needs to spend, and the terms to which he needs to agree, in order to acquire the goods/ services concerned. The assumption made regarding Party is now made regarding customer, namely that the final level beyond which he will never concede was formulated as part of his negotiating plan and therefore in his mind from the beginning of the negotiation. Any level less than this (ie more favourable to customer), which is the most to which he is prepared to agree at a point in time during the course of the negotiation, is merely an expectation of the concessions he considers necessary to make at that point in time in order to reach agreement. Customer only moves towards the upper limit of the bargaining zone as he becomes convinced of the necessity of so doing by the bargaining tactics adopted by Party. The approach is that of the man who says: 'I would be prepared, rather than lose the bargain, to pay £X but only if I am finally convinced that I cannot obtain what I want for less'.

The distinction between a change in preference and a change in belief is important to the choice which Party makes in selecting his negotiating tactics. In this model that choice is directed towards tactics which will change customer's belief and persuade him that he can only obtain a bargain on the terms and at a price level which Party prefers.

In another model, in which customer's preference function did change, Party's tactics would be directed towards securing such a change by, for example, persuading customer that his offer was worth more than customer had thought and that he could afford to pay the extra. It is a model of this nature which would be required if customer's preference function were such that the point at which he would prefer no bargain was below the lowest level which Party was willing to accept, ie there was no bargaining zone. The lower limit of the bargaining zone has been defined as that at which Party would just prefer a bargain to no-bargain, and it has been stated that in so far as Party formulated this level as part of his original negotiating strategy, he is not expected to change it over time unless some factor which influenced his original decision changes, eg the state of his order book. Specifically, the model under discussion does not allow for it being changed simply as a result of time. This is in opposition to the conclusion reached by Stevens who states 'An approaching deadline does much more . . . It brings pressure to bear which actually changes the least favourable terms upon which each party is willing to settle'[35] Zubin and Brown in their review of the *Social Psychology of Bargaining and Negotiation* also refer to experiments which have demonstrated the same point.[36]

This divergence of view seems to be due to two factors. First the incorrect initial formulation of Party's minimum position. Rubin and Brown suggest that bargainers initially inflate their minimum level and then reduce it as more information becomes available to them as to the bargain which is actually obtainable. It is accepted that some negotiators do behave in this way but normally in sales negotiations this must be wrong unless the information relates to some element which changes the worth of the bargain to Party at any particular level. If, for example, liability for consequential damages was unacceptable to Party when the tender was prepared it should still be unacceptable if Party is told he will be awarded the contract provided only that he accepts such liability, assuming always that nothing else has changed which affects the worth to party of the contract award. The evaluation at the break-even point between what is and what is not acceptable, should be made quite independently of success probability.

It is of course accepted – see Figure 4:2 – that the two are inter-dependent. If Party judges the risk, say of on-demand performance bonds, as unacceptable then this will deprive him of the opportunity of bidding into countries where they are mandatory. The same may apply to other issues such as law of the country, jurisdiction, or payment in local currency where non-acceptance of particular clauses may restrict Party's potential market or at least reduce his chance. What is argued is that, in deciding upon whether to accept the risk or not, Party is concerned with evaluating the bid as a whole in terms of its desirability and if the opinion is that the risk is unacceptable then the answer must be 'no-bid', if acceptance is mandatory, or a qualified bid if Party is uncertain whether customer will insist on the point or not. If however a qualified bid is submitted, and the decision has been made that the risk is not acceptable, then Party must continue to maintain that position. He must knowingly recognize that he runs the risk of the bid being disqualified, or pressure brought both by customer and his own agent to remove the qualification if in other respects his bid is attractive. Indeed party must ensure that his agent is fully aware of his intentions and accepts them.

Only too often, however, in practice Party does not make the evaluation in the manner suggested. His executives either engage in wishful thinking that customer does not really mean it, or console themselves with the thought that 'we will cross that bridge when we come to it'. In either case they are quite unprepared for the event when it happens and must then choose between either withdrawing, with the possible loss of a tender bond and certainly creating ill-feeling with customer and their agent, or continuing and being involved in a liability for which no provision has been made. There is also the alternative possibility that by inadequate initial risk evaluation the negotiator will be misled into believing that his management would refuse to accept a particular risk, as a result of which he continues to take that line and so loses the bargain, when in reality they would have been willing, if it was necessary for the purposes of securing the order, to accept it.

Strict definition of the minimum position is difficult and adherence to it when tempted by the prospects of contract award is even more so, but it is the corner-stone of Party's negotiating behaviour.

The second factor is the structural difference between labour relations and sales negotiations. In the former a relationship already exists between the two sides from which neither normally contemplate permanent withdrawal. Strikes and lock-outs are seen primarily as phases within a negotiation. Some agreement is therefore virtually a necessity even if it is only a maintenance of the status quo which would only apply in sales negotiations to a case of strict duopoly. Although the union may try therefore to establish a minimum, which is usually the maintenance of their member's living standards, they may be quite unable to maintain this against complete intransigence from the employers' side which by their actions the employers show they are prepared to continue indefinitely, if the only alternative for their members is unemployment or taking other work on less favourable terms. The union's minimum is therefore accordingly interactive with the strength of the employer's resistance and so can vary over time.

Level of Party's initial offer relative to the bargaining zone
From the discussion so far, two rules may be derived as to the level at which Party should submit his initial offer relative to the bargaining zone.

1   *The anticipated negotiating period is short enough for Party to ignore time costs and discount rates.* Party should submit an offer at a level which he anticipates will be equal to the maximum he believes

customer would ever accept, ie an outcome equal to what Party believes is the upper limit of the bargaining zone.

2 *The anticipated negotiating period is long enough for it to be necessary to take time costs into account.* Party should submit an offer which, when discounted to its present value and after deduction of time costs, maximizes the outcome to Party based on his belief as to customer's concession factor, and his own related concession factor, relative to time.

This offer will result in an outcome less than the upper limit of the bargaining zone; the degree to which it is less being a function of customer's expected resistance to Party's demands.

In the model, note that Party's initial demand only ever exceeds the upper limit of the bargaining zone by his expectation of the minimum concession he expects to be compelled to make to gain the maximum concessions from customer. Further, if the negotiating time is significant, his initial demand only exceeds the bargain producing the optimal outcome by the minimum concession he expects to have to make during the time taken to reach that bargain. If he were to demand more then, assuming his expectations of customer's behaviour are correct, this must result in a less favourable outcome.

In the example Figure 6:16, if Party increases his demand to £190 000 his expectation is only an outcome of £153.5 at month 7, as compared to the optimum of £156 at month 4 from a demand of £180 000. This is due simply to the fact that the marginal gain between months 4 and 7, after application of the discount factor, is less than the marginal increase in time costs.

It may be suggested that Party should make the higher initial demand with the hope of obtaining the higher pay off but aim to complete the bargaining in 4 months thus avoiding the adverse effect of the extended time costs. He could only achieve this objective by securing a change in customer's concession factor since it has been predicted that by month 4 customer will only concede £25 000. To do this would require that Party remained intransigent for longer with the substantial risk that towards the end of the 4-month negotiating period the gap between the two sides would be too wide to be easily bridged. Party would then have the choice of either conceding more rapidly in a desperate effort to reach agreement, thereby losing his credibility for the future, or facing up to the longer bargaining period and incurring the additional time costs and discount effect. Either way Party would lose.

Note also from the two rules the effect which Party's belief as to the form of customer's concession factor has on the initial demand made by Party. If Party anticipates that customer will resist strongly, so that the negotiating period is prolonged, the effect of the discount factor and the time costs will be to reduce Party's optimal demand. This will be so even if the higher initial demand pursued long enough would eventually produce a greater concession from customer.

This critical effect of Party's belief of customer's concession factor reinforces the importance of the negotiator for customer obtaining and retaining a reputation for firmness. Once established such a reputation must, within the context of the model, result in a scaling down of Party's initial demands. Equally a reputation for weakness would result in the demands being escalated.

So far the situation has been analyzed from the viewpoint of a two party negotiation – supplier and purchaser. In practice the situation is often complicated because there are two or more suppliers with whom the purchaser seeks to negotiate at the same time.

The presence of one or more competitors will primarily affect Party in his judgement as to the form of customer's concession factor. Party must recognize that customer will now believe in adding to the pressure through informing Party of the concessions, alleged or genuine, made by the other bidders. This applies of course both ways so that the process is inter-active. Party is pressurised through the concessions, purported or real, made by bidders B,C..... and vice versa. The result in general is to lower customer's concession factor and increase the negotiating period (assuming customer does not have a fixed dead-line by which agreement must be reached. The reduction in customer's concession factor and the extended negotiating period will suggest to Party (and all other bidders) that they should reduce their initial demands. However, it could also be suggested that to allow for the increased pressure from customer Party (and all other bidders) should raise their initial demands and prolong the negotiations by only conceding slowly. That will bring time-pressure on customer and result in a more favourable outcome for the successful bidder.

Figure 6:19 is an amended version of Figure 6:16 and represents the possible changes resulting from the presence of one or more competitors. Party cannot, however, now simply choose the apparently optimal outcome of bidding at £200 000 since he has to take into account competitors' actions. Assuming that his competitors have

200	12	30	170	0.06	160	1.5	18	142
190	10	25	165	0.05	157	1.5	15	142
180	8	25	155	0.04	149	1.5	12	137
170	6	20	150	0.03	146	1.5	9	137
160	4	15	145	0.02	142	1.5	6	136
150	2	10	140	0.01	139	1.5	3	136

Figure 6:19 Possible changes resulting from the presence of other competitors

approached the problem broadly in the same way as Party then each has two alternative strategies; bid high to gain the optimal outcome; bid low to maximize the chance of success. This is illustrated in the game theory type matrix in Figure 6:20.

Competitors

	High bid 200 – 190		Low bid 160 – 150	
High bid 200 – 190	Possible gain 142	Possible gain 142	Certain loss	Certain gain 136
Low bid	Certain gain 136	Certain loss	Possible gain 136	Possible gain 136

Party

Figure 6:20 Game theory matrix

Party's maximin strategy and Opponent's minimax strategy (see p. 30) is to bid low since it gives each of them the possibility of obtaining the contract at a value to them of 136. Neither can take the risk of bidding high since this would expose them to a certain loss if the other bid low. This is based on the premise that customer is otherwise indifferent as to which firm he places the order with and having received at least one low bid will save himself the trouble and his own time costs by concentrating on the low bidder.

The bidding problem in this situation is a version of the prisoner's dilemma game (see p. 35) so that although the strategy choice low bid strictly dominates that of high bid and is the unique equilibrium pair the bidders would stand to gain by a co-operative agreement between them to bid high. The chances, however, in practice of any such agreement being honoured are remote, and so, recognizing that at least one bidder may defect, all the others are bound to follow suit.

Other bargaining situations
It is now possible to apply the principles defined as being of general application to the individual bargaining situations which were separately identified and listed on p. 121.

Competitive bidding, single opportunity
Because Party has identified the bidding situation as competitive, after submission of the initial offers the upper level of the bargaining zone will be the lowest of the bids submitted, provided this is below the level at which customer would just prefer agreement to no bargain.

Any bids above that level will be ignored. The bottom level of the bargaining zone for Party is the lowest level at which he would just prefer a bargain to no bargain.

Party's objective is to secure the contract at a level within the bargaining zone which maximizes the discounted outcome after deduction of the anticipated time costs, if these are judged to be of significance.

For the moment it will be assumed that there is no customer bias either in favour of Party or of any competitor, ie customer is treated as being indifferent to the firm to whom he awards the contract.

In deciding on the level at which to bid in order to achieve his objective, Party must consider the probable bidding behaviour of the firm he identifies as likely to be the lowest competitor. Using again the example in Figure 6:16 it is supposed that Party identifies firm X as being the company likely to put in the lowest competitive bid and his estimate of the probability distribution of the level of that bid is as shown in figure 6:21.

Bid	Probability	Expected bid
140	0.1	14
150	0.4	60
160	0.3	48
170	0.2	34
		156

Figure 6:21 Expected value of the lowest competitor's bid

Given a bid by firm X at £156 000 Party then estimates the likely outcome, assuming that he is not competing. From figure 6:16 Party could expect this to be about £150 000. This is the outcome for which Party's initial bid would be £160 000. Provided that a bargain at £150 000 is above the bottom limit of the bargaining zone then Party should submit an initial offer of £160 000.

Relaxing the assumption that customer is indifferent to the firm with whom he places the business means that Party must make allowance in deciding on his bidding level, for any non-price bias either in his favour or against him. If in the example Party were to believe that he had a 10 per cent non-price advantage then he could raise his bidding level to £180 000.

In complete contrast therefore to the policy adopted when the bidding strategy was quick kill it is proposed that in a situation of hold back or Uncertainty Party should always bid marginally above the expected value of the lowest anticipated competitive bid. This will ensure that Party does not reduce what would otherwise be the upper limit of the bargaining zone, provided always that such a bid would not be above customer's maximum acceptable level and would be above the minimum acceptable to Party.

It is interesting to see what happens when both Party and firm X follow this rule. In the example Party would bid at £160 000 based on his expectation of a bid by X at £156 000. If, however, X has correctly deduced Party's bidding level then this will lead X to bid at say £165 000. This is an illustration of the self-replacing decision rule considered on pp. 27. If Party is right in his expectations, then X must be wrong in his.

The real sufferer, however, is customer since the only result of the application of the rule will be a steady escalation in the level of the initial demands. That is the price which customer pays for either deliberately adopting a hold-back strategy or at least leaving the bidders in a state of uncertainty in which, as demonstrated earlier, they must in their own protection add a negotiating margin.

Competitive bidding, multiple opportunities
The importance has already been stressed of the effect on the concession factor of the reputation which the negotiator has earned for either being strong or weak. Where the negotiation is one of a series of opportunities it is expected that in the first encounter both sides would be concerned to demonstrate their firmness. Neither would have optimistic expectations of the concessions which the other would make.

This is the equivalent in commercial negotiations of the phenomenon of *pattern bargaining* in industrial relations. One union–employer collective agreement sets the pattern for the remainder of the industry and as one would expect it is that first agreement over which most of the tough bargaining occurs. It is not just a matter of the actual terms negotiated but the manner of their achievement which will be important the next time the two sides meet, since this will decisively affect the expectations which each will have of the other's concession factor. In formulating his initial demand for the first of a series of multiple opportunities Party will be in something of a dilemma. On the one hand he will wish to secure the most advantageous outcome possible, in order to provide a favourable precedent for the future. On the other hand he will be conscious of the difficulties involved in obtaining concessions from customer and the need to avoid making any significant concessions himself for fear of being characterized as lacking in firmness.

In resolving this dilemma it is proposed that Party should in general give greater weight to his negotiating reputation than to the absolute terms of the bargain. Although not easy, precedents in terms of price level or acceptance of particular contractual obligations can usually be distinguished on the next round of negotiations. Changes in design, provision of additional features, escalation in wage and material costs, assumption of extra risks can all provide convincing reasons why the price level has changed. But a negotiator's reputation once lost is almost impossible to recover.

Non-competitive bargaining, Party's position dominant

According to the rule stated on p. 102, if Party's situation is dominant then within the limitations of the domination relationship Party can set his offer at a level which maximizes its worth to Party at the time of agreement and refuse to make any concessions. He can, therefore, increase his demand to the level at which any further increase would postpone the time of agreement by a period, such that the marginal increase in time costs and the effect of the discount factor would more than offset the gain in terms of the actual bargain realized.

In considering any two demands q_n and q_m such that q_n is greater than q_m but will take T_n time to achieve, which is longer than time T_m, then Party should demand q_n provided that:

$$q_n - q_m > C(T_n - T_m) + r(T_n Q_n - T_n Q_m)$$

As before C represents the time costs and r is the discount rate.

It is recognized that the harshness of this policy towards customer if followed to extremes could easily create an emotional reaction which would more than offset any temporary gain which Party might achieve. This point is further considered in Section 7.1.

Non-competitive bargaining, party's position subordinate

Party is obliged to negotiate within the rules established by customer. These may be formal rules, such as those applied by Public Authorities and Government Departments to noncompetitive tendering, or informal rules related to the motivation and behaviour of the individual buyer concerned. Party's initial demand must be such that demonstrably it satisfies the rules, whilst within the restraints imposed by the rules, it leads to an outcome which is optimal for Party. In this instance it is the manner in which Party's demand is structured, as much as the absolute level, which will determine Customer's concession factor and therefore the eventual outcome.

From a study of the rules Party should identify:

1 The items in the rules to which he must conform. If the buyer always expects to negotiate a 5 per cent discount then this must be allowed for. If there is an artifical limitation on profit which Party finds unacceptable, but with which he must comply, then he must look elsewhere within the structure of the bid to compensate for this.

2 Areas outside the rules where he can expect to secure an

advantage. Material quantities are often more difficult to check than rates and prices. A negotiator may, for example, be expert at haggling over rates per ton for steelwork but lose out overall because of his inability to assess the tonnages involved.

6.2 PROCUREMENT

The issue of the selection by the purchaser of an initial offer only arises when the purchaser has elected to use a hold-back strategy. A hold-back situation is classified as the case when the purchaser seeks to bargain directly on price and also the other case in which he seeks to do so indirectly through bargaining on those terms of contract which significantly affect risk, eg penalties, warranty liability and terms of payment.

In arriving at his decision as to the level at which to make his offer the purchaser faces the same basic problems as those which confronted the supplier; the more favourable the terms demanded the longer it is likely that the negotiations will take and the higher will be the time costs. From the purchaser's viewpoint the time costs will essentially be:

1   The loss of revenue or additional expenditure in which the purchaser will be involved due to the delay in starting work and therefore in completion. Postponement of the opening of a new productive facilitiy will mean a loss in earnings, at the same time involving the purchaser in paying interest charges on capital already expended. Delay in completion on non-revenue earning capacity, eg new office premises, will prolong the period before the benefits to be derived from such capacity can be realized.

2   If the tender is not on a fixed price basis, the escalation costs resulting from the work being completed later and therefore, in a time of inflation, during a higher cost period. Even if the particular contract being negotiated is on a fixed price some extra cost may arise if the delay causes postponement of related works to a later period. For example, if the purchaser spends six months negotiating a fixed price contract, the tender being valid for six months, he will not incur any additional costs under the contract. But if after the award of that contract the purchaser plans to place separate contracts for say foundations and off-site facilities the six-month delay will certainly cause these contracts to cost more.

3   Actual costs of the negotiation itself in terms of the allocation of staff involved in both the buying or contracts departments and staff in other departments called upon to provide support.

Unless the particular contract involved is subject to price escalation, then, provided that the negotiations are concluded within the validity period of the tender, the time costs with which the purchaser is concerned are wholly independent of the value of the contract. The extra costs or loss of revenue are a function only of time and the cost/revenue factor concerned and, in general, can be treated as linear with time. It follows that in many instances a potential concession is simply not worth the effort and time costs which would be required to secure it; a conclusion which if appreciated by the supplier must encourage him to remain intransigent.

The overall bargain

In developing his reply to an initial offer presented by the supplier the purchaser should be concerned with the worth to him of the overall bargain and not with whether any one particular element appears to be out of line. Treating costs, overheads and profit as separate negotiable entities seems wrong in principle and can lead only to distortion. It is interesting to note that support for this view is to be found in the American Policy Instructions to contracting officers on price negotiations:

> Profit or fee is only one element of price and normally represents a smaller proportion of the total price than do such other estimated elements as labour and material. While the public interest requires that excessive profits be avoided, the contracting officer should not become so preoccupied with particular elements of a contractor's estimate of costs and profit that the most important consideration, the total price itself, is distorted or diminished in its significance. Government procurement is concerned primarily with the reasonableness of the price which the Government ultimately pays and only secondarily with the eventual cost and profit to the contractor.

Further, there is the danger to the purchaser that unless he can bring equal pressure to bear on all elements at the same time, which is unlikely, what he gains in one direction he will lose in another. The supplier may, for example seek to compensate for a reduction in the rate of profit or overheads allowed by increasing material estimates through, say, adjustment of scrap allowances, or increasing labour estimates by, say, reducing the effect of learning.

Negotiation with a single supplier

The Purchaser would be expected to respond to an initial offer made by the supplier rather than make the first move himself. He will, therefore, have the advantage of knowing the maximum which he might have to pay and is in a better position to assess the concessions which he could anticipate the supplier making.

As before the example will be simplified by limiting it to price alone. Following the example set out in Figure 6:14 it will be assumed that the supplier has proposed his apparent optimal demand of £180 000. In order to develop his response the purchaser needs to establish:

1 The time costs; these will be assessed at £2 000 per month representing the loss of profit which would be incurred by a delay in completion.
2 The maximum level at which he would prefer a bargain to no bargain. It is decided that this is £165 000.
3 The related outcomes and negotiating periods which he would anticipate over a range of possible replies within the limitation that no outcome is acceptable over £165 000. These together with the related time costs are set out in Figure 6:22

Purchaser's response	Expected negotiating time	Expected bargain	Time costs	Expected outcome
(£'000s)	(months)	(£'000s)	(£'000s)	(£'000s)
140	8	150	16	166
145	4	155	8	163
150	2	160	4	164
155	1	165	2	167

Figure 6:22 Expected outcome to the purchaser arising from his initial response to the supplier's offer

It will be seen that the Purchaser's optimal outcome is given by a response of £145 000, which should lead to a bargain well within his upper limit of £165 000. If, therefore, the purchaser's estimate of the supplier's concession factor is wrong, and purchaser has to concede more than he anticipated, he can still do so and remain within an acceptable limit as far as the actual bargain is concerned. In that event in order to minimize the effect on the final outcome, the purchaser will be compelled to either:

1 Make the larger concession at a more rapid rate so reducing the time-cost effect, but weakening his reputation as a firm negotiator.
2 Concede slowly, so retaining his reputation for firmness, but incurring the higher time costs.

Rather than risk having to take either of these courses the purchaser may prefer to select the safer response of £150 000. His choice will depend ultimately on his confidence in the estimate he has made of the supplier's concession factor.

Firm	Price		Delivery		Guarantee		Total worth of offer		Time costs	Total expected outcome
	Initial offer (£'000s)	Expected minimum (£'000s)	Initial offer (months)	Expected minimum (months)	Initial offer	Expected minimum	Initial offer	Expected minimum	(£'000s)	(£'000s)
A	185	180	13	13	95	95	185	180	2	182
B	180	177	14	13	93	94	192	182	3	185
C	170	170	16	15	92	93	196	182	2	184

Figure 6:23 Expected outcome to the purchaser of negotiating with more than one supplier

Negotiation with multiple suppliers
In this situation the purchaser would be expected to analyse each of the bids received and select from each the significant features which are most favourable to him. His initial response to each bidder will then be based on attempting to persuade each one to match those features in the other bids which are more favourable to purchaser, without changing any feature in the bidder's own bid which the purchaser regards as optimal.

In order to follow through this strategy, the purchaser must be aware of the trade off in worth of the non-price features of the bids relative to price and the extent of any concession which he is likely to obtain, otherwise he will fail to concentrate his negotiating efforts on the areas in which it will be most effective.

An example is set out in Figure 6:23 involving three competitors and three significant features: price, delivery and performance guarantee. The following trade-off values have been assumed:

1 month's delay in delivery	£1 000
1% loss in guaranteed efficiency	£5 000
1 month's time cost	£1 000

Provided that firm A can be persuaded to concede to £180 000 then the purchaser will have obtained his expected optimum outcome. However, if firm A knows that his delivery and performance guarantees are better than either of his competitors and has some appreciation of their worth to the purchaser, he has no need to make any such concession. His position is that of the quasi-dominant supplier discussed in Section 5.1. To achieve his objective the purchaser must persuade firm A that his competitors have made concessions to an extent which has brought their bids below his in overall worth.

The purchaser's initial negotiating effort should therefore be directed at:

1 Firm B to concede on all three features.
2 Firm C to concede on delivery and performance guarantees.

Only when he has obtained sufficient concessions from these negotiations should the purchaser approach firm A. This waiting period, particularly if the existence of the other negotiations is leaked to firm A, will establish in the minds of firm A's negotiators a state of anxiety which will increase their receptiveness to the Purchaser's suggestion of a price reduction. Indeed it would not be surprising if firm A were driven by this state of anxiety into approaching the purchaser and offering a reduction of their own accord.

6.3 CONTRACT DISPUTE
In a situation of contract dispute Party's initial offer should be such as to:

1   Point the way towards a settlement which would just satisfy what
    Party believes would be Opponent's minimum negotiating objec-
    tive, given that both sides were agreed on the facts of the dispute.
2   Ensure that in any settlement Party achieves at least his own
    minimum negotiating objective.

The distinguishing feature of contract-dispute negotiations as opposed
to those relating to bidding and procurement is that the two parties are
already jointly involved in a venture from which both stand to lose or
gain. As a result the degree of emotional involvement of the negotiators is much higher and the worth to either side of a particular outcome
must be conceived as much in psychological as monetary terms.
Further it must take into account the sociolegal system under which
the relevant part of the contract is being executed.

Under these conditions it is likely that there will be a substantial
difference in the worth of the subject matter of the dispute to the two
sides. Thus failure to comply with some minor requirement of the
specification may have little significance to the contractor who is
confident that it will make no difference at all to the operating
standards and performance of the equipment. To the purchaser's
engineers, however, such failure may appear both as an insult and as
something which, if they do not insist on it being corrected, could be
the cause of their being severely censured if the facts came to the
notice of their superiors.

Valuation of opponent's negotiating objective

Party's negotiators should try therefore to see how the issue in
question looks through the eyes of their opposite numbers, and in so
doing take into account variations in national temperament, social
structure and cultural background.

Ideally the factors on the matter in dispute should have been agreed
before any offer is made at all. It is dangerous to start establishing
positions unless there is common ground between the two sides on at
least the factual issues. If, however, such agreement has not been
reached, and Party is forced into the position of having to make an
offer, then he has the difficult task of assessing what he believes would
be the minimum negotiating objective of Opponent if the facts were
agreed. For example, if Party believes that Opponent is only taking a
hard line because Opponent believes wrongly that the factors are in his
favour, then Party may assess that once Opponent knows the truth,
the objective of his negotiators will be simply to get themselves off the
hook with the minimum loss of face. Under these circumstances
Party's initial offer must be aimed at allowing Opponent's negotiators
a graceful way out, preferably without exposing them to censure from
their own management.

Suppose that the dispute concerns Opponent's claim for penalty and Party's contention that he is entitled to an extension of time. In reality Party's case for an extension of time is based four-fifths on Opponent's own contractual default and one-fifth on *force majeure*. However Opponent's management are unaware of the extent of their own default and quite genuinely believe that Party is to blame. It is suggested that in his initial approach Party should stress the *force majeure* and play down Opponent's contractual default thus giving Opponent's negotiators a way out from exposure to their own management. Party would of course, behind the scenes, ensure that the significance of this move was not lost on Opponent's negotiators and that they were aware of the consequences which would follow from its rejection.

One particular circumstance because of its importance to Party as a contractor, and its unfortunate frequency of occurrence, needs particular mention and that is customer default in payment. In this event Party has the initial decision as to whether to turn the issue into an openly recognized one of dispute or to simply record the default and continue with the contract work.

The primary factors in reaching that decision are:

1　Whether Party believes that customer will ultimately correct the default provided that it is not publicized, but that if it is, then will cause adverse and possibly irrational action by customer, eg unfair calling of a performance bond.

2　The magnitude of the default relative to Party's ability to continue to provide financial support.

3　The attitude of Party's bank and credit insurers who must be advised of the default.

4　As an alternative to 1 whether or not Party believes that, by administering a sharp shock, customer can be made to realize that he must conform to the contract terms otherwise Party will take action not only as provided for under the contract, eg suspension or termination but will so advise his government which, if customer is a public agency, could cause political problems. Implicit in this is Party's belief that customer *can* pay and that the sharp shock, eg notice of intent to suspend, will be treated by customer as credible. It further follows from this that Party must never threaten and then not act if the default is not remedied, as this would totally undermine his credibility. If Party believes customer cannot pay then he must consider the alternative of arbitrary action provided this would not invalidate any insurance cover he has against non-payment ie if he has such cover he must first consult his insurers.

5　Whether or not the contract is within a legal system which provides Party with a full and fair opportunity to recover the debt, protects Party against arbitrary action by customer, and customer has assets within the jurisdiction. If the answers to these questions is 'no' so that for all practical purposes the debt is irrecoverable by action then Party can look only to his insurers and take such arbitrary action as that to which they agree to minimize the loss, if he believes customer will not or cannot pay.

Again it is stressed that in deciding on the use of tactics of this nature Party must take fully into account the factors personal to Opponent and his negotiators; in particular that of sensitivity to criticism and the emotional reaction which such criticism would be likely to generate.

Depending on the nature of the dispute, Opponent's negotiating objective, assuming that Opponent is the purchaser, will fall into one of the following categories.

Non-termination of contract

Security—Because of some failure fully to meet specification, Opponent requires guarantees or assurances on the performance or reliability of what has been supplied. His objective will be expressed in terms of:

1 Items covered by the guarantee.
2 Extent of the guarantee.
3 Time for which the guarantee is effective.
4 Consequences if the guarantee is not met.
5 Extent to which the guarantee is in full satisfaction of Party's liabilities.

Discount—Because of failure to complete the work on time or failure to meet specification, Opponent requires a reduction in the contract price, either directly by way of discount or indirectly by way of penalty. His objective will be expressed in terms of:

1 Amount of the discount.
2 Extent to which payment is in full satisfaction of Party's liabilities.

Rectification—Because the work does not comply with the specification, Opponent requires it to be modified or additional facilities provided. His objective will be expressed in terms of:

1 Extent of the work to be carried out.
2 Time within which the work must be carried out.
3 Extent to which the rectification is in full satisfaction of Party's liabilities.

It will be understood that the three categories are not mutually exclusive. Thus Opponent may consider that the default by Party is sufficiently serious for him to require both security and discount.

Termination of contract
Opponent's objective will be expressed in terms of:

1   To the extent that work is not complete to costs of repurchase from another supplier.
2   Minimizing his liability towards Party in respect of money which he already owes to Party or which Party is entitled to in respect of work in progress, etc.
3   Recovery of damages covering delay in completion of the contract and consequential loss of revenue or additional expenditure incurred by Opponent arising out of the cancellation.

Opponent's objective is therefore unlikely to be singular. There will be a number of objectives, each of which in some measure will be related one to another, so that a concession by Party on one will be prejudicial to his negotiating position on another. Not all of Opponent's negotiating objectives will be of equal importance to him. He may, for instance, value the giving by Party of a guarantee more highly than the recovery of a discount if his primary concern is that of ensuring system reliability.

It is Party's task to seek out Opponent's value structure and to discover in which way he can satisfy Opponent's minimum negotiating objective in a manner which is least prejudicial to himself.

Party's negotiating objective
It follows from the discussion of Opponent's negotiating objective that in any contract dispute one or more factors will stand out as being of major importance quite independent of actual cash payments. Party's offer should be structured in such a way as to ensure that as a minimum his objective in relation to these factor(s) is achieved. In considering how Party actually does this two cases may be distinguished:

1   Party believes his principal objective to be directly opposite to that of Opponent.
2   Party believes that his principal objective is either of secondary importance to Opponent or its existence may even not have been appreciated by Opponent.

Party's and Opponent's objectives direct opposites
Leaving aside actual monetary payments, this is the less common case and will only occur when there is one central issue to the dispute, the

loss or gain of which virtually ends the matter. An example would be an admission by Party that Opponent was entitled to terminate the contract for Party's default when Party was liable under the terms of the contract for substantial and easily proven consequential damages.

Even if Opponent does not initially raise the issue directly, Party must bring it out into the open. In so doing Party would make it clear that any settlement to be acceptable must satisfy him on this point; a line to which he would consistently stick.

Party's objective of secondary importance to or not appreciated by Opponent
It has been indicated already that there may be a difference in the worth of the dispute to the two sides. Equally each may have a totally different principal objective. As an example consider a dispute regarding the quality of work carried out by Party. Opponent's principal objective may be simply to obtain rectification of the work plus an extended guarantee period which would provide him with security. Party may be quite willing to meet him on these issues but will try to ensure, as his main objective, that he is not penalised for delay or does not lose his performance bond. Neither of these are of primary interest to Opponent and even may not have occurred to him.

Party should conceal his anxiety and deliberately avoid raising the matters which concern him until as least the final meeting. Even then he should treat them as of minor importance and, if possible, as mere formalities.

It is not suggested that when dealing with a sophisticated negotiator this strategy will deceive Opponent. By not raising the issues initially Party will not have brought them openly within the scope of the negotiation. He will therefore have allowed the negotiator for Opponent the opportunity to ignore them. This is an illustration of the process of tacit communication and coordination. Party has tacitly agreed to meet Opponent by not raising the consequential issues; Opponent has tacitly agreed that in return for Party's concession on Opponent's negotiating objective he will give Party the assurance he wants in terms of the final bargain.

The difficulty in practice is how can Party be sure, without open communication, that he has correctly understood Opponent's intentions? If Party assumes, as he should, that Opponent is at least as much aware as Party of the importance to him of the concealed issue, then Opponent's behaviour may be explained in one of the following ways.

1   Opponent is deliberately not raising the issue until a late stage in the negotiations so that he can use it then as a lever to exert maximum pressure on Party.

2 Opponent is willing not to raise the issue at all as a major
   negotiating point.

Since Party cannot openly ask Opponent which tactic he is employing,
and even if he did could not necessarily believe Opponent's answer,
how can he satisfy himself as to which explanation is correct? The
same dilemma may face Opponent. If he has decided on tactic 2, how
can he do so in a way which Party will find credible while at the same
time not totally committing himself in case, if the negotiations are not
going successfully, he wishes to change his mind?

Recognizing the dilemma Party can arrange to give Opponent the
opportunity to raise the issue and at the same time collaborate with
Opponent in defining their agreement on all other points. In so doing
he creates the situation in which if Opponent were to raise the
concealed issue as a major negotiating issue at a late stage, Party
could legitimately withdraw from the agreements already reached and
accuse Opponent of bad faith. Party therefore uses the development of
a bargaining situation first as a means of testing Opponent's intentions
and secondly as a method of ensuring that it is no longer in Opponent's
interests to change his mind.[37]

Determination of the level of the initial offer
The basic approach to the establishment of the initial demand in a
contract-dispute situation is similar to that adopted for bidding and
procurement. Party assesses what he believes the outcome will be,
based on his judgement of Opponent's range of negotiating objectives
and his concession factor, and selects the demand which he believes
will lead to the optimal outcome. It has been seen that these objectives
are not as clear cut as in bidding/procurement and that the value which
one side puts on a particular issue may differ widely from the value
which it possesses for the other.

Time costs will only be significant where the dispute concerns a
major financial claim or the payment of other money is dependent on
the issue being settled, eg release of retention money dependent on the
settlement of a dispute relating to spares.

More so, however, than in bid/procurement negotiations Party
must consider the effect which any concession will have on the future
and that it is the ultimate not the immediate cost associated with any
action which is significant. The right little concession made at the right
time can be very useful in avoiding future difficulties. The wrong little
concession made at the wrong time can be very costly to Party in the
encouragement which it gives to Opponent to ask for more, and the
precedent it gives him on which to base future demands.

Because there will normally be a number of issues involved, the
importance of which will vary, it is essential that in formulating his

initial demand and his belief as to Opponent's concession factor Party assesses the worth to him of each issue in terms of money (or utility values if the amounts involved are of sufficient significance). The importance of each issue can then be compared and the demand structured so as to achieve the optimal outcome.

Such comparison will also indicate any anxiety issues which the form of Party's initial demand should be designed to protect. Emphasizing the point made earlier (p. 151), Party's initial demand is a function of a total negotiating plan which forsees a particular outcome based on Party's judgement of Opponent's concession factor, and the concessions which Party considers will be necessary for him to make.

This process of formulating the initial demand is illustrated with the following simple example.

Party is five months late in completing a contract for Opponent. Responsibility for the delay is disputed since neither side is wholly to blame. The defects liability period runs for twelve months from the original date for completion, extended by any period for which Party is in default. During the period of delay spares to the value of £500 have been used on maintaining the plant which Opponent considers should be paid for by Party, as free replacement of defects, and Party asserts should be paid for by Opponent since their use only became necessary through maloperation of the plant by Opponent's staff. Liquidated damages for delay are at the rate of £1 000 per month and Party assesses the cost of extending the defects liability period at £200 per month.

Party prepares the following analysis of the position:

1   Negotiating area. Liquidated damages: £1 000 per month to a maximum of £5 000. Defects liability period: £200 per month to a maximum of £1 000. Spares: £500.
2   Negotiating objective. Party's preferred objective £3 000; minimum acceptable £4 500. Opponent's expected minimum objective £2 500; expected preferred objective £5 000.
3   The anxiety factor. This is clearly the penalty. If the preferred negotiating objective is to be achieved then the penalty payment must not exceed £2 000 on the basis that at least £1 000 will have to be conceded on the other two points. If the minimum negotiating objectives is to be achieved then assuming the other two points have to be conceded completely the penalty payments must not exceed £3 000.

Additionally a concession on the period of delay will automatically involve a similar concession on defects liability. However, the converse is not necessarily true. A concession on a longer defects period could be traded for a lesser penalty.

In deciding on his initial offer Party has the choice of either:

1 Offering the limit to which he is prepard to go on penalty, making it clear that this issue is not a matter for further negotiation, whilst at the same time indicating a greater flexibility on defects liability.
2 Saying nothing, or reserving his position on penalty and making an offer only on spares and defects liability.
3 Making some offer on each issue but indicating on which he would prefer the initial negotiations to be concentrated.

Unless the negotiating position on penalty is considered to be very strong, so that the offer could be kept down to say £2 000 as a maximum, the preference would be for alternative 3. The penalty is a major issue for both sides and as such must form an important part of the negotiations. On the other hand, unless his position is very strong Party would not wish to commit himself to too firm a position too early. The negotiating plan would therefore be:

1 An initial offer of
   (a) The minimum penalty thought to be acceptable and not regarded as insulting, say, £1 000.
   (b) Acceptance of defects liability for half the disputed period which would cost £500.
   (c) Half the value of the disputed spares which would cost £250.
2 To concentrate the subsequent negotiations first on the penalty issue, conceding slowly and reluctantly to £2 000. At that point make no further concessions on penalty but offer the balance of the defects period for a final settlement. This would leave half the value of the spares as a final 'sweetener'. The cost therefore of the final bargain on this basis would be £3 500.

NOTES
1. J. G. Cross, *The Economics of Bargaining* (New York: Basic Books, 1969) pp. 48–50.
2. J. G. Cross, op. cit., p. 178.
3. See, in particular, F. Edelman, 'Art and science of competitive bidding', *Harvard Business Review* (July/August 1965). P. Brigham, 'Pricing strategy', *Building Technology and Management* (October 1969). P. Kotler, *Marketing Decision Making* (London: Holt, Rinehart and Winston, 1971), pp. 348–53, and other sources quoted therein.
4. For a discussion on pricing objectives see P. Kotler, *Marketing Decision Making* (London: Holt, Rinehart and Winston, 1971), p. 336 ff.
5. This is true for production contracts but may not be so for

research or development contracts. There Party's main purpose will often be to obtain the technical and longer-term marketing benefits which would result from carrying out the contract work, and the profit resulting directly from the contract would be of minor importance. Such benefits could include: access to customer's knowledge, the opportunity to develop a new product, the ability to secure or retain market leadership through having a technical lead over the competition.

6. From the equation on p. 23

$$U(£16\,000) = (1 \times 0.8) + (0 \times 0.2) = 0.8.$$

7. In monetary terms EV of the gamble, 80% chance of gain £24 000 and a 20% chance of lose £2 000 $= (24 \times 0.8) + (-2 - 0.2) =$ £18 800.

8. My attention has very recently been drawn to the utility curves derived by J. H. Willenbrock in his study of highway building contractors in Pennsylvania: 'A comparative study of expected monetary and expected utility value bidding strategy models', Thesis, College of Engineering, Pennsylvania State University (March 1972).

The general form of the curve derived by Willenbrock shows the same risk aversive tendency as that which I predicted for the neutral condition. However, Willenbrock does not deal with the issue of the manager's preference function related to his target or business plan margin. For this reason, his curves tend to be flatter and do not display either the sharply decreasing marginal utility below the target or business plan margin level, or the slow rate of increase in marginal utility above that level, which is characteristic of the curves developed here.

It is also not clear which considerations lead the contractors in Willenbrock's study to be more or less risk aversive, other than the size of contract and its relation to their total annual business. There is no reference made to their taking into account either contractual risks or marketing factors. However, this may be due to the narrow base of the study which was concerned solely with highway construction contractor's bidding for that type of contract work in Pennsylvania.

9. The line manager's intuitive judgement is supported by the expected utility analysis carried out using the marketing manager's subjective estimates of success probability:

Bid margin	Conditional utility	Success probability	Expected utility
10%	9.5	0.5	4.75
5%	8.8	0.7	6.16
Break even	7.0	0.9	6.3

10. This assumes that the customer is behaving rationally and will

not adjust the worth to him of a given factor, say delivery, so as to enable him to accept the lowest-priced bid. It also ignores factors of personal motivation (see Section 7.2)

11.   It is in this respect that the method proposed here differs from that suggested by S. Edelmann in his paper 'Art and science of competitive bidding', *Harvard Business Review* (July/August 1965). The bias in his comparable table Exhibit VI to that shown in Figure 6:7 is a constant. This may be justified in the type of case he was considering but is not in my experience true for capital-goods contracting.

12.   K. Simmonds, 'Competitive bidding—deciding the best combination of non-price features', *Operational Research Quarterly* (March 1968), pp. 5–14.

13.   It is for this reason that the chances of success with long tender lists are so low and why bidding under such circumstances tends to produce very low initial prices and subsequent contract disputes over 'extras'.

14.   This is based on the assumption that once Party has secured one bid in the series that his capacity has been filled. If the first offer fails then we re-estimate for the second offer with n equals 2 and if that again fails then for the third offer we are back to the individual bid situation.

15.   Note that the monetary values of the two profit contributions must be added together first *before* converting to a utility function. As noted earlier (p. 26) two utility values under risk cannot be added together.

16.   No significant loss would have been suffered in the event of non-receipt of the award, and to simplify presentation of the calculations the effect of losing the bid has been omitted since it would have a nil value.

17.   It will be in the situation in which a major objective of Party's bid is to weaken a competitor's position in the market or deny him entry into the market (see p. 123).

18.   This follows strictly from the definition of quick kill as an offer which it is anticipated customer will accept without further negotiation. It is recognized in practice that, although there may be no bargaining on price or other major terms, minor issues may still have to be settled, and in this sense Party has some limited influence on the time scale. More important perhaps is the case in which Party's bid, although the lowest, is above customer's budget and to increase the allocation would take a significant time. In negotiating with customer revisions to the scheme which would bring it within budget, Party should certainly take account of the time costs referred to here.

19.   See the discussions on p. 109 for the reasons why Party in a state of uncertainty should select hold back.

20. If Party deliberately inflates his demand by an excessive amount, and this is recognized by customer, then Party will be compelled to concede at a rapid rate to the true negotiating area or run the risk of losing the bargain entirely. Thus the length of the negotiating period will not be increased because of the additional padding and, indeed, may even be reduced, particularly if customer reacts emotionally against Party's behaviour.

21. D. G. Pruitt and J. L. Drew, 'Effect of time pressure, time elapsed and the opponent's concession rate on behaviour in negotiation', *Journal of Experimental Social Psychology*, vol. 5 (1969), pp. 50–52.

22. D. G. Pruitt and D. F. Johnson, 'Mediation as an aid to face saving in negotiation', *Journal of Personality and Social Psychology*, vol. 14 (no. 3, 1970) at p. 245.

23. J. G. Cross, op. cit., p. 45.

24. J. G. Cross, op. cit., A. Coddington, *Theories of the Bargaining Process* (London: George Allen and Unwin, 1968).

25. A. Coddington, op. cit., p. 78.

26. This is the attitude of the rational bargainer. If emotional factors are admitted then it seems more likely that customer will treat Party's bid as a cue to his own level of aspiration, and be content with the minimum bargaining necessary to satisfy his personalistic motivation. See Section 7.1 and R. M. Liebert, W. P. Smith, J. H. Hill and M. Keifer, 'The effect of information and magnitude of initial offer on interpersonal negotiation', *Journal of Experimental Psychology*, vol. 4 (1968), pp. 431–41.

27. See J. C. Harsanyi, 'Bargaining in ignorance of opponent's utility function', *Journal of Conflict Resolution*, vol. 6 (no. 1, 1962), pp. 29–38.

28. R. E. Walton and R. E. McKersie, *Behavioural Theory of Labor Negotiations* (New York: McGraw-Hill, 1965), p. 88.

29. R. A. Baron and R. M. Liebert, *Human Social Behaviour* (Homewood, Illinois: Dorsey Press, 1971), pp. 431–32. In particular, see D. G. Pruitt and D. F. Johnson, 'Mediation as an aid to face saving in negotiation', *Journal of Personality and Social Psychology*, vol. 14 (no. 3, 1970), p. 246: 'People will be more reluctant to make concessions when the other has been unyielding than when he has been yielding, presumably because they feel it is the other's turn to concede'. The authors also point out that this matching of concessions in frequency was not found under low time pressure because as they suggest: 'there is not much incentive to concede under low time pressure regardless of the other's concession rate'.

30. See the examples quoted in T. C. Schelling, *The Strategy of Conflict* (London: Oxford University Press, 1963), p. 67.

31. E. Peters, *Strategy and Tactics in Labor Negotiations* (New

London, Connecticut: National Foreman's Institute, 1955).

32. See B. M. Bass, 'Effects on the subsequent performance of negotiators of studying issues or planning strategies alone or in groups', *Psychological Monographs General and Applied* (no. 614, 1966).

33. J. C. Harsanyi, 'Bargaining in ignorance of the opponent's utility function', *Journal of Conflict Resolution*, vol. 6 (no. 1, 1962), pp. 29–68.

34. O. J. Bartos, 'Concession making in experimental negotiations', Scientific report for the American Air Force Office of Scientific Research (November 16 1964). A. R. Caggiula, *The Reduction of Group conflict: Group Goal Determinants* (Delaware: University of Delaware, 1964). L. E. Siegel and S. Fouraker, *Bargaining and Group Decision Making* (New York: McGraw-Hill, 1960). J. M. Chertkoff and M. Conley, 'Opening offer and frequency of concessions as bargaining strategies', *Journal of Personality and Social Psychology*, vol. 7 (no. 2, 1967), pp. 181–85.

35. C. M. Stevens, *Strategy and Collective Bargaining Negotiations* (New York: McGraw-Hill, 1963), p. 100.

36. J. Z. Rubin ad B. R. Brown, *The Social Psychology of Bargaining and Negotiation* (New York: Academic Press, 1975), p. 122 ff.

37. For a more general discussion of the problems of credibility in communication in negotiation, see E. Goffman, *Strategic Interaction* (Oxford: Blackwell, 1970), pp. 102–12.

7

THE PSYCHOLOGY OF NEGOTIATION

The account so far given of the development of a negotiating plan has been largely based on a normative approach to the negotiating process. This has applied particularly to the selection of negotiating objectives and strategies. Both Party and Opponent have been assumed to be concerned solely with choosing that which will be optimal in terms of corporate welfare after taking into account limitations, imposed by lack of knowledge and computational facilities, and scarcity of search resources. No distinction has in general been drawn between the negotiator as a person and the firm or corporation by whom he is employed, although it has been recognized that the personality of the individual will affect many of the variables in the decision-making process, eg shape of the utility function and estimation of subjective probability (see p. 19).

The analysis would, however, be seriously incomplete if it did not consider how far the propositions put forward will in practice be subject to modification by reason of the psychology of the individual negotiators. In so doing the analysis moves from a normative theory of negotiation to a behavioural description of the negotiating process and of the interplay between the characters involved. Now the interest is not in what Party should do, but in what the negotiators for Party can be expected to do, given their personality characteristics and their social-cum-ideological background.

The following are identified as the primary areas in which the psychology of the negotiator will have a significant effect:

1 Setting and fulfilment of personalistic as opposed to corporate objectives
2 Conflict and adjustment in the negotiators motivation
3 The negotiator's belief pattern
4 Personality interaction between individual negotiators

7.1 PERSONALISTIC OBJECTIVES
The needs of a negotiator, expressed in psychological terms, do not differ in principle from those which are possessed by other humans. This proposition may appear so obvious that it is not worthwhile stating. A common error, however, is to assume that those selected to

undertake important commercial, industrial or political tasks are in some way different from normal people and then to be constantly surprised and somehow disappointed when it is found out that they are not. It is just because of this that explanations for the events of history are to be found more often in the personality characteristics of the principals concerned than in the grand strategy which is afterwards supposed to have directed their decisions.

Following the classification suggested by Maslow the following are identified as the needs which supply the negotiator's personalistic motivational drive.[1]

1 Security.
2 Self-esteem achieved through the satisfaction of others.
3 Self-esteem by satisfying the negotiator's evaluation of himself.
4 Self-actualization by the fulfilment of the negotiator's professional potential.
5. The need to know and understand.

This list of needs is in descending order of dominance so that generally the rule holds good that until the more basic need has been satisfied to a point which the individual finds acceptable then the next need will not operate, or only weakly, as a determinant of behaviour. A negotiator in a position where he considers that his security is threatened is unlikely to be worried about earning esteem. It follows that in developing negotiating tactics based upon Party's views as to Opponent's needs regard should primarily be had to the one which Party considers to be most basic.

Security
In general psychological terms the need for security expresses itself in the individual's preference for being within a stable ordered society surrounded by familiar things. The strength of this need is easily demonstrated by putting an individual in conditions which expose him to the unknown, eg taking a town dweller and making him cross an area of countryside which is strange to him on a dark night. He is at once disoriented and his immediate reaction is to seek means of escaping back to that which provides him with the comfort of familiarity. Until that need has been satisfied it will dominate his entire thinking.

One particular instance of the operation of the security need is found in the behaviour of purchasers both in the domestic and the industrial field when deciding on the firm from whom to purchase or re-purchase.

The domestic buyer tends to rely heavily on buying goods of a well-known brand or from a source on which, based on advertising or from post experience he believes he can rely, even if the price is higher than that offered elsewhere. The more substantial the potential risk associated with the purchase, due to the nature or value of the goods concerned, the stronger this tendency will become.[2]

Equally the industrial buyer will tend to place repeat orders with the same supplier so avoiding the risks associated with the introduction of a new source and will tend actively to seek to implement a change only if the existing supplier becomes unsatisfactory. Again this tendency will be stronger the more technical the nature of the goods, so the buyer must press his case more strongly with his colleagues in the technical department in order to obtain their consent to any such change, and also the tendency will be stronger the more insecure or relatively junior in status the buyer feels his own personal position to be in the company hierarchy.[3] True initiation of change, ie without the necessity for such being forced upon him, is only likely to come from the buyer whose need for security has already been satisfied, and who is reasonably assured of the esteem of his colleagues and seniors.

The consequences of this for the industrial marketeer, wishing to introduce his firm as a new supplier, are that the he must first discover whether the buyer feels secure or not, and, if not, plan his campaign initially on the basis of working to satisfy that need.[4] He must minimize the apparent risk by offers of free trials or supply on a sale and return basis, arrange (through the buyer) technical demonstrations for the engineers, suggest to the buyer ways in which he would gain personally in prestige, etc. The existing supplier on the other hand must be continually alert to the possibility of losing the business and seek to counter this by showing the buyer how exposed he would be if he did make any change; the risks he would be running with a new product which was not proven for his particular purposes, or by buying from a firm not acquainted with the problems of the buyer's particular industry.

The negotiator's need for security is shown also in the demand for adhering to past precedents; the request by Opponent that Party should accept the contract on the same terms as those which Opponent has agreed previously with other firms. That this demand, which is frequently made, originates from a need to achieve security is indicated by the way in which the strength of the demand varies with the experience and confidence possessed by the negotiators. The greater their familiarity with understanding of the matters under negotiation, the range of possible bargains and the effect which each would have, the more willing they will be to move away from a strict adherence to the terms of past contracts. Conversely the greater their uncertainty as to the effect of any change to what had previously been agreed, the more difficult it will be to persuade them to make amendments.

This difficulty is reinforced if the review of the proposed contract by

Opponent's management is to be conducted, not in terms of its intrinsic merit, but by reference to whether it conforms or not to the agreements signed on previous occasions. Then, not only must the negotiator for Opponent possess the confidence to agree the new conditions himself, he must also be both able and willing to argue the case for their acceptance to his superiors. Obviously he is not likely to do this unless his need for security has been satisfied and the once unfamiliar arrangements have become well understood.

Under these circumstances, satisfying the need of Opponent's negotiator for security should be regarded by Party as a major negotiating objective but one only likely to be achieved through a process of patient education, and the attainment by the negotiators for the two sides of a state of mutual respect and confidence.

Such education must, however, not be seen as patronizing nor must confidence be eroded by behaviour which is less than honest. This applies particularly to situations in which Party represents a western contractor or supplier and Opponent a purchaser in a developing country. To the insecurity felt by Opponent's negotiators will be added the ingredients of national pride coupled with a sense of technical inferiority. The resultant mixture is explosive indeed and bitter resentment, if not complete disaster, will follow any use of hard-sell or bulldozing tactics which indicate contempt for, or display impatience with, the attitudes and arguments adopted by Opponent's negotiators.

Self-esteem achieved through satisfying others
Of all the drives which motivate the negotiator this is perhaps the one most commonly encountered, and when present will most strongly influence the negotiator's behaviour. The negotiator is aware of the reasons for its existence, and these may vary from fear that incurring the displeasure of his seniors or colleagues may cause him to be punished or despised, to the hope that achieving results more favourable than could be expected will lead to him being rewarded or praised.

In a western-style culture this motivational drive appears to be largely derived from childhood training in which the child as an individual is encouraged to gain the respect of his parents, teachers and fellow pupils through the achievement of success. Equally, antisocial behaviour is punished through public humiliation (wearing the dunce's cap was an ancient example of this). Many children have suffered anguish from being made to look foolish before the rest of a class by continued public questioning, on a subject to which clearly they did not know the answer, coupled with sarcastic comments as to their stupidity or laziness.

In other cultures development of the child takes place almost wholly within a group; family, school, youth association and state, so that respect for, and loyalty to, a group becomes the dominant factor of the young person's motivational behaviour. An individual brought up under such a system will go to almost any length to avoid acting in a manner which the group would consider unworthy.

Therefore, this drive is expected to be present in both forms of culture but to be stronger in those which place particular emphasis on the group.

When acting under this form of motivational drive, once the negotiator has secured concessions, which in his view are sufficient to satisfy that drive, his need to negotiate will cease and he will be content with whatever bargain has been reached at that point, regardless of its objective value. The only valuation which will be significant to the negotiator is his subjective estimate of the bargain he believes would cause him to gain the respect of the group with which he is concerned. Having secured that bargain he will not look further and this blinkered approach will extend to the suppression of knowledge not otherwise shared by the group, which would indicate that a more favourable bargain might have been obtained but only through the application of greater effort and perhaps at the risk of disturbing his personal relationships with the negotiators for the other side.[5]

By providing the necessary concessions in the form of preplanned giveaways, so allowing Opponent's negotiator to at least appear to have performed his function, Party can secure both his own negotiating objective and the goodwill of Opponent's negotiator. The converse is equally true. If Party refuses to make concessions and so prevents the fulfilment of his opponent's motivational drive, then opponent will become frustrated. He may then seek release from the tensions so created either through an immediate emotional outburst or by a later act of spiteful revenge such as issuing an unfavourable report, making semi-false accusations, etc.[6]

Alternatively since goal orientation tends to be retained, even against extremes of frustration, so that the individual seeks a way round the obstacle rather than abandon course, the negotiator may continue to try to satisfy his motivation even if this means adopting a pretence and deluding those whose favour he wishes to win.[7] This is made easier for him to the extent that those concerned have not themselves participated directly in the negotiations, and it is open therefore to the negotiator to influence strongly the standards by which his conduct is judged. He can report in exaggerated terms on the strength of Party's resistance and on the difficulties which he had in securing even minor concessions.

Many instances of behaviour of this type have been noted in labour negotiations when the union negotiators have reported back to their membership or delegate conference.[8] Such behaviour in my impression is no less common in commercial negotiations, and in a later discussion consideration will be given to tactics by Party which are designed to give the negotiator for Opponent the opportunity of behaving in just this way.

A negotiator may continue to act as if motivated by the need to achieve self-esteem through satisfying others long after he has earned that esteem and the original causes of the motivation have ceased to apply. The buyer who always demands a discount; the inspector who must always find something to reject; the cost investigator who must always find some item to disallow. Psychologists refer to the concept of the retention of such habits, after the motives which lead to their existence are no longer operative, as *functional autonomy.*

Whilst the original motive may not apply this does not mean that the behaviour is without any extraneous motivation. The negotiator may feel that he cannot act otherwise than in accordance with his previous pattern without running the risk of being accused of favouring a particular contractor/supplier and even perhaps of being suspected of taking a bribe. In such cases of functional autonomy in respect of the original motivation the negotiation takes on the character of an artificial exercise in role-playing, the conventions of which are well understood by both sides.

This is not to suggest that such negotiations are without value. They defuse the relations between the parties, prevent the risk of genuine emotion and permit the development between the negotiators of what Cross has referred to as 'organized cooperation'.[9] They also enable the negotiators for both sides to predict the outcome with greater certainty and to plan ahead accordingly.

In these respects such negotiations may positively facilitate the achievement of the matter of common interest to both parties to which reference was made at the beginning of the chapter; the less the time spent in haggling the sooner the project can get under way. At the same time removing all genuine tension and 'edge' from the negotiating process will result eventually in the negotiator for Party being content with the achievement of a target which, although satisfactory, is significantly less than the optimum which could be obtained. The quiet life of the agreed bargain is preferred to the discomfort of hard bargaining. The distinction, and the effect on the personalities involved, is similar to that which applies between a price cartel and a state of genuine competition.[10]

It has been suggested in this chapter that in seeking to achieve self-esteem through satisfying others, one of the effects may be to cause the negotiator's personal level of aspiration to be lower than the objective his company would set if they possessed adequate data. Further, to the extent that the company can obtain such data only from the negotiator this will lead to his suppression of that data.

If, however, the group which is significant to the negotiator engages in extensive prenegotiation planning, which includes the formulation of specific negotiating objectives, this will tend to have the opposite effect. In order to obtain the group's esteem the negotiator must achieve at least the objective so defined, to which he will therefore feel a greater commitment. This obviously imposes a certain rigidity on the bargaining process and may lead, as Bass and Druckmann found, to deadlock; certainly the negotiations can be expected to take longer.[11]

In the light of these experimental results reported by Bass and Druckmann, it may be asked why so much emphasis has been placed on prenegotiation planning, particularly since the need for agreement to be reached has also been stressed so that the subject matter of the negotiation can proceed. The answers to this criticism would be as follows:

1 The prenegotiation planning described involves equal consideration of Opponent's case and Party's case, and demands also an understanding of Opponent's utility function related to the issues involved. In the bargaining experiments referred to the negotiators concentrated their attentions largely on the in-group position, ie to a study only of Party's case.

2 In formulating his objective Party has been expected to take account of the realities of the bargaining position and to adjust what he would like to achieve to that considered practical of achievement. He has also used scales of utility values which take into account fully the time costs involved in any delay in reaching a settlement and, more important still, the consequences of no bargain.

   Although negotiating time costs were built into both the Druckmann and the Bass experiments it is difficult to tell how significantly these were regarded by the participants although Bass has suggested that, at least in his experiment which was of the same pattern as that of Druckmann, these effects were minimal. Also it is not clear how far the negotiators were influenced by the simulated effect of not reaching agreement but it seems doubtful that they felt anything like the pressures felt by commercial negotiators when the award of a major contract is at stake.

3 It has been emphasized that planning is a dynamic not a static process. It is repeated through the negotiations and Party's objectives modified as may be necessary to take account of variations in Opponent's behaviour from that which had been predicted. In the bargaining experiments planning would only appear to have been done once before the negotiations commenced. There was no opportunity therefore for the operation of the activity cycle.

It is believed that planning of the type described allows the negotiator reasonable flexibility and at the same time ensures a personal commitment on his part towards the achievement of the negotiating objective.

Self-esteem by satisfying the negotiator's evaluation of himself

Apart from achieving recognition by others an individual within a western-style culture will also seek the attainment of some goal for his own satisfaction. The goals he chooses will vary as he proceeds through life but the conditions under which he makes that choice will be determined by the decision he has already made as to the direction his path should take. Once, for example, a person has decided upon a certain course of action relative to his career he must afterwards accept the consequences of that decision or change the basic decision itself. The student who elects to go to university must accept the need to take examinations; the executive who takes the post of sales manager must accept that he will be involved in commercial negotiations. If either objects then their only alternative is to leave and pursue some other occupation. They are committed to following through any choice decision which they might make.

The significance of this commitment is that the individual's choice preference for any goal objective is made under real rather than imagined conditions and can be expected to take into account the consequential effects flowing from that choice. The student might prefer to study art rather than mathematics, both of which he is equally good at, but in a commitment situation would choose mathematics because it offered the prospects of a more secure career.

Psychologically these two situations, that of the student taking his examinations and the executive conducting a negotiation, have two factors in common. Both are egorelated, ie success is more closely related to the effort and skill of the person concerned than to chance factors. Both are achievement oriented, ie there is considerable pressure on the individual to succeed as opposed to a related situation in which, for example, he was playing a game for its own sake rather than to win.

Under business conditions which are both ego and achievement oriented, and in which the person will be committed to the choice he makes, the following propositions are made as to the level of goal objective which the individual will select:

1 The worth which the individual places upon any level will be a function of its achievement value to him and the subjective probability which he places upon succeeding at that level. Generally this function would appear to be a product of the two factors

and the individual will select the level which maximizes that function.

2   The achievement value will have a relationship to the difficulties which the individual considers are involved. In general, the greater the difficulty, the higher the individual will value the achievement.

3   The individual's estimate of his subjective probability of succeeding at any level will be biased in the direction in which his motivation is stronger. If he is strongly motivated towards achievement he will overestimate his chances of success; if he is strongly motivated towards avoiding failure he will underestimate his chances and overestimate the risks involved.

4   Success at any given level will result in the individual reassessing both the achievement value and the probability of success at that level and at those which are more difficult to achieve. Over a short range of values this will cause the individual progressively to select those levels which objectively are more difficult to achieve. With each success achieved, however, the consequence to the individual of failure in terms of public humiliation are also increased. In the end he will be driven to aim for the extreme, which is beyond that which anyone could possibly expect, simply in order to fail with minimum loss of face and so return again to his natural level.

This is akin to the phenomenon of the football team who start the season with a winning run. Everyone now expect them to go on winning and although after their first defeat the team feels an immediate depression their secondary reaction is one of relief. The tension associated with the impossibility of always winning has been lifted.

5   If the individual fails then his immediate reaction will be one of the following:

(a) If he is motivated positively towards achievement then he will repeat the effort. The apparent increase in difficulty has added to the value of the goal objective which will tend to balance the reduction in his estimate of success probability, so that the product of the two will remain roughly the same.

(b) If he is activated towards avoidance of failure his reaction will be either to reduce his level drastically so as to eliminate the risk completely, or alternatively, raise the level to a point at which failure is very probable but no blame could be attached to him on that account.

The above represents a necessarily brief summary of what is generally referred to as *level of aspiration theory*.[12] The parallel is clear between this theory and that of the maximization of subjective expected utility discussed earlier (see pp. 23–26). The level of the goal objective is obviously closely related to that of the utility which a particular result possesses at any given time.

There is a significant difference between this personalistic approach to goal setting and a range of utility values based on corporate objectives. Simon has arrived at the same distinction for a decision. If the decision is oriented to the individual's goals it is *personally rational* and if oriented to the organization's goals it is *organizationally rational*.[13] When Party assessed the utility to him under risk of any bid level, the only truly subjective factor which he considered was his attitude towards risk taking. All other factors were objective: the profit which would be realized if the bid were successful, the need to obtain the order, the contractual risks involved (see pp. 123 and 124). The function so derived represented as far as possible the corporate utility of the bid.

The level of goal objective under discussion is, however, entirely personalistic with its emphasis on achievement. The utility to a company manager of a particular bid, when he is acting under corporate motivation, is not affected by the ease or difficulty of securing the order. It is irrelevant since the resultant contract, if the bid is successful, will return the same profits, employ the same people and involve the same risks. To the sales manager, however, the challenge of the competition and the sense of exulation felt when he wins, enter very strongly into his personalistic worth assessment, so that to him the difficult order will possess a higher level of achievement value than the easy one. Two conclusions follow from this; first the sales manager is likely to apply greater effort to securing the difficult order, and secondly he is likely to overestimate his chances of success.

When acting under personalistic motivation therefore there is a tendency to aim for the highest level which it is believed can be achieved and conversely it is also believed that the level aimed at can be achieved. Beliefs are reinforced or otherwise by past record of success or failure; success encourages sights to be raised still higher; failure, particularly if it is repeated, will tend to cause selection of some lower goal.

An individual may keep some goals to himself but those which relate to his business or social life are likely to become the common property of the group with which he is involved. A husband's ambition to obtain promotion will become known to, if not shared by, his wife; a manager's ambition to become a director of his company will be known to his immediate colleagues. Although the hurt to the individual if these aims are not realized will be substantial it will be greatly increased if he is aware that his failure is apparent to the group, and the closer his ties to the group the deeper that hurt will be.

Because this group awareness of his failure is something that the individual will wish to avoid he can be expected to both:

1 Take action to prevent it happening.
2 React strongly against any person whose activities could be the cause of such failure.

Preventive action

The individual will deliberately select a target in negotiation which is lower than he expects to achieve. He will overstress the difficulties and problems to be encountered: the skill of Opponent and the strength of Opponent's negotiating position.

Provided that such behaviour is only a contrived outward show, designed to protect the negotiator from loss of self-esteem within the group under circumstances which the negotiator never seriously envisages happening (ie he does not allow it to affect his real goal or the effort which he makes to achieve it), then no harm should result. It is a pretence for which he may gain credit as being a person not inclined to exaggerate his own prowess.

If, however, the negotiator comes to believe in such a target as representing his own genuine level of aspiration then this must have the effect of reducing the effort which he puts into the negotiation, and so ultimately the absolute value of the results which he attains. He will become an expert in achieving mediocrity.

In Japan where the primary motivation is that of the shame of failure, the effect of any failure can either be, to provide an incentive to even greater efforts, or to cause a loss of confidence accompanied by anger and aggression. In order to de-fuse this potentially dangerous situation the Japanese will act to minimize direct competition, and therefore the number of occasions on which they run the risk of feeling the need to act so as 'to clear one's name'. The proverbial politeness of the Japanese is one example of this as also are their consensus methods of decision making involving people at a number of different hierarchial levels and departments within the organization so that the decision emerges from the process of consultation and is not handed down from the top. In that way there is neither loser or winner.

Retaliatory action

A negotiator expects to win and lose points; he does not expect to be humiliated in circumstances in which his humiliation is in front of, or must become known to, members of the social group whose opinions and respect he values, which would include other members of the negotiating team. If such humiliation occurs his first reaction is likely to be to regard his opponent's conduct as trickery and unfair, and to maintain that he as an honest man has been taken advantage of. If due to lack of experience or sophistication he already feels insecure in dealing with his opponent then this reaction will be even stronger.

It has been suggested that up to a certain point a negotiator will ignore such humiliation and even treat it with contempt but that after that point has been reached he will retaliate in such a way as to demonstrate the ability to handle himself.[14] The suggestion is persuasive and my experience of many negotiations throughout the world shows that people when bargaining do indeed behave in this way. The first reaction is either to ignore the insult and treat it with contempt or to deny the accusation indignantly. The second reaction is that of retaliation; Opponent must pay for his behaviour and what is even more important must be seen to pay by the members of the social group (members of the negotiating team, other office colleagues), whose valuation of him as a negotiator Party finds significant. Moreover, at this stage, Party's behaviour would not be expected to be a model of rationality. He will still retaliate even if such retaliatory action causes him to suffer an economic loss greater than the gain he would achieve if he did not take such action.

The experimental work in this field has concentrated inevitably on the short-term relationships between Party, Opponent and Party's social group, and may be summarized briefly as follows:[15]

1   Having suffered humiliation subjects will retaliate even at some cost to themselves.
2   Their retaliatory action is much stronger if the humiliation becomes known to a social group which is of significance to them, and because of the humiliation they have suffered that group regards the subjects as being 'weak'. They will be willing in that event to suffer much greater losses themselves in order to carry out the retaliation.
3   Subjects will tend to exercise restraint and not take retaliatory action if the reaction of the social group is unfavourable towards the person initiating the humiliation and sympathetic towards the subjects.

Of more interest, but more difficult from the viewpoint of experimental work is the situation in which such relationships are long term thus creating opportunities for future adjustment.

With a long-term relationship it seems likely that minor acts of humiliation will be forgotten, if not forgiven, provided that the subject is not continually reminded of them. For most people the expression 'life's too short' probably sums up their general attitude.

However, if the humiliation has been serious, if the subject has been driven through what we term his *resentment level*, then the motivational drive for retribution will continue. Resentment level is defined as the level of humiliation beyond which a subject feels a permanent sense of antagonism towards the person who inflicted the humiliation. The hurt he has suffered is something which he can neither forgive nor forget. Once an emotional state of this nature has been created, further negotiation between the persons concerned will be difficult, if not impossible. Further, it is likely that the person humiliated will be supported publicly by his colleagues against the person responsible for the humiliation, even though, internally, they may criticize his weakness.

Public humiliation by Party of Opponent is therefore a dangerous act which is likely to cause Party to suffer the greater loss, even if the original act which caused the humiliation was inadvertent.

Given therefore that Party possesses the power to humiliate Opponent, it is suggested that Party should act in one of the following ways:

1 Deliberately disarm himself so that the power no longer exists. If, for example, Opponent has made a mistake Party can ignore it and act publicly as if it has never happened. If through ignorance Opponent has already committed himself by agreeing, say, to the wording of a contract clause, Party may have to extract him from the commitment by, in this instance, pretending that he has made a mistake himself, and withdrawing the clause in question.
2 Indicate privately to Opponent that he does indeed possess such power whilst at the same time offering Opponent a way out which leaves the balance of advantage just in Party's favour, provides Opponent with some benefit, and certainly does not expose him to humiliation.

For this to succeed Party must make sufficiently credible to Opponent not only the threat, say to expose a mistake, but Party's determination to carry through the threat should Opponent not respond. It is not necessary that Opponent should believe that Party actually would execute the threat, but only that there is a sufficient risk of Party doing so, to make acceptance of Party's proposal the more attractive alternative.

In practice, in order to avoid embrarrassment, Party would minimize his open communication both of the threat and his willingness to carry it out, leaving Opponent to understand the implications behind Party's words which might be: 'I appreciate this is a problem for you. However, things cannot be left to stand as they are, but at the same time we do not want to make them any more difficult as that is not going to do either of us any good. How about if we . . .'. Notice how Party clearly implied he *could* make matters more difficult but would prefer not to, and emphasized collaboration to solve a joint problem. This is aimed deliberately at reducing the conflict and defusing emotion.

Self -actualization through professional fulfilment

If a person wishes to develop his potential to the fullest then this type of motivation is generally referred to as *self-actualization*. It is being used here in the rather narrower sense of a person whose motivation in the field of negotiation is the achievement of the highest possible level of professional attainment. Neither the 'roundness' of that person's personality nor the development of harmony between the parts of his personality are being considered here.

It might be thought that if the negotiator's motivation were so based on the need for self-expression at the highest level of professional attainment then no psychological problems of adjustment would arise. Because of his professionalism the negotiator's personal objectives would be consistent with those derived solely from a study of economic factors and the use of objective decision-making techniques. There would be total identification between his own goals and those of the organization.

Even if it is assumed that self-actualization provided the negotiator with his sole motivational drive, and this is an assumption which in practice would be made reluctantly (man is much too complex for such simplifications), that motive in itself is liable to incline the negotiator away from a purely economic and objective approach.

As stated earlier, negotiation like any other business technique is never an end in itself but only a means to an end. Further, the success of any negotiation must be judged in relation to the contribution which it makes to the welfare of the business as a whole. It may for instance be preferable in the total interests of a group of companies as a whole for a negotiator, or a claim for breach of contract against a client, to 'fail', if the final result is the award of a new contract at an enhanced profit margin to another member of the group.

Such a result would be unlikely to bring the negotiator charged with the handling of the claim any personal satisfaction and, indeed, he can be expected to react strongly against any suggestion that group interests make it necessary for him to 'lose'. He would regard this as a denial of his professional skills. On a similar basis a member of Party's negotiating team, whether lawyer, engineer or accountant, will find it hard to accept an opinion from his opposite number on Opponent's team with which professionally he disagrees, even if he is told that it is in the interests of Party's overall negotiating plan that he should accept it.

Whilst beneficial, therefore, in that the individual will not degrade corporate negotiating objectives for personalistic motives in the sense discussed, self-actualization can still be a hazard in preventing the development of the total negotiating plan which, in the case of long-term relationships, is always looking to the future.

The need to know and understand

Under conditions in which the need for security has been satisfied human beings have an urge to know and understand. This need is shown early in a child's life and its strength is closely related to intelligence. The simplest way in which Party can satisfy this need is by a well-prepared presentation of the facts supportive of his proposal in a form which is equated to the manner in which those of Opponent's staff concerned are accustomed to receiving such information. Since this need often operates most strongly with Opponent's technical staff (using that term broadly to cover engineering, law and finance), Party should seek to discover the ways in which they are familiar with data presentation and follow these, even if it means changing his own methods. In this way Party may be able to set up dialogues and develop informal alliances between his own and Opponent's technical experts so winning their support.

However, satisfying Opponent's need to know is not always the best tactic for Party to employ. Once Opponent knows then it will be difficult for him to ignore such knowledge, and if the information concerned is unfavourable to Party then it is usually better to withhold it until such time as Party has established his position more securely. On the submission of tenders which are to be publicly opened, Party's objective is to make sure that his bid is sufficiently low that it will not be rejected and that it would not embarrass the Minister or Head of the Public Authority concerned if Party were to be awarded the contract. Party should therefore structure his bid in such a way that what is read out at the public opening and reported in the press presents Party's offer in the most favourable way, burying the detailed qualifications and ommissions in a later part of the tender document. Again if Party wishes to secure the approval of a Minister or Head of a Public Authority to his proposals, say for the initiation of a project, then he should present these in a simplified and positive way avoiding qualifications which would raise doubts as to the project's viabilility. By initially minimizing the amount of detail provided Party would hope to secure a commitment before he had to enter into detailed negotiations with the authority's staff.

When Party as the purchaser is the recipient of detailed data then it can also be to his advantage to adopt the 'blind eye' response and suppress the need to know. Once he accepts the data as the basis upon which the negotiations, say in a contract dispute situation, are to proceed then he is committed to a solution which is derived from the accuracy and relevance of such data. By ignoring it however, he can use the weapons of commercial and financial power – see pp. 92–93 – to compel Opponent to accept a settlement which is quite unrelated to the merits of the case as established by the data and much more favourable to Party. See further p. 369 under the heading 'Arbitrary behaviour'.

A further use of the same tactic, working against his need to know, is when Opponent's proposals are genuinely capable of more than one interpretation, but only one is acceptable to Party. Party's response can then be to accept the more favourable interpretation setting out in his reply the basis of his understanding.

7.2 CONFLICT AND ADJUSTMENT IN THE NEGOTIATOR'S MOTIVATION

At the beginning of the chapter, reference was made to the conflict inherent in any negotiation between the need to reach agreement and the desire to do so on the most favourable terms achievable. In Section 6.1 this was amplified by showing the relationship between the time spent in negotiation and the terms obtained; that the more favourable bargain takes longer to achieve.

These parameters of the negotiating situation necessarily create a conflict in the mind of the negotiator. He is motivated to achieve two positive goals which are mutually opposed; the optimum terms and the certainty of agreement today. As a result he is placed in the conflict situation which is generally referred to as *approach–approach*, in which there is a choice between two positive incentives; holding out for optimum terms carries the risk of losing the bargain altogether; reaching agreement today involves the risk of doing so on terms which are unfavourable.

Therefore the negotiator has also a dual conflict of *approach–avoidance*; the choice between two aspects of a goal, the one positive and the other negative. This situation can be represented diagrametically as shown in Figure 7:1.

Figure 7:1   Approach–avoidance situation for the negotiator

The strength of the negotiator's tendency to approach or avoid is clearly related to the strength of the motivational drive concerned, although both tend to be stronger the nearer they are to the goal objective. Although it is not so obvious, experimental results have established that the strength to avoid increases more rapidly than that of approach as the subject nears the goal objective.[16]

This is confirmed in relation to negotiation by the following observations derived from my own experience:

1   In the early stages of negotiation a sales negotiator will be willing to argue strongly for the best terms. The positive aspects of achieving favourable terms are immediately attractive; he knows there is no question of an immediate agreement and also that the risk of losing the bargain altogether at that stage is equally remote.
2   As the number of items left for discussion diminishes he will become unwilling to argue strongly in favour of any point to which the buyer appears to be seriously opposed. The fear of losing the bargain altogether will become the dominant motivational drive.

Ambivalence of this type is typical of situations in which the decision to resist, or to take a strong line, is first expressed at a time remote from the point at which we will be faced with the consequences of following through that decision. At a distance the real advantages to be gained are the attraction whilst the disadvantages are seen as hypothetical. 'Let's cross that bridge when we come to it' is the favourite expression of those who think this way.

Later as the time for final action or decision approaches, the consequences, once so lightly discarded, loom large, and we are compelled to change course even at the risk of suffering some humiliation.

The negotiator's internal conflict is not, however, lessened by final agreement being reached. The brief moment of exhileration is quickly followed by the longer period of doubt and self-criticism, even of remorse.

As a defence against such anxieties, and in order to retain self-esteem the answers are rationalized. Opponent is credited with greater strength or skill; the need for preserving goodwill is given as a reason for not having pressed home the advantage possessed. The process as a whole is illustrated in Figure 7:1.

Such rationalizations are helpful in moderation because they enable an adjustment to take place and a return to other business without an obsession with failure. They only become harmful if they are used as reasons for lowering the level of aspiration.

It is necessary, however, to be aware of this conflict of motivation problem when developing a negotiating plan. By setting limits on the negotiator's authority the motivation to obtain favourable terms is reinforced and the tendency to snatch at early agreement is lessened.

7.3 THE NEGOTIATOR'S BELIEF PATTERN
The negotiators for both sides prepare their plans and later come to the negotiating table with a series of attitudes concerning their opposite numbers, their respective organizations and the subject matter of the negotiation. These attitudes will influence strongly the negotiator's initial approach and his reaction to any proposals put forward by the

other side.[17] The subsequent conduct of the negotiations, if they are prolonged or the first in a series of many, may provide the opportunity to modify some of these attitudes. Specific ways in which this may be achieved will be discussed in Chapter 9 and Part 4. The immediate concern is to identify these attitudes and how they arise, and examine the effect they will have on the negotiator.

Attitudes towards the negotiator for opponent
The attitudes which the negotiators for Party will have towards those for Opponent will be derived from:

1   Any previous direct experience of negotiating with Opponent's negotiators.
2   Information obtained from others who have negotiated with Opponent.
3   Prejudices which they have developed towards the character and class of person whom they believe the negotiators for Opponent to be.[18]

Prior experience
Distinction must be made between prior experience of the actual individuals who will be involved on behalf of Opponent and prior experience of negotiating with others in Opponent's firm or in the industry to which it belongs.

When the prior experience relates directly to the persons concerned then it may be of positive value in enabling Party to prepare for the encounter ahead. Even then great care is required. At previous meetings the negotiator for Opponent may have been playing a part, acting the part of the 'hard guy' to allow his colleague to be conciliatory. (See the discussion of the negotiating tactic of 'partners as opposites', p. 374.) On another occasion he may appear in his natural role of a reasonable fair-minded individual.

If, however, the experience is a generalization 'buyers in Opponent's industry demand discounts', based on what happened at the last two negotiations, this provides no certain guide for action. Because the last two buyers encountered in that industry wanted a discount, it cannot be stated that *all* buyers in Opponent's industry want a discount. Unless this can be stated, it cannot be inferred that Opponent's buyer will want a discount. To make such an inference would be committing what the logicians call 'the fallacy of composition'; asserting that what is true of a part is also true of the whole. (It would not of course be unreasonable to assume there was a good chance that he would ask for a discount and therefore to allow for this in the pricing.)

Prejudices

The less intimately people are known the more they tend to be categorized by reference to such factors as their job, their income, the house/district in which they live, the school to which they went and the one to which their children go, the clubs and societies to which they belong, etc. From these 'labels' Party tends to draw a composite picture and assumes that those whom he identified as fellow members of a particular socio-economic group will share with him common values and beliefs. If Party finds that he does not belong to a particular group, but nevertheless it is one for which he has high regard and to which certain virtues are ascribed, then he will similarly assume that all members of the group possess those same virtues. Conversely if the group is one for which Party has little regard, or with which he may actually consider himself to be in conflict, then he will assign to its members all the failings he associates with that group.

Generalizations of this type which identify a person with a certain grouping, and then give that person a character based on prejudices for or against that grouping, are widespread and would appear to be found in the very young. Haire and Morrison have reported, for example, on an experiment in which high-income group children judged a union man to be significantly more lazy, stupid, greedy, communistic and uselesss than did low-income children.[19] The experiment was conducted in 1957; if it were repeated today I would suspect from my own limited researches that, although the general conclusion would remain the same, a higher proportion of the high-income children would tend to favour the union representative in preference to the one from management. This would, however, be a simple anti-establishment, anti-authority vote based on a feeling of being *against* rather than any positive feeling *for*, and would quite likely be reversed when the children became adults.

In practice generalizations of this type are made continually; placing people into categories and drawing conclusions from this as to their character, for example, 'Managers are sound chaps. John is a manager, therefore John is a sound chap'. The inference is logically sound but the truth of the inference depends wholly on the first generalization which can only be based on very limited knowledge and be entirely subjective. Party may believe it, but he would find it difficult objectively to justify his belief, and a union negotiator who had never met John and was told only that he was a manager might have a very different picture of him.[20]

Therefore, in preparing for a meeting with the negotiators for Opponent, whom they have not previously met, the negotiators for Party should listen to the views of others and consider such of their own past experience which is relevant but, equally, they should keep an open mind. In particular they should not draw firm conclusions as to the likely behaviour of Opponent's negotiators because they happen to belong to a certain 'class', although, naturally, the more statistically significant their experience of a common behaviour pattern of people in that class the more they should in a game-theory sense maximize their security', by preparing for that common pattern to be repeated.[21]

Attitude towards the organization

The attitude most commonly encountered in the buying–selling relationship, which is related to the corporation employing the negotiator, is that of paternalism. This is used to describe the attitude of the buyer who considers that, because of the poverty of his country/ industry relative to that of the supplier, the supplier should show favour to him; that it should be regarded by the supplier as a privilege to have the opportunity of being paternal towards the buyer. This type of thinking exists most strongly when the buying country/industry believes that the fulfilment of their requirements will satisfy some social 'good', eg expansion of their hospital services. The supplier is expected to take, as at least part of his reward, the awareness of the contribution he has made towards that country/industry's develop-ment.[22]

Attitude toward the subject matter of the contract

As an attitude, paternalism is strongly associated with the idealism of intrinsic value; the belief that the creating of something of value to the community, a bridge, a hospital, has a value in itself; that neither side should seek to use bargaining tactics or to take advantage of each other; that the bringing into being of the new facilities is of greater importance than the supplier earning maximum profits, or the buyer squeezing the price or exacting penalties, and that the two sides through their recognition of this mutuality of interest should be in cooperation, not conflict.[23]

My own experience in the contracts department of a nationalized industry showed a widespread belief that a value existed in the subject matter of the contract which had nothing to do with economics.

This belief was not confined to the buying side; it existed as much among the industry's traditional suppliers so that profit maximization was neither expected nor demanded. In this instance there was a two-way paternal relationship since the same suppliers also believed that they had a right to be protected by the buyer when the demand for their products slumped because of a down-turn in the fortunes of the nationalized industry concerned.

It is expected, therefore, that the negotiator will bring with him a particular attitude towards the organization and towards the subject matter of the contract. This may be expressed solely in economic terms; that he is there to obtain the best bargain which he can, always taking long-term considerations into account where these are relevant. At the other extreme he may see the contract as one of social adjustment; the means whereby the needs of those for whom he feels socially responsible are satisfied.

7.4 PERSONALITY INTERACTION BETWEEN NEGOTIATORS

Stephenson has stated that the evidence accumulated to date, both from studies of actual negotiations and from laboratory experiments, suggests that 'successful negotiation stems from the character of the personal relations established by the negotiators'.[24] He was writing particularly of management–union negotiations and within an American context. (It is unfortunate that in recent years almost all of the behavioural work in this field has orginated in the United States.)

The above argument is disputed since in the commercial world of buyer-seller success in negotiation is derived from both:[25]

1 Very careful research and effort in the building of the total negotiating plan, which must include means for the establishment of good personal relationships with the other negotiating team.
2 The carrying into effect of the negotiating plan, amending and developing it as necessary in a controlled manner as the negotiation proceeds, including the achievement of such good personal relationships.

As indicated at the beginning of the chapter, because commercial negotiation is a micro-economic activity involving in the ultimate possibly only two people, the interrelationships between those two people, and how they react to and against each other is of major importance. Without advantageous interaction negotiating success on a long-term basis is unlikely; with it, success is achievable within the limits imposed by the economic factors discussed earlier and the terms of the negotiating plan. Good interpersonal relationships between negotiators are therefore an essential ingredient for negotiating success; all that is disputed in regard to Stephenson's statement is that they are the only requirement or that the establishment of good personal relations between negotiators necessarily ensures negotiating success.

Good interpersonal relationships

This term has been used so far without giving it a definition. The suggestion is that it involves the negotiators for each side in:

1 Recognizing the legitimacy of the position adopted by the other.
2 Respecting the integrity of the other.

Legitimacy of interest

The nature of the bargaining relationship between the parties has been expressed to be primarily distributive. The contractor wishes to carry out the work for the most favourable price he can obtain and at minimum contractual risk; the purchaser wishes to have the works constructed for the lowest price consistent with the technical/delivery standards he requires and with the maximum protection he can obtain against the contractor's default. Both have opposing interests and it is anticipated that the attitudes adopted by each will reflect this. Each will try hard to defend his position, and will expect the other to act similarly, but provided each recognizes the legitimacy of that position then such attitudinal behaviour will do no harm to their interpersonal relations.

The difficulty lies in the term *legitimacy of interest*. As Walton and McKersie have demonstrated many of the emotional problems which have bedevilled American labour relations have arisen because there has been no accord between management and union on what are the legitimate interests of each.[26] I have observed similar difficulties in commercial negotiations. For example, so long as the purchaser is willing expressly to waive his right to claim consequential damages for defects after delivery, bargaining on the actual wording of the defects clause can proceed amicably. However, if the purchaser does not accept that exclusion then the bargaining will be characterized by deep bitterness since the contractor will never accept the legitimacy of the purchaser's right to be able to claim such damages. Other similar examples would be requirement by the purchaser for the contractor to supply manufacturing drawings or to disclose actual costs incurred.[27]

Integrity

It is not expected that the negotiator will always tell the truth or tell all of the truth. However, the deception is expected to be one which is determined by the structure of the bargaining situation, and the extent of and motive behind the deception are expected to be consistent with the legitimacy of the negotiator's position.

A deception can be said to be determined by the bargaining situation when it is required to counter the position or tactics adopted by, or expected to be adopted by, the other side.[28] For example, in price negotiations the buyer would be foolish to reveal the actual level of his purchasing budget at a time when he suspected the supplier's price still included a margin for negotiation; he would use a figure which was substantially lower. His motive would be consistent with the legitimacy of his position and would be recognized as such by the supplier.

A distinction is drawn between acts of deception which flow naturally from the structure of the bargaining situation and those which are free acts, in the sense that they are not predetermined by that structure. A promise made to undertake some future act which was never intended to be implemented, but was made solely for the purpose of obtaining some benefit from the other side, would be a *free act*. An example would be a promise by the buyer to award the supplier future business if the supplier will give the buyer a discount on the present order, when the buyer knows, but the supplier does not, that there is no prospect of future business.

As a generalization it is maintained that each party to a negotiation will expect that the other may exercise deception when giving information and will accordingly apply their own judgement to such information when evaluating its significance. Moreover, to the extent that a negotiator adopts a position or tactics the obvious counter to which is deception, he is assumed to accept the use of deception as legitimate within that framework, falsehood ceases to be a falsehood when it is understood on all sides that the truth is not expected to be spoken.[29]

Expressions of intention to act in a particular manner which are designed to influence the other party's actions will be expected to be made in good faith at the time, although they may be subjected to reconsideration in the light of subsequent events. The distinction is important; a negotiator's effectiveness depends largely on his reputation of integrity. It is suggested that this will not be impaired by factual distortions within the framework determined by the negotiating structure, which will be anticipated by the other side, but may be destroyed by the expression of false intentions. This appears to be due in part to moral upbringing, and in part to the advantages derived from being classified as people whose word can be trusted.[30]

Interpersonal attitudes

Rubin and Brown[31] have provided a useful concept which they refer to as a negotiator's 10 (Interpersonal Orientation). A negotiator with a high 10 is responsive to his interpersonal relationship with his opposite number. He is sensitive and reactive to how the other behaves. A person with a low 10 is non-responsive to such relationships and is concerned only with his own interests and achieving his own objective without regard for the other. A further distinction is drawn in this analysis between high 10 negotiators who are competitively orientated, ie are out to take advantage of the other and are suspicious of any apparent generosity on his part and those who are cooperatively orientated, ie are prepared to trust the other and to behave themselves in a trustworthy manner eg reciprocate concessions.

The following table sets out the result of the possible pairings of the 3 types.

	Party	Opponent	Results
1	High 10 competitive	High 10 competitive	Party will respect Opponent as being someone similar to himself. Bargaining will be tough but professional and the outcome will be largely a function of the relative power positions of the two sides. Social relationships will develop between the two but be confined to business ie they will lapse if the business relationship itself terminates.
2	High 10 competitive	High 10 cooperative	Party will respond to Opponents cooperative acts by exploiting every possible advantage which Party possesses. Opponent can be expected initially to react with hurt surprise 'I would never have believed anyone could behave like that'. Later his reaction will take one of two forms. First he may turn vicious and respond aggressively even if it means losing the bargain. Secondly he may avoid any outward show of resentment and take the best bargain he can get this time. Either way he will determine if possible never to have any more dealings with Party. If he is compelled to have further dealings then he will change to being strongly competitive from the outset. Party's gain will at best therefore be one good bargain.
3	High 10 competitive	Low 10	Opponent will act solely in his own interests regardless of Party's behaviour. Since he is not interested in Party as a person Opponent will tend to re-act to Party's competitive-

ness as if it were solely the result of the structure of the bargaining situation. The negotiations will be difficult because whilst Opponent would accept an outcome which satisfied his own interests, Party would only accept it if it gave Party a bigger share of the cake. So the classic 50/50 split could be acceptable to Opponent, if it met his objective, but be rejected by Party.

4	High 10 collaborative	High 10 competitive	This is the reverse of 2 above
5	High 10 collaborative	High 10 collaborative	The bargaining period will be short with both sides concentrating on essentials and not interested in scoring points. The outcome will be one which is recognized by both sides as fair but will not be optimal for either. Since the two sides will have enjoyed dealing with each other repeat business can be expected.
6	High 10 collaborative	Low 10	Opponent having no interest in Party's attempts at collaboration will pressurize him to the point at which Opponent has secured his own objective assuming this is feasible given the relative power structure of the two sides. As in 2 above Party may become so frustrated at Opponent's misunderstanding of Party's moves that he explodes emotionally and the negotiations either terminate or continue with Party embittered and suspicious.

7	Low 10	High 10 competitive	This is the reverse of 3 above.
8	Low 10	High 10 collaborative	This is the reverse of 6 above.
9	Low 10	Low 10	Both party and Opponent are now interested solely in achieving their own ends. They will behave rationally themselves and expect the other to do likewise. Their negotiations will therefore be coldly impersonal. They will recognize the validity of an argument from the other side only if it is supported by power or it is in their overall interests to do so eg by creating a trade-off situation which gives them what they want. Negotiations will be prolonged as both sides test the other to the limit. Also because of their low 10 the two sides will lack any mechanism for informal or 'off-the-record' discussions over dinner or the golf course and they will be unable to trust each other as persons.

It is not suggested that in real life we often meet people who are at either end of the 10 continuum or are either wholly competitive/collaborative. However, it is important to discover at least the general direction which the tendencies of the negotiator for Opponent take, and match our own team accordingly, avoiding cases 3 and 6. Even if we lack knowledge of the particular negotiator for Opponent we can often obtain a guide from the national characteristics of Opponent's country. As a generalization if negotiators from that country can be expected to be concerned over 'losing face', would regard Party's negotiator as having insulted them were he to raise his voice in real or apparent anger or would be seriously disturbed if they felt that Party by his behaviour was being insensitive then we should not select a negotiator with a low 10 and that range of characteristics is to be found in many countries in Latin America, Southern Europe and the Far East. The importance of this point is that persons who are low 10's do not change irrespective of the person with whom they are negotiating. They are insensitive to the other's behaviour and will go on behaving as if the world consisted only of persons like themselves. A naturally co-operative high 10 will change his behaviour according to that of the person with whom he is dealing so that if it is competitive he will change to being competitive and more strongly so than if it were his natural manner of behaviour.

Effect of the psychology of negotiation on the negotiating plan
The effects which the psychological factors discussed in this chapter may have on the development of Party's negotiating plan, according to the principles considered in Chapters 3 and 4, can be summarized as follows:

1   Definition of the objective. To the extent that Party's position is dominant Party may need to limit his objective so as to avoid opponent becoming antagonistic or resentful.
2   Strategy selection. In order to satisfy the personalistic motivations of Opponent's negotiators Party may need to build 'giveaways' into his offer. Although rationally his choice should be quick kill he will need to change to hold back.
3   Level of the first offer. This is influenced by two main factors.
    (a) Party's estimates of the subjective probability of success and utility value of any offer will be influenced by the levels of aspiration of Party's negotiators. Party must ensure that these estimates are 'balanced' by having them prepared by two or more executives who differ in their achievement values and motivations.
    (b) In deriving Opponent's concession factor (see pp. 156 and 157) Party must consider the psychological factors which will influence Opponent's negotiators: their likely personalistic motivations and levels of aspiration.

The attitudes and personalities of Party's potential negotiators, and those whom Party believes will be negotiating for Opponent, will influence Party in the choice of his negotiating team, taking into account the structure of the negotiating situation and the objectives which party wishes to attain. This point is considered further in Chapter 9 under the heading 'Selection of the negotiating team'.

NOTES
1.   A. H. Maslow, 'A theory of human motivation', *Psychological Review*, vol. 50 (no. 1, 1943), pp. 370–96.
2.   See R. A. Bauer, 'Consumer behaviour as risk taking', *Proceed-*

*ings of 43rd Conference of the American Marketing Association
(1960)*, pp. 389–98.
3.   See R. F. Shoaf, 'Here's proof—the industrial buyer is also
human', *Industrial Marketing* (May 1959).
4.   This assumes that the buyer or purchasing officer is identified as
playing a significant part in making the decision on the supplier from
whom the company purchases. Again the extent to which this is so is
likely to vary with the technical content of the item concerned and its
importance to the company's business. In general the higher the
technical content the less the buyer's influence of the actual choice of
supplier, although he may still play a significant part in the subsequent
contract negotiations. See the interesting study by H. Buckner, *How
British Industry Buys* (London: Hutchinson, 1967), and G. T. Brand,
The Industrial Buying Decision (London: Cassell/Associated Business Programmes, 1972).
5.   This can be regarded as equivalent to H. A. Simon's 'satisficing'
hypothesis in which the negotiator divides the utilities of all perceived
outcomes into satisfactory and unsatisfactory, and then acts so as to
achieve that outcome which meets the criterion of satisfactory for the
minimum expenditure of effort. The term effort here includes search
resources so that once a course of action is found which is regarded as
satisfactory no further search will be made. For example, see W. H.
Starbuck, 'Level of aspiration', *Psychological Review*, vol. 70 (no. 1,
1963), pp. 51–54.
6.   Union leaders who are elected by their members for the precise
purpose of bargaining are always placed in an extremely difficult
position when the offer made to them initially is, in fact, management's final offer. The practice by management of acting in this way
(often referred to as Boulwarism, after the man who developed it at
General Electric in the USA) always gives rise to emotional resentment in Union leaders who are thereby deprived of the opportunity of
demonstrating to their members that they have acted effectively on
their behalf. This applies irrespective of the size of the offer. This was
clearly the case in the miner's dispute in UK in the winter of 1973/4.
The package offered by the NCB had extracted all that could be
offered within the limits of the Government's phase 3 policy, to the
point at which it was described by the Union's leader as: 'having done
more than scrape the barrel; it has scraped some of the paint off the
outside too'. Unfortunately the very extent of the initial offer had left
the NCB nothing to bargain with and the subsequent reaction of the
Union's leaders was predictable to an offer which, as one of them
stated, 'was an offence to everyone's negotiating instincts; there was
scarcely any room for manoeuvre'.
7.   N. L. Munn, *Psychology* (London: Harrap, 1966), pp. 228–29.
8.   See the examples quoted in R. E. Walton and R. E. Mckersie, *A

Behavioural Theory of Labour Negotiations (New York: McGraw-Hill, 1965), pp. 327–29.

9.   J. G. Cross, *The Economics of Bargaining* (New York: Basic Books, 1969), p. 177.

10. It has been proposed by R. M. Cyert and J. G. March, *A Behavioural Theory of the Firm* (New Jersey: Prentice-Hall, 1964), pp. 119–20, that a major objective of businessmen is to control their environment and eliminate uncertainty. One way of doing this is for contracts to be negotiated which impose no strain on either party. The delivery period contains slack so the penalty clause can be accepted; the price contains a substantial margin for profit so that costs are not under severe pressure; the equipment is proven so performance guarantees present no problems.

Pressure by the purchaser to tighten on these factors must initially create stress as the contractor's organization adapts in order to respond. New methods and procedures will be adopted to speed manufacture; cost savings will be introduced to safeguard profit; new developments will be perfected to improve performance standards. The same must apply to the commercial negotiators. Because of the pressures imposed on them by their superiors the standards by which the group judge the negotiators' achievements must rise, which in turn must compel the negotiators to demand more of themselves. They will look for new safeguards in the wording of clauses, tighten up on ambiguities and avoid leaving loopholes. But this will only happen if the bargaining is 'for real' and that in turn will only happen if the other side has elected to adopt an aggressive policy of maximization.

11. B. M. Bass, 'Effects on the subsequent performance of negotiators of studying issues or planning strategies alone or in groups', *Psychological Monographs General and Applied* (no. 614, 1966). D. Druckmann, 'Dogmatism, prenegotiation experience and simulated group representation as determinants of dyadic behaviour in a bargaining situation'. *Journal of Personality and Social Psychology*, vol. 6 (no. 3, 1967), pp. 279–90, and D. Druckmann 'Prenegotiation experience and dyadic conflict resolution in a bargaining situation', *Journal of Experimental Social Psychology*, vol. 4 (1968), pp. 367–83.

The Druckmann 1968 experiment was based on a collective bargaining negotiation between management and the union on four issues: wages, off-the-job training, hospital plan and paid vacation. The extract given below from Table 1 in this article shows the differences in negotiating time, differences apart at the end of the negotiations and the amount which the negotiators yielded from their starting positions. Five minutes simulated one day of negotiation and a 30 minute deadline was imposed.

Mean and standard deviations for two conditions of prenegotiation experience on three measures of conflict resolution.

Condition	Speed of resolution (minutes)		Average distance apart		Average yielding	
	mean	SD	Mean	SD	Mean	SD
Prenegotiation formulation of strategy	102*	0.018	2.02	2.018	7.365	0.909
Study by the team of the issues but without strategy formulation	31.6	0.030	0.458	0.714	7.77	0.357

*In order to take account statistically of contracts which ended in deadlock the harmonic mean was used and this figure is inflated by the number of such deadlocks.

An extract from Table 2 of the same paper shows the number of unresolved issues for the same negotiation and the same two prenegotiation conditions.

Number of dyads with 0,1,2,3 or 4 unresolved issues.

Condition	Number of unresolved issues				
	0	1	2	3	4
Prenegotiation formulation of strategy	3	2	2	1	4
Study by the team of the issues but without strategy formulation	7	2	1	1	1

12. For more detailed studies see N. J. Feather, 'Subjective probability and decision under uncertainty', *Psychological Review*, vol. 66 (no. 3, 1959), pp. 150–64, and W. H. Starbuck, 'Level of aspiration', *Psychological Review*, vol. 70 (no. 1, 1963), pp. 51–60.
13. H. A. Simon, *Administrative Behaviour* (London: Macmillan, 1959), pp. 75–76.
14. See M. Deutsch and R. M. Krauss, 'The effects of threat on interpersonal bargaining', *Journal of Abnormal and Social Psychology*, vol. 61 (1960), pp. 223–30, and 'Studies of interpersonal bargaining', *Journal of Conflict Resolution*, vol. 6 (1962), pp. 52–76; I. Goffman, 'On face work', *Psychiatry*, vol. 18 (1955), pp. 213–31.
15. An interesting example is that conducted by B. R. Brown at Columbia University and reported in 'The effects of need to maintain face on interpersonal bargaining', *Journal of Experimental Social*

Psychology, vol. 14 (1968), pp. 107–22.

Subjects were required to play a variation of the Deutsch and Krauss trucking game. In this game each player has two routes over which he could send a truck, one much shorter than the other. If he goes over the short route he can make a profit, the amount of which depends on the time taken; to go over the long route inevitably means incurring a loss. Whilst, however, the long routes for each player are independent, those for the short route have a section in common which is so narrow that only one player's truck can proceed at a time. In the Brown variation there were toll gates either end of the common section, which could be used by the player given control of the gates to stop the other player's vehicle indefinitely, until he agreed to pay the toll. Alternatively the other player could refuse to pay and go the long way round.

The experiment was so arranged that the experimenter had control of the gate for the first ten trials and charged the subject high tolls relative to the subject's potential earnings. Subjects were therefore exposed to high frustration. The position of experimenter and subject relative to the toll gate were then reversed. The subjects were given a schedule of tolls they could charge, relative to the costs they would incur, structured so that the larger the toll the more the cost to the subject. They were faced therefore with the dilemma, often found in commercial practice: the stronger the retribution sought, the higher the costs will be.

Two situations of audience response to the results of the first ten trials were then fed to the subjects:

1   The audience were highly critical of the subject for having been made to 'look like a sucker'.
2   The audience realized that the subject had been put in a difficult position in which he had done his best.

The results of the experiments as Brown has stated 'leave little room for doubt'. When bargainers have been made to look foolish and weak before a salient audience they are likely to retaliate against whoever caused their humiliation. Moreover their retaliation will be chosen despite the knowledge that doing so may require the sacrifice of all or large portions of the available outcomes, ie the subjects' profits.

16. J. S. Brown, 'Gradients of approach and avoidance responses and their relation to motivation', *Journal of Comparative and Physiological Psychology*, vol. 41 (1948), pp. 450–65.

17. Milton Rokeach's definition is adopted: an attitude is 'a relatively enduring organization of beliefs around an object or organization predisposing one to respond in some preferential manner.'

18. This means an attitude that is firmly fixed and resistant to change.

19. M. Haire and F. Morrison, 'School children's perception of labour and management', *Journal of Social Psychology*, vol. 46, pp. 179–97.

20. Haire conducted an experiment in which managers and union representatives were introduced through photographs and written descriptions to Mr B, an ordinary middle-aged, reasonably well-dressed man with no distinguishing features. The view which each took of Mr B differed widely according to whether they were told he was a representative of management or of a union. M. Haire, 'Role perception in labour management relations: an experimental approach', in *Social Perception* edited by H. Toch and H. C. Smith (London, Van Nostrand, 1968).

21. 'Class' is used here in the sense of belonging to a certain group who may be considered as negotiators to have certain defined characteristics, eg lawyers, accountants, buyers, salesmen and to sub-groups of these who belong to a particular country, industry or firm.

Sherif in a provoking study has shown how intergroup relations can be seriously affected by sterotyped images: 'group prejudices and derogatory images of other people, though products of historical processes forming part of a people's cultural heritages may exert a fateful influence on the ongoing process between groups. *In the context of immediate encounters the past becomes a heavy hand*'. M. Sherif, *Group, Conflict and Cooperation* (London: Routledge and Kegan Paul, 1966).

22. A parallel could exist here with the wage negotiations of certain employees in the public sector, eg nurses who are expected to take part of their reward in vocational satisfaction.

23. I was reminded of the existence of this attitude recently when, after giving a talk on negotiation to young engineers at a nationalized industry staff college, I received a letter from the course tutor which read in part: 'Some of the course doubted whether tactics in negotiating were legitimate and if used were dishonourable. One course member went so far as to say that young engineers should not be exposed to such ideas.'

24. G. Stephenson, 'Intergroup Relations and Negotiating Behaviour', in *Psychology at work* edited by Peter B. Warr (Harmondsworth: Penguin Books, 1971), pp. 347–73.

25. This is measured, as before, in terms of the contribution which the negotiation makes to the achievement of the overall corporate objective.

26. R. E. Walton and R. E. McKersie, *A Behavioural Theory of Labor Relations* (New York: McGraw-Hill, 1965), pp. 196–98.

27. An exception would be a Government contract which included condition SC 48, which provides for the disclosure of such costs under certain defined conditions.

28. Machiavelli in *The Prince* (London: Folio Society), p. 95, suggests the same thought: 'A prince cannot observe all those things which give men a reputation for virtue because in order to maintain his state, he is often forced to act in defiance of good faith . . . he should have a flexible disposition varying as circumstances dictate . . . he should not deviate from what is good if that is possible, but he should know how to do evil if that is necessary.'

29. H. Taylor, quoted in *The Negotiation of Government Contracts* (North Dodsworth, Covine, California: Procurement Associates, 1970), pp. 1–6.

30. For an interesting discussion of this problem, see I. Goffman, *Strategic Interaction* (Oxford: Blackwell, 1970), pp. 126–30.

31. J. Z. Rubin and B. R. Brown, *The Social Psychology of Bargaining and Negotiation* (New York: Academic Press, 1975), p. 158 ff.

PART TWO

Organisation and administration

8

THE NEGOTIATING ENVIRONMENT

Negotiations do not take place within a vacuum. They are conducted under a system of law and within a particular economic, cultural and political framework. To the extent that they are international that framework will be derived from two or more sources which will, to a degree, be in conflict one with the other. It is only to be expected that the side who believes themselves to be in a dominant position will seek to conduct the negotiations only taking into account their own framework. Specifically if the purchaser is an overseas ministry or corporation then they will seek to impose their framework on the contractor largely to the exclusion of his own. Resistance to such pressure may be feasible if the foreign purchaser is requiring government supported credit and/or aid or if the contractor is able to offer project financing on the back of an off-take agreement for the product which the scheme is designed to produce. By such means the contractor may be able to insist on the inclusion of particular provisions derived from his own framework, eg arbitration under International Chamber of Commerce Rules. But even then there is often the problem in many territories of mandatory legislation which overides contract provisions. Staying with the arbitration example there is always the problem of the enforcement of any award for which application must be made to the local courts and there may even be laws prohibiting overseas arbitration without judicial consent or, as in Iran at the time of writing, the consent of Parliament under Article 139 of the Iranian Constitution.

As a general rule on an overseas construction contract, the contractor must expect that both the initial negotiations and those which arise subsequently out of the performance of the contract will take place largely within the environmental framework of the territory concerned. Knowledge of that environment and the ability/willingness to apply that knowledge are therefore essential to the achievement of a successful outcome to the contract. Note that it is the outcome of the contract which is significant, not just the initial negotiations. Many a firm has found out to their cost that what they thought was a negotiating triumph in securing a bargain based on their own terms, has turned into a disaster when the contract has had to be performed. Fine words in a contract do not alter local ways in which business is conducted or the rules and practice to which it is subject.

Additionally, the environment includes the totality of these factors related to the foreign country, its economic and physical resources, infrastructure, climate and geography which will affect the way in which the work can be performed and the programme of implementation. In turn these factors will affect both the cost and the importance of specific contractual terms. It is only possible for these to be assessed if the negotiator is fully informed as to their applicability.

The logical sequence of the process of learning and application may conveniently be considered under the following headings:

1　Identifying all issues which may be relevant.
2　Selection of those issues relevant to the particular negotiation.
3　Acquisition of detailed knowledge of the relevant issues.
4　Deciding on how the strategic planning should take into effect such issues.
5　Deciding selection of appropriate tactics and the composition of the negotiating team.

8.1　IDENTIFYING ALL ISSUES WHICH MAY BE RELEVANT

The following list identifies those environmental factors which may be relevant:

The political system
1　The extent of state control of business enterprises.
2　If state control exists how is it organised:
　(a) Centrally or regionally
　(b) What are the limits of delegated authority from the centre
　(c) With which state authority/enterprise must the negotiations take place – ie are there more than one, and if so what are their inter-relationships?
3　What is the extent of political interest in the particular project:
　(a) Who is interested
　(b) What are the respective powers of those who are interested?
4　What is the stability of the present regime? It is likely to change in the life-time of the Project?
　(a) When are elections scheduled to take place and is the project in question an election issue?
5　What are the political relations between the governments of the seller and purchaser?
　(a) how susceptible are these to the acts of the others (eg the showing of the film 'The Death of a Princess' or human rights activism)
　(b) Are they likely to change if there is a change in the political persuasion of the government of either country?

6   Is it likely that:
      (a) One's room is bugged or telephone tapped, or conversation recorded
      (b) Attempts will be made to compromise one sexually?

Religion
1   What is the predominant religion of the country of the purchaser? (Note that religion in this context is to be interpreted as including communism.)
2   Does that religion influence significantly the conduct of:
      (a) Political affairs
      (b) The legal system
      (c) Nature, or country of origin of products which may be purchased
      (d) Social relations and individual behaviour
      (e) Entry of personnel having particular nationalities or other religious beliefs/political affiliations
      (f) Incidence of holidays and working hours, eg Ramadan

Legal system
1   What is the legal system? Is it codified or derived from the English common law?
2   Is it mandatory to accept that the contract must be governed by the purchaser's legal system?
3   What is the level of enforcement of laws and regulations in practice?
4   To what extent are the courts and the judiciary independent of the executive?
      (a) What level of influence in practice could the purchaser or a major sub-contractor exercise over the judiciary?
5   What is the time-scale for court proceedings?
6   What means exist for the enforcement of court judgements?
7   Is there any procedure, and if so what, for the enforcement of foreign judgements/arbitral awards?
8   Is the purchaser's legal system such as to:
      (a) Inhibit his negotiations in making agreements, granting concessions etc
      (b) Restrict the authority of those able to conclude, award or amend contracts to specified officers of the purchaser's corporation?
9   Is there a reliable local firm of lawyers independent of the purchaser?
10   Is it necessary legally to establish a local company to carry out local work? If so, what are the rules in particular on the proportions of overseas to local shareholding, fees for management service and remittance of profits?

11 What are the relevant laws on employment, and social security? How are those applied to foreigners? Is there a required ratio of local foreign staff? Must an engineer be employed who is a member of the local engineering institute? These may differ if you establish a locally registered company as opposed to operating, if this is permitted, as a foreign company.

The business system
1 How is business conducted? is it primarily between the principals of firms (as is largely true of the Arab world) or are all levels involved (as is the case in Japan)? Is there any real delegation of authority?
2 Is everything expected to be put in writing (as in Eastern Europe) or are verbal agreements treated as binding? What significance is given to contracts?
3 Do professional advisers eg lawyers play a major role in negotiations and the decision making process as in the USA, or are they regarded as subordinates whose primary function is to 'get the words right'?
4 Are formal meetings conducted only between the leader of both teams with the other team member only speaking if they are specifically asked to do so?
5 Is industrial espionage practised? How careful must one be with locking away papers or even not bringing them at all?
6 Is bribery necessary to secure and/or carry out business? If so, how is it operated and what are the usual terms?
7 Can contracts be negotiated with one firm or must they by law, or as a matter of practice, be put out to competitive bid? If the latter, what are usually the key criteria for securing the award? Is it just a matter of price?
8 Do negotiations proceed in two stages, first the technical and then the commercial (as in Eastern Europe and China)? Are negotiations conducted by levels each of which will expect to obtain some concession?
9 In what language is business conducted? Can documents be in two languages, one of which is English and both be of equal validity?
10 Will negotiations be with an export/import agency, as often happens in Eastern Europe or direct with the operating company? Even if direct there may be a purchasing department involved who can be expected to have different motives to the actual users.

The social system
1 What is the level of formality expected in terms of dress, use of first names, use of titles etc?
2 Is business conducted only in the office or also after-hours eg over a drink or dinner or a golf-course?

3 Do social meetings involve wives and visits home or is all entertaining done in restaurants, clubs etc?

4 What is expected in the way of gifts?

5 Do people willingly accept criticism in front of others or only in private? How important are questions of honour or loss of face?

6 Are there particular issues eg matters of religion or politics or sex which are openly discussed here?

7 Do women participate in business and if so is it on terms of equality with men?

The financial and fiscal system

1 What is ECGD's financial rating of the territory concerned? What country limit has ECGD established?

2 What is the country's debt service ratio? Has the country applied to the IMF for assistance and if so what result?

3 How large are the country's foreign exchange reserves? On what commodities does it primarily depend for foreign earnings?

4 Is the territory's currency freely exchangeable? If not what are the restrictions?

5 What is the country's record on honouring payment obligations including likely delays?

6 Can one obtain Letters of Credit confirmed in London?

7 What procedures have to be gone through with the Central Bank or Ministry of Finance for obtaining payments in foreign currencies?

8 What are the applicable tax laws, in particular on what does the liability for tax depend? Can tax be limited to work performed in the country concerned? Are there any double taxation conventions in force and if so with which countries?

9 Is the remittance of the final payment subject to the issue of a tax clearance certificate? If so how is this obtained and how long does it take?

10 Can profits earned by a local company be remitted overseas? If so what are the rules and procedures?

11 What are the regulations on the payment of customs duties or can the contract be duty exempt?

12 Are there any other fees such as stamp duties, taxes or invoices which the contractor will have to pay?

Infra-structure and logistical system

1 What is the availability in the territory concerned of:

(a) Necessary labour both skilled and unskilled

(b) Professional staff

(c) Materials for construction

(d) Constructional plant

(e) Maintenance facilities

(f) Competent and financially sound sub-contractors?

2   What restrictions are there on:
    (a) Importation of staff labour
    (b) Importation of materials which are made locally
    (c) Importation of plant?
3   Will the contract be negotiated and administered in the local
    language? If so, what is the availability of reliable and secure
    translators?
4   What are the local logistical problems relating to:
    (a) Port unloading facilities and waiting time
    (b) Road and rail access to site relative to the foreseen size and
          weight of loads to be transported
    (c) Internal air transport if this has to be by the national airline
    (d) Customs clearance, particularly at peak holiday periods?
5   What problems are foreseen relating to weather such as:
    (a) Rainy seasons
    (b) Winter, snow and frost
    (c) High summer temperature
    (d) Dust
    (e) Earthquakes
    (f) High humidity?

Each of these may affect the programme or the design and therefore
the cost of the works.

8.2 SELECTION OF THOSE ISSUES RELEVANT TO THE NEGOTIATION

The selection of issues relevant to a particular negotiation is a matter
of obtaining an understanding of the points referred to in the previous
section related to the territory in question and of recognizing both the
degree of their importance and the extent to which they are interrelated.

Obtaining data

The sources of generalized data sufficient to understand whether a
problem exists or not include:

> *Within the UK*
> The Department of Trade
> Chamber of Commerce and Trade Associations
> Councils or Committees established for the particular territory
>   or region, eg Committee for Middle East Trade
> Banks having a particular interest in the territory or region
> Friendly UK firms already trading with the country
> Newspaper and journal articles

Overseas
Any local company established by your own company or within
   the group of companies to which you belong
The local British Embassy or High Commission
Local Banks
Your own agent
Other businessmen operating in the territory
Your own observation and experience
Local newspaper and journal articles

   In collecting and assessing data it is essential to bear in mind any
bias which may exist in the person from whom the data is obtained and
hence in the data itself, which will cause the data to appear either more
or less favourable to your company. Bias may arise because:

1   The person providing the data may have an interest in your future
    actions. So anyone concerned to promote trade between your
    company and the country/purchaser in question will tend to
    minimize risks and present opportunities as favourably as he can.
2   The person wishes to please you, so he will tell you what he
    believes you would like to know. This is particularly true of the Far
    East.
3   The person does not really know the answer to your question but
    cannot bear to lose face by admitting this. Again particularly true
    of the Far East.
4   The person may genuinely believe he does know but his information
    is incorrect because he consistently fails to obtain data from
    reliable and objective sources. This will usually apply to data
    based on the cocktail party gossip of those who rely on the
    Embassy circuit instead of going out to learn the hard facts.
5   The person who, while appearing to support your interests, is in
    reality concerned to support those of one of your competitors or
    even your customer since he believes showing favour to them will
    bring him the greater reward.

   Essentially the gathering of data is an intelligence-type operation in
which a number of separate facts are collected and fitted together to
form a composite picture which is coherent and 'hangs together' in a
way which is likely to resemble reality. But the emphasis here is on the
facts being separate. All too often Fact A is regarded as being
supported by Fact B when in reality they are both derived from a
common source. The opinion of the commercial counsellor on a
matter, and an article in the local financial journal on the same subject,
are not supportive of each other unless both have obtained their data
from unrelated sources. What is more likely in practice is that either
(a) the counsellor read the journal or (b) the journalist obtained the
copy from the counsellor or (c) they both met separately with a senior
official of the central bank.

8.3 ACQUISITION OF DETAILED KNOWLEDGE OF RELEVANT ISSUES

Unless the company is already operating in the territory, there is only one way in which such knowledge can be obained and that is by one or more visits to the territory concerned made by suitably qualified personnel from the company's staff. The key factors which will make such visits successful are:

1   Time spent beforehand in preparation and obtaining as much generalized data on the territory and issues in question as possible.
2   Having a limited number of meetings set up in advance with those likely to be able to provide access to the data required.
3   Allowing enough time for meetings being cancelled and for other and further appointments/visits being made.
4   Getting out of the hotel and officials' offices and seeing something of the country first-hand.
5   Retaining an objective and enquiring mind and not allowing particular events or limitations to affect one's judgement.
6   Writing up reports as one goes along, recording the facts impartially and refraining from making judgements until one is able to do so in a balanced manner.
7   Not relying on second-hand data but insisting politely on being referred to primary sources.

8.4 DECIDING ON HOW STRATEGIC PLANNING SHOULD TAKE ENVIRONMENTAL ISSUES INTO ACCOUNT

Rules for making such decisions are:

1   Do not expect the overseas country to change its methods of doing things for your benefit or because their way is not the way you do it.
2   If you can avoid asking them to change and adopt new methods, do so. If you cannot, say because their current specfications would exclude your firm's products, then (a) you must give them reasons beneficial to themselves why they should change and be sure they can see the way in which they will benefit, and (b) you must allow them time in which to change.
3   Look positively at ways in which you can reduce risks which cannot be avoided. Examples could be:
    (a) Split the contracts into on- and off-shore to minimize tax, payment and currency exchange risks, taking your profit off-shore;
    (b) Use local contractors and hire locally available plant to minimize your build-up of assets in the country;
    (c) Employ your topline staff on the contract to ensure that things do not go wrong even if the job is only of small value;

(d) Make sure your agent is paid on a basis which will ensure that he has continued interest in your receiving payment throughout the job up to the issue of the final certificate;

(e) If you can, start with a smaller valued job to give you territory experience;

(f) Allow time and money for overcoming the frustrations which will occur in customs, with inland transport, petty pilfering, etc.

(g) Do not ignore the customer at top level after he has given you the contract. The man who sold him the job and, hopefully, got to know him should visit him regularly to provide reassurance on progress and make him feel you still need him.

4   If in doubt, if the risks are not for you or not commensurate with the reward you can expect to earn, decide this at the earliest possible moment before you have incurred too many costs and abort. Do not vacillate and hope it will all come right somehow. It will not and the less whole-hearted your commitment the greater the risk of disaster.

8.5 SELECTION OF APPROPRIATE TACTICS AND THE NEGOTIATING TEAM

The table set out below gives the suggested rules to be followed:

Do		Do Not	
1	Be sensitive to the local social, business and religious customs	1	Go native
2	Be aware of the local political scene and how it may affect both your project happening and your chances of success	2	Involve yourself in any form of political activity or express publicly your opinion on political affairs
3	Behave courteously and be respectful to ministers and officials	3	Be subservient or allow yourself to be intimidated or over-awed by their status or by the shock tactics they may use to impress upon you their superiority or power
4	Prepare yourself in advance for all meetings and stay calm	4	Be surprised at the unexpected or allow yourself to get flustered
5	Take every opportunity to get out and about and talk to people	5	Succumb to local temptations!
6	Have as team members those whose personality and technical abilities are likely to fit	6	Allow your expert, however brilliant, to patronize the client or try to teach him his

in with those with whom negotiations will be conducted

7 Be flexible and willing to
   adjust to their conceptions
   provided you can still obtain
   your objectives even if the
   means are different

8 Be careful on security of your
   papers and discreet in referring
   to people particularly your
   contacts by name

9 Listen to your agent's advice
   with an open mind

10 Be patient

business

7 Be rigid and insist that yours
   is the only way

8 Be eager to show off your
   limited knowledge

9 Try and teach him his business
   or impose your preconceived
   ideas

10 Leave the territory unguarded
   at critical stages even if you
   miss a board meeting or your
   holiday

9

THE NEGOTIATING TEAM

9.1 CHARACTER AND COMPOSITION OF THE TEAM

Although Party and Opponent have been referred to throughout Part One as if they were single entities, in Chapter 7 on the psychology of negotiation emphasis has been placed on the importance of personalistic motivation and interpersonal action between negotiators when considering a behavioural as opposed to a normative description of the negotiating process. These factors apply equally to relationships between negotiating team members. Therefore the performance of Party's team depends as much, if not more, on the way in which its members function togther as it does on the technical expertise which each individual member possesses.

In considering the character and composition of the negotiating team it is necessary to look beyond technical skills to the personality and temperament of the proposed members and the way in which these are likely to interact between themselves and with the anticipated members of Opponent's team. The character and composition of the negotiating team must therefore be such that:

1   The members have the technical expertise to deal effectively with the whole of the area which it is foreseen that the negotiations will cover.
2   The members are compatible in temperament with one another and with those whom it is believed will represent Opponent.

Size of the negotiating team

The area covered by any contract negotiation may be divided broadly into four sectors:

1   Commercial: price, delivery, commercial policy on risk taking
2   Technical: specification, programme, methods of work
3   Legal: contract documents, terms and conditions of contract, insurance, legal interpretation
4   Financial: terms of payment, credit insurance, bonds and financial guarantees

If the scale and importance of the negotiation justifies it then the negotiating team for each side would comprise a negotiator qualified in, and responsible for, each of those areas. These four persons would then constitute the permanent team for the negotiation, and would be supplemented by other specialists on particular issues as they arose, eg production methods, inspection, installation. For negotiations of lesser significance one negotiator would double for another and cover two areas, after having been fully briefed on the subject with which he was less familiar. Thus the legal negotiator might cover the financial area, and the commercial negotiator, if he had an engineering background, might assume responsibility for the technical area. Alternatively the commercial negotiator might cover both his own and the legal plus financial areas, with an engineer to support him on the technical side.

On lesser negotiations therefore the team of four could be reduced to two; it should not be reduced to one, no matter how well-qualified the negotiator concerned. It is demanding too much to expect the same person on his own to:

1   Present his own case and study Opponent's visual reactions
2   Listen to and makes notes on Opponent's reply
3   Plan and present his response to Opponent's reply
4   Consider the possible outcomes on each point, and their effect on the bargain as a whole and develop a trade-off strategy
5   Identify and conclude the final bargain
6   Record the final bargain

Additionally the presence of a colleague will give the negotiator the advantage of:

1   Being able to employ team tactics.
2   Not having to develop all the arguments on his own. It is more effective for arguments on different points to be developed with differing styles.
3   Having someone to support him in the case of sickness or overtiredness. This is particularly valuable when negotiating away from home base.
4   Having someone with whom to share his problems. This is again especially valuable when operating abroad with poor communications back home and faced, inevitably, with the doubts and uncertanties present in that type of situation.

It is preferable that a negotiator has the support of an assistant or trainee to make notes, do calculations and remind him of any points which he has missed, and thus not leave him to handle the whole bargaining process by himself. If a company maintains that they cannot afford to send two people then really they should not be in the business to which the negotiation relates.

Equally, however, the negotiating team should not be too large. At any time it should not exceed five, although they will not necessarily be the same five over the whole period. If a basic team of three is assumed, one commercial, one legal and one technical, then this might need to be augmented on a major negotiation at different stages by specialists from the engineering, production or finance functions. Beyond five it becomes extremely difficult for the team to be kept under control and for its activities to be directed towards a single outcome. Separate and uncoordinated discussions are likely to start between the functional specialists on both sides, and arguments are likely to develop between the members of the team themselves during the negotiating session. The retention of a united front and the direction of all argument towards a single goal are essential preconditions for an effective team operation and with more than five permanently in a team these are most unlikely to be achieved.

In certain industries with which I have been associated, it has been the practice to involve in the negotiations both local and higher levels of management, plus representatives from all staff functions. An assembly of as many as 25 people cannot be referred to as a negotiating *team* because it is certainly *not* a team. Arguments between assembly members are numerous and based on the lines of traditional disagreement between staff functions or the entrenched views of their representatives. The practice may be effective as a means of communication, so that everyone concerned is informed about the proposals under consideration, but it is highly ineffective for the purpose of negotiation and from that viewpoint has nothing to commend it.

It will be noted that the preceeding paragraphs have referred to the negotiators and also to functional specialists. A clear distinction is drawn between those whose function on the negotiating team is to negotiate and those who are there to provide specialist advice or information. A quality assurance manager may for example be asked to join the team when matters affecting his function are being discussed but is not his task actually to carry out the bargaining with Opponent. That would be the task of the commercial negotiator who would look to the quality assurance manager to provide him with the necessary specialist support.

A further distinction is drawn between the risk-taking function of the commercial negotiator and the functions of the other specialists who do form part of the negotiating team. These other specialists have a dual task to perform. They negotiate with their opposite number on the wording or interpretation of the documents with which they are specifically concerned. However, when the issue raised is one which involves commercial risk then their function is to act as an adviser to the commercial negotiator and to apply his policy decision. Take the simple example of a warranty clause. The commercial negotiator will ask his lawyer to interpret for him the risk which acceptance of Opponent's proposals would create, and then take the decision on the policy line which he wishes to adopt. As necessary he argues this policy line with his opposite number but leaves it to the lawyer to express that policy in the form of an amended clause and argue the drafting of this with the lawyer from the other side.

These distinctions are important since much of the criticism which is made of functional specialists as negotiating team members arises from a lack of clear understanding of the role which they are there to perform. The major problems arise when such specialists stray away from their proper role and start to take the risk decisions which are the prerogative of the commercial negotiator. It is not lawyers who lose suppliers contracts because of their legalistic attitude but commercial negotiators who do not keep lawyers in their proper place and attending to their proper function.

Selection of the negotiating team

As part of their normal business function purchasing and sales departments can be expected to provide people to take part in negotiations. Despite the relative lack of attention given to the subject in textbooks on either purchasing or selling, negotiation is a major part of the activity of both departments. Although the academic training of the junior may be deficient in the theory of negotiation, he is likely to be introduced to the subject in a practical way from quite early on in his career, and his further advancement may well be dependent upon the degree of success he achieves.

It is not so, however, with other departments. Negotiation does not form part of the professional training of an engineer, lawyer or accountant nor is it an activity in which the individual will necessarily be engaged for any significant portion of his time or one which will influence his future chances of promotion. One cannot therefore expect to be able to take any engineer, lawyer or accountant away from his office desk and send him straight out on an overseas contract negotiation. Accordingly, if a company is likely to require the services of these professional people as members of negotiating teams, they should arrange for them to receive the necessary training.

In addition to his professional abilities the person should be selected on the basis of his suitability *as a negotiator* for the negotiation in question. If it is a major negotiation then he would be expected to have significant negotiating experience, and be judged to be compatible with the other members of the team and with what is known of the attitudes of Opponent's team. If the negotiation is of lesser significance then it might be judged a suitable opportunity for someone of less proven ability to gain experience. The important factor is that the selection is made positively from the viewpoint of the best interests of the company in regard to that negotiation and for the future. It may for instance be decided that one negotiator specializes either in a particular product or with a particular customer, so that a sense of continuity is achieved. Alternatively if the company identifies its market as a particular overseas country with its own peculiar environment then one or more negotiators should be trained as specialists in all aspects of that environment and encouraged to obtain at least a colloquial knowledge of the local language.

When referring to someone's ability as a negotiator the following qualities seem to be the most important:

1 Sound technical knowledge of his own discipline and of the techniques of negotiation.
2 Understanding of the product or service involved in its relationship to his discipline/function. Thus the lawyer engaged on contract negotiation should have sufficient knowledge of the subject matter of the contract to appreciate the practical significance of the clauses which he is negotiating.
3 Facility of expression.
4 Ability to listen to what the other side are saying and analyse their arguments objectively.
5 Willingness to look at issues from the viewpoint of the other side.
6 Capability to stay in command of himself even when exposed to severe pressure.
7 Mental/physical stamina and a sense of determination.
8 A sense of humour.
9 Readiness to retain a sense of proportion and stay with the main issues and not be diverted onto side lines.
10 Possession of a 'feel' for the relationship of the negotiating point with another and being willing to trade one for another.
11 Ability to get on with people of differing nationalities, religions and social classes and to avoid nationalistic, racial or social prejudice.

To what extent can these qualities be taught and to what extent are they determined either genetically or by the social conditioning to which the individual has been subjected from birth?

Clearly 1 and 2 must be taught; the remainder are a function of the individual's personality and the environmental influences to which he has been subjected. In practice it is my view that by the time people start to carry out commercial negotiations their personality and attitudes have been so far developed that they are unlikely to undergo significant change. Therefore, whilst a person can refine himself and gain experience of the way in which others behave, so that he develops a sense of either anticipation or understanding of their actions, he will still retain the essential personality and attitudes with which he emerged as an adult.

Imaginative training may develop any particular characteristic, such as ability to understand the other's viewpoint, to the extent that it is latent within the individual. It is argued that such training is unlikely to create the ability where previously it was non-existent.

The role of the agent

The role of the agent will vary widely between two extremes. At the one end of the spectrum is the agent who is solely a 'contact man' with those who are supporting Party in their efforts to secure the business. At the other is the agent who permanently represents Party in the territory or with a particular customer, has some knowledge of Party's products/services and is able and willing to provide Party with a range of services such as translation, office and communication facilities, assistance with local legal and taxation advice and joins the negotiating team at least for certain meetings.

The agent whose function is limited to being a 'contact man' will not be a member of the negotiating team as such, although he will be involved in any discussions between the team leader and those who are assisting Party and stand to benefit, should Party be successful. Because of the delicate nature of his role it would not be appropriate for him to become involved in the formal working sessions. His task lies outside these in the informal discussions which may be necessary so that Party can attain his objective. He is also there to brief the team leader on how to handle particular situations or personalities.

The agent whose role is wider can be co-opted as a member of the negotiating team although this will generally be one of his younger staff rather than the principal himself. If the language eg Chinese, is totally unknown to any of Party's team then he may act as the interpreter. Certainly he should be there to check on any interpretation being done by customer's interpreter. The difficulty in practice is that the agent only stands to gain if Party is successful in obtaining the contract and he has therefore a vested interest in Party making the concessions necessary for this purpose. He will be resistant to Party taking a tough line which could cause the business to go to a competitor and will often seem to Party to be more on customer's side than his own. There are other difficulties as well. The agent, especially in the Far East, will almost never tell you directly any bad news. He wants you to be happy and therefore will tell you what he believes you want to hear. Somehow he will have an explanation for each reverse and 'a cousin' who can put matters right. It is up to the team leader to see through this and get to the truth, otherwise time and money will continue to be spent on what is a lost cause. Also can you be sure that he is working for you alone and is not also involved with one of your competitors? Or again the ubiquitous 'cousin' who is the source of information in the customer's office may be receiving as much information about your proposals as he is providing about customer's plans.

These problems have to be anticipated and guarded against both in as careful selection as possible in the first instance and with continued attention subsequently to testing him as you go along. This will either prove him to be the right man whom you can reasonably trust or provoke him into taking an unexpected holiday. One such person, known to the author personally, who was a very non-devout Muslim, suddenly decided when the going got rough to disappear on the Haj!

But despite all the above the agent in many territories is essential to success. It is rare for the team leader or other members of the negotiating team to be sufficiently familiar with their opposite numbers or others who are part of the decision making process, that they can ever become part of the local 'old-boy' network. They will never be able to obtain access to genuine 'inside' data or exercise informal influence on the decisions to be reached. Only the agent has the possibility of belonging to the 'right' local family or tribe or of having been in the same year at college with one or more of the decision makers, and can take advantage of the reciprocation of favour for which such links provide the framework. Only he may be able to get you that vital appointment ahead of the crowd or ensure that it is your proposal which the real decision maker has in front of him at the appropriate moment.

9.2 APPOINTMENT AND DUTIES OF THE TEAM LEADER

Appointment

In discussing this topic at seminars on negotiation is has been suggested to me that the question of *choosing* a team leader does not really arise; he chooses himself because of the position which he holds in the company or organization concerned. Reference has been made specifically to the sales manager and chief buyer as two obvious examples.

There are many occasions when these two managers will act as leaders of their respective teams, but there are also numerous other occasions when an alternative candidate will be proposed. Some examples drawn from my own experience are set out below and the reader is left to make his own choice.

Subject matter of negotiation	Candidates for team leader
Purchase of raw materials for production process	Raw materials buyer Plant manager Production manager
Purchase of major item of capital plant	Purchasing/contracts manager Chief Engineer Divisional manager or other line executive
Major sales contract	Marketing/sales director or manager Senior line executive from managing director downwards Project manager designate for the contract
Contract dispute	Project manager Contract administration manager Sales manager or other executive who originally negotiated the contract

When deciding whether or not to appoint an executive as a negotiating team leader, two criteria by which he should be assessed are suggested, as follows:

1　His ability to lead a negotiating team as opposed to any purely technical skills which he may possess.
2　His degree of personal responsibility for the profit or loss which may follow from any decision taken during the negotiations.

Specifically a person should not be selected for either of the following reasons:

1　He can be spared, having nothing else to do at that time.
2　He is *the* technical expert on the product.
3　He happens to be the senior manager concerned with the outcome of the negotiation.
4　He once knew personally the territory concerned or members of team for the other side.

Although it has been indicated that the team leader does not have to be a technical expert on the product upon which the negotiation is centred, it is not suggested that either buying or selling is a mystique on its own which can be conducted without any product knowledge at all. The leader for a sales team who cannot answer any of the buyer's questions directly, but must refer him to one or other of his colleagues, is unlikely to earn the buyer's respect.[1] Equally the buyer without product knowledge can too easily be fooled in a situation in which an informal alliance develops between his own and the supplier's technical experts. Such alliances are not uncommon in industries in which the engineers, although commercially on opposing sides, were trained together, are members of the same professional Institute and have collaborated together technically in finding solutions to common problems.

The negotiating team leader should possess therefore sufficient knowledge of all the problems involved in the negotiation; commercial, technical and contractual to enable him to make an intelligent contribution to each item discussed and to direct and coordinate the activities of the functional specialists.

Duties

The specific duties of the team leader are to:

1 Select the remainder of the negotiating team.
2 Prepare the negotiating plan.
3 Conduct the negotiations and in particular take all decisions on:
 (a) Timing and level of concessions.
 (b) Selection of items to be traded-off against each other.
 (c) Calling of team review meetings.
 (d) Requests for an adjournment.
4 Make the bargain with the other side.
5 Ensure that the bargain is properly recorded.
6 Issue the negotiating report.

Additionally, as a leader, he has the more general functions of leadership to perform: of generating enthusiasm in his team, maintaining their morale under all conditions and by his own example obtaining from each the maximum contribution which he is capable of providing.

The team leader is there to lead and, within the scope of his authority, to make decisions. Certain of those decisions will involve the question as to whether a particular risk should or should not be taken, and the team leader can expect to receive advice on the issue concerned from the appropriate specialist on the team. Ultimately the decision is for the team leader to take and he must be permitted to go against the specialist advice if he considers this necessary.

It is in this respect that the departmental organization of a company can be prejudicial to the proper conduct of negotiations. The specialist will come from one of the functional departments, eg engineering, law, finance. Whilst his technical advice, must be considered by the team leader (or the specialist dismissed from the team as being someone in whom the leader has no confidence), this does not mean that the leader must act upon that advice. The engineer may, for example, advise that the company's product does not conform with a particular requirement of the buyer's specification. But the decision whether to ask for an amendment prior to contract and risk losing the business, or to take the risk and seek to negotiate a concession during the course of the contract, should that become necessary, is for the team leader to take. If he is in any doubt he refers back to his own line manager.

9.3 VISITS BY SENIOR PERSONNEL

A problem which often arises on major contract negotiations abroad is whether or not at some stage to involve a person senior in the company hierarchy to the team leader such as a group board director. In negotiating contracts with overseas ministries, government corporations and similar bodies it may be necessary to do this in order to gain access at the highest political level. It also may be appropriate if the assistance is being sought of a minister from the UK government to visit the territory concerned to support Party's efforts. The following are the suggested guide lines for such visits which can be helpful but which can equally be disastrous:

1   The advisability and timing of the visit should be left to the negotiating team leader.
2   The visit must be handled in such a way to reinforce and not derogate from the authority of the team leader. There should be no suggestion of opening úp a new line of communication with the visiting director so that he can be used to over-rule the team leader's decisions. This applies both to the client and to the agent.
3   The visiting director must allow himself time to be briefed and for the possible postponement of appointments. His schedule must be kept flexible and not oveloaded with a rapid succession of meetings. If necessary he must be prepared to stay an extra few days to secure that vital appointment remembering that the people he wants to see will have many other important matters to deal with.
4   The local British embassy must be informed in advance of the proposed visit and intended meetings with ministers and their support enlisted.
5   The visiting director must take the trouble even if it is only on the outward journey to inform himself of the basic political, economic, religious and social facts relating to the overseas territory.
6   Never must the visiting director appear as patronizing to the local minister or senior government officials whom he meets. He may be at or near the head of a major UK company but there are many other companies in the world. There is only one President or Prime Minister of that territory. His approach should be courteous and respectful but firm on the points he wishes to establish.

NOTE

1. The importance of product knowledge in a sales situation has been stressed by G. Brand in *The Industrial Buying Decision* (London: Cassell/Associated Business Programmes, 1972), p. 98, where he points out that failure by the seller to provide information requested by the buyer only frustrates the development of their relationship.

10

COMMUNICATION AND SECURITY

10.1 COMMUNICATION

The communication which is referred to here is that between a negotiating team operating away from home base and their home management. The need to communicate arises from the requirements of the negotiating team and the home office.

1 The negotiating team require:
   (a) Factual information
   (b) Specialist advice
   (c) Management decisions
2 The home office requires reports on how the negotiations are proceeding.

Preferably such communications should be minimized, for the following reasons:

1 Communication links are not necessarily secure (see p. 251).
2 The need to communicate inevitably imposes a delay in the negotiating team being able to make a decision. This puts Party at a definite disadvantage against a competitor who is able to make decisions on the spot, and creates a bad impression on the foreign buyer. The criticism is frequently made by overseas buyers of the lack of authority of British negotiators as compared with their European competitors and in my experience this criticism is often justified.
3 It is difficult for a negotiating team to be able to convey an adequate impression of the problem with which they are faced and of the atmosphere within which the negotiations are being conducted. When therefore they receive the advice and/or decision from home base it is frequently inappropriate in the particular circumstances.
4 Frequent reference back to home base weakens both the negotiating team's own morale and their standing in the eyes of the overseas buyer.

In preparing his negotiating plan positive action should be taken therefore by the negotiating team leader to reduce the need to communicate with home office to an absolute minimum. In so far as information and advice are concerned the following suggestions are made as to how this can be achieved:

1   The necessary back-up data is assembled to enable answers to be given to each question which it is foreseen that Opponent may raise. For this purpose all prior correspondence, notes of meetings, etc, should be reviewed and note taken of issues which have arisen on similar negotiations in the past.
2   Points on which it is known that any competitor may be regarded as superior to Party are similarly reviewed and information put together to rebut such criticisms.
3   Supporting information and precedents which may be helpful in negotiation are collected. Some examples would be:
    (a) Precedents of clauses from other contracts.
    (b) Copies of official records showing changes in wages and material costs since the last order/tender with this particular purchaser.
    (c) Specimen test specifications of the type which will be provided to the purchaser on inspection and acceptance.

4   Sufficient data is assembled to enable price changes resulting from simple amendments to the specification to be calculated on the spot. This would include unit rates and prices for such work as cabling, trenching and plant installation. In particular the detail of the steps by which the costs have been developed into a selling price must be available in a form convenient for easy reference. A suggested format is given in Figure 10:1.
5   If the contract is to be subject to other than English law, advice is obtained in advance from a local lawyer so that the effect of any major differences can be assessed. Similarly the taxation position is investigated to ascertain whether or not the supplier will be subject to sales tax, tax on profits earned in the foreign territory, etc.

The requirement for reference to home management for decisions can be reduced if not eliminated by the way in which the negotiating brief is prepared (see Chapter 11).

There are, however, two major exceptions to the general rule of minimal communication.

1   The opening phase of the negotiation shows that no bargain is foreseeable within the terms of the negotiating brief. This is discussed in detail in Section 16.3.
2   The negotiations are prolonged and interim action is required to be taken at home. In that event the safest course is to send back the

Plant and materials

| Unit cost ex-works | Quantity | Total ex-works cost | Freight and insurance | Duty | Commercial overheads | Profit | Agent's commission | FBCD premium | Interest and bank charge | Selling price |

Installation

| Basic man-hour rate | Premium rate | Living allowance | Total man-hours | Total cost | Commercial overheads | Profit | Agent's commission | EC premium | Interest and bank charge | Selling price |

Plant hire

| Basic hire rate | Fuel | Total weeks | Total basic cost | Freight and insurance | Total cost | Commercial overheads | Profit | Agent's commission | Interest and bank charge | Selling price |

Figure 10:1 Make up of selling price

member of the negotiating team within whose field the action required falls. If it is a question of approaching ECGD to obtain their approval to the terms of payment provisionally agreed with the buyer then the financial negotiator should return. If the technical discussions have resolved the issues on the equipment to be supplied and delivery is tight then the technical negotiator might return home early to enable editing, and even advance ordering, to proceed whilst contractual discussions continue.

It is recognized that this course of action may be expensive and at times inconvenient, but it is the only sure way in which the correct information is likely to be transmitted. In addition, secondary questions, which the receipt of such information generates back home, can be answered first hand and with the minimum of delay.

Reports for home office

Inevitably management at home are concerned to know of the progress their negotiators are making. Managers who are accustomed to daily contact with their staff, by telephone if not face to face, do not take kindly to a situation in which they feel out of touch. They hate the uncertainty of not knowing.

Reporting is not necessarily an easy matter. It has all the disadvantages enumerated earlier as applying generally to communications and the special problem of being concise without being misleading. If delivery is a key issue and the team leader reports back that he has settled for a period which hardly satisfies Party's minimum negotiating objective, the manager is at once concerned. He wonders why the negotiators have not done better. At best he will react to the situation by requesting clarification and suspending judgement until it is received. At worst the manager will jump to the conclusion that the negotiator has let him down and will initiate panic action accordingly, possibly to the extent of flying off immediately to the scene of the negotiations.

In fact the negotiating team may well have achieved an acceptable result, for example, by tying the delivery promise to the performance by the purchaser of certain obligations, such as the supply of full technical data to enable Party to proceed within stated time scales, which the negotiator knows in practice the purchaser cannot achieve. The shorter delivery promise may be a device to enable the purchaser to place the order within authority he has already received from his Board and without having to go back for revised authority which would lose the buyer face and perhaps lead to the negotiations being reopened with a competitor.

The old saying 'no news is good news' applies also to negotiations. If these are proceeding within the negotiating brief then there seems little point in the negotiator saying so. However, security was earlier identified as a motivational drive (see p. 191), and if the home manager's need for security can be satisfied by a simple telex saying 'Discussion proceeding. All well' then no harm is done. But for the reasons already given, any detailed reporting by telex or telephone on specific issues is strongly opposed; it leaves far to much room for misunderstanding. The manager ought to be able to work on the basis that the team leader will only come back to him in specific terms if he finds that he cannot satisfy the terms of the negotiating brief.

Throughout this chapter reference has been made to the negotiator communicating with his manager, and this has intended to imply a single line of communication between the negotiating team leader and the manager having the profit and loss responsibility for the contract. Parallel lines of communication between other team members and their respective functional departmental heads should not be permitted. If say the lawyer on the team wishes to communicate with the company's legal adviser then he should do so through the team leader and the message should similarly be relayed at the other end from the manager to the legal adviser.

This may sound a laborious and even time-wasting procedure but it is essential if the team leader is to retain control of the negotiations. To start with he must approve of the need to communicate and check the security aspects. Secondly any request for advice is bound to contain a mixture of pure professionalism and commercial risk taking. For example, the drafting of a clause on exclusion of liability for consequential damages must be related to the degree of risk that such damages could be recovered and the company's attitude towards the taking of that risk. This is not a matter which the lawyers can settle on their own, and any telex to home office for advice needs to describe both the practicalities and commercial implications of the risk issue as well as the legal position on recovery of damages.

Finally the team leader should never be put in the position in which a team member has communicated with his functional chief at home and obtained support for his views which he then uses as a weapon in argument against the team leader who may well, in the company's hierarchy, be junior to the functional head.

The rule as to a single line of communication between the team leader and his line manager at home is one therefore that should never be broken.

10.2 SECURITY

The problems with security are that no one takes it seriously until he has personally be involved in an incident in which he has been the victim, and if it is going to be taken seriously this demands constant care and attention especially at moments of relaxation.

A person's approach to security will differ according to whether he believes that deliberate attempts will be made by others to obtain confidential information from him or that people may simply take advantage of an act of carelessness. The first instance is generally rare, confined to certain territories and reasonably well publicized. The negotiator knows in advance to expect bugged hotel rooms and searches of his luggage, and to avoid contact with local nationals whose objective may be to obtain evidence of compromising behaviour.

Much more difficult is the territory which is seemingly innocent and in which therefore the negotiator is liable to be that much more careless. If asked the question directly, 'Would you expect Opponent to take advantage of a lapse in your security?', the negotiator may well reply 'I suppose he might'. This would still not prevent him from going to lunch and leaving papers in Opponent's office in an unlocked briefcase!

Security in those circumstances is very much a matter of habit and it is suggested that the negotiator should adopt the following habits:

1   Do not talk business in a place where conversation can easily be overhead and there is no idea of who is listening. This applies especially to aircraft, trains, hotel lounges and chauffeur-driven cars. Do not assume that others can only understand their own language.

2   Do not put temptation in Opponent's way. Specifically do not:
    (a) Leave papers on the table in his office or conference room when at lunch. If they are left in a personal office or conference room make sure Opponent cannot re-enter first.
    (b) Ask him to make copies of any document or arrange for him to do any typing, unless it is in order for him to take an extra copy for his own use.
    (c) Have the negotiating brief with the figures clearly displayed open on top of papers. He may be very good at reading upside down.

3   Do not trust hotel porters with cables or hotel/public telex operators. This may run the risk of the message being sold to the competitor or the foreign buyer. In some countries this is a recognized trade.

4   Do not assume that people employed by a personal agent or local company are necessarily to be trusted. Their nationalistic ties with the foreign buyer may be stronger than their commercial loyalty or they may simply be underpaid.

5   Do not leave business papers lying about in public or hotel rooms, and do keep those of a strictly confidential nature securely locked away.

Sometimes the negotiator may be offered information of a confidential nature regarding either the competitor or the buyer. How should he react?

It is suggested that the first reaction should be one of suspicion. Is the information a 'plant' intended to mislead the negotiator? Remember it may be so, even though the actual informant believes it to be genuine; he may have been deceived as well.

Only if there is complete satisfaction that the information is genuine would it be prudent to use it and even then with the greatest of care. If it really is genuine then this is a source of further information which will have to be concealed. Neither competitor nor Opponent must ever be allowed to suspect the transference of information. Alternatively if it is after all a 'plant' the person concerned must not be allowed to think he has succeeded; preferably he should remain in a state of uncertainty.

An example would be a case in which Party had been supplied with information as to Opponent's budget. In negotiating the price Party would act initially as if he believed the budget to be higher than the information indicated. If the information is indeed correct then Party can allow himself gradually to be persuaded by Opponent that he cannot afford to pay more than the lower figure. If the information is false then Party's figure will be nearer the truth and he will have minimized any reduction in the upper level of the bargaining zone (see p. 145). Party will also have taught Opponent that he is not easily fooled.

The use of codes

Communications between the negotiating team operating abroad and their home office may be subject to surveillance by the authorities of the country in which the team is operating, as well as possible exposure to the team's competitors. Items which are politically sensitive or commercially revealing should be coded, therefore, in a way which will at least make it difficult for either the authorities or competitors to interpret and would not expose the team or their agent to political action. Such issues would include:

1 Names of any persons who are politically or commercially sensitive. This would include Party's agent, government ministers Party's competitors and top personnel within customer's organization.
2 Price level and discounts.
3 Acceptability or otherwise of particular propositions.

If any form of coding is to be used then it should be easy for the recipient to interpret, not be capable of being misunderstood and still make sense as a message. The last point is important since otherwise it may not be accepted for transmission and could certainly arouse strong suspicions.

The need for coding must therefore be identified at the planning stage of the negotiations and the system to be used agreed between the team leader and his home manager. Code names may be given to persons whose identity is sensitive and a numbers translation agreed.

An example of the use of a simple code might be:

Coded message. Uncle still not well. Paul believes another visit to hospital may be necessary. Will make arrangements tomorrow. Do not worry as condition still amenable to treatment.

Translation. Customer still not satisfied. Agent's contact man thinks further discount necessary and will make offer tomorrow. Proposals still within negotiating brief.

11

THE NEGOTIATING BRIEF

A distinction is drawn between the negotiating brief which consists of the instructions given to the team leader by management and the negotiating plan which is developed by the negotiating team and represents the manner in which they propose to implement those instructions.

The negotiating brief is prepared in writing and signed by the manager having profit and loss responsibility for the outcome of the negotiations in question. It may vary in form from a short informal memorandum to a more lengthy formal paper. In general the simpler and shorter the brief the smaller the risk of misunderstanding and the greater the chance that the instructions will be followed.

Although the preparation of the brief is the responsibility of management its terms must be acceptable to the team leader as representing feasible target at which to aim and allowing him sufficient latitude within which to negotiate. He and possibly other team members should participate in the formulation of the brief in the manner suggested on pp. 52–53.

The brief should:

1 Define the negotiating objective in terms of the major issues to be discussed.
2 State the minimum acceptable level for each of the major items.
3 Establish the time period within which the negotiations should be concluded.
4 Identify the team leader and other members of the negotiating team.
5 Set up the lines of communication and the reporting system.

The format of the Brief will be common to each of our negotiating situations, selling, procurement and contract dispute, although the details to be included will obviously vary. The example and notes which follow deal with a brief for a sales negotiating team about to go abroad to negotiate an export contract for which their company has earlier submitted a tender.

11.1 THE NEGOTIATING OBJECTIVE

Price level

The negotiating objective will usually be expressed in terms of the expected return on sales, taking into account the risks involved in performing the contract.[1] If any of these risks are changed then the degree to which the margin may be changed should also be expressed. The risks referred to are those which were listed earlier when the determination of the bid utility value was under discussion.

If it is assumed that the original tender was submitted with a margin on sales of 35%, this might be broken down as:

Commercial overheads	15%
Profit	12.5%
Risk contingency	5%
Negotiating margin	2.5%

It will be remembered that in arriving at the level of the first offer it was established that Party would submit a demand which was optimal in relation to his estimate of the concessions he would be compelled to make in favour of Opponent, in order to obtain the maximum likely concessions from Opponent, and the time it would take to achieve this outcome. Therefore it can be assumed that Party has settled on 2.5% as his estimate of the concession he will need to make to opponent in order to obtain a price which contains a margin of 32.5%, with the negotiations being completed within the validity period of the tender.

The negotiating objective on price level would be stated as: 'To achieve a margin of 32.5% within the validity period of the tender and without addition to the risks allowed for in the tender.'

The major risks for which allowance has been made in the build-up of the margin might be:

Terms of payment

The buyer's terms of payment are less favourable than those normally obtained by Party on export business. The down payment is only 5% and there is 10% retention money held during the two-year warranty period. Additional interest charges included in the commercial overheads are 2½%

Delay penalty

The delivery period requested by the buyer is four weeks shorter than Party would prefer and the penalty rate is 1% per week. The delivery quoted by Party in his tender is four weeks longer than the buyer's period and in addition Party has allowed in the risk contingency for penalty of 4%

Warranty
Party's normal warranty period is 12 months. Since the Buyer is asking for 24 months Party has included 1%.

The negotiating objective in relation to contractual terms might then be stated as:

1   Increase the down payment from 5% to 10%.
2   Eliminate the holding of retention money during the warranty period; offer instead a bank guarantee.
3   Secure the delivery period stated in the tender.
4   Obtain reduction in the warranty period to 12 months.

For each of these objective secured Party would be willing to grant the buyer a discount up to the contingency allowance included in the tender but only if such a reduction were demanded by the buyer. Altern- atively if such a reduction were not demanded by the buyer then, if necessary, any surplus contingency could be used either to secure some other advantage or to add to the discount on price level. The important words here are 'if demanded' and 'if necessary'. The negotiating brief would make it clear that Party does not give any concession voluntarily but only in response to pressure.

11.2 MINIMUM ACCEPTABLE TERMS
The negotiating brief for these might read.
Price level
Maximum reduction in profit after concession of the negotiating margin, provided that the negotiations are concluded within tender validity period is 5%.

No reduction permitted in risk contingency except against elimination of risk concerned.
Terms of payment
Buyers terms of payment can be accepted subject to commercial overheads remaining unchanged.
Delivery
Shorter delivery can be accepted provided penalty contingency retained.
Warranty
Longer warranty period can be accepted again provided that risk contingency secured.

11.3 TIME PERIOD FOR NEGOTIATIONS
Normally Party would only have allowed in his costing for the effect of time costs as defined on p. 148 up to the end of the validity period of his tender. Any delay in obtaining the contract after that date must

therefore necessarily erode his margin although, depending on the incidence of cost increases, particularly those relating to labour, the effect need not be linear.

However, the negotiating team should be given as much time as possible within which to complete the negotiations in order to avoid the incidence of time pressure (see p 306), and the trade off in the reduction in margin because of time costs and time spent on negotiation should be made clear. In the example the brief might state:

The tender validity expires within one month. Extension of validity would cost approx ½% for the first month and 1% per month after that. After three months it would be necessary to requote since delivery could no longer be maintained. Aim should be to conclude negotiations in 2 months at the maximum.

Time costs trade off:

1 month negotiating period	0% time costs
2 months	½%
3 months	1½%

11.4 THE NEGOTIATING TEAM

The brief should state the names and job titles of the team members and indicate any duties they will be required to perform outside of their own function. In the example the brief might read:

Team Leader: Mr Jones Export sales manager
Team members: Mr Brown Assistant manager system engineering
                        Mr Smith Assistant legal adviser

Mr Brown will cover all production aspects in addition to engineering and is responsible for obtaining instructions from the production manager for this purpose. Mr Smith will look after ECGD requirements and is responsible for obtaining necessary instructions from the export credit manager.

11.5 COMMUNICATIONS AND REPORTING

The brief might state:

Mr Jones will report to me on this negotiation and I will be responsible for advising functional and departmental heads of any issues affecting them. In my absence Mr Williams will assume this responsibility. No reports are expected, provided that negotiations can be concluded within the terms of the brief, until the team has been away for two weeks.

Signed ....
General Manager
Engineering Contracts Division

NOTE

1.   Contribution margin would be preferable but as noted earlier (see p. 122) the figure is unlikely to be available from the company's accounting system. Percentage margin rather than an actual amount is used since there are likely to be small changes in quantities of materials/services to be provided which will affect the total price. Only if these variations became large would the company normally wish to reconsider the percentage figure. If the value were reduced significantly then the percentage would be liable to be increased and vice versa.

12

THE NEGOTIATING PLAN

The functions of the negotiating plan are to:

1 Define the initial strategy
2 Develop the supporting arguments
3 Identify the data required to support such arguments
4 Allocate responsibility for the collection of such data
5 Decide on the location for the negotiations
6 Ensure that the appropriate administrative arrangements have been made

12.1 DEFINITION OF INITIAL STRATEGY

Party has submitted an offer

In relation to each issue which has been identified as forming part of the negotiating area, Party is likely to have at least some knowledge of Opponent's views. Obviously he knows that his own initial offer is not wholly acceptable. There are then broadly three possibilities:

1 Opponent has replied with proposals of his own. Alternatively, if Party has taken objection to a term of Opponent's call for bids, Opponent has stated that he insists on that term. In either event the negotiating area is defined.
2 From discussions with his agent or preliminary informal encounters with Opponent, Party has been advised on the items which Opponent disputes and why, but not the precise terms which Opponent is going to demand.
3 Party merely knows his own offer is in some respects unacceptable to Opponent.

In regard to 1, Party's initial strategy is to defend the position he has taken in his offer. Specifically he does not make any concessions (see p. 275).

With situations 2 and 3, whilst similarly defending his own position, Party must explore Opponent's views and seek to identify the width of the gap between the two sides and the intensity with which Opponent objects to Party's proposals.

In all three instances Party must seek to reassess his preliminary estimate of Opponent's concession factor. In the negotiating brief example Party would seek to establish whether or not his estimate of 2½% for the price concession factor and one month for the negotiating period was correct or not.

Party has received an offer
If Party has received an offer his initial strategy will depend upon whether or not he has already made any reply which defines the terms Party would be willing to accept.

1 Party has replied stating his own terms. The negotiating area is defined and Party's initial strategy is again to explore Opponent's position without making concessions.
2 Party has not replied with a statement of his own terms. Party's initial strategy is to persuade Opponent to reveal the strength of his own commitment to the terms of his offer, whilst making the minimum disclosure of his own position.

12.2 SUPPORTING ARGUMENTS
The actual arguments which Party will use to support his strategy on any issue will be particular to that issue and to the negotiation in question. An example may clarify the way in which it is suggested that Party should approach the problem. Let us take the issue referred to earlier in the previous section on the negotiating brief of the delivery period.

Party has tendered a longer period than that asked for in the call for bids. To a large degree, Party's selection of arguments will be dependent on his views about the strength of Opponent's commitment to the shorter period. If Party believes Opponent is not strongly committed and the shorter period was in the nature of a 'try-on' then Party will present a non-detailed factual statement on his design/ manufacturing/installation programme and state that, having re-viewed the position, he cannot shorten the period. He will not encourage detailed discussion on any particular section of the pro-gramme.

Going to the other extreme if Party believes Opponent is commit-ted, perhaps politically, to the shorter period so that any absolute denial of its acceptability would cause an emotional reaction with overall adverse consequences to Party, then his arguments must be rather different. Whilst still defending his original demand he would present the supporting programme in some detail in specific areas on which he was prepared to negotiate. In this way he would hope to lead Opponent into an integrative bargaining exercise on specific propos-als for shortening, say, the testing and shipping periods. Alternatively he might deliberately highlight a specfic area of high risk which would lead to a suggestion that the period could be shortened if Opponent were prepared to assume this risk himself, for example, interference to installation work due to bad weather. This latter type of approach is to be preferred if Opponent's commitment is genuinely political, and his only real concern is his ability to be able to say that the contract has been placed for the shorter period without the need to disclose the contractual provisions on which the delivery is based.

As a third alternative Party may find if Opponent's commitment is weaker than he thought that Opponent will ultimately give away and accept the longer period rather than assume some risk or obligation for himself. The argument 'We could agree to shorten the delivery period if you were prepared to . . .' is often more successful than the blunt rejection of Opponent's arguments.

The essential point is that whatever the issue the arguments are directed towards meeting Party's belief as to Opponent's views and problems and not related to Party's problems, which are no concern of Opponent. It is not a valid argument to say as a supplier that the price cannot be reduced because of the level of costs. The costs are the supplier's problem, not the buyer's. If the buyer wants a particular service, say new product development, or expects the supplier to take a particular contractual risk, it is a valid argument to say to the buyer that he must be willing to pay for it, since if the supplier does not undertake the service or contractual risk that becomes a problem for the buyer.

12.3 SUPPORTING DATA

From the nature of the argument to be presented will come the definition of the supporting data required. Continuing the delivery example, clearly a programme in PERT network or bar chart form would be needed. However, the actual periods allocated to certain activities would vary according to the decision reached on the type of argument to be presented. A checklist of the type of supporting data which might be required in each of the three negotiating situations is given in Appendix 6. The plan needs then to allocate responsibility for the collection for such data and its presentation in the format required by the negotiation.

12.4 THE LOCATION OF THE NEGOTIATIONS

For both sides there is usually a strong preference for 'playing at home'. The environment will be familiar, it is easier to bring in additional support, the 'home side' are in charge of the administrative arrangements including those for hospitality, there is the psychological advantage that 'they have come to you', and the saving in costs for hotels and air fares.

However, there are some advantages in 'playing away'. The

negotiators can devote their whole time to the negotiation without being distracted, it avoids the risk that Opponent can argue that he does not have authority since there is the option if he tries that of insisting on going to the top, the team leader does not have his own management on his back and is able to exercise a greater degree of freedom within the overall scope of his negotiating brief.

12.5 ADMINISTRATIVE ARRANGEMENTS

If Party is 'playing at home' then it is up to him to ensure that the arrangements for the meetings have been made in a way which is conducive to agreement being reached. Specific points to be considered are:

1 The choice of the meeting room. It should be large enough to accommodate comfortably all taking part, well ventilated and should not have a telephone.
2 There should be at least one side room which can be used for an adjournment meeting which should have a telephone.
3 A secretary should be available in a nearby office for taking messages, arranging for photo-copying and typing up draft proposals.
4 If appropriate visual aid facilities should be available and although most negotiators will have a pocket calculator with them, a larger machine with a print-out facility is often useful.
5 Refreshments should be ordered in such a way that they create natural breaks. Ideally they should be served in an ante-room to give a chance for informal discussions.
6 The table and seating plan should be worked out in advance. The authors own preference is to avoid having a 'head of the table' and to have the two sides opposite each other with the respective team leaders in the middle.

If the Party is 'playing away' then unless he is fortunate enough to have a subsidiary company operating in the territory or he can arrange facilities through his local agent, he must be prepared to operate on his own and to provide his own back-up. He should therefore give attention to the following:

1 Typing facilities. It is a great advantage if one member of the team can type reasonably well so that drafts and telexes, etc, can be produced quickly. A typed telex is much more acceptable to a foreign telex operator and therefore much more likely to be sent that day than one in an unfamiliar form of handwriting.
2 Headed note-paper and visiting cards. The latter may have to be specially produced to give the senior members of the team titles which will impress Opponent as to their status. In many countries a manager is a nothing compared to a director.

3 Staying at a hotel which has the best available business facilities. The team leader should if possible have a suite so that one room can be used for private discussions.
4 Reference data as suggested in Appendix 6. This should be supplemented by a file of newspaper and magazine cuttings appropriate to the project in which Party is interested, which is updated daily. A typical file might contain data on:
   (a) Economic situation in the country
   (b) Recent finance deals concluded or financial offers made on other projects
   (c) Inflation
   (d) Rates of pay for grades of local staff and labour
   (e) Union activities
   (f) Reports on the industry in which Party is operating
   (g) Local contractors of possible interest to Party
   (h) Changes in laws, insurance regulations, workers benefits, etc
5 Other portable office equipment such as typewriter, calculator with print-out facility, stapling machine, punch, file covers, typing ruled and graph paper, ruler, scissors, eraser and visiting card file. The author's own practice is to have one brief case which contains permently all of these items, other than the typewriter, and to add to it with experience, so that one can operate to the greatest degree practicable independently of local facilities which may either not be available, expensive or in the case of typing constitute a security risk.

13

CONDUCTING THE REHEARSAL

As the final stage of his preparations for the negotiation Party needs to test out his plan in a rehearsal for the live performance. If the time can be allocated and the importance of the negotiations justify it, the rehearsal should be made a formal negotiating session with a team representing Opponent drawn from the appropriate departments within Party's organization. It is surprising how often a session of this nature can develop more 'needle' than the real event.

13.1 VALUE OF THE REHEARSAL
The value of a mock negotiation of this nature is that not only will it expose any weaknesses in Party's negotiating plan, it will also constitute a training exercise for Party's negotiating team. The whole performance can be recorded on video-tape and later played back to expose deficiencies in technique of which the participants were totally unaware, for example, irritating mannerisms, poor control of facial expression, muddled presentation of arguments, excessive use of English colloquialisms in talking to foreigners.

This is the ideal and it is appreciated that time and expense may not permit it to be achieved, although I hold strongly the view that it is only by training of this nature that a company's success ratio in negotiation can be improved significantly. Considering its importance to a company's profitability it is remarkable that the need for training in negotiation continues largely to go unrecognized, except for the type of training which consists of learning from mistakes made in practice, the cost of which must exceed that of any training programme.

However, if a full session cannot be arranged the team leader should insist as a minimum on a colleague playing the part of a 'devil's advocate' and using the arguments which he thinks Opponent will adopt in order to attack Party's case. This may cause the team leader to recognize the need to change the presentation or strengthen certain arguments and identify the requirement for additional supporting data. Scrutiny by the 'devil's advocate' of such data which the team leader is intending to show Opponent will often reveal inadequacies or the inclusion of statements which Party would find embarrassing.

PART THREE

Structure and sequence of the negotiation

14

THE APPROACH

The actual conduct of the negotiation itself will now be considered. The approach will be partially normative, in the sense that it will seek to indicate ways in which Party, as a rational negotiator, should act so as to optimize the outcome in his favour, but reasoning will be based on assumptions as to the manner in which the negotiators for Opponent can be expected to behave, based on the practical experience of observed behaviour.

It is recognised that this means that the rules for Party may assume actions by Opponent which are less than optimal and that such rules would come therefore within the category of self-replacing decision rules as defined and discussed in Section 2.4. As such the approach could be criticized on the grounds that Opponent may be underestimated and that surely there is no right to assume that he is any less rational or skilled than Party.

Firstly it may be pointed out that the decision rules for Party will allow for wide gradations in Opponent's behaviour from the largely emotional to the largely rational, and with Opponent's choice of tactics varying from extremes of naivety to extremes of sophistication. Secondly that actual experience shows that large variations do exist in both the negotiator's motivation and negotiating skill, and that it is essential for Party to have the knowledge and ability to operate effectively against either end of the spectrum. Remembering that negotiation is not an end in itself, and allowing for the existence of opportunities for future retributive action, it can be as disastrous for Party to employ sophisticated tactics against a naive Opponent as the other way round.

14.1 STAGES OF THE NEGOTIATION
The period covered by the negotiation proper, as distinct from its planning, may be divided into five stages:

1 The opening
2 The review of the opening
3 The follow up
4 Identifying the bargain
5 Concluding the bargain

As Warr has pointed out, the stages of a negotiation may be considered as an example of the sequential phases through which any social group passes in the course of its development.[1] In stage 1 the negotiators are getting to know each other and identifying the issues involved. In stage 2 these issues are reviewed and the negotiating plan modified as necessary to take account of any factors disclosed in the opening of which Party had not previously been aware. As suggested by Warr this may well be a time of friction within the negotiating team, as the members come to realize the extent to which they may have to depart from their personal opinions if agreement is to be reached.[2] Stage 3 covers the broad period of bargaining in which concessions are made and advantages gained, so that the gap between the two sides is narrowed to the point at which Stage 4 begins and the form of the final bargain is identified. In stage 5 the last concessions are made and the bargain concluded.

Although the negotiation has been divided into these stages for the purpose of analysis, it is not suggested that in practice there are sharp dividing lines between them. One phase may overlap with another. But, by examining the primary activities on which the negotiators are involved, it should be possible at any time to determine the stage the negotiations have reached. It is most important that the negotiators themselves should know at which stage they are working so that they can direct their energies to the solution of the problems with which that stage is concerned, and not either anticipate the next stage too soon or leave one stage uncompleted when moving to the next. It is as wrong to start making concessions in the opening as it is to be trying still to identify the issues when looking for the form of the final bargain.

NOTES
1.   P. Warr, *Psychology and Collective Bargaining* (London: Hutchinson, 1973). The stages suggested by Warr are (1) getting organized, (2) breaking up, (3) accepting a common goal, (4) finding solutions, and (5) the final decision. Broadly allowing for the differences between collective bargaining and commercial negotiations these stages are in line with those suggested in this chapter.
2.   P. Warr, op. cit., p. 160.

15

THE OPENING

It is assumed that the preparation and planning for the negotiation has been carried out in the manner described in Part Two and that the time has now arrived for the initial presentation of Party's case in accordance with the terms of the negotiating plan. Party may be in the situation that he is required to either take the initiative and submit a proposal himself or to respond to one already provided by Opponent. In either event there are three possible ways in which he may proceed (although it may be found in practice that one or more of these are eliminated by the rules under which the negotiation is being conducted):

1 Submit a written proposal/answer without supplementing this by verbal discussion.
2 Submit a written proposal/answer to be supplemented by face to face discussions.
3 Present verbal proposals at a meeting.

15.1 WRITTEN PROPOSAL/ANSWER WITHOUT DISCUSSION

It is suggested that a written proposal/answer which is not to be supplemented by discussion should be submitted only when:

1 Party has no other choice under the rules of the negotiation, eg tendering to a strict public authority which does not permit discussions with tenderers during the adjudication period.
2 Party intends the written proposal/answer to be his initial move and also his last. An offer of discussions, whether expressed or implied from the wording of the proposal/answer, will be taken by Opponent as a clear indication that the terms offered do not represent Party's final position. If they do, or Party wishes to give the impression that they do, the document should be complete in itself and drafted in such a way that:
   (a) If it is a proposal, it can be replied to on a simple yes/no basis without the need for clarification.
   (b) If it is an answer, it can be accepted without qualification in the terms in which it has been presented.

Whilst a written proposal has the obvious advantages of being complete, and permitting the expression of complex ideas in a detailed form which Opponent can read and reread until these have been fully assimilated, it has certain serious disadvantages:

1   It is a permanent record of Party's adoption of a certain line of action. As such it will give rise to a feeling of commitment and make it more difficult for Party at a later stage to make concessions.[1] This difficulty will be reinforced if Party has circulated the document widely within his own organization.[2]

2   Any written presentation is necessarily 'cold' and although English is a wonderfully flexible language it is often difficult to choose words which convey precisely the meaning intended and avoid misunderstandings or the giving of offence. This becomes even more difficult when the document has to be translated and the finer shades of meaning will inevitably become lost in the process.

3   People tend to use more formal expressions and therefore state their positions with greater apparent firmness in written as opposed to verbal proposals.[3] Again, if the proposal is to be circulated within Party's own organization, Party may feel it necessary to defend or explain his position at length which in turn will increase the degree of commitment he feels to that position.

As an example of the difference between written and verbal expressions of the same idea compare the two statements:

We regret that we are unable to see our way clear to . . .

I'm sorry, but I don't really see how we are going to . . .

Putting aside for the moment considerations of the need to maintain good interpersonal relationships between negotiators as a basis for a long-term continuing business relationship between Party and Opponent, it can be argued that the extent to which the use of formal communications is a disadvantage will vary inversely with the strength of Party's case. Experiments conducted by Morely and Stephenson have shown that the stronger Party's case the more he stands to gain from a formality in communications between the two sides.[4]

The more formal the communication medium the more the negotiations will be centred upon objective interparty issues and the less time will be spent by the negotiators on self-presentation. Conversely the less formal the communication system, the more the negotiators are dealing face to face and the less easy it is for the stronger side to remain totally adamant and refuse any concessions. Interpersonal feelings between negotiators will tend to create what has been termed the *norm of reciprocity*, so that to some degree concessions will be made on emotional grounds which it would be difficult to justify on a strictly objective appraisal.[5] It is much easier to say no by letter, or even over the telephone, than it is to a person's face, particularly if that person is someone with whom one has already developed some form of interpersonal relationship.

However, reintroduction of the factor of a continuing business relationship between Party and Opponent reduces significantly the value to Party of this approach. The deliberate minimization of the element of interpersonal contact will prevent Party from reaching informal agreements or understandings with Opponent, will deprive Party of access to information which Opponent is only willing to release informally, and result in the contracts concluded being interpreted and applied strictly according to their legal terms.

Each of these factors must prove detrimental to Party's long-term interests. For instance, he can never be sure when the time will come that the only real safeguard which he has against the imposition of severe claims/penalties will be the goodwill existing between himself and Opponent; goodwill which has arisen out of the multitude of interpersonal relationships developed at all levels between his own and Opponent's staff.[6]

Given therefore the expectation of a continuing business relationship between Party and Opponent it is suggested that Party should:

1 As a norm seek to develop close interpersonal relationships with the negotiators for Opponent.
2 When the issue is significant, and he does possess the stronger case, increase to some degree the formality of the negotiation, perhaps by introducing a negotiator who is less well known to Opponent and who is sufficiently senior to merit Opponent's respect.
3 Conversely, if Party has the weaker case then he should maximize the informality of the negotiations, eg seek face-to-face discussions between negotiators whose interpersonal relationships are the best developed.

15.2 WRITTEN PROPOSAL/ANSWER SUPPLEMENTED BY VERBAL DISCUSSION

The advantages to be derived by Party from the submission of written proposals in advance of a meeting with Opponent are as follows:

1 They will provide an agenda for and give coherence to the discussion.
2 They will enable Opponent to consider the points raised, prepare for them and seek prior claification of any items on which he is in doubt.
3 If the proposals embody any complex drafting, they allow this to

be studied and, as necessary, permit advice to be taken from specialists who would not normally attend the discussions.

4   They provide a definite expression of the commitments into which Party is willing to enter.

By defining the issues in advance, and giving time for preparation by Opponent of his negotiating plan, the submission by Party of prior written proposals can mean a greater chance of decisions being reached in the meeting, and within a shorter time than would otherwise be the case.

This will only be so if the gap between Party's proposals and those of Opponent is narrow and there is a substantial overlap between their respective minimum objectives. If the gap is wide, and little or no overlap exists between the respective minimum negotiating objectives, then the submission of written proposals in advance, to which Party now feels a degree of commitment, will have the reverse effect, making agreement more difficult to reach and certainly prolonging the negotiations.

These conclusions are supported by the experimental work of Bass to which reference has already been made (see p. 218). He found that where the two sides had both prepared strategy plans then, provided their strategies overlapped, this produced quicker results than if no such prior planning had taken place. However if their strategies were largely opposing, and no initial overlap existed in their minimum objectives, then the result was either deadlock or the negotiating time was substantially extended. He attributed these results to the degree of commitment which the negotiators felt to the strategy plans they had developed in their own groups. It is submitted that the effect of a feeling of commitment will be largely the same, regardless of how the commitment has arisen.

A possible disadvantage of the presentation of written proposals in advance, in addition to those referred to on p. 270, is that giving Opponent advance notice enables him to prepare his plans with that much more knowledge of the line which Party intends to follow. If the negotiators for Opponent are inexperienced or naive, then giving them no advance warning may tempt them to deal with the issue unprepared, rather than admit their on inadequacy, and as a consequence lead them to concede more than they would have done had they been forewarned.

However, any advantage gained by Party in this way will only be temporary if the negotiators for Opponent, either on further reconsideration by themselves, or after censure by their own management, decide that they have been 'tricked'. This can only result in their passing through the resentment level (discussed on p. 201) and feeling a sense of continuing personal antagonism against the negotiators from Party whom they consider to be responsible.

15.3 VERBAL PROPOSALS ONLY

The advantages to Party of relying wholly on a verbal presentation at a meeting without the submission of any prior written statement are as follows:

1   Total flexibility. The negotiator can change his mind right up to the moment when he deals with the actual point concerned and even then he can strengthen or weaken his treatment of the issue dependent on his judgement of how the negotiations are going.
2   Exploration before commitment. The negotiator can test the reaction of Opponent to a certain line before irrevocably committing himself to it.
3   Use of emotion. The negotiator can use emotion in order to emphasize a particular point or to disarm criticism and avoid giving offence.
4   The association by Opponent of the integrity of the proposals with the personal integrity of Party's negotiator. A person's belief in the validity of a statement is strongly influenced by his belief in the veracity of the person making the statement.

Bacon expressed much the same thoughts when he suggested that to 'deal in person is good when a man's face breedeth regard; or in tender cases where a man's eye upon the countenance of him with whom he speaketh may give him direction how far to go: and generally where a man will reserve to himself liberty either to disavow or to expound'.[7]

The disadvantages which are inherent in the concept of flexibility are:

1   Use by the negotiator of Opponent's actions, remarks or even facial expressions, as a cue to the level which the negotiator selects for any demand and the firmness with which he pursues it. Lacking any definitive commitment in the form of a written proposal known to Opponent, the negotiator for Party must rely primarily on personalistic motivation—his own level of aspiration—for providing him with support. To that extent he is much more vulnerable to determined resistance by Opponent which, as discussed earlier, may cause a progressive reduction in the negotiator's level of aspiration.
2   It is easy for the negotiator to lose the thread of his argument and to be diverted on to side issues.
3   It is difficult to present complex points involving figures or detailed drafting without at least some written back-up.
4   Misunderstandings may arise and apparent agreement be reached without genuine understanding. This is particularly likely to happen if the parties do not speak the same native language.

5   Not having had advance warning Opponent may listen politely and then withdraw until he has had the opportunity to consider the points made and prepare his answer.

15.4 CONCLUSIONS

Drawing the various advantages and disadvantages of the three possible methods of presentation together the following guide lines are suggested:

1   A written statement should only be submitted, whether as a prelude to discussions or not, if:

 (a) It is known that it will not give offence. If there is any doubt on this point then the draft, or relevant parts of it, should be cleared informally with the chief negotiator for Opponent before formal submission.

 (b) The negotiator is either totally committed to the points made in the proposal, so that he is prepared to lose the bargain rather than withdraw, or he is indifferent to withdrawing the points or modifying them, if this is necessary to secure the bargain.

2   If no prior written proposal is made then a statement summarizing the main items of Party's presentation and giving details of figures and particular points of drafting should be available both for use by the negotiator and as a handout (possibly in a censored edition) for Opponent. To the extent that this brief has been prepared as part of the preparation of the negotiating plan, and endorsed by Party's management, it will provide the negotiator with a significant commitment and a strong reinforcement of his level of aspiration.

3   Any written proposal, whether given in advance or not, should refer only to those points which the negotiator wishes to disclose at that time in the negotiation, since agreement on point A may be difficult or impossible to obtain if Opponent realizes in advance the line the negotiator intends to take on associated point B, especially if B raises emotional issues.

 Where a draft contract is being tabled for negotiation this may be difficult to avoid but certain clauses can still be left blank to be supplied later, the drafting of these only being finalized when the attitude of Opponent to the remainder of the draft as presented has been discovered.

15.5 EXPOSING THE NEGOTIATING AREA

Party's objective at the opening stage of the negotiations may be described as exploration without commitment. He wants to ensure that the whole of the area to be covered by the negotiation is exposed, together with Opponent's views on each point. But at the same time he does not want to be drawn into making too firm a commitment of his own position on any individual issue; specifically he will wish to avoid at this stage any partial agreement or concessions.

Figure 15:1 below is a suggested guide to the way in which the negotiator should behave in the opening phase.

Do	Do not
When a written statement has been submitted by Opponent	
1 Challenge each point, asking why Opponent made it.	1 Speculate on Opponent's reasons or put words into his mouth.
2 Appear ignorant, even if this is not true, and let Opponent justify his case.	2 Try to be clever and show depth of knowledge by answering questions put to Opponent.
3 Note his answers and reserve the position.	3 Agree immediately even if agreement will be reached in the end.
4 Make certain each point has been fully understood even if this means going over the ground twice. This applies particularly if native languages are not the same.	4 Snatch at what appears to be a favourable bargain or interpretation of Opponent's views.
5 Test out the strength of Opponent's views of each point so that later on the probability of Opponent sticking to his position under pressure can be assessed.	5 Be drawn into lengthy arguments on any individual point from which it may be difficult to withdraw.
6 Be aware of the interrelationship between different contract points and the possible counter arguments which will be developed if success is achieved on any particular one.	6 Be conscious only of the particular point under discussion and of the immediate benefits to be derived from succeeding on that point alone.
7 Appear calm and quiet.	7 Betray feelings by showing anger, surprise or delight at Opponent's remarks.
8 Correct Opponent if he is proceeding on a false belief as to a factual position for which you are responsible.	8 Improve Opponent's judgement unless it is advantageous.

Figure 15:1 Guide to negotiator's behaviour in the opening phase

When Party has submitted a written proposal

1 Limit answers to Opponent's questions to the minimum and seek to persuade Opponent into talking again as soon as possible.

1 Elaborate at length on motives.

2 Test out the strength of Opponent's objections by seeing if he will withdraw them without requiring any corresponding concessions.

2 Concede anything or be drawn into trade-off negotiations before all points have been discussed.

3 Behave generally as described in points 6, 7 and 8 above.

When no written statement has been submitted by either side

1 Identify all the points to be discussed.

1 Let the discussions ramble on without any defined order.

2 Cover each point in sufficient depth for both sides to be aware of each other's position.

2 Concentrate the discussion on one point to the exclusion of all others.

3 Keep the discussions exploratory.

3 Be drawn into definite commitments either in the form of making a firm concession or taking up a position from which it may be difficult later to withdraw.

4 Behave generally as described in points 6, 7 and 8 above.

Figure 15:1 (concluded)

NOTES
1.   See P. C. Vitz and W. R. Kite, 'Factors affecting conflict and negotiation within an alliance', *Journal of Experimental Social Psychology*, vol. 6 (1970), pp. 233–47, in which the authors describe experiments in bargaining conducted by telephone and by written communication.
2.   Of course, this may be done deliberately by Party as a negotiating tactic (see p 376).
3.   This was certainly the case in the experiments referred to by P. C. Vitz and W. R. Kite in note 1. In my own negotiating experience, there is a continual need to review and rephrase the drafts of written proposals to try to overcome this tendency to harshness of expression

and the inclusion of gratuitous phrases of exaggeration. A quote from one of the written messages in Vitz and Kite's experiment serves as an example: 'I cannot agree that *under any circumstances* our contributions are to be based upon resources'. The words italicized add nothing to the argument, are unlikely to be true, and are almost certain to annoy the other side. All they achieve is to make it more difficult for the person initiating the message to negotiate away from that position in the future.

4.   E. Morely and G. M. Stephenson, 'Interpersonal and interparty exchange: a laboratory simulation of an industrial negotiation at the plant level', *British Journal of Psychology*, vol. 60 (no. 4, 1969), pp. 543–45, and 'Formality in negotiations: a validation study', *British Journal of Psychology*, vol. 61 (No. 3, 1970), pp. 383–84.

5.   This norm states that (1) people should help those who have helped them and (2) people should not injure those who have helped them. A. W. Gouldner, 'The norm of reciprocity', *American Sociological Review* (April 1960). Opportunities will arise during the development of interpersonal relations between negotiators for one to be of assistance to the other even in such simple matters as arranging transport or accommodation, providing secretarial facilities, etc. Such assistance at once places the recipient under some obligation to reciprocate.

6.   A. W. Gouldner in his article 'The norm of reciprocity', *American Sociological Review*, vol. 25 (1960), p. 161, suggests that one important function which the norm performs is that of establishing stability given significant power differences between two persons and groups. The invoking of this norm by Party, as a contractor, in the relationship between himself and a purchasing authority is a clear example of this. Even if Party's first order defence of non-contractual liability fails, he can still rely on the second order defence: 'You should not impose the penalty because of the assistance which I provided to you in connection with . . .'.

Party may also suggest that he will withdraw in the future from his previous willingness to provide benefits if the purchaser does not recognize the moral obligations arising from those provided in the past. Assistance and benefits in this connotation do not refer to gifts or bribes but to services which a contractor regularly undertaking work for a purchaser performs without specific charge, eg technical consultancy on maintenance problems or the development of new specifications, sponsoring attendance at technical conferences. See also S. Macauley, 'Non-contractual relations in business', *American Sociological Review*, vol. 28 (1963), pp. 55–66 for further examples.

It could also be implied (Gouldner does not mention this) that the norm of reciprocity would only be invoked provided that the person doing so considered that he himself was without significant normal guilt. Thus the contractor would not utilize his second line of defence, if the delay giving rise to the penalty claim was clearly due to his own negligence, but only if the default was in the nature of a legal technicality. On this hypothesis the reciprocation extends also to the social character of the acts involved.

Macauley makes somewhat the same point when he refers to a supplier having a commitment to conform to his customer's expectations which is largely independent of legal sanctions. The supplier is expected to produce a good product and stand behind it.

7.   Sir Francis Bacon, 'Of negotiating', in *Essays of Sir Francis Bacon* (London: Grant Richards, 1902), p. 134.

16

REVIEW OF THE OPENING

If it is assumed that Party is presenting the initial proposal then at the end of the opening phase Party should be in a position to:

1 Know those parts of his offer which Opponent is likely to accept.
2 Know those parts which Opponent is unlikely to accept.
3 Deduce, from the line taken by Opponent in his criticism of Party's offer and from Party's own question of Opponent, the strength of Opponent's opposition on any issue.
4 Predict the general form of the optimum bargain to Party on each issue or groups of related issues which Opponent is likely to accept.

Before proceeding further with the negotiations, therefore, Party should first review the results achieved from the opening phase and decide into which of the following three categories the negotiations can be placed:

1 A bargain acceptable to both sides is immediately identifiable.
2 A bargain acceptable to both sides is foreseeable but will require further negotiations to achieve.
3 No bargain is foreseen which would be both acceptable to Opponent and would meet Party's minimum negotiating objective.

16.1 BARGAIN IMMEDIATELY IDENTIFIABLE
This is the simplest case and the one in which Party may be tempted to merge the opening phase into the later commitment stages of the negotiation without allowing the opportunity for intermediate bargaining. Sensing the narrowness of the gap between his own position and that of Opponent, Party may jump at once to the point of making proposals for a final settlement.

Whilst recognizing the temptation, it is one which for the following reasons Party should resist:

1 By making an immediate proposal, which must represent some concession from his initial offer, Party may encourage Opponent to believe that by prolonging the negotiations he can achieve

further concessions from Party.

2   By appearing over eager Party may lead Opponent to believe that Party has some personal reasons for wanting early agreement. Again this would suggest to Opponent that he could achieve more by holding out longer.

3   Unless Party retracts, any further negotiations will start from the level of his settlement proposals which can only be disadvantageous to Party. However, the withdrawal of any offer must create emotional antagonism towards Party and lead Opponent to demand more than he would have done otherwise, as a penalty on Party for his behaviour. Either way Party will stand to lose.

Accordingly even if the bargain is immediately identifiable Party should still allow time for the working out of the negotiating process. This proposition may be illustrated with a simple example.

Suppose that Party has made an initial offer of 100 to which Opponent has responded with a counter offer of 90. If asked separately their belief as to the settlement figure it is highly probable that both would reply 95. If Party makes an immediate offer of 95 it is likely that Opponent, for the reasons given above, will respond with an offer to split the difference at 97.5.

On the other hand if Party's first negotiating proposal is 92.5 to which Opponent responds with 97.5, thus establishing a pattern of mutual concessions, Party can then propose a further mutual concession of 2.5 so arriving at a final bargain of 95.

Following his review of the opening, it is proposed that Party should decide on some intermediate step which will:

1   Act as a signpost to Opponent of the form of the final bargain.

2   Provide the opportunity for Opponent to make a responsive concession.

3   Allow Party to judge his next move according to whether Opponent makes a responsive concession or not.

4   Commit Party to the minimum concession only which is necessary to obtain the desired concession from Opponent.

16.2 BARGAIN FORESEEABLE

Review of the negotiating area

Provided that the opening sessions have fulfilled their primary objective of disclosing all the items to be covered by the negotiations, it should now be possible to identify the total negotiating area. This may be considered graphically as being formed in length by the points to be negotiated and in height by the distance separating Party from Opponent. Assuming for the moment that each issue can be expressed in terms of its financial significance to Party, a series of rectangles of varying heights will be obtained which when placed side by side will constitute the negotiating area.

This is illustrated in Figure 16:1 which is based on the negotiation of a contract between Party (a supplier) and Opponent (a buyer) in which there are four major items under discussion: price, terms of payment, delay penalty and warranty. Opponent's initial offer, ie the bargain which Party could make now, is represented by £0 on the horizontal axis. Party's initial offer is represented by the upper level of each rectangle (the width of the rectangle has no financial significance).

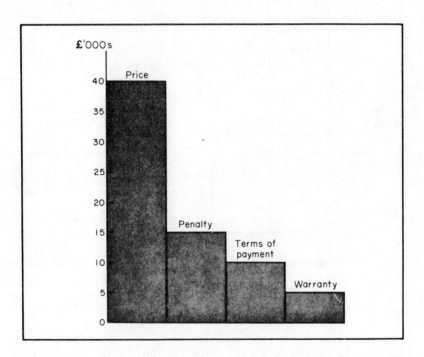

Figure 16:1 The negotiating area: initial position

The negotiating area is made up of four sections:

1 Price: £40 000
2 Terms of payment: £10 000
3 Penalty: £15 000
4 Warranty: £5 000

The total difference between the two sides is £70 000. If now as a result of further discussions the gap is narrowed, this is shown by reducing the size of the bargaining areas as illustrated in Figure 16:2 in which Party has made a concession of £10 000 and Opponent one of £5 000, on price, and Party has made a concession of £5 000 on penalty.

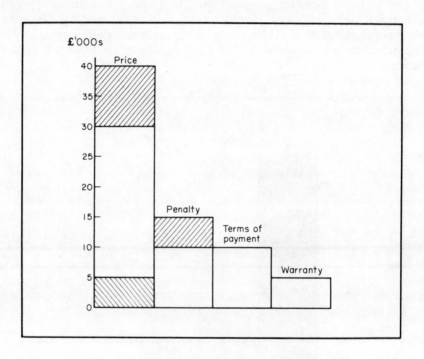

Figure 16:2 The negotiating area: after negotiation

The advantages of a visual presentation of this form, particularly as an aid to management briefing, are:

1   It gives an immediate picture of the scope of the negotiation in terms of the issues to be negotiated and their financial consequences.
2   It shows clearly the relative financial values to Party of the differing issues and the significance of each to the bargain as a whole.
3   As the bargaining proceeds and the gap between the two sides is narrowed the effect is easily indicated at any time and the updated chart can form the basis of any management review.

It is not, of course, practical to treat all bargaining issues in this way, since with certain contract clauses, eg *force majeure*, the differences cannot easily be expressed in direct financial terms. For these issues it is suggested that the format of the review should be a chart on which the primary differences between the two sides are highlighted on a side-by-side comparison.

Resistance points

Already it has been indicated that the degree of resistance which will be offered by either side on any substantive issue is not a linear function over the scale between the opening demand and the point at which agreement is just preferred to no bargain. Within the negotiating area therefore, both as a whole and in relation to each major issue, there will be a number of resistance points to which the intensity of party's adherence will vary considerably.[1]

Therefore as part of the review stage, based on his original planning and what he has learned from the opening, Party should seek to establish the resistance points for each major issue. Later information gained from Opponent's behaviour may cause Party to change this assessment but it is essential that he starts off with a clear concept of his own plan and his own intentions. In deciding on the degree of resistance which he offers at any point, Party will consider two values. Firstly, his valuation of the expected cost of making the concession demanded by Opponent compared to the consequences which Party would expect to ensue from his not making the concession. Secondly, his belief about the value which Opponent attaches to securing that concession, and Opponent's estimate of his chance of success.

In assessing these values Party will make an estimate of:

1 The loss he would suffer, either now or in the future, if he were to concede the point.
2 The probability of incurring the loss were he to make the concession.
3 The loss he would suffer, if by maintaining his resistance, this were to result in the negotiations ending in no bargain.
4 The probability of the negotiations ending in no bargain were he not to make the concession.
5 The value to him of the bargain without making the concession.[2]

He will then combine these estimates into the two equations given below which establish the expected values of the two alternative courses of action, *concede* and *not concede*.

EV of concede = Value of the bargain without the concession	−	Conditional loss from making the concession	×	Probability of the loss occurring[3]

| EV of not concede = Conditional loss from no bargain | × | Probability of no bargain if concession not made | + | Value of the bargain without the concession | × | Probability of bargain if no concession made |

Further information on the construction of these equations and the points to be taken into account in their application are given in Section 16.4.

This method may be applied to the example given in Figure 16:1. It is assumed that the value to Party of his original offer was £50 000 and that of no bargain was –£10 000. Party then selects, say, three possible concession steps, estimates at each step the subjective probability of no bargain should he refuse to make the concession, and calculates the expected value of the two courses of action. The results are as shown in Figure 16:3.

Concession step	Value of concede	Probability of no bargain	Expected value of not concede
£'000s	£'000s		£'000s
50–45	45	0.7	8
45–40	40	0.5	17.5
40–35	35	0.2	30

Figure 16:3 Comparison of the value of concede and the expected value of not concede

On the evidence of this figure Party would be expected to:

1 Fix a final resistance point at £35 000 and not to concede below that. This would still be so even if he would prefer a bargain at £30 000 to no bargain.
2 Set up a resistance point between £40 000 and £35 000 from which he would only concede under great pressure.
3 Establish a strong line of resistance around £40 000.
4 Be prepared to concede to £40 000 without too much hesitation provided that his concession were being reciprocated by Opponent.

Applying the conclusions drawn from Figure 16:3 to the diagram in Figure 16:1 the review would now show the negotiating area for the price factor broken down into a series of steps, corresponding to the resistance points selected. If the same is done for Opponent and the two price rectangles set side by side, the result is as shown in Figure 16.3. Clearly this latter diagram indicates that although a bargain is possible the negotiations will be concentrated primarily within the narrow limits of the shaded area and will be protracted.

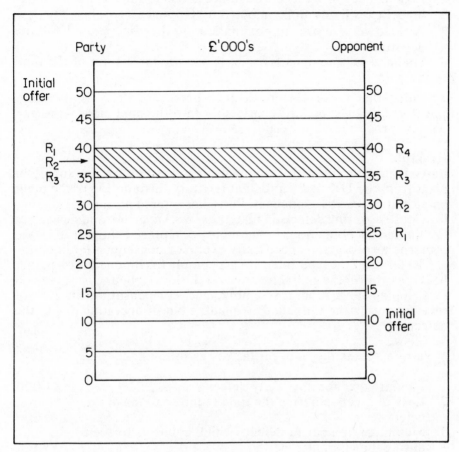

Figure 16:4 Resistance points on price for Party and Opponent

Because of this it would in practice be wise to check the conclusion of the review by substituting utility for monetary values and taking time costs into account in the manner described on p. 158.

The same type of approach is applied to the other negotiating areas and an example which follows relates to warranty costs and consequential liability. Finally all the areas are brought together to ensure that the negotiating plan with which Party moves forward into the next phase takes account of the total concessions which he foresees as being necessary to achieve the preferred outcome.

At the conclusion of the review stage Party should have achieved the following objectives:

1   Defined the negotiating area.

2   Established his points of resistance and made an estimate of those he believes likely to be adopted by Opponent.
3   Arrived at a close approximation of the time period for the negotiation.
4   Updated his previous forecast of the probable form of the final bargain.

Provided that these objectives have been met Party is then in a position to move forward confidently into the next-stage—the bargaining proper.

Example
Party is negotiating with Opponent for a contract for the supply of plant from the UK to a far distant territory, installation of the plant being undertaken by Opponent. Party has offered his normal guarantee clause covering defects in materials, workmanship and design but has limited his obligations to the supply of replacement parts CIF the overseas territory and specifically excluded consequential liability.

The terms of the guarantee are acceptable to Opponent except that he is pressing for the guarantee to cover the local labour costs involved in stripping down and reassembly, and compensation for loss of revenue during the time that the plant is out of operation due to the defect.

Party assesses the relevant factors as follows:

1	Labour costs for any likely defect	£1 000
2	Loss of revenue during the time required to make the defect good	£10 000
3	Maximum number of defects which could be forseen during the guarantee period	3
4	Probability assessment based on anticipated operating conditions of three such defects	70%
5	Contribution margin which would be earned by contract award	£50 000
6	Loss which will be incurred if contact not obtained	£20 000
7	Probability of loss of contract if Party does not agree to request for inclusion of labour costs in the guarantee	80%
8	Probability of loss of contract if Party does not agree to the inclusion of consequential damages	20%

Party requires to decide on the degree of resistance which he will offer to Opponent's request.

Inclusion in the guarantee of labour costs
Expected value of concede $= £50\,000 - (£1000 \times 3 \times 0.7) = £50\,000 - £2100 = £47\,900$
Expected value of not concede $= (-£20\,000 \times 0.8) + (£50\,000 \times 0.2) = -£16\,000 + £10\,000 = -£6\,000$

Clearly Party would be willing to make the concession although equally he would seek to secure some concession from Opponent in return.

Inclusion of consequential liability

Expected value of concede=£50 000–(1×3×0.7)+(£10 000×3×0.7)=£50 000–£23 100=£26 9000

Expected value of not concede =(–£20 000×0.2)+(£47 900×0.8)=–£4000+£38 300=£34 300

Party should now take the decision to resist extremely strongly Opponent's proposal that Party should be liable for consequential damages arising out of a defect during the guarantee period.

However, it is noted that the expected values from the two equations would be approximately equal if the probability of losing the contract by refusing to make the concession were to increase to 30%. It might be argued therefore that, if as the negotiation proceeds Party becomes more convinced than before that Opponent would not place the contract with Party unless he makes the concession, then Party should at some point prefer the strategy concede.

Before that conclusion can be reached it is necessary to compare an expected value of the contribution margin for the contract of £26 900 with Party's negotiating objective and the point at which he would prefer no bargain.

It would also be possible for Party through his negotiating behaviour to influence Opponent in his decision. Opponent will already know that he is asking for a major concession. If Party remains firm, so indicating that he does not believe Opponent will break off negotiations for failure to obtain the concession, then Opponent is likely to continue to probe Party's defences but without making any definitive commitment which would restrict his choice of action. Opponent's decision will reflect his belief as to Party's belief in what he, Opponent, is going to do.

16.3 NO BARGAIN FORESEEABLE

It happens not infrequently that as a result of the review of the opening it becomes clear that no bargain is foreseeable within the terms of the negotiator's current authority. If the negotiator finds himself in this position there are three possibilities open to him:

1 Break off negotiations and withdraw.
2 Continue and seek revised authority.
3 Influence opponent to seek revised authority.

Break off negotiations

No negotiator likes to break off discussions particularly if, as a supplier, he knows that there are competitors waiting in the wings only too eager to take his place. So this is a last resort which at this stage in the negotiations should be selected by Party, whether as a supplier or a buyer, only if *all* the following conditions are satisfied:

1 ' Party knows that he is in a strong position and that Opponent must contact him again if the business is to proceed.
2   Party believes that this is the only way in which to convince Opponent to change his mind.
3   The issues involved are fundamental and if Opponent will not give way then Party genuinely would prefer no bargain.

Later, of course, Party may have no option but to withdraw if he is satisfied that Opponent will never concede on issues on which Party would rather face the consequences of no bargain than accept. But this is a conclusion to which Party should come slowly and with reluctance. Few statements made early in a negotiation should be taken at their face value.

The same principles should govern Party's conduct in a case of contract dispute. As indicated earlier (see Secton 4.4) few firms like the idea of taking their disputes to law or arbitration. The difficulties and costs involved in obtaining and enforcing a favourable judgement are too formidable especially if the contract is for export. No matter how great the problems or the degree of patience required the attempt to arrive at a negotiated settlement should be continued until all hope is lost.

Continue and seek revised authority
This the more normal course for Party to follow. The negotiation is kept going on minor issues while the negotiator communicates with his management and seeks a revision to his authority which he believes will be sufficient to secure eventual agreement. In referring the issue back to management, the negotiator will be expected to make his own personal recommendations to management as to the action they should take, based on the range of bargains which he forsees as being possible to achieve, the time it would take to do so and the value to Party of such bargains in comparison with that of no-bargain. Because of his proximity to the negotiating table and to Opponent, the negotiator must be careful, when expressing his views, to avoid becoming so emotionally involved with securing agreement, or identifying himself so closely with Opponent's viewpoint, that he loses objectivity. It is only too easy for a negotiator widely separated from his home base in terms of time and distance to 'go native'.[4]

The interesting point arises as to whether the negotiator should allow Opponent to be aware that he is seeking revised authority or should endeavour to conceal this fact.

There is the obvious disadvantage that by disclosing his actions the negotiator admits that his company may not be totally committed to the position which he as the negotiator had adopted, and implies that their value system may be such that they would prefer making at least some concession to Opponent's viewpoint rather than accept the outcome of no bargain.

Having made this admission once, the negotiator must expect that Opponent will not in future, attach the same degree of belief in the negotiator's firmness of purpose, especially if management's answer is to relax the restrictions previously placed on the negotiator's powers. Naturally, this relaxation of restrictions becomes known to Opponent, at least in principle if not in degree, through the manner in which the negotiator subsequently conducts his case. Opponent will become more inclined to doubt the negotiator's word and to insist on his referring back any issues of significance. Clearly, if this process of reference back and amendment to the negotiator's power is repeated too many times, the negotiator's position will be destroyed.

To prevent this happening Party's management must demonstrate their support for the negotiator and their general commitment to the terms which he is seeking to secure. They may do this by:

1 Sending written messages of support to the negotiator which he can either show openly to Opponent or allow him to 'discover' them.
2 Selectively refusing to make any concessions. The negotiator deliberately refers back (and allows Opponent to know he has done so) an issue on which it has already been predetermined that Party's management would not depart from the negotiator's stand.
3 Demonstrating that any concession had to be secured from the highest authority within the company and must be treated as a total exception. Again the negotiator should be provided with evidence that this is so in a form which he can produce for Opponent.
4 Sending out a 'hard-line' support man from head office to take the pressure off the negotiator and to prove that Party, as a company, solidly supports the negotiator in the job which he is doing.

A related point is the effect of Opponent's knowledge that the negotiator is seeking revised authority based on his estimation of the negotiator as a person with whom to deal. Amongst sophisticated bargainers it is well accepted that an individual negotiator does not possess *carte blanche* to deal on any terms he chooses. There are always limits placed on his authority and provided that these appear reasonable to Opponent he is not likely to think any the worse of the negotiator because he becomes aware of their existence. He will not consider that his pride or status have been offended because he has been called upon to bargain with a negotiator who is acting under instructions.

However, this is not always so with unsophisticated negotiators, especially those whose own authority is largely absolute either because they are sole proprietors of their own business or princes of their territory. They may react emotionally to any admission by the negotiator that he must refer back on any issue for further instructions, and demand that if *he* does not possess the necessary authority then Party should send someone who does.

If this difficulty was foreseen in advance then it would be expected that Party would send someone who was sufficiently senior in the company, with sufficiently wide terms of reference and enough technical support, to be able to complete the negotiations without the need for reference back, even if ultimately this means no bargain. It is stressed that possessing wide terms of reference is not a matter of merely having the authority to make concessions; it is having the authority to make judgements as to whether the terms on which agreement is possible are to be preferred to no agreement at all.

If the problem was not foreseen in advance, and the negotiator does not in consequence possess the necessary authority, then three choices are open to him:

1 Admit his position and risk the strong possibility that he will be asked to withdraw.
2 Exceed his authority.
3 Seek to communicate with his management without this becoming known to Opponent.

It is obviously impossible to lay down a single rule for deciding which of those three choices is the correct one in every case. However, the first preference would be for choice 3 but, if this was judged impractical, then choice 2 would be selected. The reason for avoiding any admission of lack of authority, and being compelled to withdraw, is that this would place any other negotiator who is brought in subsequently in a very difficult position. The very fact that another negotiator had been brought in would imply that Party was willing to make, at least in part, the concessions which Opponent was demanding.

One advantage that the negotiator may be able to secure by allowing Opponent to know that he is waiting for revised authority is that he can use the waiting time to identify and collect together all other significant issues which are in dispute and on which he requires concessions from Opponent. When he does receive the revised authority, the negotiator exchanges these concessions from Opponent for the ones which Opponent wants and which are the subject of the revised authority. During the waiting time, the more the negotiator has been able to build up in the mind of Opponent's negotiator the enormity of the concession for which he is asking, the higher the exchange price Party will be able to secure. On one occason in which I was involved in a situation of this type the chief negotiator for Opponent replied to the terms of the exchange proposal with the question: 'Mr Marsh, you want the lot?' to which the reply was simply 'Yes.'

Obviously if the request for further authority is refused and Opponent remains adamant then the negotiator has no further options open to him; he must withdraw.

Influence Opponent to seek revised authority

As a course of action this is often used in conjunction with the two courses just discussed rather than on its own. Indeed the primary aim of breaking off the negotiations is to compel Opponent to reconsider his demands.

Equally whilst Party is seeking revised authority he should at the same time be working to persuade Opponent at least to modify his demands to some degree. Party's primary methods of achieving this are:

1   Holding firm as long as he can to his own position.
2   Convincing Opponent of the major injury which Party would suffer by agreeing to Opponent's terms. As suggested previously it is in Party's interest to exaggerate this injury in order to justify the demand for a larger concession from Opponent in return.
3   Seeking to make the individual supporting members of Opponent's negotiating team understand Party's real difficulties, and using these members as allies to work on Opponent's management. The most effective allies for Party in this respect are the professional advisers to Opponent, such as lawyers and engineers, who can usually be relied on to take a more objective line.
4   Persuading Opponent that the benefits he would gain from achieving his demands would be appreciably less than Opponent believes. Again reference behind the scenes to Opponent's professional advisers can be helpful in achieving this. Information can be 'leaked' to them which Party indicates he would not reveal officially, and because the information is presented in this way it is more likely to be believed to be true.

16.4 SUPPLEMENTARY NOTES ON THE EQUATIONS WHICH ESTABLISH THE EVs OF CONCEDE AND NOT CONCEDE

In establishing the values to be incorporated in these equations the following points require to be noted:
1   In the same way as an army will fight desperately to defend a

mountain pass or river bank, because they know that the plains beyond do not offer any easy opportunity for re-establishing a defensive position, so a negotiator will resist strenuously any proposal which, on acceptance, would make it difficult for him to find another line of resistance.

Consider the issue of consequential damages for defects during the warranty period. Whilst the negotiator for Party can argue with conviction the commitment of his company to the non-acceptance of the principal of consequential liability, once he concedes that principal, no natural line of resistance is left. He may press for a financial limit to be placed on the liability but he has the disadvantage that no one figure has any greater significance than another. Some might suggest a percentage of the contract value, or even finally the contract value itself, but there is little logic in this since no relationship exists between the value of the contract and the buyer's potential loss of earnings due to an outage in the system or plant concerned.

A similar situation arises when Opponent wishes Party to accept responsibility for, say, the quality or standards of performance of materials supplied, but is unwilling to give Party the freedom to decide on the source of supply. Responsibility and the authority to make decisions go together and if Party allows himself to be driven from this position there is no naturally-defined stopping point. All manner of complex and often unworkable proposals could be made but no one proposal possesses any greater degree of validity than the rest.

In placing a negative value therefore on the concession Party must make a realistic assessment of what the concession would mean and where he could realistically expect to be able to establish his next line of resistance.

2   If the concession would establish a precedent for other contracts then Party should add another term to the equation for concede, which would represent his estimate of the conditional loss he would be likely to incur in the future, as a result of the concession, multiplied by the subjective probability of incurring that loss. For example, if the concession would increase the risk of warranty costs by say £10 000 per contract, and Party considered there was a 50% chance of incurring those costs, for say 3 contracts over the next 5 years, then he should add £15 000 to the value of the expected loss.[5]

3   If, however, Party belives that he can offset at least part of the loss he would suffer from making the concession by trading with Opponent for a matching concession, then Party should add to the equation concede the term: value of off-setting concession × probability of obtaining that concession.[6] Party's belief on this point will be a function of his estimate of:

(a) The value which Opponent attaches to securing the concession.
(b) The extent to which Opponent considers he needs to make a matching concession in order to secure the first concession from Party.

4   When Party is considering a second concession on the same issue, having already conceded the first, then the value of the bargain term in both equations must be adjusted by deducting the expected loss due to the first concession.

5   In deciding on the probability of incurring the loss due to the granting of the concession, Party must distinguish between the case in which the loss must follow the concession, eg a concession on price, and the case in which the granting of the concession merely creates the risk of incurring a loss, eg increasing the rate of the delay penalty. In the latter the risk is the joint probability of the delay arising and the penalty being claimed, ie the probability of delay multiplied by the probability of a claim being made. (It is well known that many buyers hesitate to claim delay penalties for fear of putting up future prices whilst a few apply strictly the terms of the contract.) The risk of a claim being made is obviously greater if the buyer has in his possession retention moneys or a performance bond (see Section 4.4).

6   In respect of such risk concessions, including warranty costs, sums payable on termination for default, etc, Party's assessment of the probability of the loss occuring is largely a reflection of his belief in his own efficiency. The more confidence he has in the product and services which he is offering the lower this probability factor becomes and the greater the degree of risk which he can afford to take. Equally in these circumstances, Party must expect that Opponent will bring pressure to bear on him to make concessions by referring to Party's proven record of success.

Party will be in a particularly difficult negotiating position if he is at the same time seeking to justify the award to him of the contract, at a price above that of the lowest tenderer, on the grounds of his greater efficiency and proven record of reliability. The more he resists making concessions which increase his contractual risks the more he casts doubt on his confidence in his ability to perform.

7   The smaller the chance of Party securing alternative business which would utilize the same productive capacity during the same time scale, the higher the conditional loss from no bargain. This is one valuation which may change during the course of prolonged negotiations because of the failure by Party to achieve success on other tenders (see p. 146). As a consequence Party's valuation of the loss

due to no bargain will increase until at the extreme it equals the contribution to be obtained from contract award.

8   Party's estimate of the probability of no bargain should he fail to give the concession is a function of his belief:

(a) Of the importance which Opponent attaches to securing the concession. This has been discussed already under point 3 but again it may be stressed that Party must view the issue through Opponent's eyes and take full cognizance of Opponent's emotional attitudes and the level of aspiration of his nelgotiators.

(b) Of the alternatives which are available to Opponent in the event that the negotiations end in no bargain. However much Opponent may desire the concession he should not rationally break off the negotiations if the worth to him of any alternative is less than that of the bargain without the concession.

(c) As to whether Opponent will behave rationally or alternatively will allow his actions to be determined by the need to satisfy the personalistic motivational drives of his negotiators.

NOTES

1.   In order to avoid any possible confusion over terminology it must be indicated that the term *resistance point* is being used with a different meaning to that given by Walton and McKersie in their *Behavioural Theory of Labour Negotiations*. In their terminology resistance point is the point at which the negotiator would finally just prefer a bargain to no bargain; it represents his minimum settling point. In the present use of the term, however, it indicates a point on which the negotiator feels sufficiently strongly to make it the subject of hard bargaining; the degree of his feeling and therefore the degree of his resistance increasing as the consequences of any concession become more serious until the point is reached at which he would prefer no bargain to any further concessions.

2.   If the accounting system of the firm will provide the information, this should be the contribution which would be earned by the contract. If this information is not available then the gross margin is probably a sufficient approximation.

3.   If the loss does not occur then the value is zero and, therefore, the other term in the probability expression has been omitted.

4.   In reported experiments it has been shown that members of a group consistently over-value their own products. Two principal explanations have been suggested for this. Firstly, through participation in the group activity a member develops a better understanding of the factors which have led the group to the adoption of a particular solution in preference to any other; this may be termed a cognitive bias. Secondly, that emotional identification with, or attraction to, the

group is responsible for creating the bias.

In terms of a negotiating team, especially if operating away from home base, both causes of bias are likely to be operative. Through having worked together, the team will have formed a social group with a common experience. In going through this process the team will have become emotionally involved.

However, the social group may not be limited in membership to those who are permanently assigned to the negotiating team. Head office staff who join the negotiations and act in a manner which the team judge to be helpful may be admitted to membership. So also may members of Opponent's team in situations in which the outcome of an integrative bargaining session has resulted in the choice of a solution which is preferred by the group to that proposed by Party's head office who, on this occasion, are seen by the negotiating team as an 'out group'.

See C. F. Ferguson and H. H. Kelley, 'Significant factors in over-evaluation of own-group products', *Journal of Abnormal and Social Psychology*, vol. 69 (no 2, 1964), pp. 223–28, and M. Sherif, 'Experiments in group conflict', *Scientific American* (November 1956), pp. 276–77.

5.   This assumes a competitive situation in which Party cannot expect to be able to add the anticipated loss to his future tender prices.

6.   Again, the other term in the probability expression has been omitted as its value would be zero.

17

THE FOLLOW UP

It is in this stage of the negotiations that each side starts significantly to adjust its demand and attitudes to the observed behaviour of the other. The primary emphasis, therefore, is on adjustment and because each knows this, their initial behaviour is likely to contain a strong element of bluff although, as suggested earlier, bluffing too strongly can be self-defeating.

This is also the stage in which the unity of the negotiating team will receive its first severe test. One team member may regard Opponent's violent criticism of his proposals as largely bluff, and so maintain strongly that Party should stand its ground. Another may feel with equal conviction that from Opponent's viewpoint the criticisms are justified, and that agreement will not be reached unless Party's original proposals are modified in a way which will substantially meet the criticisms. Therefore, temporary alliances may well be formed across the negotiating lines. Whilst this is inevitable behind the scenes, the team leader should never permit such alliances to appear openly at the negotiating table unless as part of a tactical ploy (see p. 374). However, it is necessary to recognize that interaction between the members of the negotiating team plays a major part in the adjustment process and that the degree to which Party moves towards Opponent is to some degree a function of the personalities of the negotiators and the discipline established by the team leader.

The process by which the two sides adjust to one another within the framework of the variables which lead Party initially to prefer one demand to another is now considered. The form of Opponent's concession factor and therefore the value of the outcome achievable, the time which will be taken to reach that outcome, the costs associated with that time, and the major strategic weapons at Party's disposal (commitment and threats) will all be discussed.

17.1 REAPPRAISAL OF OPPONENT'S CONCESSION FACTOR
It will be remembered (p. 149 ff) that Party's initial demand was optimal in relation to:

1 His expectation of Opponent's concession factor.

2   His expectation of his own concession factor necessary to secure that concession from Opponent.
3   The time at which Party anticipated that a bargain would be reached related to his own and Opponent's initial demands and their respective concession factors.
4   The costs associated with the time taken to secure agreement.

It is necessary to consider now the manner in which Party's demand may change, according to whether his expectations regarding Opponent's behaviour prove to be correct or not. There are three possibilities:

1   Opponent acts in accordance with party's expectations.
2   Opponent concedes more and/or faster than Party had expected.
3   Opponent concedes less and/or slower than Party had expected.

Opponent acts in accordance with party's expectations
In order for Opponent's initial behaviour to be in accordance with Party's expectations, Opponent must have selected a negotiating strategy which will also lead at time T_{ij} to an outcome O_{ij} (using the same notation as that on p. 149). Accordingly, although Party and Opponent differ in their initial demands, they have both independently selected the same outcome. Assuming that Opponent has behaved rationally in the choice of his concession factor, it must also follow that Party has made a mistake. He has assessed a concession factor for Opponent as a *maximum* whereas, in fact, it represents the *minimum* which Opponent considers necessary to exact a maximum concession from Party.

By the same reasoning Opponent is equally mistaken in his beliefs. The concession he has assessed as Party's *maximum* is that which Party judged would be the *minimum* he would have to allow to Opponent in order to obtain the *maximum* which he believed Opponent would yield.

A simple numerical example to illustrate this behaviour is set out in Figure 17:1.

	1 Original demand	2 Assumed maximum concession factor	3 Expected outcome	4 True maximum concession factor	5 True level at which bargain preferred to no bargain
Party	100	−4	96	−6	94
Opponent	90	+6	96	+7	97

Figure 17:1 Comparison between true and assumed concession factors

Party as the supplier makes an offer of 100 to which the buyer responds with an offer of 90. This defines the bargaining area. Column 3 shows that both sides expect that the bargain will be made at a price of 96, and both make the same assumptions regarding the other's maximum concession factor and their own minimum required to achieve this. In fact, both are wrong. Both could have adopted a harder initial line. The buyer could have tried to force the price down to 94 and the supplier to push it upwards to 97.

Generalizing, it may be stated that in any case in which at the commencement of the bargaining a negotiator's expectations as to his Opponent's concession factor are immediately fulfilled, then the negotiator has underestimated the maximum concessions which his Opponent would make. As a corollary to this, if either Party or Opponent are correct in their estimation of the other's true concession factor, their actual behaviour will differ from that which the other expects. In Figure 17:1, if Opponent knew that under pressure Party would concede to 94 then his initial approach would be considerably harder than Party had expected, since Opponent would only plan on making a concession of 4 whereas Party has anticipated his making a concession of 6.

Coddington has proposed that in any satisfactory model of the bargaining process a bargainer does not revise his decision when his expectations are fulfilled.[1] However, it has just been demonstrated that given a rational opponent, the fulfilment of Party's initial expectations must mean that Party has underestimated Opponent's concession factor. Does this mean that in this particular case Party should exhibit inconsistency and change his strategy even though his expectations have been fulfilled?

Provided Opponent stays with his strategy, Party can be confident that, as a result of the initial moves, his own strategy will lead to the outcome associated with his original demand. Although Party now knows that this outcome is less than optimal in terms of its value at the time of agreement, a more favourable outcome derived from Party's adoption of a hard-line strategy would take longer to achieve and therefore would be subject to a reduction in terms of its present value, due to the effect of the increased discount factor and time costs.

Party also knows that any change he makes in his strategy is likely to cause Opponent also to make a change. This could be more favourable to Party, ie Opponent could increase his concession factor or alternatively Opponent could react unfavourably from Party's viewpoint by hardening his line of resistance. The latter is more probable. Rationally Opponent already has some guide to Party's true concession factor from Party's first moves; emotionally he is likely to react on the lines: 'All right, if you want to make things tougher, two can play at that game.'

The result of the initial moves may be regarded as having created a temporary balance between the demands of the two sides. If the balance is confirmed by their next moves this will point the way to a specific outcome on which the two sides will focus their attention and coordinate their expectations. If the initial balance is disturbed by Party's change of strategy neither side will be able to recognize immediately any such focal point, and time will be required for exploratory probing before balance can be restored at some new level.

Accordingly, in practice, unless the anticipated improvement in outcome is significant and the adverse effects of the delay in reaching agreement are small, there will be little incentive for Party to change his strategy *provided that Opponent does not change his*. If Opponent were to change to a harder line and to concede less than Party had expected in return for his own concessions, then Party would be compelled either to change strategy himself, so prolonging the negotiations, or to make more concessions and so lower the value to Party of the outcome. Either way Party would lose. The same reasoning could be applied to opponent and at this point a similarity begins to appear in the situation facing the two sides and that of the two collaborators in the zero sum game.

The decision problem facing Party is now represented in game-theory form to see whether suspicions are confirmed. This is shown in Figure 17:2, the data for which is based on that previously used in Figure 6:16 for arriving at Party's original optimum demand. The assumption is made that if Party switches to his hard-line strategy then he increases the value of the outcome to 170 but it takes longer to achieve; 5 months if Opponent does not change his strategy and 8 months if he does. Conversely if Opponent changes to a hard-line strategy, but Party does not, it is assumed that Party will reach a lower outcome than that originally predicted, but that it will only take 3 months to reach agreement. While the actual figures used in Figure 17:2 are arbitrary the assumptions on which they are based as to the circumstances under which the value of the outcome to Party will be increased or reduced, or the time for agreement extended or shortened, would seem to be of general validity.

This is in fact the situation considered earlier on p. 33. Party's maximum strategy is clearly a_1, stay with his original choice, since, even if Opponent does change to a hard line, Party is still better off on present values than if he had selected a_2. However, as in the earlier discussion and for the same reasons, Party could still be tempted to change strategy if he believed that Opponent would not, and some people might well decide to take this gamble.

The preference would be to stay with strategy a_1 and the argument to support this choice would be that the selection of the hard-line strategy would carry with it, in most bargaining situations, a higher than 50 per cent risk that Opponent would follow suit and Party would finish up, therefore, with outcome a_2b_2 which is the one he would most prefer to avoid. Party would have to be convinced that both the risk of this happening was very small, and also that Opponent would not become resentful and determined to exact retribution on a future occasion, before changing to the hard-line.

		Opponent	
		Stays as predicted b_1	Changes to hard line b_2
Party	Stays with original plan a_1	156	153.1
	Changes to hard line a_2	158.25	151.2

Figure 17:2 Decision problem: stay with present strategy or change to hard line

Assuming it is decided to stay with strategy a_1 then it is necessary to try to ensure that Opponent also stayed with his initial strategy, so that the outcome became a_1b_1 which might be termed the 'cooperative choice'. It is suggested that Party should approach Opponent informally along the following lines.

We both want the best bargain we can get. The way for us both to achieve that is to continue the way we have started. If, however, you start to play it tough then I can do the same which will benefit neither of us. We both have to live so let's be sensible and not too greedy.

Party's decision rules
From the above analysis it is suggested that Party should adopt the following decision rules:

1 Party should only change to a hard-line strategy if this is clearly optimal against any likely probability distribution of Opponent's strategy choice, and will not reflect adversely on Party on a future occasion.
2 In any other case Party should stay with his original strategy choice.
3 If Party does decide to stay with his original strategy then he should 'signal' Opponent to do likewise with the threat of switching to a hard line if Opponent does not agree.

Whilst the analysis has been made by considering Party's decision-making process in relation to the reaction of Opponent to Party's initial demand, the reasoning used is quite general and, therefore, the above decision rules can be applied at any stage in the negotiations. They are especially important to remember in the final stages of the negotiation when the temptation to defect, to ask for that little bit more, seems for some negotiators to be especially strong and can be the cause of serious delays and loss of Opponent's goodwill.

Therefore the answer to the question of whether Party should show inconsistency in his decision making or not, is that Party should at each time make that choice which is optimal in relation to the knowledge which he possess at that time. To the extent that as the bargaining proceeds his knowledge increases this may cause him to change his strategy, even if his expectations have been fulfilled, if he believes that to do so will be advantageous.

Opponent concedes more and/or faster than Party had expected
As established in the previous section, Opponent's initial response to Party's demand, when judged from Opponent's viewpoint, represents Opponent's estimate of his minimum concession factor necessary to obtain a maximum concession from Party. If Opponent now concedes more or faster than Party had expected this must mean that his real concession factor is even greater.

Party therefore is not wrong in his estimation of Opponent's concession Factor by the visible gap between his expectations and Opponent's actions but by the far larger gap between his expectations and Opponent's true concession factor. Assume that in the example in Figure 17:1 Party had expected Opponent on the first bargaining concession to concede 2 and in fact he concedes 3. Party can now reason that if Opponent is willing initially to concede 3 then this must mean that his maximum concession factor is probably of the order 8–9 and not the 6 which Party had originally estimated.

Party accordingly revises upwards his expectations as to Opponent's concession factor, in line with the maximum to which he now believes that Opponent will concede and the time it would take for Opponent to obtain such a concession. This in turn leads Party to revise downwards his belief as to the minimum concessions which he needs to make and so to harden his bargaining line.

The process is an accelerating one in which each concession by Opponent reinforces Party's belief as to the maximum to which Opponent will concede, and so strengthens Party's determination to stand firm, and this in turn persuades Opponent that he has no alternative but to go on conceding. So it continues until Opponent has conceded to the level of his point of final resistance, provided that this is less than Party's then current demand. If it is greater then Opponent must at some time accept Party's current demand.

In a purely theoretical model it would be possible to allow for Party actually increasing his demand so that if he were prepared to allow the negotiations to go on for long enough the end point of the bargaining sequence would always be Opponent's final resistance point. As stated earlier (see Chapter 6) it is considered that to increase a demand during the course of the negotiation would create such an emotional disturbance that it could not be to Party's advantage to do so. Accordingly this possibility is dismissed.

It may also be objected that although opponent originally conceded more than Party had expected this does not mean that he must continue to do the conceding. Could he not at some stage stand firm himself and compel Party to concede? What if Opponent made a mistake by conceding too much all at once and this has led Party to assume a far larger maximum concession factor for Opponent than is really true? In the extreme, what if Opponent has already reached his point of final resistance?

The difficulty is that, by his initial action, Opponent has persuaded Party to a revised expectation of the final bargain to which Party may already now be committed in the sense either that he has advised his management of the revised outcome, which he now anticipates being able to achieve, or at least the negotiator will feel a personal commitment to the other members of the team as a result of the planning meeting at which they revised their strategy.[2] If Opponent now tries to change from conceding to standing firm he will simply not be able to convince Party that, after having made those early concessions, greater than Party had expected, he now means his present intransigence. Party's refusal to believe that Opponent's change of plan is genuine will be reinforced by the humiliation which the negotiator for Party would suffer were it true. In terms of his personal reputation he cannot afford to allow it to be true, and the best means available for preventing it, is to stand firm and to demonstrate that he intends to continue to stand firm.

This is one example in contract negotiation of the moral of the old Aesop fable of the boy who cried wolf. A person cannot suddenly change his behavioural pattern and expect to be believed; not at least unless he can relate the change to some external event, the truth of which is easily demonstrable, eg as a buyer, being prepared to show a lower quotation, received late, to the supplier with whom negotiations are in progress. Merely to say the quotation has been received will be taken as bluff.

In the situation under discussion, Party can be expected to assume that Opponent is bluffing, in the absence of any overt act by Opponent proving the contrary. He will make this asumption, either because he genuinely believes it to be true, or because he cannot afford to allow himself not to believe it. So long as Party does this, and Opponent prefers the outcome represented by Party's demand to no bargain, then Opponent has ultimately no alternative but to give way.

This conclusion emphasises the key importance of limiting the amount of initial concession. It must be no greater than the minimum which the negotiator believes is essential to initiate the bargaining process and exact the maximum concession from the other side. Any doubts as to the level of the concession should be resolved downwards. It also confirms the conclusion reached earlier (see pp. 154 and 155) that exaggerated demands do not operate in favour of the side who make them, since it is more difficult to minimize the initial concession when the demand has been artificially inflated.

Whilst the effect of the time cost have been allowed for in this representation of the bargaining process, in that Party's demand has been assumed to be optimal after taking these into account, no allowance has been made for the tactical effect of either side being under a time restraint, eg the existence of a defined date by which the buyer must place the order. Clearly the pressure resulting from any such restraint will have an effect on both the tactics employed and the eventual outcome, and this is an issue which will be dealt with in Section 17.2.

Opponent concedes less and/or slower than party had expected
If Party discovers that Opponent is taking a harder line than Party had expected then there are two possible explanations for this:

1   Party was correct in his original estimation of Opponent's genuine concession factor but Opponent is bluffing.
2   Party was wrong in his original estimation of Opponent's concession factor.

The consequences which flow from these two alternatives, Party's reaction to Opponent's failure to behave in the manner anticipated and Opponent's response to Party's reaction, are set out in decision-tree format in Figure 17:3.

The crucial decision for Party is whether Opponent is bluffing or not. The only real way for Party to determine this directly is for Party to adhere to his original plan, make the concessions he had intended to make, but beyond this to remain intransigent. The danger to Party of adopting this strategy is that he becomes so committed to a firm line that, if he is wrong and Opponent is not bluffing, the concessionary move by Party when it does come involves much greater loss of face and reputation for firmness (see p. 150 ff). As a result Party may find it difficult to re-establish both his credibility and a firm line of resistance. Often he will feel compelled for just this reason to take a stand on some issue of doubtful validity on which otherwise he would have been prepared to concede.[3]

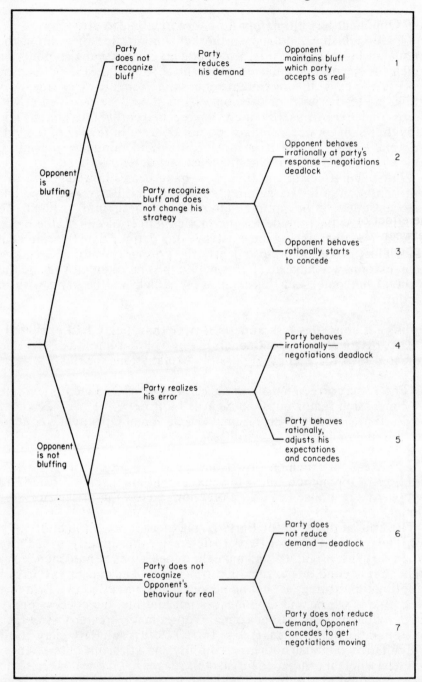

Figure 17:3 Decision tree—Opponent concedes less or slower than anticipated

In order to minimize this risk Party, whilst holding firm but with the minimum of defined commitment, should seek to discover indirectly the extent, if any, of Opponent's bluff. He may do this by informal discussions with Opponent's negotiators, by cross checking his assessment of the strength of Opponent's negotiating position from neutral sources and by looking for outward signs of the true attitude of Opponent's negotiators in terms of their personal behaviour. If the senior negotiator really has booked his flight home tomorrow, when home is 5 000 miles away from the scene of the negotiations, then this is some indication of how he feels.

Assuming that Opponent is not bluffing and Party behaves rationally this will cause Party as in branch 5 (Figure 17:3) to adjust his expectations downwards and lower his current demand. What will be the effect of this on Opponent? This will depend on the relationship between the amount/rate at which Party does concede related to Opponent's expectations. There are again three possibilities:

1	Party concedes at the amount/rate expected.	1 Opponent adheres to his original strategy.
2	Party concedes less than Opponent had expected.	2 If Opponent believes Party is not bluffing and behaves rationally, then Opponent adjusts his expectation and lowers his demand. This is what Cross has described as the general case of a convergent bargaining process.[4]
3	Party concedes more than Opponent had expected.	3 Opponent amends his strategy by hardening his line and the negotiating process follows that described previously.

Irrational behaviour

Even if Party's diagnosis is correct it does not necessarily follow that the negotiations will proceed smoothly. It has been indicated in branches 2 and 4 (Figure 17:3) that the negotiations may deadlock due to irrational behaviour. Being caught out or persuaded that he has made a mistake may create the reaction of: 'It was worth a try', accompanied by a philosophical shrug of the shoulders. Alternatively the negotiator may react by showing stubbornness, a wilful refusal to face reality and by taking refuge in insults and rhetoric.

The patient coaxing of colleagues and the urge of economic necessity will both be needed in order to compel the negotiator into a more responsive attitude. Party's own negotiators can assist by finding some small concession to smooth Opponent's way back to the bargaining table and by refraining from open signs of delight or triumph at Opponent's discomforture.

Finally being *right* in one's diagnosis and following this with the *right* response does not necessarily lead to the most favourable outcome. In branch 7 by failing to recognize that Opponent is not bluffing and, therefore, failing to respond to Opponent's intransigence by making concesions, Party compels Opponent to reconsider his level of demand. If Party had known why Opponent was adhering to that level of demand, for example that this was the minimum figure which he had been instructed by his management to achieve, then Party by reason of his improved understanding would in all probability have moderated his own demand.[5] The negotiator's attitude would have been that there was nothing to be gained by pressing the point further as it was not going to be conceded, and that he was wise to accept the position and take what he could get.

It is in the hope of indicating this type of attitude that negotiators use commitment tactics by saying that, for example, they personally see the force of the argument but are bound by other decisions, other instructions or regulations.

Unfortunately negotiators over the years have debased the coinage of commitment tactics by bluffing; by pretending to commitments which either do not exist, or are far less restrictive than they have stated. Again the parallel may be drawn with Aesop's fable of the boy who cried wolf. If a negotiator wishes to be believed, when genuinely he is committed, he should not pretend to commitments when the falseness of his position can easily be exposed.

17.2 THE INFLUENCE OF TIME

So far, discussions on the effect of time have considered only the time costs incurred by Party as a result of the duration of the negotiations and the discounting effect due to the later receipt by Party of the benefits from the negotiations. It has been shown how the greater advantages which may be gained from prolonged bargaining must be balanced against these time costs and the discount factor so as to optimize the outcome. When doing this no specific limit has been placed on the time available for the negotiations, and both this, and the time actually taken, have been assumed to be a function of the bargaining process itself.

Time limits, at least at some stage in the negotiations, are the rule rather than the exception in commercial practice and will affect the conduct of the bargaining in two ways:

1   Strategically by defining the negotiating period and compelling the negotiator at some predetermined point in time to change his

strategy from that of hold back to quick kill.
2   Tactically by the pressure created on the negotiator himself through the need to make decisions against a defined deadline.

Strategic effect
In considering the strategic effect of time limits on a negotiation it is necessary to distinguish between:

1   The situation in which the time limit is established at the outset, is known to both sides, and constitutes therefore a negotiating time framework.
2   The situtation in which no specific time limit exists initially, but one is subsequently created unilaterally by one side issuing a demand for the negotiations to be completed by a defined date, often accompanied by a statement as to the terms upon which he requires agreement to be reached.

Negotiating time framework
The following axioms related to the behaviour of the two sides will apply to any negotiation which is conducted from the outset within a defined time framework.

1   The higher the initial concession rate of either side relative to time, the less favourable the bargain they will secure.[6]

2   Both sides should therefore initially only make minor concessions or none at all.

3   At some period before the deadline both sides should make a series of moves designed to permit identification of a final bargain which is acceptable to both of them. These moves may be concessionary, or a repeat of earlier offers, depending on the bargaining strength of the two sides.

4   The side with the weaker bargaining strength is the one which is under greater pressure to reach agreement by the deadline, ie the one which has more to lose if the end result is no bargain.[7]
    If at the end of the final time phase of the negotiations Party as the weaker side would prefer Opponent's initial offer to no bargain, then Party must accept that offer. Specifically Party at that time will act so as to maximize his security and will not offer a compromise, which there must be some probability Opponent might reject, so bringing the negotiations to an end without agreement having been reached.
    In order to reduce the risk of being faced with the choice between Opponent's initial terms and no bargain, Party in the penultimate

phase of the negotiations will make some concessionary move designed to secure reciprocal concessions from Opponent.

5 The more even the bargaining strength of the two sides the later each can leave it before making a concessionary move. Each will be aware that the other knows he would prefer a bargain to no bargain so both will expect that ultimately they will come to terms.

If the practice of making late mutual concessions happens several times then this will become the norm of the two sides negotiating behaviour and it would be unthinkable for either of them to depart from this, either by making concessions too early, or by failing to make the concessions needed for agreement to be reached, even if this happens only minutes before the deadline is due to expire.

6 The length of the period referred to in point 3 should be just sufficient to allow Party and Opponent to reach agreement, taking into account any difficulties in communication.

If the period is too short, because neither side has made any move soon enough for the concession-making process to operate, then the side with the weaker bargaining strength having failed to set up a position of potential compromise will be exposed to the time-threat of accepting the other side's offer as it stands, or run the risk of no bargain.

If the period is too long, because one side has made a move too early, then this will be treated by the other as a sign of weakness and encourage him to remain intransigent, thus reducing the opportunity for reciprocal concession making and increasing the chances of no agreement being reached at all. The move will be misinterpreted because it was made at the wrong time.

17.3 THREAT STRATEGY

Strategic effect and time threats

The imposition by either side of a time limit to the bargaining process necessarily carries with it a threat should the time limit be passed without agreement having been reached.

The function which this threat performs is related to the incentive to carry out the threat which the negotiator who is threatening would have, should his demands not be met.

If the demand represents the minimum negotiating objective of the negotiator who is threatening, so that he would prefer no bargain if it were not accepted, then the primary function of the threat is to convey that message to the other negotiator. The threat tells the other negotiator the scale by which the negotiator who is threatening values the terms of the proposed agreement.

One difficulty with the threat as a means of communication is that there is no commercial equivalent to 'cross my heart'. The person to whom the threat is made can only estimate whether the negotiator who is threatening really would prefer the implementation of the threat to no bargain, and he may get it wrong. This problem of the belief of the reality of the threat by the person threatened is crucial to the whole concept of threat strategy and will be discussed again.

If the threat does not succeed, suppose now that the alternative would represent a worse outcome to the negotiator who is threatening than accepting the bargain available without the use of the threat. The primary function of the threat then becomes to deter through 'its promise of mutual harm'.[8] The negotiator has no incentive to carry out the threat, whether his demands are met or not, although if they are not met he may be compelled to do so in order to maintain the other side's belief in his firmness of purpose.

The severity of the deterrent effect of any threat will depend upon:

1 The extent of the commitment which the issue of the threat places upon the person making it.
2 The belief of the person to whom the threat is addressed that if he does not accede to the other's demands then the threat will be implemented.
3 The injury which would be suffered by the person to whom the threat is made, if he accedes, in comparison with the loss he would suffer by resisting, were the threat to be carried out.

The threat as a commitment
The making of a threat in itself creates a commitment on the person who makes it to carry it out, should his demands not be met. The degree of that commitment which will be visible to the person to whom the threat is made, will be in proportion to:
1 The extent to which both the demand and the threat are specific. The more they are specific the less room there will be for adjustment, either in the demands or the threat itself, and so the greater the degree of commitment. Conversely the looser the phrasing the greater the opportunity of subsequent 'interpretation' and therefore the smaller the commitment. Compare these two statements:

We must made the decision today. You have until 12 o'clock to accept the terms we have offered or we shall place the business elsewhere.

We cannot go on discussing any longer. You know the terms of our last offer. If we cannot reach agreement on these then we shall have to consider seriously placing the business with another firm.

The first statement is explicit both in terms of the demand and of the time scale in which it must be accepted. The commitment is total. If the supplier does not accept, there is no alternative left to the buyer. He must give the order to another company. To do otherwise would destroy the buyer's reputation for firmness and his credibility as a negotiator.

It follows from this that the buyer is unlikely to risk making a threat of the type in the first statement without the intention of carrying it out, and having the ability to do so in the form of an alternative source of supply. *These facts must be known to the supplier.* The second statement, however, is much less clear. No specific time limit is mentioned and the reference to 'reaching agreement on the terms of the buyer's last offer' indicate some flexibility in the buyer's position. The commitment is that much weaker.

2   The authority and reputation of the person making the threat. The more senior the negotiator, and the greater his reputation as being 'a man of his word,' the stronger the degree of commitment.

3   The norms of social interaction prevailing in the business society within which the negotiation is being conducted. The commitment which a negotiator feels for a statement he has made depends, in part, on the expectancy which he believes others will have as to the likelihood of his telling the truth. If in a particular context it is recognized as legitimate to bluff, and no particular shame attaches to being caught out, then the commitment which a negotiator has to a verbal expression of intent will be small. If on the other hand the negotiator is operating within a business community in which his value as a negotiator is related strictly to the trust which others place in his word, and the penalty for being caught out is never to be believed again, the negotiator's commitment is absolute. He cannot afford to act otherwise than in accordance with his expressed intentions.

It is expected that in such a situation the negotiator would normally use statements in which the degree of commitment was only weakly defined and he had room left to manoeuvre. When, exceptionally, he made a definitive commitment then this would be regarded as a positive signal of his intentions to carry out the threat should the other side not accede.

The belief of the person threatened

A threat which is designed as a deterrent will clearly be ineffective if the person to whom it is addressed does not believe it will ever be implemented. Party's belief that Opponent will implement a threat, should Party not accede to his demands, will be related to:

1   The character of Opponent's negotiator and the consistency of his conduct on other occasions.

2   The loss of reputation for bargaining firmness which the negotiator

for Opponent would suffer were he not to carry out the threat, again taking into account the business environment within which the negotiation is being conducted.

3 Any overt act of commitment made by the negotiator for Opponent from which he would find it difficult to withdraw, eg publicizing his intent to third parties.

4 The value to Opponent of securing the concession to which the demand is related. Would he benefit to an extent which makes the threat sound sensible?

5 The economic loss which Opponent would incur were he to carry out the threat. As a factor in Opponent's decision-making process this will clearly be in conflict with 2 and 3 but, whilst a generalization is difficult, it is believed that in any continuing relationship between Party and Opponent, the negotiator's reputation will be of greater importance than the economic loss. Expressed in another way, the negotiator is not likely in such a situation to put his reputation at risk unless he has already weighed the economic costs of threat implementation and decided they were worth risking.

The loss which would be incurred by Party

The general nature of a threat associated with a time limit is that if Party does not accede then Opponent will terminate the negotiation. Therefore, the comparison lies between the value to Party of the bargain after making the required concession and the value of no bargain. As indicated in Section 16.4, a distinction must be drawn between a concession, such as discount, which is a certain reduction in value, and a concession, such as agreeing to an increased rate of penalty, which only creates the risk of loss.

Party's strategy decision after Opponent has made a time threat

Rationally is is proposed that Party should make his decision on whether or not to concede to Opponent's demand by comparing the two courses *accede* and *stand firm*, and selecting that which possesses for him the greater value.

If it is assumed that once Party has given the concession, agreement is reached without further bargaining, then the value to Party of accede is simply that of the bargain after taking into account the effect of the concession.[9] The value of stand firm, however, is not a certainty since it depends upon Opponent's reaction to Party's decision. It can be expressed therefore only as an expected value according to the following equation:[10]

$$(U_1 \times p_1) + (U_2 \times p_2); \; p_1 + p_2 = 1$$

in which:

U_1 = value of the bargain without the concession.
U_2 = value of no bargain.

p_1 = the probability of withdrawing his demand and agreeing to Party's terms.

p_2 = the probability of Opponent carrying out his threat and breaking off the negotiations.

The use of this decision rule clearly involves Party in some risk, in the way described earlier in the discussion of the use of expected value techniques, whenever the value to Party of the bargain, after accepting Opponent's demand, is higher than that of no bargain (see p. 27). Nevertheless it is believed that it does represent in a quantified form the way in which most negotiators intuitively approach this problem in practice.

An alternative to the decision rule maximize security would mean that Party would choose the strategy accede in any case in which the value of this course exceeded that of no bargain. In general the adoption of this rule would be far too defeatist. It should only be considered in exceptional circumstances in which Opponent's commitment to the threat is regarded as very strong, and therefore the risk of its being invoked is high, and the importance of securing the bargain even after granting the concession is too substantial for risks to be taken.

Repeat bargaining between Party and Opponent
However, if Party were consistently to adopt the decision rule of selecting the course which maximized expected value, and his dealings with opponent were on a continuing basis, then Opponent would soon come to anticipate Party's decisions. By carefully selecting the threat, and ensuring that Party was aware of his commitment to carrying it out, Opponent would ensure that Party's decision was always to concede.

Party's defence to any such tactics by Opponent would be to pre-empt Opponent by:

1 Defining in advance Party's own commitment to any issue on which he anticipated that Opponent might develop a threat strategy.
2 Acting in a manner so as to avoid the gap on any major issue which Opponent would be likely to use in conjunction with a threat being too wide too late in the negotiations. The narrower the gap towards the close of the bargaining period, the less Opponent will be likely to stake his reputation or risk having to implement the threat, should Party stand firm. By the same reasoning the lower is Party's credulity in the threat being fulfilled if he does stand firm.

Accordingly, if a time limit is foreseen in advance, at the penultimate stage in the bargaining Party should ensure that on any issue which could be made the subject of a threat he has made an offer which he considers is sufficiently attractive to Opponent to justify a compromise.

3 Randomizing his response to Opponent's threats by challenging Opponent on certain occasions even though the rational decision would be to concede. The effect of this will be to confuse Opponent in his attempts to build up a picture of Party's value structure and prevent him from making reliable estimates of the probability of which course Party will select.

Emotional response to the use of threats

The issue of a threat is an overt assumption on the part of the person making it that he has a power relationship with the person to whom the threat is addressed that allows him to make the demand which the threat carries and to expect the other person to obey. In considering the emotional reaction of the person threatened two conditions are distinguished:

1 The existence of a power relationship which the person threatened finds acceptable in terms of his perception of the status differential between himself and the negotiator making the threat.

2 The arbitrary assumption, by the negotiator who is threatening, of a power which the person threatened may be compelled to obey, but which he does not regard as legitimate and so does not respect or accept.

Under condition 1 the right to issue the threat is acknowledged and no sense of resentment will arise. Under 2, however, there will be a very strong feeling of resentment which is likely to give rise to an emotional outburst. A typical reaction would be: 'I will *not* give my agreement to those terms even if we do lose the order. It will serve him right too. He will have to pay more if he buys from anyone else.'

In this type of reaction the person threatened is concerned primarily with the results of his actions on the negotiator who is threatening and not with the effect on himself. He may be willing to accept significant punishment on his own behalf provided only that he can obtain the satisfaction of inflicting at least equal punishment on the negotiator who is threatening.

It has been suggested that the person threatened may regard the threat as legitimate if he regards the goal which the negotiator who is threatening is seeking to obtain as legitimate.[11] This is especially so if, because of the identfication of the means with the end, the person threatening is willing to regard the threat as depersonalized. If, as the negotiator for Party, I can say that I understand and accept what the negotiator for Opponent is trying to do and that I bear no personal grudge, then clearly I regard the threat he is making as legitimate, and will not feel emotionally disturbed because of it.

However, I may feel that he is going beyond his true function. If according to my standards he is trying to be greedy in order to satisfy his own personal motivation beyond a point which I can recognize as being reasonable, then I will react emotionally against any such threat.

The difficulty arises in practice because the standards of the two negotiators are seldom the same. Small differences may be tolerated but if the standards of the two negotiators are widely separate then emotions must be aroused, and the possibility of discovering an agreement which both sides genuinely accept that much reduced.

17.4 THE TACTICAL EFFECT OF TIME

By defining in advance the time limit within which the negotiator for Party is required to make an irrevocable decision, Opponent at once places the negotiator under pressure, the degree of which will be related to:

1   The importance of the decision
2   The time available
3   The extent of isolation of the negotiator

Importance of the decision

The more important the decision the greater the pressure which the imposition of a time limit creates. The negotiator, aware of the consequences of a wrong choice, will want the maximum opportunity to investigate, consider alternative courses of action and the wider issues involved, and to consult his superiors and colleagues.

Because of the time constraint he will be restricted to a greater or lesser degree in the extent to which he is able to follow through any or all of these opportunities. He will be compelled to act in some measure in a manner contrary to that in which he has been trained and even possibly to override the instructions he has received.

Inevitably there will be conflict between the demands of the system, the ordered method of the company's negotiating control procedures, and the requirements of the negotiating situation itself. Under these circumstances the negotiator's behaviour would be expected to follow the sequence now decribed.

1   Initially the negotiator will react emotionally against the dissonance of the situation conflict into which he has been placed. He will describe it in exaggerated terms and put the blame on the negotiators for Opponent or his own head office whom he will criticize severely.[12]

The psychological function of this outburst is to provide the negotiator with a defence mechanism. By defining the position as one of impossible difficulty, for which he is not responsible, he has lowered his own level of aspiration and provided justification for others to judge his actions according to that level. Despite the difficulties, if he is successful he will receive great credit; if he fails he will hope to escape censure.

2   The negotiator then seeks some course of action which minimizes the conflict between the system, or his instructions, and the demands of the negotiating situation. Within the time available, he tries to obtain revised instructions and to avoid commitments, which he knows would be totally unacceptable to his company, by redefining them in a way which appears to meet Opponent's demands but still provides Party with essential protection.[13]

Finally, he concedes to the limit he believes he could justify subsequently.[14]

3   Having acted, he reduces the dissonance which still remains by altering his valuation of any possible course of action which he did not select, but which was attractive to him, so as to make it less attractive.[15]

Suppose that he took the decision not to accept Opponent's demands on delay penalty, because these exceeded the company's norm for such clauses, but was nevertheless tempted to do so on the grounds that he personally did not believe the risk involved was substantial. He will now support this decision by changing his belief in the risk of paying penalty; from being a low risk it will now become significant.

Time available

Clearly, in terms of making a final decision, the shorter the time allowed to the negotiator the greater the pressure to which he is subjected. From a personal viewpoint, he resists that pressure by adjusting his level of aspiration to that which he believes is the optimum he is likely to achieve within the time available.[16] Having made this adjustment he is no longer concerned with the amount of time involved, which then becomes a parameter of the decision-making process.

For example, if there is inadequate time to consult the company's head office lawyers on the drafting of the contract, the negotiator adjusts his level of aspiration for the preparation of the contract documents, downwards, from that of a legal expert to that which would be expected of a layman experienced in contract matters working on his own. Having made that adjustment, and in so doing provided himself with a defence against future criticism, the negotiator acts to achieve that level of competence without worrying about the improvement which could have been achieved had time been available for consultation.[17]

However, because the negotiator is successful in his defence to Opponent's time pressures in terms of enabling him to proceed with the bargaining without being subject to severe personal stress, this does not mean that there is no objective loss in efficiency. On the contrary, although the negotiator may rationalize away his inadequacies to himself, the inefficiency caused by such inadequacies still exists and will be reflected in the terms of the final bargain.

Time pressure often has an adverse effect by compelling hurried decisions, inadequate reviews, etc, all of which give rise to the risk of some vital point being overlooked. To a considerable extent, the negotiator can guard himself against this risk, if only he will take action to do so in advance, and before the time pressure becomes effective. For example by:

1 Planning communication links with home base and ensuring that the right people will be available at the time when they will be needed.
2 Anticipating concessions for which Opponent may ask and having approved answers available.
3 Ensuring that essential data for rapid reassessment of price or delivery periods are available.
4 Taking advice in advance on technical issues which may arise, whether these are of engineering, law or finance.

Extended negotiations

Time pressure can also be created in the opposite way by Opponent deliberately extending the negotiations so that the negotiator for Party is left uncertain about Opponent's real intentions. This tactic is most effectively used by a purchaser who is negotiating with two or more overseas suppliers.

The sales negotiator who wants to get down to business and conclude the bargaining is frustrated by the buyer's unwillingness to come to any firm decisions, by meetings being postponed, requests made for alternative or additional quotations, etc. He becomes fed up with life in the foreign hotel, despite its superficial glamour, suffers frequently in health from the effects of eating unusual food and the nervous strain of waiting and wondering, with the added worry of the effects of a prolonged absence from home on his domestic life.

These conditions, together with his natural desire to obtain the order, create an almost irresistible temptation to the negotiator to do anything, if only it will produce a definite answer. The purchaser obviously hopes that the 'anything' will take the form of significant concessions perhaps much greater than the negotiator is authorized to make, and often his hopes will be realized. The negotiator will make the concession for much the same reason as a political prisoner confesses; for the relief which he obtains from so doing. There may be problems in the future in justifying his actions but for the moment these are shut out by the release from tension which he now experiences.

Later when the negotiator does have to justify himself he would be expected to act again in the way suggested by the theory of cognitive dissonance and overestimate the disadvantages of the alternative courses of action which he rejected.

Is there any way in which the negotiator faced with this type of situation can be helped? From my own experience the answer is yes. There are steps which management can take and the most important are:

1 Sending a negotiating team which is tough, experienced and compatible.
2 Providing the negotiator with strong support from home base, eg quick and realistic answers to his queries.
3 Keeping in regular contact with the negotiator.
4 Giving management encouragement to the negotiator and giving credit to him for perserverence whilst sympathizing with his difficulties.
5 Helping out with domestic problems, for example, ensuring that a young wife with a baby is visited, that she is kept in touch and does not feel neglected.

If support of this type is given then it has been known for the position to be reversed; for the purchaser to have procrastinated too long so that eventually he comes under time pressures himself due to his need to get the order placed.

Natural breaks
Apart from any time limits imposed by Opponent, time pressures are also created by natural breaks in the negotiations, especially if these are associated with social occasions.

When Opponent has already made a concession during the morning bargaining session Party will come under some pressure to reciprocate before the break for lunch particularly if the two sides are lunching together. He will want the atmosphere to be relaxed rather than tense, for Opponent to feel good towards him rather than the reverse. Opponent can be expected to back up the pressure by making some remarks such: 'Look, let us at least see if *something* can be settled before we break. I have given way on X, how about Y? Can you agree to that so we can achieve at least that much for a morning's work?' If Party does not make the concession before lunch then he will be under even more severe psychological pressure to do so immediately after lunch. In such circumstances, continued refusal by the negotiator to make any sort of concessionary move must have the effect of alienating Opponent and even members of Party's own negotiating team. They want the negotiator to respond to an atmosphere of goodwill by making the responsive concession.

Whilst pressures can be created by the existence of natural breaks they can also be induced by withholding a break. For example, Opponent, as the side who would normally have called the lunch recess, continues the arguments throughout the recess period. If Party raises any objection he is at once put in the wrong by being told that if only he would be reasonable and agree then everyone could go to lunch.

Degree of isolation
Pressure on the negotiator becomes more intense the further he is isolated from his colleagues. This point has already been referred to in Section 9.1 when discussing the dangers of a one-man negotiating team.

Man is a social animal who requires contact with other humans in order to operate effectively. The negotiator's needs are support, to review and reinforce his judgement, and balance, to correct any lack of proportion in his thinking.

If he is deprived of these needs by being isolated, and unable to communicate effectively with his home base, the negotiator soon becomes vulnerable. At the same time, if he is subjected to time pressures the situation can easily become one which it is beyond the capability of the negotiator to handle in a rational manner. He may then become either verbally aggressive, attacking the negotiator for Opponent whom he treats as responsible for the situation, thus providing himself with a defence mechanism, or apathetic, refusing to participate further in a cooperative manner.

The measures to prevent this type of situation from arising are the same as those suggested previously dealing with extended time pressures.

17.5 MODIFICATION OF THE NEGOTIATING OBJECTIVE
Party's original negotiating objective was formulated as the optimum outcome which he could foresee in relation to:

1   Opponent's expected resistance to a range of possible demands.
2   The time which would be expended to secure each outcome over the range of those foreseen as possible, and the related time cost and discount factors.
3   The desirability to Party of each outcome over the range of those foreseen as possible including the negative value of no bargain.

As a result of the initial contacts between the two sides it is probable that Party will have been led to modify factors 1 and 2. The way in which this modification may occur has already been discussed in Section 16.2.

The desirability to Party of each outcome should not have changed as a result of the initial encounters between Party and Opponent, unless, by his conduct, Opponent has satisfied Party that some factor which influenced Party in his original valuation was incorrectly assessed.[18] Two examples of the way in which this could occur would be:

1 Opponent makes it clear that Party's chances of securing worthwhile follow-on business are dependent on Party's willingness to establish local manufacturing facilities. Party had not previously taken this point into account in assessing either his current costs or future returns.
2 Opponent explains that Party's interpretation of his terms of contract is incorrect, and that they are much less onerous than Party had believed, and Party is willing to accept the explanation.

Party is now in a position to draw together the three factors listed at the beginning of this section, as modified by the experience which he has gained from the initial contacts, and to reassess the potential outcomes over the spread of issues with which the negotiation is concerned, and the time which it would take to achieve each of these. This will enable Party to determine the conditional value for each outcome and to estimate the probability of success. Applying the techniques used previously Party can arrive at an expected value for each outcome and select the negotiating strategy which maximizes this expected value function. An example of this method of analysis is as follows.

Party as a supplier is negotiating the terms of a major contract, following the submission of a competitive tender, and his selection as the firm with whom the Purchaser intends to place the contract. Based on his tender and from the initial discussion with Opponent, Party prepares a table (Figure 17:4) covering the major items being contended and the range of possible outcomes.

Party combines these items into possible outcomes, assigns a utility value to each and estimates the probability of that outcome being achieved and the time it would take. Utility values are on a scale 0-10, 0 representing the value of no bargain and 10 that of the most advantageous bargain which Party can foresee. The utility value of the time costs and discount factor is assessed using the method described on p. 163, the scale selected being from 5 representing immediate agreement to 0 greater than 4 months.

The weighting to be given to the time factor relative to the

Item	Upper limit	Lower limit
Contribution margin	35%	30%
Delivery	24 months	22 months
Delay penalty limit	10%	15%
Consequential damages	not acceptable	not acceptable

Figure 17:4 Table of major items covered by the negotiation

achievement of the outcome will reflect not only the costs involved and the discounting loss, but also Party's need to secure the business quickly in relation to his forward order book and work on hand. This latter will also affect the degree to which the utility scale for the time factor is non-linear. In practice it will normally be found that Party is not seriously concerned with the extent of the negotiating period until it reaches some critical point, after which his concern will increase rapidly.

The expected value of a negotiating strategy is then found by multiplying the utility value of the bargain having taken time costs into account by the success probability.

The results are set out in Figure 17:5. In this example it has not been necessary to consider the possibility of no bargain since Party has already indicated he prefers strategy 1, which represents Opponent's current offer, by assigning to that strategy the utility value 2.

It is important to note that the key variable in estimating probabilities is the time over which the negotiations are conducted. Party's only justification for increasing his estimate of success probability of, say, outcome 3 from 40% to 60%, if he adopts strategy 4 in preference to strategy 3, is that strategy 4 involves extending the negotiations from 2 to 4 months.

On the basis of the figures in Figure 17:5 Party should clearly chose strategy three and aim to complete the negotiations in not more than 2 months. Based on that choice Party is able to decide on:

1 His degree of commitment and/or concession rate on each point.
2 Issues which he can expect to trade off one against another.

Also he can formulate what he now believes will be the shape of the final bargain.

17:6 MAKING THE NEXT MOVE
In making his next move following from the opening, its review and his decision on the follow-up strategy choice, Party's primary concern is with the degree of commitment he attaches to any issue. Commitment in this sense means that Party adheres strongly to a defined viewpoint.

It has been established already that firm commitment by Party,

1 Strategy number	2 Contribution margin (%)	3 Delivery (months)	4 Penalty limit (%)	5 Utility value of bargain	6 Time for negotiation	7 Time cost utility value	8 Conditional value of strategy col. 5 + col. 7	9 Success probability
1	30	22	15	2	0	5	7	1.0
2	32.5	23	12.5	6	1	4	10	0.8
3	32.5	24	10	8	2	3	11	0.4
4	35	24	10	10	4	1	11	0.2

Expected values EV

Strategy

1 1.0 (2 + 5) = 7

2 0.8 (6 + 4) + 0.2 (2 + 4) = 9.2

3 0.4 (8 + 3) + 0.5 (6 + 3) + 0.1 (2 + 3) = 9.4

4 0.2 (10 + 1) + 0.6 (8 + 1) + 0.1 (6 + 1) + 0.1 (2 + 1) = 8.6

Figure 17:5 Expected value of a series of possible strategies

which is demonstrated as such to Opponent, is likely to cause Opponent to reconsider his own estimates of success on the issue in question, and possibly to scale down his demands or his commitment to them accordingly. By demonstrating the strength of his commitment to any issue Party communicates to Opponent the importance which that issue possesses for Party. If he is successful in demonstrating a strong commitment, Party will cause Opponent either to concede outright or increase the value of the concession which he offers in exchange, unless Opponent is prepared to accept the risk of no bargain.

However, extreme firmness of commitment will only be an embarressment to Party if he is compelled by pressures generated by Opponent, or by external events, subsequently to withdraw. The loss of credibility which he will suffer will be even more serious than the immediate impact of the withdrawal on the outcome of the particular negotiation.

Party is therefore in the dilemma that if he is not firm enough he will not convince Opponent; if he is too firm, or firm on the wrong issue, he will lose credibility and will not be believed when later on he does genuinely intend to stand firm. The virtue of firmness lies only in its ability to be convincing to the other side.

In terms of the development of the negotiation the opportunities open to Party, in order of their weakness of commitment, may be stated broadly as follows.

1 Exploratory talks. Party gives no indication of his commitment to any particular position but continues to explore the issues under negotiation as he did in the opening phase.
2 Negotiations on fringe areas only. Party concentrates the serious negotiations and adopts a position of commitment only on minor issues; all major issues are put on one side for later discussion.
3 Negotiation on fringe issues; trade-off position developed on major issues. Party negotiates and may reach agreement on minor issues; on major issues Party defines his position with varying degrees of commitment and seeks to develop an overall trade-off situation which will lead to a final bargain. This may be one single 'package' but is more likely to be several.
4 Repetition of initial offer on major issues; bargaining limited to fringe areas. Party makes it clear that in his view the negotiations are only about the fringe areas. Having defined his position on the major areas in his offer he is not prepared really to discuss these in any detail; he is willing only to restate his position from which he is not prepared to move.

Unless due to the commercial structure of the negotiation either Party or Opponent is in a position of significant bargaining superiority, the negotiations, when viewed from either side, would be expected to fall generally into category 3. Categories 1 and 2 are only a matter of 'putting off the evil day' and indicate a substantial weakness in Party's position. Category 4 can only properly be adopted by Party if he is in a position of major strength. To select it he must be confident that Opponent, faced with total intransigence on all major issues, will in the end concede.

The process of commitment will be progressive. On very minor points there may be almost immediate agreement unless any of these are retained as 'straw issues' (see p. 381) for use as bargaining counters at a later stage. On more significant points Party and Opponent will reiterate and expand on their previous proposals with varying degrees of commitment but without closing the door totally on the possibility of finding some way in which their respective viewpoints may be reconciled.

Some of the points already made in discussing the strategic aspects of the negotiation are relevant to the issue of how commitments can be made with varying degrees of firmness, and it may be useful to recapitulate these here:

1   A written commitment is firmer than one made verbally.
2   A commitment will be firmer:
    (a) The more formally it is made.
    (b) The more senior the negotiator by whom it is made.
    (c) The more final the terms in which it is made.
    (d) The more specific the terms in which it is made.
3   A commitment can be increased by supportive action which is demonstrable as such to the other side.
4   Discussion of a proposal in advance within Party's own organization, and in particular its adoption as part of Party's negotiating plan, will increase Party's commitment to that proposal, and this commitment can be used by Party to demonstrate to Opponent the impossibility of Party agreeing to anything else.
5   Commitment may be increased by reference to the authority or requirements of third parties.
6   Maximum commitment can often be demonstrated by a minimum response—a simple yes or no said with sufficient conviction is more effective than a long speech.

Once commitments have been convincingly demonstrated, individual trading off of points may then take place, on terms which will allow both sides to claim that they have secured their own underlying objectives, whilst giving recognition to the other's viewpoint. As an example, consider a case in which Opponent and Party were negotiating on the times for various activities to be included within the overall contract completion period. Party as the supplier might agree to Opponent's proposals for a 4-week testing period at Party's works prior to shipment, provided that Opponent agreed to complete custom's clearance of the equipment for which he was responsible within 30 days instead of his original 45.

By these means the gap is gradually narrowed until only the really major issues remain. On these two the outlines of compromise may now be clear, although at this stage both sides will remain outwardly wedded to the stand which they have taken. If that is so, then Party and Opponent are ready to move to the final phase of first identifying and then reaching the ultimate bargain.

NOTES

1.   A. Coddington, *Theories of the Bargaining Process* (London: George Allen and Unwin, 1968), p. 93.
2.   See the discussion of Druckmann and Bass's experiments, Chapter 7, note 11, p. 200.
3.   I have noted how some negotiators with whom I have dealt will immediately follow a concession with taking a hard line on some point of minor significance as if to say: 'Now do not misjudge me; just because I gave in a few moments ago does not mean I am a soft touch; I can be tough as well, when I want to be; so just remember that.'
4.   J. G. Cross, *The Economics of Bargaining* (New York: Basic Books, 1969), p. 51.
5.   L. E. Siegel and S. Fouraker, *Bargaining Behaviour* (New York: McGraw-Hill, 1963), found that, in general, increasing the amount of information available to the bargainers, as to the profits to be derived by their opponent, led to their adopting a pareto-optimal strategy as opposed to one which simply maximized their own profits. The experiments conducted by Druckmann and by others have suggested that where the negotiators for Party and Opponent have engaged in bilateral prenegotiation discussions which have concentrated on an understanding of the problem issues, then this has facilitated the concluding of agreements. In the experiments of Bass, the only group to achieve agreement on all contracts working against a time deadline was that in which there had been prenegotiation study with opponents, but the favourability of the contracts negotiated was significantly less to Party than those in which there had been either unilateral study or study with others than the negotiators from Opponent. D. Druckmann, 'Prenegotiation experience and dydadic conflict', *Journal of Experimental Social Psychology*, vol. 4 (1968) pp. 367–83 and B. M. Bass 'Effects on the subsequent performance of negotiators of studying issues or planning strategies alone or in groups', *Psychological Monographs General and Applied* (no. 614,

1966), especially the results described in Table 1.

6. Intuitive judgement that this should be so is supported by experimental evidence. See, in particular, B. M. Bass 'Effects on the subsequent performance of negotiators of studying issues or planning strategies alone or in groups', *Psychological Monographs General and Applied* (no. 614, 1966), p. 14. But note this refers solely to the terms obtained from the negotiations, and does not take into account time costs.

7. The negative value of no bargain to Party will only change during the course of the negotiations if one of the factors upon which the valuation was made itself changes, eg if he is a supplier, the state of Party's forward order book, or, if he is a buyer, the loss he would suffer in time and cost of placing the business elsewhere.

The valuation should not be changed for emotional reasons such as the personal involvement of Party's negotiator's and their motivation for success. The valuation does not necessarily change with any alteration in the terms of the bargain now foreseen from those which Party assumed when he made his decision to open negotiations with Opponent. Again it should only be changed if the alteration directly affects some point which was relevant to the initial valuation, eg to Party as a supplier, a change in the scope of work which significantly affects the volume of production for some item or section of the contract.

8. T. C. Schelling, *The Strategy of Conflict* (London: Oxford University Press, 1963), p. 35.

9. In making a valuation of the bargain after the concession, Party may need to take account not merely of the immediate contract but of the longer-term effects of any precedent. If the longer-term effect would be serious Party must make an adjustment (see p. 292).

10. As the demand is associated with a time limit, after which negotiations are to be concluded, no other alternative is allowed for. If Party considered that the time limit might be extended to allow for further negotiations then he could consider the alternative of compromise, making some offer part way between Opponent's demand and Party's existing terms. This would imply that Party did not believe Opponent was serious in his time threat, in which event Party would be likely to gain more by standing firm and making Opponent reconsider his proposals.

11. See 'Threats in interpersonal negotiations,' H. H. Kelley, *Journal of Conflict Resolution,* vol. 9 (no. 7). The whole article is a thought-provoking analysis both of the use of threats and of the problems involved in the conduct of bargaining experiments, and the conclusions which may legitimately be drawn from them.

12. In a number of reported experiments significant stress has been placed on the differences in loyalty to a negotiating plan between a

negotiator operating on his own and one who has participated in group formulation of negotiating strategy. This loyalty factor has been shown to be particularly strong in situations in which the group possesses an influence over the negotiator's own future personal career. See B. M. Bass, 'Effects on the subsequent performance of negotiators of studying issues or planning strategies alone or in groups', *Psychological Monographs General and Applied* (no. 614, 1966), and the reports to which he refers.

However, it is suggested that a distinction should be drawn between a group loyalty, which the negotiator is willing to give and finds personally acceptable, and a loyalty to which the negotiator is required to conform by the demands of the company system, but which he as an individual does not necessarily find personally acceptable, eg a loyalty demand to head office. In the latter his primary loyalty will be to the company unit with which he is most strongly involved and to which he is most closely identified. When what he believes to be the interests of that unit and the demands of his head office are in conflict, his initial reaction will be to conform to the interests, as he believes them, of his unit. Later, if he is compelled to conform to head office requirements he will place the blame on head office for whatever he perceives to be the adverse outcomes of the negotiation, irrespective of the relationship of those outcomes to the conflict situation. Head office becomes the scapegoat with whom he identifies all adverse factors.

13. An example from my own experience concerned a negotiation in a foreign country in which the negotiating team, of which I was a member, was required to give immediate written answers to a series of propositions or withdraw from the negotiation. One of these propositions was for a three-month reduction in the delivery period! The answer given was to agree to the proposal but to provide that the delivery period started from the time when all technical information necessary to perform the contract was available, which in practice would have exceeded three months.

14. His belief will be in part a function of the tightness of the company's control procedures. As was indicated earlier (see p. 53) it is only by these controls being tight that inquests can be avoided. The negotiator, particularly if isolated from home base, needs the reinforcement of control procedures and a firm negotiating brief.

15. This follows the theory of *cognitive dissonance* developed by L. Festinger, described in *Scientific American* (October 1962).

16. Experimental evidence has shown that under conditions of high time pressure negotiators do set themselves lower minimal goals, and that their concessions are larger and more frequent than under conditions of low time pressure. D. G. Pruitt and D. F. Johnson 'Mediation as an aid to face saving', *Journal of Personality and*

Social Psychology, vol. 14 (no. 3, 1970) pp. 239–46.

17. The assumption is made that either the company's control procedures do not insist on the contract being reviewed by their lawyers or that if they do, the negotiator has decided to override them on the grounds that to insist on such review would cause the loss of the bargain. Again following the theory of cognitive dissonance it would be expected that the negotiator having made such decision would adjust his belief of the value of consultation with the lawyers, so that it became minimal. He would not allow himself to believe that a course of action which he had rejected possessed any significant value.

18. Of course, it may have changed as a result of a change in some factor peculiar to Party which was relevant to Party's original valuation, eg if Party is a supplier, a change in his forward order book which makes securing the current order either more or less desirable.

18

IDENTIFYING THE BARGAIN

18.1 SIGNALLING TO OPPONENT

It was indicated earlier that one of the difficulties which faces a negotiator is that of making his words credible. Since bluffing is universally recognized as an essential element in the real-life bargaining process, Party expects Opponent not to believe all that Party tells him. Further, Opponent knows that Party does not expect him to believe everything and would regard him as a bargaining simpleton if he did. Opponent is therefore constrained in two ways from believing what Party tells him. Firstly, in general, he has no absolutely reliable means of knowing whether Party is telling the truth or not. Secondly he is afraid of losing his own reputation as a negotiator with Party if he permits himself to be too easily deceived.

As the negotiations proceed, and each side makes concessions from the original starting position, the probability that they are telling more of the truth must increase. If either side actually does reach their minimum negotiating objective on any issue then they would actually be telling the truth if they stated they would prefer no bargain to making further concessions, But how is Opponent to know this? How is he to distinguish Party's protestations, that he can concede no further, from those which Party made earlier and from which he subsequently did concede?

The communication of credibility is a difficult task as many an unfortunate person has found when subjected to torture in order to compel him to disclose information of which he was ignorant. This is the serious disadvantage of any process of compulsion and perhaps of physical torture in particular; it may force a man to talk but cannot ensure that he will tell the truth.

How then do negotiators distinguish the truth from untruth; how do they know when they have secured the most favourable bargain which is open to them within the time scale concerned?

One answer is that they do not make the distinction; they continue to be deceived all the way through the negotiation and the end bargain does not on any major issue represent the minimum negotiating objective of either side. This was the conclusion reached by Ann Douglas in the four cases which she studied in American Union—Management negotiations and is supported by my own experiences in the field of commerce.[1]

However, the end deception may be more apparent than real. The bargain which is negotiated constitutes, in Diesing's words, 'the terms by which the parties are to live together'.[2] He was referring to collective bargaining between unions and management, but in this respect the principles are identical with those which apply to long-term relationships between supplier and purchaser.

Since the bargain is of this nature, and because the implementation of the contract will afford the opportunity for either side to work for the adjustment of the terms, if they feel aggrieved, there is an incentive for both sides not to inquire too closely into whether the bargain really does represent the most favourable outcome they could achieve. The attitude of the negotiator might be described as that of the man who says:

The bargain is good enough, even though I probably could achieve more. I know he is cheating a little, and if it makes him happy that's fine, but I've won the points I really wanted. It will probably help things along later; at least he will not be trying to score points.

Although this may represent the attitude of the negotiator at the time the bargain is made, it is not one which he will necessarily wish to disclose to his own management, or even later admit to himself. To his management he will rationalize the bargain as the best that was achievable; to himself he will adjust his beliefs so that they correspond to and support the action which he took. If this adjustment indicates that he may have been deceived the negotiator will look for a scapegoat which may be Opponent or someone in his own organization.

The way in which the negotiator's attitude may change is illustrated by the three statements set out below which describe the way in which the same negotiator might represent the same bargain, first at the time at which it was made, then later to his own management and finally to himself.

1   At the time of making the bargain: 'I agree to a bargain of 100 although I suspect Opponent would drop to 98, but a bargain at 100 satisfies my minimum negotiating objective, should keep him happy and ensure there are no problems in the future'

2   To his own management: 'I settled for 100 which is well within the negotiating objective and shows a saving of £X on the earlier contract. I doubt if any further reduction was feasible and in any event could only have been secured at the expense of quality.'

3   Later to himself: 'I agreed to 100 because I thought it was the lowest to which he would go on the basis of his cost figures. He could have deceived me on that. If I find out he did he'll get no mercy next time.'

Another more positive answer to the question is that negotiators do keep certain words, phrases and manners of expression or behaviour intact in terms of honesty. They do so not because they feel constrained for any ethical reasons against telling untruths but for reasons of operational necessity.[3] As Diesing has expressed it: 'There must always be some way to communicate one's true position without deception and without misunderstanding.'[4]

However, as stated by Goffman, there must be strict limits placed on the use of such signals since otherwise the negotiator might be tempted to misuse them, and statements unaccompanied by such signs would carry little weight.[5] The limitation is created very largely by the norms and structure of the negotiation itself. In the early stages Opponent will bluff and exaggerate, and the negotiator for Party will expect this and act similarly.[6] Later as the bargaining moves to the stage of identifying particular concession-exchange situations, the negotiator will expect to receive signals from Opponent which are genuine indicators of his position.

When a negotiator recognizes that he has received such a signal he knows that a bargain is available to him on those terms, and that any other terms could only be secured, if at all, by the use of any power threat available to the negotiator. However, this would only be likely to result in driving Opponent through his resentment level, so creating problems for the future (see p. 202).

The actual form of signal used will clearly vary from one negotiator to another but some which I have encountered in practice are as follows:

1　The negotiator states his position with the minimum of argument and includes some phrase indicative of commitment and the absence of bluff: 'That is my final position. It is now up to you'.
2　The proposal is complete and made in absolute terms; there are no loose ends.
3　The negotiator has left himself with no way out, other than to break off the negotiations, if his proposals are not accepted.
4　The negotiator's tone of voice is one of complete finality and his demeanour impassive. He looks straight at Opponent and does not shuffle about, fidget, whisper to colleagues or engage in other forms of displacement-type activity which would be indicative of tension associated with lying.
5　The negotiator's answers to any questions from Opponent are as brief as possible, often just a simple yes or no.

One method which the negotiator can use to be convincing to Opponent on a particular issue is to transfer it from the area of intercompany relations to that of the interpersonal relationships between himself and his opposite number. By so doing he changes the norms of social morality from those which prevail between competing organizations to those which provide the basis for dealings between persons within the same social relationship group. In effect the negotiator identifies himself and his opposite number as members of the club. During this period of identification the norms of morality which govern the negotiator's behaviour towards his opposite number, and according to which he expects his opposite number to behave, are those which apply between club members. Since it would be unthinkable for one club member to be dishonest to another, irrespective of how they treat outsiders, the negotiator by his actions has commited himself to telling the truth and equally has bound his opposite number to do the same.

This process will normally take place outside both the formal negotiating arena and the formal negotiating session, for example, at a coffee break or during prelunch drinks. The negotiator signals his intentions to his opposite number by treating him with a much higher degree of familiarity. He will use Christian names, perhaps take him by the arm, and will adopt a more intimate style of speech. If they have the same professional backgrounds or other common links the negotiator will refer to these.

18.2 COMMUNICATION AND COORDINATION
In analysing the reasons which lead the negotiators finally to settle on one figure, or one set of words, in preference to any others, there is a distinction between:
1 Power point coordination
2 Focal point coordination

Power point coordination
This refers to the situation in which the outcome is selected because it is preferred by both sides to no bargain and also represents the value which each believes the other only marginally prefers to no bargain, within the time period concerned. It is the outcome therefore which both sides believe is the minimum the other would accept within a specific time scale.

The buyer agrees to a price of £100 because he was willing to pay up to £102 but believes the supplier will not sell today for less than £100. The seller agrees to £100 because he was in fact prepared to sell for not less than £98 but believes that the buyer today will not pay more than £100.

The beliefs of the two sides as to the other's minimum figure may or may not be true; in general, as in the example given above, it is maintained that they are not true. My experience over many years, first as a buyer and latterly as a seller, is that in almost every case the other side could have obtained more had they pressed their case further, although certainly the outcome would have taken longer to achieve. If that is Party's experience of Opponent there is no reason to believe that his experience of Party is any different.

The explanation for this failure to maximize advantage appears to lie in the reasons which have created the negotiator's belief. He can rarely have any independent knowledge as to whether Opponent is willing to concede further or not. He must rely on the history of previous dealings with Opponent, the way in which the negotiations have proceeded and his observations of what Opponent says and does. His belief is accordingly entirely subjective and therefore subject to the family of motives which influence negotiating behaviour, some of which will favour proceeding further and others which will be in favour of settling now. The members of this family, which have been discussed already, are briefly identified in Figure 18:1.

Motives in favour of negotiating further	Motives in favour of settling now
1 Increasing the negotiator's self-esteem, and that in which he is held by others of significance to him, by obtaining further gains.	1 The diminishing marginal utility of further gains and the adverse influence these may have on future relationships with Opponent.
2 Satisfying the negotiator's need for self-actualization by achieving a better bargain.	2 The time it will take to secure further gains and the related time costs/discount factor.
3 Creating a more favourable precedent for the future.	3 The need for achieving certainty.
	4 The desire to end the conflict and establish or re-establish harmonious relationships with opponent.

Figure 18:1 Table of negotiating motives

The negotiator's belief as to whether Opponent will concede further or not is a blend of prediction and motivation, in which the interpretation placed by the negotiator on his observatons of Opponent's conduct is conditioned by the motives which influence the negotiator's own behaviour.

As the negotiations proceed and some concessions are made the degree of influence exerted by any particular motive will change. Initially the negotiator's need for achievement of esteem will pull him strongly towards holding out for better terms. However, once the negotiator's minimum negotiating objective has been secured, the influence of this particular motive will decline and that of another, say the fear of disturbing long-term relationships with Opponent, will begin to influence the negotiator more strongly.

This change in motivation will in turn influence the way in which the negotiator interprets Opponent's behaviour. Initially he will disbelieve and therefore ignore Opponent's protests that he cannot accept some particular term but later he may be prepared to listen more closely and offer Opponent a compromise; one that is designed not only to protect the negotiator but which will also, in the negotiator's judgement, satisfy Opponent's own motivation.

Provided that the negotiator's esteem motivation for continuing the negotiation is satisfied, to the point at which it ceases to be a matter of concern to him, no problem of dissonance will arise from his acting in a manner which will satisfy his other motivational drives. Suppose, however, that the esteem motive remains unsatisfied although the negotiator also recognizes that on balance other considerations, such as time costs, the need to obtain work for the company, preclude him from negotiating further. He will resolve the dissonance so created by 'interpreting' the resistance shown by Opponent to mean that however long the negotiations had continued he could not have secured more from them. He will adjust his interpretation of Opponent's behaviour so that it eliminates any feelings of personal inadequacy which he might otherwise have possessed. Additionally he may look for a scapegoat, a previous precedent set by another negotiator, or a rash statement made in the tender for which he was not responsible.

Therefore, it is never recognized, in the objective sense, by the negotiator, that Opponent will not concede further. He arrives at this belief in the compound way, from a mixture of observation and motivation. The influence of motivation has been discussed but how about the actual observation itself; what are the signs for the negotiator to read?

It is suggested that the following three signs are the most significant.

Continued repetition of a simple demand without change
By repetition Opponent increases his commitment to the demand. This implies that Opponent is willing to risk no bargain should Party not agree and, therefore, securing the demand is a part of Opponent's minimum negotiating objective.[7]

Establishment of a chain of logic which cannot be broken
If Opponent can demonstrate that a chain of logic exists which supports a particular demand, this establishes a commitment to the achievement of that demand. Opponent would suffer too serious a loss

of esteem were he to abandon the demand after having made such a demonstration.

As an example of this type of commitment, in negotiating the terms of a supply contract I demonstrated that it was illogical to apply the same warranty terms to equipment, the failure of which would put the entire system out of operation, and to equipment which if it failed would only affect system operation to a minor degree. Having established this principle I was committed to the achievement of its acceptance by Opponent.

Absence of any partial fall-back position
It is unlikely that Opponent will concede a demand if he has presented it in such a way that his only alternative to achieving success is capitulation. By denying himself the comfort of a fall-back position, which would allow him a partial gain at the expense of a partial concession, the negotiator puts himself into a situation in which he must either succeed or suffer serious humiliation. He is therefore strongly committed against making any concession.

Many examples could be drawn from other fields of human behaviour in which people have deliberately thrown away a safety mechanism in order to provide themselves with the strongest motivation for the achievement of their objective. The young swimmer who deliberately ventures out of his depth and throws away his plastic ring, the man with 'prospects' who takes on financial commitments slightly beyond his means and who must therefore ensure that the 'prospects' do materialize.[8]

Focal point coordination
Focal point coordination refers to the situation in which each side recognizes that the *same* outcome would satisfy their minimum negotiating objectives and would provide a fair and reasonable settlement of the difference between them. If proposed to each of them by an independent mediator, each would separately agree that the point constituted a fair bargain.[9]

The conditions necessary for focal point coordination to occur are:

1   The two sides share a social and ideological background which is sufficiently common for them both to possess the same general views as to what is fair and reasonable.
2   The gap between the demands of the two sides is such that a solution which both recognize as fair and reasonable is identifiable as being preferred to any other mutual choice.

For example, if there is a prominent solution which balances almost equally the demands of the two sides, and both belong to a society which adheres to the equity of equal shares, then both are likely to identify a 50/50 split as being an acceptable outcome.[10]

It is stressed that both conditions 1 and 2 must be satisfied if focal point coordination is to occur. For instance, if the buyer is concerned only with purchasing at the lowest price, and is uninterested in whether this policy in the long run provides sufficient rewards for suppliers to invest in efficiency, then focal point coordination will not arise, since the ideology of the two sides will be too sharply opposed. It is also worth noting in this context that different pairs of negotiators for Party and Opponent may differ in the focal point at which they coordinate or even whether or not they do coordinate.

The negotiators' attitude towards what he regards as a focal point on which to coordinate will depend upon:

1   His professional background. Coordination is easier if the two negotiators share the same background.
2   The extent to which his motivational drives for security and esteem have been satisfied. The less the negotiator feels the need to prove himself the more likely he is to be fair.
3   His emotional bias for or against the negotiator for the other side. Any prejudice against the other is bound to influence the negotiator to be less fair; conversely a favourable bias towards the other person will tend to influence the negotiator towards wishing to be fair and therefore he will more easily recognize a potential focal point.
4   His emotional bias for or against the principle which the other side is seeking to establish. Again any prejudice against the arguments being presented by the other side must prevent the negotiator from taking an objective approach.

Factors which will lead the two sides to recognize a particular outcome as a focal point will be:

1   A precedent set at a previous negotiation, the results or operation of which both sides have been satisfied.
2   The rounding down of a demand, usually so that the last two digits of a four-figure number, the last three digits of a five-figure number and the last four digits of a six figure number are zeros. A supplier will often take advantage of this to arrange the price in such a way that the buyer reacts to the presentation accordingly. The fewer the number of zeros with which the price ends the more prominent the reduction to round numbers becomes as a focal point, eg £462 265 is a more powerful signal to coordinate at £460 000 than £462 200.
3   The gap between the demands of the two sides is not too large and

can be divided in a manner which is intuitively appealing, eg 1:1 (50/50), 2:1 (⅔/⅓), 3:1 (75/25).

4   The existence of some formula, however crude, for apportioning the difference or relating payments, the facts for the calculation of the formula being easily ascertained and not in dispute. The formula in this case takes on the nature of a scapegoat, as it does to some extent in factor 3. It becomes in itself the justification for the bargain and is at hand to take the blame should the bargain be criticized.

As suggested in the comment on factor 2, it is common negotiating strategy for Party to structure his demand or his response to Opponent's demand, in such a way as to create a situation which points towards a focal point. If the invitation is accepted by Opponent, the bargaining is then concerned with the identification of the actual focal point upon which to coordinate and not with the principle of acceptance or non-acceptance of Party's demand/response.

Party's strategy choice

The capability of the two sides to coordinate at all is primarily a function of the compatability of their needs. If these are compatible to a degree which makes coordination feasible, then the type of coordination and the point at which it occurs will be a reflection of the ideology and personality characteristcis of the negotiators involved.

In deciding on his negotiating strategy, therefore, Party is not a free agent. He is restricted in his choice by factors related to Opponent, at least some of which Party cannot hope to change, eg Opponent's social and political ideology. If Opponent's belief system is such that he regards securing the most favourable price as more important than incurring delays to the project through protracted negotiations (often the case with buyers in certain Communist countries), then Party must expect Opponent to be much more strongly· motivated towards continuing the negotiations than his Western counterpart. Because of this need to secure concessions from Party, Opponent can also be expected to go on for a longer period of time refusing to believe Party's argument that he cannot make further concessions. The conditioning effect of motivation on belief is not confined to one ideology alone.

Under these circumstances focal point coordination is clearly impossible and power point coordination something to which Opponent will only move slowly and with reluctance.

Party makes his choice, therefore, taking into account his belief of Opponent's attitudes. If these are in sympathy with coordination on a focal point, Party's original demand and subsequent concessions are directed towards that focal point which represents the most favourable outcome Party believes he can secure.

Alternatively, if Party considers Opponent will not be sympathetic towards a focal point, Party's strategy will be to convince Opponent of Party's commitment to the achievement of some outcome which he believes is just acceptable to Opponent, within a time scale which makes that outcome optimal to Party.

18.3 POLICY ISSUES

In their search for a solution upon which to coordinate, a factor which may inhibit the two sides is any issue of which the acceptance or non-acceptance would involve the negotiator in departing from a policy rule. If the rule is in the nature of a social custom then, under extremes of pressure, the negotiator may give way and correct the dissonance so caused by an adjustment of his belief as to the respective values of the custom and the bargain he has made. However, if the rule is a command which the negotiator (say, for Opponent) is compelled to obey, no concession is possible and Party's continued insistence on the point must cause the negotiations to deadlock.

The alternative is to search for a solution which does not directly involve any point of principle, but is concerned solely with practicalities. In a dispute between two nations over their rights in regard to a disputed piece of territory, to raise the issue of sovereignty directly must cause an emotional deadlock. Provided that the negotiators concentrate on such practical matters as customs formalities, entry and exit documents, work permits, etc, a workable compromise may be achieved.

The same type of problem will arise in negotiations with government departments or quasi-governmental organizations. Sometimes the rules of these bodies have the force of law, for example, the Armed Services Procurement Regulations of the USA. In other instances, as with the standard contracting procedures of the British government departments and nationalized industries, they are a matter of departmental orders which, whilst lacking the force of law, are regarded as binding by the officials concerned and only subject to amendment with difficulty and at the highest level. To depart from them in a particular case would create a precedent which it would then be difficult, particularly for Ministry officials, to refuse to others.

The commitment of the government body to these rules clearly strengthens the bargaining position of the government negotiators.[11] They cannot concede the issue and their lack of authority is demonstrable to the commercial negotiator who knows that if he raises the issue directly he cannot succeed.

By the establishment of such rules the issue is transferred outside the negotiating arena and converted into a parameter of the negotiating situation, inside which the commercial negotiator must seek means to achieve his objective. If the negotiator is bound by a government accountancy formula for determining his overheads, he must look elsewhere for the recovery of these cost elements which the formula disallows. Instead of arguing the principal of whether a particular element of overheads should be allowed or not, the negotiator bargains on a percentage figure, as a figure, without reference to the elements of which it is constituted. This can be taken a stage further and the price, as a whole, negotiated without any settlement being reached on particular cost items, wage rates or profit margins, on which, if taken individually, the official negotiator may be unwilling to commit himself for fear of offending some rule or creating a precedent for the future.

NOTES

1.   A. Douglas, *Industrial Peacemaking* (Columbia: Columbia University Press, 1962), p. 199.

2.   P. Diesing, 'Bargaining strategy and union—management relationships', *Journal of Conflict Resolution*, vol. 5 (no. 4) footnote to p. 376.

3.   Moral repugnance against lying arises only when to lie would be contrary to the social behavioural norm established by society for the particular circumstances in question. Society has not designated bargaining in general as an area in which there is a social norm against the making of self-disbelieved statements. On the contrary (see Section 7.4) it has been proposed that it is an accepted part of negotiating behaviour to make such statements, and no condemnation will be made of the person making them provided that they arise naturally out of the negotiations.

It is only certain acts, eg shaking hands to seal an oral bargain, which society treats as a commitment from which it would be socially unacceptable for the negotiator to seek to withdraw.

4.   P. Diesing, 'Bargaining strategy and union-management relationships', *Journal of Conflict Resolution,* vol. 5 (no. 4), pp. 375–76. See also I. Goffman, *Strategic Interaction* (Oxford: Blackwell, 1970), p. 128.

5.   I. Goffman, *Strategic Interaction* (Oxford: Blackwell, 1970), p. 129.

6.   This provides one of the reasons for negotiation. Each side must bargain, and must bluff in order to bargain, because they have no alternative means for testing the truth of the other's statements. If either were to fail to bargain then they must suffer. This is illustrated by the following matrix which describes the outcomes to be expected by Party, according to whether he bargains or not, following the submission of an offer by Opponent, and according to whether Opponent's offer was a bluff or already had been reduced to his minimum negotiating objective. The assumption is made that by bargaining

Party will eliminate the bluff element in Opponent's offer to zero, and that Opponent will not reduce his offer below his minimum negotiating objective, in the case in which he has not bluffed, so that in this instance Party will incur costs due to time and the discount factor, without any corresponding gain. The figures are in £'000s.

	Opponent	
	Believes Party will bargain so has bluffed	Does not believe Party will bargain so has not bluffed
Party Bargains	0	−1
Does not bargain	−10	0

Clearly unless Party can be *certain* that Opponent has not bluffed then Party must bargain. This would only arise from the structure of the negotiating situation, eg submission of a competitive tender to a strict public authority (see p. 105).

7. An interesting example of this occurred in the 1973 Common Market negotiations on farm prices, in which the German negotiator Herr Ertl only managed to convince the EEC Commission that his country's real interests are the protection of the German farmers, irrespective of how good an investment in agricultural terms they might be, by stubbornly refusing to change his negotiating position on the border tax payments which protect German farmers.

8. For other examples see T. C. Schelling, *The Strategy of Conflict* (London: Oxford University Press, 1963), p. 19. Schelling also makes the point that the negotiator increases the effect of the commitment by making it clearly visible to Opponent that he has no fall-back position.

9. For an example of a solution proposed by a mediator which provided a focal point on which the negotiators could coordinate see T. C. Schelling, *The Strategy of Conflict* (London: Oxford University Press), p. 63.

10. This was certainly the case in the experiments in price negotiations reported in L. E. Siegel and S. Fouraker, *Bargaining and Group Decision Making* (New York: McGraw-Hill, 1960), and confirmed in their later work *Bargaining Behaviour* (New York: McGraw-Hill, 1965).

11. This was the declared intention of the United States Congress when they passed the cost or pricing data law, under which it was made mandatory for the contractor to furnish the government negotiators with adequate cost or pricing data.

19

CONCLUDING THE BARGAIN

19.1 THE FINAL REVIEW

Immediately prior to the session at which the negotiator believes the final bargain will be reached, it is essential that he conducts a review for the purpose of:

1 Identifying *all* the points which are still outstanding.
2 Deciding on the bargain on each point which he expects to achieve, and the limit on each point to which he is prepared to concede either singly or in combination with other issues.
3 Determining any particular tactics to be used.
4 Deciding on the arrangements for recording the bargain.

The duration and formality of this review will depend on the magnitude of the negotiations. It may be only a twenty-minute recess towards the end of a single day's bargaining; it may be a formal meeting, at which a director or general manager of the firm is present, before the negotiator and his colleagues depart for the final round of talks.

Irrespective of the form of the review, it is the time at which the final decisions must be made and the alternative of no bargain squarely faced. The approach to the review should therefore be in terms of the value of the agreement to Party as a whole. Each outstanding point, on which the policy has been to resist Opponent's demands, should be re-examined to see whether Party really would prefer to walk away and lose the bargain rather than to concede. This is the time at which narrow departmental interests *must not* be allowed to prevail. This is not suggesting a policy of concession but one of realism in relation to Party's overall business objectives. Contractual risks may be unpalatable to the lawyer and every effort made to avoid the more serious ones, but, in the end, a contract should only be turned down if an evaluation of the risk shows that it is unacceptable relative to the contract as a whole and to the totality of Party's business circumstances.

19.2 THE FINAL CONCESSION

It has been indicated already that Party's dilemma in making a concession is that of retaining a reputation for firmness whilst indicating a willingness to 'meet' Opponent, and so encourage him to reciprocate. In the concluding stages of a negotiation the timing and magnitude of the final concessions are of major importance.

19.3 TIMING

If the concession is made too early Opponent will believe that it is merely another one 'along the road' and so be encouraged into demanding more and conceding less himself. If it is too late then, unless its value is very significant, it will get lost and make little or no impact on Opponent.

For the purpose of timing it is suggested that the final concessions should be divided into two parts. The major part should be made at a time which allows just sufficient opportunity for Opponent to review and consider prior to the deadline.[1] One minor concession should be held in reserve as a final 'sweetener', if it becomes absolutely necessary, and offered at the very last moment.

The essence of the manner in which the final concessions are made is the emphasis placed on their finality. The negotiator must at this point be able to communicate credibility.

19.4 MAGNITUDE

The communication of credibility is dependent as much on the magnitude of the final concession as on its timing and the manner in which it is made. If it is too large, Opponent is unlikely to believe that it represents Party's last word, unless Party has very carefully prepared the ground in advance. If it is too small, it will be regarded by Opponent as trivial, perhaps even insulting, so that Party will have gained nothing.

One major factor in determining the size of the final concession is the level of the person in Opponent's organization to whom it is to be made.

With certain organizations, it is normal for the final negotiations to be held with someone from Opponent's management of signficantly higher seniority than the officials with whom Party has been negotiating to date. If Party foresees this then he should ensure that he is in a position to make a concession which is:

1 Large enough to just satisfy the higher dignitary in terms of his need to maintain his position.
2 Not so large that he censures his officials for having failed to do their job and insists they continue the negotiations further.

After he has made his final concession Party must remain firm. It is to be expected that Opponent will test the strength of Party's determination by tactics such as insulting language, walking out or telling Party to leave. Any weakness by Party at this stage will immediately be exploited by Opponent and Party will have lost his credibility.

19.5 COUPLING
One of Party's fears in making his final concession is that it will not lead to a responsive concession from Opponent but will only encourage Opponent into continuing his resistance.

Unless Party's concession is a total acceptance of Opponent's current demand, Party must signal to Opponent either prior to, or in the course of making his final concession, that he expects Opponent to respond. Two of the ways in which Party may give such signals are as follows:

1   The negotiator in presenting the concession suggests that it is his own idea for which he may well get into trouble with his company. Therefore, he could only agree to such a bargain provided that Opponent reciprocated so that he had something to sell to his management when he returns home. 'I am willing to agree to your proposals on the rate of delay penalty although probably I will be heavily criticized for it, but you will have to help me on the *force majeure* clause.'
2   The negotiator does not give the concession directly but indicates his willingness to do so against a concession from Opponent. 'I have thought over the proposals on inspection and quite frankly I do not see a lot of difficulty there, providing an agreement can be reached on the time for delivery.' The phrase 'I do not see much difficulty there', or words to the same effect, has come to be something of a standard signal that the negotiator is willing to concede the point not now but in the future.

19.6 ENSURING AGREEMENT IS GENUINE
One of the difficulties in negotiation is to ensure that the two sides have identical understanding of what is being said. Differences in terminology, the use of words which are terms of art to one side, but not to the other, and differences in language, all contribute to misunderstandings. It is never more important than at the time when the bargain is being made that the two sides should have identical understanding of the terms to which they are agreeing.

The following is a guide to some points which commonly cause difficulties and in respect of which the negotiator should be especially careful.

Price
1   Is it fixed or can the contractor recover for increases in labour and material cost?

2 Does the price cover taxes, duties and other statutory charges? If so, and these are increased during the period of the contract, who pays the increase?
3 Is the currency fixed against exchange-rate fluctuations?
4 Is it clear what the contract price does *not* include?

Completion
5 is completion clearly defined? Does it include customer testing of the plant/system?
6 Can a completion/acceptance certificate be issued if minor items are missing which do not affect system/plant performance?
7 Can completion be by sections and is this clearly set out?

Specification
8 Are the purchaser's obligations clearly defined for the issue of permits, licences and approvals of drawings, etc, with time periods for the performance of each?
9 If any general standards of national or international institutions are referred to, is it clear which issue of these applies and which parts are relevant to the contract?
10 Are the materials/equipment tests both in factory and on site clearly defined with their tolerance limits and testing methods?
11 Is it clear who has the responsibility for customs clearance, delivery of goods to site, off-loading and storage?
12 Is it clear who has the design responsibility for both the permanent and any temproary works?

Claims settlement
13 What is the scope of the settlement?
14 Is the settlement a final bar to any future legal proceedings?

Points such as these, so far as they apply to any particular negotiation, and any others judged relevant, should be gone through thoroughly to ensure that there is a genuine meeting of minds between the two sides. It may be objected that this gives either side the opportunity to back-track and reopen a point already settled. It is admitted there is a risk of this, but it is judged to be a less serious risk than that of entering into a bargain which genuinely is interpreted quite differently by the two sides.

19.7 RECORDING THE BARGAIN
Depending on the nature of the negotiations there are a number of ways in which the bargain may be recorded; the fundamental point is that it is recorded in writing and initialled by the two sides before they depart. The possible methods of recording are:

1   Notes or clauses are read over and agreed between the negotiators as each point is settled. Normally this method is used when the negotiations are concerned with the commercial clauses and specifications for a complete contract.
2   Notes of the day's discussions are prepared by one side in the evening and presented for agreement as the first item of the next day's agenda. Only when these have been agreed do the negotiations proceed. This is laborious but recommended for prolonged negotiations particularly in certain communist countries.
3   Notes of the discussions are prepared by one side and presented for agreement at the end of the negotiations. This is the easiest method provided that the negotiations only last 2 or 3 days.

The meetings should never be allowed to break up without an agreed written record. The practice of one side issuing minutes days or even weeks later has nothing to commend it, and only causes more argument as the minute writer is so easily tempted into recording what he would have liked to have been said and not what actually was said.

NOTE
1.   The closer to the deadline, the less the time left to Opponent to review and the greater the time pressure brought on Opponent. The lateness in timing will have increased the credibility of Party's offer as being truly 'final'. But, whilst rationally sound, the tactic may create an emotional outburst if Opponent believes he is being 'crowded', and only serve to increase the difficulties of reaching a bargain.

PART FOUR

Negotiating tactics

20

ATTITUDINAL TACTICS

Tactics are generally thought of as specific ploys which are used in certain defined situations to achieve some advantage in much the same manner as conventions are used in bridge. This certainly describes one class of tactics which are referred to as situation tactics (see Chapter 21). However, there is another class of tactics, which relate to the attitudes the negotiators for the two sides have towards each other, and therefore referred to as attitudinal tactics.

In adopting such tactics, Party is concerned to create the conditions under which the personal interaction between the negotiators leads towards agreement on terms which are closer to Party's viewpoint than to Opponent's and at least satisfy Party's minimum negotiating objective. Further, and in a long-term continuing relationship between the two sides, a factor of almost equal importance is that this result is achieved without Opponent being left with a feeling of resentment.

In any negotiation the negotiators for the two sides are each playing a particular role, both within the confines of the negotiation and outside in the broader context of their in-company relationships. For instance, the negotiator may be playing the role of buyer, and within that role he knows that he is expected to achieve certain results which will come to represent at least his minimum level of aspiration. Clearly this role and that of the negotiator representing the seller are to some degree opposed, for example, in terms of the price to be paid and the period for delivery.

Equally this opposition is not total; if it were negotiation would become impossible and no agreement would be reached. Opposition will exist in varying degrees and the factors which will determine the extent of this opposition are:

1   The way in which the negotiator 'sees' the role character. Because he is playing the role of buyer he may believe he must demonstrate his toughness by humiliating the seller. That is to say, in taking the role he adopts the attitudes which he believes are appropriate to that role.
2   The negotiator's own personality, and the extent to which this is in sympathy with, or opposed to, his views of the role character. If the personality of the mythical negotiator who 'sees' the buyer as a

hard man is domineering, then his role attachment will be much stronger than that of someone else who is himself naturally unassertive.

3 The negotiator's own level of aspiration relative to that of his opponent. Given the power balance between the two sides, and the issues involved, then, in general, the higher the levels of aspiration the greater the degree of opposition.

4 The personality interaction between the two negotiators; the degree to which the negotiator feels that his opposite number:

(a) Understands the negotiator's own situation and needs.

(b) Is the type of person for whom the negotiator can have respect and with whom he can do business.

The tactics which are designed to modify these four factors, so as to improve the chances of reaching agreement on terms which are favourable to Party, may be classified as *positive* and *negative*.

A positive tactic is one which is intended either to reinforce behaviour by Opponent, which is already favourable to Party, or to change Opponent's behaviour in the desired direction by emphasizing the rewards which Opponent will obtain from so doing.

Negative tactics are those which are intended either to deter Opponent from some forseen course of action, which would be unfavourable to Party, or to change his behavioural direction away from its present course, by actually penalizing Opponent, or at least indicating the penalties he will suffer unless he does change.[1]

20.1 IN THE OPENING PHASE

At the commencement of any negotiation the initial attitudes of the negotiators for the two sides will range between reserved cordiality and concealed hostility depending on the extent to which:

1 The negotiators are already known to, and have respect for, each other.

2 The results of the last negotiation and the outcome of the contract, if any, which followed from these, and how far the result satisfied the negotiator's personal motivation.

The manner in which the negotiator makes his first approach, and the tactic he selects, will be based upon his judgement as to the form which these attitudes take. The possible situations and the appropriate tactical choice are analysed as follows:

Situation	*Class of tactical choice*		*Example of tactic to be employed*
Negotiators known to, and respected by, each other. Last negotiation satisfied both sides.	Mild, positive	1	Questions designed to identify the sharing of common business interests: 'How are your plans going for . . .' 'I was interested to see the progress you have been making in . . .'
		2	Questions and/or statements intended to re-establish close personal relationships. 'How are (wife's name) and the children?' 'Have you been playing **any** (golf, tennis, etc.) **lately?**'
Negotiators known to and respected by each other. Last negotiation did not wholly satisfy Party.	Mild, positive plus Mild, negative	1 2	As for the previous situation. Use of statements to indicate negotiator would have a personal problem if he does not achieve a better result than he did last time: 'I'd better say straight away John that I cannot afford a repeat of what happened on (name of last contract). If we are going to get anywhere, and I am sure we will, I hope you have come pre-

Situation	Class of tactical choice	Example of tactic to be employed
		pared to be a little more flexible.' Note this approach identifies the problem as one which is personal to the negotiator and he appeals to his opposite number on a personal basis, but with just the hint of a threat behind his words.
Negotiators known to each other but Party does not respect Opponent.	Strong, positive plus Strong, negative	Use of statements to emphasize benefits to be gained by not repeating the past coupled with definite threats should Opponent not respond. 'I am sure we both want to make progress so I suggest we ignore past negotiations and concentrate on the present and future. We have got some firm proposals to make which are intended to be constructive. I suggest we discuss these with an open mind and see how far we can reach. If, having done that, you still do not feel they can form the basis of an agreement, we shall have to decide where we go from there. Maybe we shall have to take the matter upstairs and call in (refer to managing director or

Situation	Class of tactical choice	Example of tactic to be employed
		other relevant person of superior authority) and get him to talk to your Mr. . . . I would prefer that not to happen and so, I am sure, would you so let us see if we can get there on our own.'
Negotiators not known to each other personally but Opponent has had previous dealings with Party's company. 1 Previous dealings regarded by the negotiator as having been satisfactory.	Mild, positive	Use of statement to indicate that the negotiator is aware of the satisfactory nature of the previous dealings and to identify personal points of mutual contact. Use of questions to discover points of common interest and to bring the negotiator into the family of personal relationships which exist between the negotiator for Opponent and other members of Party's firm.
2 Previous dealings not regarded by the negotiator as wholly satisfactory, so that he wishes to avoid these being treated by Opponent as a precedent for all	Mild, positive plus Mild, negative	Use of questions and/or statements which will lead to the establishment of a personal relationship, but which will also indicate to Opponent that the negotiator has taken over from

Situation	*Class of tactical choice*	*Example of tactic to be employed*
aspects of the current negotiation.		those with whom Opponent dealt before, and does not necessarily accept as a precedent the terms of the earlier bargain. The selection by the negotiator of one or more issues upon which he takes a tough line to serve as a warning to Opponent that the negotiations will not be so easy this time, and the sooner his attitudes changes the better.
Negotiators not known to each other and no recent personal contacts between other members of their respective firms.	Strong, positive	The use of questions aimed at discovering points of common interest and identifying any strongly held beliefs. Not all these questions would be asked at once but as the opportunity arose during initial periods of conversation, over drinks or during lunch/dinner. These questions might cover 1 Length of time with company and area of responsibility. 2 Previous company and position held. 3 Professional background. 4 Outside interests,

Situation	Class of tactical choice	Example of tactic to be employed
		eg golf, tennis, sailing.
		5 Family: children, education, etc.
		Having asked the questions, the negotiator volunteers in reply information about himself and his own business/ social situation which emphasizes points of mutual interest or contact. Points upon which the negotiators differ or lack mutual interest are minimized.

20.2 IN THE LATER PHASES

It has already been suggested that one of the factors which will affect Opponent's attitude towards Party is his level of aspiration, and that Opponent will select a level which maximizes the product of his personalistic utility function and the probability of achieving that level (see p. 197).

Since the higher Opponent's level of aspiration, the greater his opposition to Party, it must be in Party's interest to reduce Opponent's aspiration level, and so develop in Opponent an attitude more favourable towards Party's viewpoint. Therefore Party's attitudinal tactics will be those which the negotiator considers are the most appropriate for persuading Opponent that the utility he would gain, and/or his chance of obtaining that outcome, are less than he thought.

Some possible means which Party can use for this purpose are now considered.

Changing Opponent's utility valuation

One course of action would be to persuade Opponent that in the long term he personally will lose more than he will gain if he insists on demanding a particular outcome.

As an example, consider a contractor who is negotiating with a construction authority which is insisting on a more onerous penalty clause than the contractor wishes to accept. One argument against the authority could be that if the particular line on penalty is insisted upon and Party is forced to agree, then to protect himself, Party would be compelled to apply strictly all the administrative procedures on variations, extensions of time, etc, during the course of the contract. That would increase Opponent's administrative work and costs. It would also reduce flexibility and could affect the good relations which have existed between the site staffs in the past which could be detrimental to the contract. Opponent should be asked if he really believes that this insistence is in his own interests and be reminded that he may soon have complaints from his local staff.

A second method is to offer Opponent an alternative bargain with reasons which he can use to justify its acceptance both to himself and to others and, at the same time, making it clear that Opponent has minimal chance of obtaining the outcome for which he has been pressing.

The following is based on my experience. An exporter had been arguing with an overseas buyer that acceptance of certain high-technology equipment should be at the exporter's works; the buyer had been arguing that he only ever accepts goods on delivery to site. There were three remote sites involved.

The exporter finally proposed provisional acceptance at his works and final acceptance at the buyer's central depot, with the buyer having the right only to repeat the exporter's factory tests according to the exporter's test procedures and specifications. If the tests were not carried out within 30 days of the equipment's arrival at the depot, acceptance would be deemed to have been given.

The proposal was accepted by the negotiator for the buyer although he knew that they had no intention of carrying out the tests, since to do so would have meant purchasing additional and expensive test equipment. However, the proposal satisfied the negotiator's aspiration level in that:

1　It appeared on paper to be an improvement on the exporter's original proposal.
2　It retained the principle of final acceptance only being given after the equipment had been delivered to the buyer's country.
3　It satisfied the objections of the buyer's legal department since it followed closely enough past precedents from other contracts. (They were, of course, unaware that the right existed only on paper and the negotiator for the buyer had no intention of telling them.)

Naturally the negotiator for the exporter emphasized the above points in presenting and discussing his proposal and, at the same time, made it clear that he had no intention of agreeing to acceptance at site with the delays and uncertainties which that would involve.

Success in using tactics which are intended to persuade Opponent to modify his utility function depends on selecting the right person in Opponent's organization to whom to present a particular line of argument. In the first example, it would have been little use presenting that argument to a lawyer who would probably believe that strict adherence to contractual procedures is a good idea. To an engineer or commercial negotiator acquainted with the way in which contracts are actually run in practice, the argument is highly persuasive.

A third course of action is to persuade Opponent that his valuation conflicts with commercial equity. Already the view has been expressed that negotiators the world over do not like to be criticized by their opponent for being unfair (see Introduction). In companies which have established written purchasing procedures there is often to be found some phrase such as 'fair and reasonable' or 'fair and equitable' to describe the approach which the buyer should take in negotiation, for example, see the Ford Motor Company Policy guide extracts from which are set out in Appendix C to *The Industrial Buying Decision*.[2]

Despite the widespread use of such phrases it is difficult to arrive at a definition of what constitutes fair commercial conduct which would command universal acceptance. The moral basis upon which one human being should deal with another in a business sense has been, and still is, the subject of much ethical speculation. Where moral precepts have been derived from religion they appear too unrealistic to provide practical guidance, although it is interesting to note that the major religions of the world do not appear to differ significantly in their general attitudes.[3] The suggestion which seems most nearly to approach enlightened commercial practice is that of Professor Stace: 'the proper degree of unselfishness in my dealings with you is that degree which will result in both you and I receiving a fair and equitable share of the available satisfaction'.[4]

Into the definition of what is fair, this imports the concept of sharing the benefits which are available in an equitable manner, but still leaves undefined the question of the proportions in which the sharing is to take place. Professor Stace's words are reminiscent of those used by Nash in describing his formulation of a fair division between two rational bargainers and certainly Nash has provided one answer to the problem.[5]

It can however be argued that the Nash solution is only fair in an ethical sense if there is economic symmetry between the negotiators. If their economic roles are asymmetrical then, as Luce and Raiffa have pointed out, this will be reflected in the shape of their utility functions.[6] If each then behaves rationally and adopts the Nash solution this must result in the negotiator whose economic position is weaker, and his need accordingly the greater, receiving the smaller share!

Contract price £'000s	Profit share supplier	buyer	Supplier's utility	Buyer's utility	Utility product
20	5	0	1	0	0
19	4	1	0.95	0.1	0.095
18	3	2	0.9	0.3	0.27
17	2	3	0.7	0.6	0.42
16	1	4	0.4	0.8	0.32
15	0	5	0	1	0

Figure 20:1 The Nash Solution

This may be illustrated by the following example. It is agreed between a buyer and a seller that the shop cost for a contract is £15 000. The buyer's budget allows him to spend up to £20 000. The buyer is a large corporation and the supplier is a small firm desperately short of work. The respective utility functions for the two firms relative to the £5 000 to be split between them are set out in Figure 20.1 which also shows the product of these. The Nash solution would give a profit of £2 000 to the supplier and £3 000 to the buyer.

The form of the supplier's utility function (which shows that he is indifferent to a certainty of profit of 1 and a gamble with a 40% chance of a profit of 5 and a 60% chance of a zero profit) clearly reflects his urgent need for orders. Given that the buyer's utility function is more or less linear with money, or shows a slight risk preference in favour of taking the gamble, as in the example, the result of applying the Nash solution must be an outcome which favours the buyer.

Although it is not pretended that negotiators in the real world base their strategies on knowing the Nash solution, it is contended that their preference functions, if both behave rationally, and consider only their own interests, will lead them to an outcome which is very close to that proposed by Nash. Only if the economically stronger party includes the needs of the weaker when making the assessment of his preferences from which his utility function is derived, can the effect of asymmetry be corrected. He must consciously consider the results of his own preference choice on the other negotiator so that his reasoning would be on the lines: 'I know I would prefer a gain of 3 for myself but that would only leave 2 for him which hardly seems fair. After all, I can afford to pay the extra 1 more than he can afford to lose it.'

It is recognized that such reasoning implies an interpersonal comparison of utility values which previously have been regarded as inadmissible. Once ethical considerations are introduced which require Party to have regard to the effect of his preference choice upon Opponent, and to modify that choice if he feels that it would produce an unfair result, then it seems inevitable that such comparisons must be made.

Fairness requires that both sides take the interests of the other into account when placing a value upon the achievement of any particular outcome, even when there is no other compulsion to do so.[7] The gain which Party would achieve from success on a particular issue is balanced with the detriment which would accrue to Opponent, and Party only insists on a demand which balances his own essential interests with his view of what is essential for Opponent. He can then argue that he has been fair in limiting his demand to X, that he could have asked for Y which would have been much worse for Opponent, and that Opponent should now respond by moderating his own demand and showing similar fairness.

It follows that if Party wishes to use the tactic of appealing to the principle of fairness to persuade Opponent to moderate his demands, he must first demonstrate fairness in his own conduct. Further, his argument will be that much more persuasive, and difficult to rebut, if he can establish that in showing fairness to Opponent he did so from a feeling of moral duty in the Kantian sense and not from any reasons of expediency or self-interest.

A fourth method is to change Opponent's views about the point at which he would just prefer no bargain to reaching agreement.

This can be done most effectively by actions which are outside the scope of the actual discussions between Party and Opponent. In referring to political negotiations Ikle and Leites instance the strengthing of forces or military advances during armistice negotiations.[8] An example from the commercial field would be the buyer who ensured that catalogues and samples from a firm's principal competitor were prominently displayed when that firm arrived for discussions, or who held a purported conversation with the competitor arranging a meeting to discuss his quotation, which he allowed the firm to overhear.

Earlier it was argued that in a normative sense moves such as these should not alter the point at which agreement is preferred to no agreement. Certainly they may cause Party to moderate his not so essential demands and to adopt a less ambitious approach to the negotiations. But the level of the break point should be changed only if one of the factors which were used to assess that level itself changes and the desirability of obtaining the order, or denying it to a competitor, should not change due to an alteration in Party's belief as to his chances of success.

In discussing the negotiator's level of aspiration (see p. 199) a distinction was made between the value of securing a bargain to the company and the value to the negotiator personally. The value for the negotiator is a function of the significance of the bargain to him in terms of personal achievement. If that value is considerable then, as the negotiator's estimate of success probability declines because of the tactics adopted by Opponent, the fear of losing the bargain completely will lead the negotiator to reassess the value of a bargain on less favourable terms. By being willing to agree to such terms, which previously he had treated as unacceptable, the negotiator hopes to restore the level of success probability.

Since at that stage the negotiator's predominant motivation will be the avoidance of 'failure', his estimate of success probability related to any specific set of contract terms will be lower than an objective assessment.[9] He will therefore tend to over react and so propose acceptance of terms more onerous than necessary.

From a behavioural point of view, therefore, tactics which cause the negotiator for Party to believe there is a serious danger of no bargain are likely to influence the negotiator into lowering the level at which he would feel compelled to break off the negotiations, unless he is restrained from so doing by the terms of his negotiating brief.

Changing Opponent's assessment of success probability

In an ego-orientated and commitment situation such as a commercial negotiation, a negotiator's subjective assessment of success probability will be related primarily to:

1 Past experience and precedent.
2 Cues provided by the behaviour of the opposing negotiator.
3 The degree of support provided to the negotiator by his own company.

Since the assessment is subjective it will be biased by the wishes and fears of the person concerned.[10] More specifically this bias will be a function of:

1 The negotiator's motivation for success. The stronger his achievement orientation, the more optimistic his assessment; conversely the stronger his motivation towards avoidance of failure the lower his assessment.
2 The attractiveness of attainment. The more attractive the end objective, the more optimistic his assessment. Note that this end objective is the negotiator's personal one which may differ widely from that of his company.
3 The consequence of failure. The more serious these are the lower will be the negotiator's assessment.

Clearly certain of these factors are wholly within the negotiator's own control or that of the company which employs him. In varying degrees, other factors can be manipulated by his opponent. These factors and the way in which such manipulation may occur are now considered.

Cues provided by Party's behaviour
Apparent strength of commitment–The stronger Opponent's beliefs that Party is totally committed to a specific position, the lower will be Opponent's estimate of his own success probability. Since Opponent cannot know in any absolute sense the true strength of Party's commitment he must infer it from Party's behaviour. The signs which will guide him in making that inference are:

1 Party's choice of language. The simpler and more direct this is the stronger the commitment.
2 The degree of precision in Party's definition of his position. The less the ambiguity the stronger the commitment.
3 The openness of Party's statements. Statements made in front of colleagues are more binding than those made privately.
4 Party's willingness to state his position in writing. A written statement is always a stronger commitment than one made verbally.
5 Gestures by Party which support his commitment, for example, putting his papers in order, sitting back with arms folded seemingly unmoved by any verbal attack.
6 Exhibiting patience and a willingness to wait, for example, not booking a return flight, not contacting Opponent to arrange further meetings but leaving Opponent to contact Party.
7 Not leaving open any obvious line of retreat. Party should have a fall-back position but he should not reveal it unless forced to by the strength of Opponent's position.

By giving these signals, Party will seek to demonstrate to Opponent the high degree of commitment which Party feels toward the negotiating position he has adopted. At the same time Party will recognize the Opponent may be trying to do exactly the same. In his reaction to Opponent's words Party would be wise to be guided by the advice of Bacon who wrote: 'The Sinews of Wisdom are slowness of belief and distrust; that more trust be given to countenances and deeds than to words; and in words rather to sudden passages and surprised than to set and purposed words.'[11]
Demonstrating a lack of anxiety—There is a distinction between indicating a firm commitment to a specific position through personal attachment and demonstrating anxiety. Some apparent personal involvement is necessary if a commitment is to appear credible. But the involvement should be supported by reasoned argument on the lines that if the other side could only understand the problem then they would agree with the proposition. The involvement is intellectual rather than emotional. In presenting an argument on this basis the negotiator also shows a certain indifference to whether the other side

believe his argument or not as it will make no difference to its validity or to his commitment which he has no intention of changing.

However, any indication by the negotiator that his commitment is based on fear of the consequences should he not be successful, and not on reasoned argument, must immediately expose the weakness of his case. I can argue against a high rate of delay penalty on the ground that it exceeds any probable loss that the buyer might suffer and is contrary to normal commercial dealing in that type of business. I cannot argue that it is too high because I am afraid I might have to pay it. If I do, the buyer will respond by saying that there is even more reason for having the penalty since, clearly, I am not confident on my delivery and only a penalty spur will compel me to complete on time.

In order to reduce Opponent's estimate of his chances of success Party should blend commitment with a measure of indifference. Conversely, irrespective of his inner feelings, the negotiator should never reveal anxiety or use arguments which have as their base fear of his own or his company's inadequacy.

Adjusting the attractiveness of the bargain

Since Opponent will tend to overestimate his chances of securing any bargain which appears to him to be attractive, and conversely will tend to underestimate the success probability of one which appears to be unattractive, it is in Party's interests to present the range of possible bargains in a way which will lead Opponent to regard as attractive the outcome which best satisfies Party's negotiating objective.

Party may do this in two ways.

1   Leading Opponent to propose a solution to a point of difficulty rather than Party proposing it himself. This is an example of what is commonly referred to as the NIH factor (Not Invented Here). Opponent will value more highly a solution which he believes he has thought up for himself than one suggested by Party.

Party therefore guides Opponent in the right direction by narrowing the range of options but leaves the final choice to Opponent.

For example, Party as an exporter is negotiating the delivery terms of the contract with an overseas buyer. Party's major negotiating objective in relation to this clause is to persuade the buyer to waive the requirements that the goods are shipped on the national shipping line of the buyer's country, which is notorious for the infrequency of its sailing and the unreliability of its service. Party's argument might be that he appreciates the buyer's wish for delivery to site to be effected in 12 months, but the facts should be examined. It has been agreed that 10 months is a reasonable period for manufacture, including 1 month's factory testing which the buyer wishes his engineers to observe. Buyer is insisting on the use of his shipping line, to which there are no objections, but his shipping agents say that realistically 6 weeks should be allowed for delivery to port of entry. In addition 5 weeks should be allowed for custom's clearance and 1 week for onward delivery to site, giving a total of 13 months. This period will have to be adhered to unless buyer can suggest anything.

Party has narrowed the options open to the buyer to the point at which he waives the factory test, removes the restriction on the shipping line or makes a special deal with the customs authorities. Party knows that in practice the buyer is unlikely to do the first and has no power to do the last. Therefore he has really no alternative but to remove the shipping line requirement if the 12-month delivery period is to be achieved. He does not ask for this directly but leaves it up to the buyer.

The buyer might reply that it looks as though the shipping question will have to be re-examined since nothing can be done about the time for customs and the month really is needed for testing and to familiarize the engineers with the equipment. If Party is allowed to use a line of his own choice, would he be willing to guarantee delivery in 12 months?

Party should of course know the answer to this question but equally he should not admit it since to do so might lead to the buyer becoming suspicious. It is suggested that Party should reply in a way which will strengthen the buyer's commitment to the idea and reinforce it as having been his suggestion. The reply could be that the idea had not been considered in any detail since until Opponent made the suggestion it was thought to be out of the question. Clearly it would help, and it looks as though the 12 months might be possible, but it will be looked at as a matter of urgency and the answer will be confirmed tomorrow. In the meantime discussions can proceed on the basis that the 12 months can be agreed upon under that condition.

2   Over emphasizing the apparent importance to Party of securing a particular point when Party's real objective is the direct opposite. Sometimes this is colloquially referred to as 'pulling the pig's tail' since the usual result of that activity is that the animal pulls as hard as it can in the opposite direction. The same result in intended here; namely that Opponent will become convinced that this is just the point he must secure and will direct all his efforts to doing so.

As an example, consider an issue that has arisen as to whether an installation activity should be priced as a firm lump sum or on a man–day basis. The contractor would prefer the lump sum as this would avoid the purchaser becoming involved in the details of the operation and allow the contractor greater flexibility.

Initially the contractor suggests, and argues, for the man–day basis, pointing out that the work involves risks which will be difficult to allow for in his pricing. The more the contractor points out the risks the more the purchaser becomes convinced that the contract should be on a firm lump sum, so that he knows his commitment in advance. Eventually the contractor 'concedes' leaving the negotiator for the purchaser pleased with his 'success', and convinced that he has obtained the better bargain.

Had the contractor argued for a lump sum in the first instance, the purchaser would have been suspicious that the price was too 'fat' and might well have proposed a man–day basis. Also by leaving it to the purchaser to suggest the lump sum the contractor is in a better position to argue for the inclusion of a reasonable allowance for contingencies. The contractor might argue that he suggested a man–day basis but it was unacceptable for the very reason that risks are involved and the total commitment is difficult to calculate. This is understood and appreciated, but by the same token contractor's price must now include an allowance for those risks.

NOTES

1.   There is an obvious relationship between these tactics and the learning process of *operant conditioning*. This process is described briefly in E. R Hilgard et al, *Introduction to Psychology* (New York Harcourt, Brace and Jovanovich, 5th edition 1971), p. 196 ff. The application of the process to union-management negotiations is considered in R. E. Walton and R. E. McKersie, *Behavioural Theory of Labor Negoitations* (New York: McGraw-Hill, 1965), pp. 185-270.
2.   G. T. Brand, *The Industrial Buying Decision* (London: Cassell/Associated Business Programmes, 1972).
3.   See R. Wood, *The Principles and Problems of Ethics* (St. Louis: Herder Book Co., 1962), which sets out to give the ethical views of Christianity, Eastern Orthodoxy, Islam, Buddhism and Confucianism, and gives those relating to commercial dealings on p. 134: 'There must be equality in exchange; the amount of profit must be within reason; goods of necessity must be priced so that people can afford them; to price so low as to force a competitor out of business is unethical.'
4.   W. Stace, *Concept of Morals* (London: Macmillan, 1962), p. 134.
5.   'Now since our solution consist of rational expectations of gain by the two bargainers, these expectations should be realizable by an appropriate agreement between the two. Hence there should be an available anticipation which gives each the amount of satisfaction he should expect to get.' J. F. Nash, 'The bargaining problem', *Econometrica*, vol. 18 (April 1950) 155–62.
6.   R. D. Luce and H. Raiffa, *Games and Decisions* (New York: Wiley, 1957), p. 130.
7.   In the example the buyer would not be acting from the principle of fairness if his motive in allowing the supplier a price of, say, £18 000

was the fear that at any lower price the supplier might get into financial difficulties, and so fail properly to implement the contract. The distinction between performing an act from a moral duty, as opposed to following enlightened self interest, was well described by Kant in the following passage from his *Theory of Ethics,* quoted in R. H. Popkin and A. Stroll, *Philosophy Made Simple* (London: W. H. Allen, 1969), p. 38. 'It is always a matter of duty that a dealer should not overcharge an inexperienced purchaser; and wherever there is much commerce the prudent tradesman keeps a fixed price for everyone so that a child buys of him as well as any other. Men are thus honestly served; but that is not enough to make us believe that the tradesman has so acted *from duty* and from principles of honesty; his own advantage required it; it is out of the question in this case to suppose that he might besides having a direct inclination in favour of the buyers so that, as it were from love, he should give no advantage one over another. Accordingly the action was done neither from duty nor from direct inclination but merely with a selfish view.'

8.   F. C. Ikle and N. Leites, 'Political negotiation as a process of modifying utilities', *Journal of Conflict Resolution*, vol. VI no. 1 p. 19.

9.   See J. W. Atkinson, 'Motivational determinants of risk-taking behaviour', *Psychological Review,* vol. 64 (1957), p. 367, and the earlier discussion in Section 7.2.

10.   'The expectancy level of the psychological future is also affected by the wish and fear level of the psychological future.' See 'Level of aspiration', in *Personality and The Behaviour Disorders* (New York: Ronald Press, 1944), p. 367.

11.   Sir Francis Bacon, *The Advancement of Learning*, edited by D. W. Kitchen (London: Dent), p. 190.

21

SITUATION TACTICS

Situation tactics may be divided into two classes: offensive and defensive. Offensive tactics are those which are designed to take or retain the initiative. Defensive tactics are not merely the counter to these but the springboard from which a counter-offensive can be launched. Therefore, both are concerned with the initiative, ie:

1 The order in which items are taken
2 The points on which to exert pressure
3 The degree of pressure exerted
4 The basis upon which the issues are argued
5 The time over which the argument lasts

Purely defensive tactics are ruled out since, if Party were to adopt such an approach, this would leave it open to Opponent continually to switch his attack from one point to another in search of the weak point in Party's defences. Given that no defence is ever perfect, ultimately a weak point will be found upon which Opponent can then concentrate his attack.

Students of military history/tactics will recognize the analogy which can be drawn between negotiation as a form of conflict and warfare, and indeed many of the principles governing the use of situational tactics and military tactics are similar.

21.1 OFFENSIVE TACTICS

Asking questions

Probing questions
Party's first use of questions is as a means of probing Opponent's defences; a reconnaissance in military parlance. Having discovered what he believes may be a weak point in the propositions which Opponent has put forward Party wishes to be sure that it really is a weak point before he launches a major attack.

Such a question is deliberately phrased in general terms. Thus a buyer having reviewed a seller's quotation may start off the discussion by saying: 'We have had a look at your quotation but before we get

364

down to details perhaps you could explain rather more fully the way in which you have arrived at the increase in price over the last contract.'

A question of this type asking for general clarification is most difficult to answer directly. The supplier does not know whether the buyer agrees generally with the item as stated in his tender or not. Any overall reply may merely provide the buyer with fresh points on which specifically to direct his attack. In fact this is the idea of the question.

The supplier's correct response is therefore the *counter question*, designed to compel the buyer to limit the scope of his inquiry and to reveal more of the buyer's own position. The supplier's reply might therefore be on the following lines: 'I am sorry if there is a difficulty here; I thought we had stated the general position quite clearly in our offer. However we will be pleased to try to clarify any particular points about which you are unhappy. What in particular is worrying you?'

Notice that the supplier in addition to asking the buyer to be more specific has made the suggestion that the buyer must be dissatisfied with some aspects of the quotation. This is included in the counter question in order to elicit from the buyer one of the following statements:

1 He is not really unhappy with the supplier's offer but just wants some more information.
2 He is unhappy with the offer and the reasons for this concern.

In this way the supplier seeks to regain the initiative. Counter questions are really part of defensive tactics and their general use is discussed in Section 21.2.

Specific questions
A question is defined as specific when it can be answered only by supplying a piece of data, the nature of which is determined by the wording of the question itself, as in the following examples: 'What labour and material price indices did you use to calculate the escalation allowance in your price?' 'What is your programme for manufacture and testing?' 'How long will it take to produce the layout drawings?'

The rules for framing an attacking question are:

1 Keep it short and simple
2 Do not disclose all the facts
3 Never suggest an answer to the respondent

Perhaps the most effective attacking question of all is the single word 'why?'

In the example just considered the buyer does not refer to the ratio between the movement in the manufactured goods index and the movement in the price of semiconductors, nor the extent to which the weighting given to various elements in the construction of the index allows for semiconductors. The supplier is left to provide his own answers which can then form the subject matter of a further attack.

In the description of the use of the question as an offensive tactic three consecutive stages have been identified:

1 The probing question: intended to gain information.
2 The specific question: based on the information gained from 1 and data already known; designed to force an admission.
3 The attacking question: based on the answers to 2 and other data; designed to force a concession.

It should also be clear that specific and attacking questions are never asked 'blind'. The questionner already knows in advance that the answer, at least in part, will support his line of attack.

The yes/no question
Some questions are so worded that the only answer to them can be a simple yes or no; others can be replied to in that way if the respondent wishes.

If the use of a question of this type gives the questionner the response for which he is looking then nothing can be more effective. He has obtained a direct admission without equivocation. However, if he obtains the reply he does not want, it is extremely difficult for him to reopen the issue and any opportunity that was available for compromise has been lost.

The reason is that a simple yes/no is the strongest commitment into which a negotiator can enter. In the example quoted at the end of Section 16.3, after I had said yes, there was no way in which the negotiator for the other side could proceed except to adjourn the discussions. On the side which I was representing there was total commitment in that word to the propositions which had been made.

In another instance I was asked to break down a total price quoted for the services of men and the hire of equipment into these two elements. The answer was a straightforward no without any reason being given. Faced with this answer the buyer let the matter drop and turned the discussion onto another topic. He really had no alternative except to discontinue the negotiations.

A yes/no question should never be asked therefore unless the questionner has prepared the ground in advance and is satisfied that the answer he will obtain is the one which he wants to hear. Ideally it is an explicit confirmation of an understanding at which the two negotiators have already informally arrived.

Questions like these, to all of which there are factual answers, can run the questionner into a dead end unless he has already prepared supplementaries. If he cannot challenge the reply given he is bound to accept it and that line of questioning is then exhausted. As a corollary, therefore, a specific question should be only asked in one of the following situations.

1   The questionner believes the subject area to be a weak spot and has already prepared follow-up questions with which to continue the attack.
2   The question is designed merely to confirm a position with which the questionner is generally satisfied.

For example, the question on labour and price indices might be asked by a buyer if, as a result of his initial probing, he believed that the seller had used indices which were more favourable to the seller than those which the buyer considered appropriate to the seller's type of business. If the seller's reply confirmed this then the buyer's supplementary questions, which he had already prepared, would be directed at the inappropriateness of the indices selected. Continuing the example, the buyer's supplementary question after the seller's reply might be: 'You have chosen as the material index that for manufactured goods used generally in industry, whilst some 70% of your material costs must be semiconductor devices. How can you possibly justify this?'

Note that the nature of the question has now changed from one which was purely designed to extract information to one which has set up a direct attack. This type of question is referred to as an attacking question.

Attacking questions
Any question which includes phrases like: How can you justify that? How can that be valid? What justification can there be for that? is classified as an attacking question.

Pressurizing individuals
In the same way as there will be weak points in Opponent's arguments there will be weak members in Opponent's negotiating team. Individual team members may be vulnerable to:

1   Flattery
2   Coercion
3   Blackmail

Flattery

This is the weapon used against someone junior or inexperienced when party believes that the person concerned, rather than admit he does not know, will express an opinion or make a decision and that such an opinion/decision will be favourable to Party. The opinion/decision is likely to favour Party since, because of his junior status/inexperience, the team member involved will not want to be 'difficult'. This is especially true of junior professional advisers when faced with experienced commercial negotiators. In these circumstances there may even be a tendency for the commercial negotiators for the two sides to form a group against the professional adviser whom they may jointly regard as being outside of their 'club'.

The type of remark which may be made by Opponent would be: 'This is something on which we would value your advice Mr Jones. Do you see any problem here? We see no problem, but then we do not have your expertise in these matters.'

If this is Mr Jones's first experience of a major negotiation he will need considerable moral courage to reply that he does see a problem. This is when he needs a great deal of help from his team leader who must firmly resist any temptation to align himself with the negotiator for Opponent: he must act to protect his own colleague and provide him with cover. He could do this by replying for Mr Jones: 'It is hardly fair to expect Mr Jones to answer that off-the-cuff. I suggest we let him think about it and come back to the point after coffee/lunch.'

The team leader will then use the natural break to go over the point with Mr Jones in private.

Coercion

Coercion is the opposite to flattery and may be used against a junior team member who is standing in for his chief. He may be asked: 'We have always dealt with Mr Smith before, and he has never taken this line. Are you sure you have his backing over this, Mr Jones?'

Again the team leader must intervene and answer the question himself instead of leaving it to Mr Jones who may well be embarrassed. He could do this by saying: 'Let us leave Mr Smith out of it shall we. He is not here, so it is not very helpful to ask whether he would approve or not. Mr Jones is here and I have every confidence in him. As far as I can see, the line which he has taken is perfectly reasonable, but if you do have any specific points of criticism Mr Jones and I are willing to listen.'

By identifying himself with the argument which Mr Jones has used the team leader diverts the pressure onto himself and commits himself to the support of Mr Jones so integrating him more closely into the team. At the same time the commitment is not total; he leaves himself with a line of retreat by suggesting that both of them are willing to consider criticisms. But these have to be specific, which once more puts the ball back into Opponent's court.

Blackmail
This is a tactic which may be used against the team leader himself and describes the situation in which Opponent seeks to make use of some personal relationship which he alleges he has with the Chairman, Managing Director or other senior officer of Party, to threaten the negotiator that if he does not behave reasonably then he will be in trouble. In practice it is seldom put in quite those words but the inference is clear.

So, the seller in dealing with the professional buyer may take the line: 'You may not be aware that I had dinner with your Mr X last week and he made it clear he took a great interest in this project and expected that we would be participating in it. Indeed, he seemed surprised that we had not signed up already. I only mention that in order to let you know that your own top management are all in favour.'

The team leader must immediately call Opponent's bluff if he is to retain credibility as a negotiator. One way would be for him to reply: 'If you would like me to arrange an appointment for us both to see Mr X, I would be pleased to do so, although I do not think it would be very helpful. However, in the meantime, I suggest we get ahead with our discussions.'

Arbitrary behaviour
Sweet reason is not necessarily the best form of argument. Sheer arbitrary behaviour can be more effective.[1] Once a negotiator's behaviour becomes in our terms 'irrational' he is outside the value system and untouchable by the arguments normally used.

If a buyer indicates that he does not care about whether costs have risen or not, he is just not going to pay more for the goods under this contract than he did last time, this may be a more effective tactic than arguing about changes in labour/material costs, allowances for increases in productivity and the other factors which are usually treated as forming an integral part of such negotiations. It will certainly present the negotiator for the supplier with a difficult form of challenge in which his statistical data on cost increases, so carefully compiled are valueless.

The point about so-called 'irrational' behaviour is that it relies for its effectiveness on the other side continuing to behave rationally. General Amin was certainly, in the eyes of the countries who received the expelled Asians, behaving irrationally. But his action was effective because he relied on our behaving rationally by our own standards, which we did both in meeting his deadline and in providing the refugees with a home.

If a man says: 'Give me a £100 or I will kill that child', and from the circumstances and his appearance it is judged that he will carry out the threat, then it is likely that he will be paid the £100. But suppose normal value standards are discarded and his adopted; suppose he is told 'Very well go ahead and kill the child', that at once alters the bargaining situation. Level terms are resumed again. No longer because of his irrationality does the person uttering the threat possess any advantage.

To return to the example of the 'irrational' buyer. If the supplier continues to try to argue on the rational grounds of unavoidable cost increases, he must lose. Either he will be forced to accept the buyer's terms or lose the bargain.

Supposing the supplier says 'Fine, I will take the contract at the old price, but if I find I cannot meet the costs then, unless you increase the price, do not expect me to deliver. Further at that stage you will have no chance of obtaining the goods from anyone else in time to meet your production schedule. It will do you no good to sue me; it will be too late and by the time you get an award of damages, if you do, there will not be any assets left in the company.'

Both sides have now introduced irrationality into the bargaining game and the rules have been stretched to the point at which there are virtually no rules, and the uncertainty involved is too great for the continuation of normal business relationships.[2]

The lesson is clear. Irrationality, short term and in small degrees, may pay; extended in time or extent and opposed in equal measure it must fail.

Making Opponent appear unreasonable

One method of challenging the validity of a proposition is to find a case in which application of the proposition would be manifestly absurd. The person advancing the proposition is then challenged to redefine it in more limited terms which will avoid the absurdity. It is closely related therefore to the method of logical argument known as the *dialectic* in which a *thesis* is stated, a contrary case known as the *antithesis* is then produced, and the reconciliation of the two produces the *synthesis*.

An example of *the dialectic* would be as follows:

Thesis: The contractor is responsible for any delay to the contract work

Antithesis: Responsibility presupposes control; a contractor cannot therefore be responsible for events over which he has no control, eg war or riots.

Synthesis: The contractor is responsible for delays to the contract work except when these are due to causes beyond his control.

One frequent application of the tactic is to circumstances in which it is proposed that liability should vary in degree with some defined scale or should change significantly when some particular point is reached.

For example, in negotiating a penalty clause for failure to meet guaranteed performance limits the buyer might propose a series of steps as shown:

1   £1 000 between 89–90% purity
2   £5 000 between 88–89% purity
3   £10 000 between 88–87% purity
4   £20 000 below 87% purity

The contractor in reply could point out that a change from 88.95% to 89.05%, ie a change of 0.1%, could make a difference of £4 000 which he would claim was absurd and unfair, even assuming that one could measure to that degree of accuracy.

The outcome or synthesis in dialectical terms would probably be a much smoother relationship between percentage purity and penalty. Alternatively after it has been demonstrated that the thesis as originally stated is too wide the proposer may find great difficulty in justifying one particular synthesis redefining the proposition in narrower terms in preference to any other. If £4 000 is wrong for the change between 88.95 and 89.05%, what is right? At what point does the proposition become fair?

To take another example, the buyer might claim the right to reject a whole consignment for a single defect. The antithesis argument would be that it would be unreasonable to reject a consignment, say, of 100 items value £10 000, all of which are usable, because say the paint on one was scratched.

The first synthesis might be to limit the right to reject the whole to where the number of defects exceeded say 5%. Assuming this was acceptable to the supplier, it does not overcome the problem of what kind of defect entitles the buyer to reject. For example, does it include a paint scratch and, if so, how deep a scratch?

A second synthesis might be that the right to reject would apply only if the defect was one which affected the purpose for which the item was being supplied.

Because of its probing nature, and the use it makes of hypothetical assumptions, the adoption of the tactic by Party frequently leads to an emotional outburst from Opponent who may seek to dismiss the arguments as 'mere quibble'. If this can be avoided, or with patience overcome, the tactic is a valuable means of clarifying and delimiting broad propositions, or of causing them to be abandoned altogether if they are too difficult for precise definition.

Fishing

This describes the tactic of deliberately over stating a demand in order to discover Opponent's reaction. Party's demand would be well beyond any level he considers Opponent likely to accept.

In discussing the level at which Party should make his initial offer (see p. 164), it was concluded that, ignoring time costs, the level would be the upper limit of the bargaining zone increased by the amount of the concession which Party anticipated being compelled to make in order to reach an outcome equal to the upper limit of the bargaining zone. So that Party may follow this rule he must reasonably be aware of Opponent's concession function and the level at which Opponent would just prefer a bargain to no bargain. When the two sides have negotiated before, or have information on the terms/prices which the other has agreed in contracts with third parties, it is not difficult for either to arrive at a reasonably accurate estimate of these values, at least for the major issues.

If the two sides are largely unknown to each other then the only way for Party to discover what Opponent might accept is to overstate his demands and see what happens. Before deciding to adopt this tactic, Party must plan his next move depending upon what sort of reaction he obtains. Broadly, there are three possibilities:

Violently anti

Opponent dismisses the demand with some statement such as: 'You cannot possibly be serious. Your suggestion is out of the question. If that is the line you intend to take it would be better to terminate discussions now.' Party must have a position prepared against this type of response which will extricate him with a mimimum loss of reputation for firmness (see Section 17.1). The simplest means of doing this is for the demand to have been made by the number two in the negotiating team and for the team leader now to reply: 'Mr Jones was being serious. We are concerned about two points. However, there are always two sides to every story: you have heard ours, perhaps we can now hear yours. I am sure that when we have listened we will be able to find a way to reach some understanding.'

The response is aimed at achieving two objectives. Firstly, forcing Opponent to state his case in reasoned terms and so expose his position to further questioning and reveal more of his preference function. Secondly to prepare the way for a retreat with an alibi which protects Party from being thought weak, if Opponent's reply indicates that he is totally firm on the point, and is supported by arguments which Party cannot shift. If that does happen, then the next statement from the negotiator for Party might be, addressing Mr Jones: 'Well John, you have heard their arguments, and I must say they seem to be fairly solid I know how you feel but I think we must go over this point again and see what we can come up with.' Turning to Opponent, negotiator for Party might continue: 'Thank you for spelling it out so clearly. I think there may have been some misunderstanding here on our side. Obviously we need to consider this further amongst ourselves so perhaps we could leave it there for the moment and return to the point later.'

Reasoned reply
Opponent treats the demand as a serious basis from which to proceed to negoitate. Party immediately reassesses his estimate of the final outcome and of the strength of his negotiating position relative to Opponent's since this is obviously greater than he thought.

Apparent acceptance
This is in some ways for Party the most difficult response of all. He finds it hard to believe from what he knows of Opponent that the demand should be acceptable to him. It is highly probable that Opponent has either made a serious mistake or misunderstood what Party meant. Alternatively it is just possible that Party has misjudged the situation and Opponent's acceptance is genuine.

Party's next move therefore should be to explore whether or not Opponent has misunderstood, or made a mistake, without revealing his anxiety in a way which, if Opponent's acceptance is genuine, would cause Opponent to reconsider.

Party might use some words such as: 'This is a reasonably important point and I would just like to be certain that we are both clear on it. Perhaps it would help to do this if you were to state your own understanding of what we have just agreed. Then we can move on to the next point on the agenda.'

Asking Opponent to restate the argument should ensure that if there has been a misunderstanding this will be revealed. Also it leaves the initiative to Party to comment on Opponent's statement.

It may be asked why, if Opponent has made a mistake, Party should be concerned to have it corrected; why not simply take advantage of it and let Opponent suffer for his foolishness? The answer is that contracts are a continuing relationship, and when Opponent finds out his error his defence mechanism to internal criticism from within his own organization will be to claim that he was tricked by Party. Accordingly he will seek retribution against Party and in particular against the negotiator for Party whom he considers to have been responsible (see p. 201). He may seek to have that negotiator personally blacklisted and to secure from Party some concession by way of compensation.

Partners as opposites

It was suggested that one way in which a negotiator could be provided with a line of retreat from an extreme position was by his partner taking the responsibility. Frequently in negotiations the following kind of remarks may be heard between team members: 'You are being very difficult this morning, John. I would have thought we could have agreed to . . . I think they have a point there. Should we agree to . . . I know it is a problem for you, Bill, but perhaps you could see your way clear to . . .'

In all these instances one team member is ostensibly taking Opponent's part and suggesting to his partner that he should make a 'concession'. More often than not, the two are playing a game in which it was decided in advance that John or Bill would take the hard line, and that at the opportune moment his partner would propose the compromise to which, with a show of great reluctance, John or Bill would agree.

Naturally having obtained this 'concession' for Opponent, the partner would expect Opponent on the next negotiating point to return the favour.

Alternatively the game may be played the other way round. John may make a few early concessions on points of little significance; then on the point which really does matter his partner (Bill) will provide the firm backing; 'I am sorry John, I know you are in a very generous mood this morning but you cannot give away this one. We have given away too much already.'

John turns to Opponent with a slightly pained expression as if to suggest that there is nothing more which he can do to help and Opponent is on his own.

In cold print the game may appear obvious and even trivial; certainly not something likely to deceive an experienced negotiator. However, under the pressures generated by long and tense negotiating sessions the trick is not nearly so easy to recognize, particularly if the two negotiators have worked together on a number of occasions, so that rehearsal becomes unnecessary, and the trick a matter of habit.

There is also always in Opponent's mind a measure of doubt. He can never be absolutely sure that it is a game; perhaps the words are genuine, so that the opportunity exists to divide Party's negotiating team.

The other advantage of the tactic, if it is used on an apparently random basis, is that Opponent can never be certain just how strong Party's feelings are on any individual point. He cannot therefore judge with any accuracy the true form of Party's concession factor.

Pulling the pig's tail

Reference was made earlier (see p. 361) to the idea that one way of persuading Opponent to agree to X is to propose the converse of X. Some negotiators are suspicious of any proposal made by their opposite number. If the supplier offers to deliver cif (carriage, insurance and freight), he must be making a profit on the shipping charges; so the buyer insists on purchasing fob (freight on board). If the supplier had offered fob this must have been to reduce his liability; so the buyer insists on cif.

In this situation it is no use Party attempting to negotiate by persuading the buyer of the honesty of Party's proposals. If the personality of the buyer is what Cattell refers to as *sizothymic,* at least when he is acting the role of Buyer within a commercial environment, the attachment to that personality characteristic will be too strong.[3,4] Scrooge may have changed in *A Christmas Carol* but commercial negotiators do not have the advantage of possessing as allies ghosts which can portrary to the buyer past, present and future. So the negotiator, foreseeing the rejection of his proposal, demands the opposite to his preferred requirement.

Entering into a prior commitment
Previously the use of commitment has been discussed in terms of the negotiating framework and the need for Party to persuade Opponent of the truth of the statements which Party is making. Commitment also represents a major offensive negotiating tactic, the persuasive power of which varies with the degree to which visibly Party's hands are tied. The commitments may be listed in order of the strength of their persuasive power.

Commitment	*Example*
1 National law binding on Opponent.	Under the law regulating public contract, Opponent as a government department must insist that the contract is governed by the law of his country.
	Party has no alternative; he must either accept or withdraw from the negotiations.
2 Regulation which is legally binding on Opponent unless and until amended by some administrative or legislative body.	Standard forms of contract and/or contracting procedures are established for public authorities which require the authority of some higher council to amend.
	Opponent will clearly be

Commitment	*Example*
	reluctant to ask for amendment and the formalities will take a considerable time to complete if the request is made. Party will therefore be under significant pressure not to press for any amendment and to do so may cause him to lose the contract.
3 Standard procedures of the company/authority which are binding on the unit which is negotitating the contract. Alternatively, instructions received from some third party whose involvement is necessary to the conclusion of the contract, eg a credit insurance bureau.	Opponent's contract procedures require that the approval of some higher level, head office/ Board of Directors, is required before they can agree to Party's proposals. The negotiator for Opponent will be reluctant to ask for such approval and the head office/ Board will equally be reluctant to grant it for fear of creating a precedent. Party may therefore have to be content with a *side letter*.[5]
4 Previous precedents.	On previous contracts either with Party or other contractors Opponent has negotiated certain terms. To depart from these would show the negotiator for Opponent as weaker or less competent than those who had negotiated the other bargains. Alternatively if he had negotiated the other bargains hurriedly he could be accused of having accepted a bribe in order to show favour to Party. Party must therefore provide the negotiator for Opponent with reasons which he can use to justify his acceptance of Party's arguments.
5 Instructions from a superior.	Opponent's negotiators, having

Commitment	*Example*
	consulted his immediate superior and obtained his agreement to the negotiating plan, is in some difficulty in going back and saying the plan cannot be achieved.
	Again Party's success will be dependant largely on providing the negotiator for Opponent with reasons with which to support his request for revised authority.
	Alternatively, Party may propose that he accompanies Opponent's negotiator to discuss directly with his superior.
6 Position adopted at the outset of the negotiation by Opponent's negotiator on his own initiative.	The negotiator, for motives usually associated with earning esteem, takes a particular stand and makes it known within his own organization that he has done so.
	Later it becomes obvious that the line he has taken is incompatible with the achievement of a bargain, and the need to obtain agrement is of greater priority.
	Party must now find some way to 'get the negotiator for Opponent off the hook' as gently as he can.

It is obvious that both sides will use commitment tactics. Party will refer to a commitment to his board; Opponent to one to his higher authority. When the commitments are of different rank, the higher will normally prevail. So a commitment on Party as a contractor to comply with a requirement of his head office must give way to a law or regulation which is binding on Opponent as a purchaser. An example would be a procedural rule within Party's organization, that contracts should be entered into only on the basis of disputes being referred either to the courts of Party's country or the International Chamber of Commerce, as opposed to a regulation of Opponent's country which provided that for public contracts disputes were to be determined by the courts of Opponent's territory. To continue the example, if Party could reinforce his argument by reference to the requirements of his credit insurance bureau he might be able to secure that financial disputes are referred to the International Chamber of Commerce whilst only other disputes went to the national courts of the overseas territory. (This example is based on my own negotiating experience in the Middle East.)

So it becomes a battle to secure the stronger commitment for Party and to undermine that put forward by Opponent, by showing that it is not as strong as he has maintained, eg that there is not a law on the subject concerned; that it is only a matter of convention which can be disregarded.

21.2 DEFENSIVE TACTICS

Minimum response and pretended misunderstanding

A well-known interrogation technique is to persuade the suspect to repeat his story a number of times in the expectation that sooner or later he will contradict himself and so reveal the truth. Conversely the less a suspect says the less likely he is to give anything away to his interrogator. Many more people are convicted through the telling of their own stories than by the evidence of others.

It follows that amongst the most effective of defensive tactics in negotiation is to say only just enough to compel the other side to go on talking. The more they talk the more they will reveal; the more they will feel compelled to reveal in order to be persuasive, and the nearer they will come to exposing their genuine motives and the real level of their minimum negotiating objective. The association between minimum response and pretended misunderstanding, which is another useful defensive tactic, is that the easiest way to persuade Opponent to repeat his argument is to pretend that you have misunderstood it. As well as making Opponent go over the same ground again, this has the added advantage of giving Party more time to consider the merits of Opponent's argument, and to decide on his counter argument. So one member of Party's team may be listening to the repeat argument while the others are busy studying the implications of the argument as presented, and checking it against their prediction of what Opponent would demand and the arguments which he would advance. Therefore, having listened politely to Opponent's opening remarks, Party may make some reply to the effect that he is probably being very slow but would Opponent mind going over that again.

Also, it can be an infuriating technique. Opponent has delivered a carefully rehearsed statement expecting some sort of positive response, only to be met with a bland smile and the polite request to start all over again. He is not likely to be pleased and for this reason the repeat made under conditions of emotional stress will be that much more unguarded.

The technique is particularly effective in dealing with technical experts from whatever discipline. Few experts can resist the temptation to show off their expertise to a captive audience. But in so doing, it is virtually certain that they will give away more of the real reasons why the proposition in question is being made than ever had been intended.

Answering inaccurately
Another way of answering a question without giving Opponent the answer for which he is looking is to start the reply by some phrase such as 'As I understand your question you are asking . . .' and then go on to re-phrase the question slightly before replying to your re-phrased version. Not only does this avoid giving the direct answer but it also gives you and your colleagues time to think.

Changing the level
Specific questions where opponent is asking for detailed information can be answered by raising the level to that of greater generalization. Thus the question referred earlier of 'What labour and material indices did you use?' could be countered by your replying 'Obviously the possible effect of inflation is something we have had to consider. It is not something we are seeking to make a profit on but equally we don't want to lose'. Party would hope then to turn the discussion into more a general one on the subject of escalation and establish that Opponent did agree that escalation should be fully reimbursed before any detailed discussion on indices took place.

Side-stepping
Rather than answer opponents question directly at the time it is asked, Party may seek to side-step the issue. So in answer to a question 'Can you guarantee completion by a specified date?' Party might reply 'Here have a look at the programme, shall we, then I can show you how we have arrived at the end date and you can see for yourself the problems and the allowance we have made'.

Answering incompletely
There is no need for Party to volunteer more information in answer to a specific question than necessary. If Opponent has limited his question to asking 'Have you included for customs duties?' there is no need in your reply, assuming it is 'yes', to go on referring to your having allowed for other taxes or charges related to importation. You might want later to be able to argue that those were extra.

The 'Yes–but' technique

The outright, negative *no* represents a definitive and uncompromising commitment and should be reserved for those occasions when such a commitment is really intended. Because of its inflexibility and the risk of giving offence the use of the direct negative in certain cultures is almost unknown; there are just three versions of yes; one meaning 'no', one meaning 'maybe' and one meaning 'yes'. the shopkeeper to whom a watch has been entrusted for repair will answer 'yes' to the question of whether the watch will be ready tomorrow. Of course, it will not be ready, and the shopkeeper knows that. But to reply 'no', which is clearly not the desired answer, would mean giving offence in a face-to-face situation. So the shopkeeper answers 'yes' and hopes that it will be recognized as a form of politeness.

Social behaviour is often similar, for instance a pressing invitation to go to a party may be received from a friend. To avoid 'hurting feelings' by saying 'no', either an excuse is found or the reply is indirect by explaining that events of that date are uncertain or that someone else has to be consulted first. Again, like the shopkeeper, it is hoped that the reply will be recognized as a form of politeness and not taken at its face value.

So the negotiator faced with the direct question which he wishes to answer in the negative, but without giving offence, and without definitely committing himself, may use the technique of yes — but. Asked, for example, to agree to a reduction in the period of delivery he may reply that *yes* he agrees that the delivery period looks rather long, *but* a number of factors have to be taken into account; for instance the shortage of materials which is affecting the current level of output and also the fact that the design has not yet been finalized.

The affirmative part of the answer should appear to align the negoitator alongside his opponent and so establish the negotiator as someone who is cooperative and appreciative of the viewpoint of the other side.

The negative part of the answer is intended to identify some of the reasons which nevertheless prevent the negotiator from doing what Opponent would like him to do; in the example, to shorten the delivery. In choosing the reasons he puts forward, the negotiator should select those which are likely to appeal most to Opponent by reason of his background, personality or the position which he holds. Ideally the negotiator should use this part of the reply to lead Opponent into taking action which would overall favour the negotiator's case or at least present Opponent in the ultimate with the choice of acting in that manner or of withdrawing his request.

In the above example the negotiator, in the course of the discussion which followed his reply, might seek to persuade Opponent to settle the outstanding issues on the design and to authorize Party to order the long delivery materials on the basis that this would enable Party to reduce the delivery time. Such action would clearly increase Opponent's commitment to Party and so improve Party's negotiating position. If Opponent were unwilling to take these actions then the longer delivery must stand.

The counter question

Closely related to the yes—but technique is that of replying to a question with a question. The classic from domestic life is that of the wife who replies to the invitation to attend some social engagement with the question: 'What am I going to wear?' In contract negotiation, for example, Opponent asks Party: 'Why will you not accept that the period for installation should be 20 weeks and not 25?' Party replies: 'Can we look at this another way. On what are you basing your estimate of 20 weeks? Can we have the breakdown of that and the assumptions which you have made?'

Party's real answer to Opponent's question may be bluntly that he knows more about it than Opponent does, but this is hardly the most tactful of replies. Party therefore seeks to turn the discussion into an examination of the basis of Opponent's estimate of time, and from that to lead Opponent into admitting his own lack of experience.

A further use of the counter question is to switch the direction of an argument and to prevent attention being concentrated on one area to the exclusion of others. In a price negotiation, for instance, Opponent may be attacking one small area of Party's costs. At some point instead of replying to Opponent's questions Party might say: 'Look, could we get away from this business of the transport costs as they are only minor. Surely it's the price as a whole in which you are interested. Are you saying that is unreasonable?'

Straw issues

In legal terminology a *man of straw* is a person of no means and one from whom no compensation can be recovered. By transferring to a man of straw property which is a liability rather than an asset, the liabilities arising out of the ownership of the property may be avoided.

In negotiating terminology a *straw issue* is one which is of no value to Party in itself but which is raised with the intention that it should be lost and so provide the opportunity for Party to secure a genuine concession from Opponent in return.

As stated earlier (see p. 153) the alternating of concessions although not necessarily the matching of their magnitude, is virtually a norm of negotiating behaviour. If Party wishes to secure a particular concession from Opponent he knows that he must be willing to allow Opponent something in exchange. By including one or more straw issues in his initial demands Party ensures that he has 'something in the bank' to allow Opponent as compensation for Opponent abandoning or modifying his own initial demands.

Party can add to the number of straw issues available to him as bargaining counters by declining in the opening phases of the negotiation to agree to any of Opponent's demands no matter how reasonable these may appear to be. A major difference between the approach of a 'true' bargainer and that of the average Western commercial or legal negotiator is to be seen in the different ways in which they respond to their Opponent's initial demands. The typical Western negotiator will agree immediately to those which he considers reasonable or of little importance, and he will be impatient to move quickly to those which he regards as the real issues in dispute.[6]

A true exponent of bargaining will concede nothing during the initial stages. Each point on which he does intend to concede will be carefully reserved for later use as a means of extracting a concession from the other side. Obviously this lengthens the time spent in negotiation and increases the time costs, so in each instance the negotiator must decide on how far to follow the 'bargaining' approach in order to achieve the optimum outcome.[7] It is essential that this should be a conscious decision and not one taken in default.

In deciding on what to select as a 'straw issue', Party must view the problem through Opponent's eyes and have regard to subjective as much as objective considerations. The achievement of some concession, however minor in an objective sense, may be of major importance to Opponent in terms of selling the bargain to his own management and enhancing his own prestige.

Tactical recess

A negotiation can gain momentum from the application of incessant pressure by, say, Opponent until it reaches the point at which Party knows that his defences must break down unless relieving action is taken. The flow of the negotiations must be interrupted in an attempt to throw Opponent off balance and allow Party the opportunity to recover. Some ways in which this may be done are as follows:

1 Party finds some excuse to leave the room in the middle of Opponent's presentation of his case.
2 Party arranges for the timely arrival of coffee, tea or drinks depending on the time of day.
3 Party requests a short adjournment.

Although in case 3 the recess may be used to review the position reached in the negotiations, and to plan the next move, this is not the primary purpose of the recess. It is simply intended as a way of breaking up Opponent's attack. When the negotiations are resumed

Party may seek to continue the diversion by raising some new issue which he can pretend is related to those previously under discussion, but which he knows is likely to lead to a long and detailed argument between his own and Opponent's experts. By the time this argument is over Party would have hoped to have thought up new lines of defence.

There are several means by which stratagems 1 and 2 may be achieved. A junior member of the team leaves the room ostensibly to go to the cloakroom but in reality to tip off the team leader's secretary, so that five minutes later the leader is summoned to take a long-distance telephone call. The team leader may arrange with his secretary that if he calls her to perform some apparently innocent assignment, unconnected with the negotiations, this is in fact a signal to interrupt the meeting within the next few minutes either by calling him out or by bringing in refreshments.

Wearing out Opponent

Negotiation is a tiring business. It demands intense concentration, patience and the exercise of mental agility, very often under conditions which are totally unfavourable, for example, in rooms which are too hot and with inadequate ventilation. The negotiator may not be able to relax for long when the day's arguments are over; he may need to continue the discussion with his colleagues. If operating away from home base he will have the further problems of reporting back on progress and requesting further information and assistance, overcoming in the process any difficulties due to poor communications and time difference between his own country and the one in which the negotiations are taking place.

These natural hazards may be added to by tactics which artificially prolong the negotiations and/or deprive the negotiators of the limited opportunities which they do have for rest and relaxation. The apparently friendly evening hospitality extended to the visiting negotiator may be only a trap to keep him out of bed until well past midnight, and try to ensure that when he does get there it will be with the makings of a hangover. Naturally the leading negotiator for the other side will regret that he is unable to join the party and delegate the social task to a colleague not otherwise closely involved in the discussions.

So the days pass in interminable arguments and the nights are shortened, until it is exhaustion, rather than Opponent's skill in debate, which is the determining factor in shaping the final outcome.

The ethics of such tactics may seem dubious but their lineage is an ancient one. Bacon in his essay on Cunning wrote: 'When you have anything to obtain of present dispatch, you entertain and amuse the party with whom you deal with some other discourse that he be not too much awake to make objections.'[8] It is important to be aware of such tactics and to guard against their employment by others.

Taking Opponent into confidence

The difficulty which a negotiator may have in persuading Opponent that he is telling the truth has been pointed out several times. It is, however, only by doing so that the negotiator can enlist the support of Opponent in turning the issues which divide the two sides into an exercise in problem solving. If Party is up against a genuine difficulty in complying with some requirement from Opponent, provided Party can convince Opponent of the reality of that difficulty, and the efforts which he is making to resolve it, then this may be a far more effective tactic than trying to hide the truth and find excuses.

But when Party does decide to adopt this approach he must be completely honest and hold nothing back from Opponent. To attempt to enlist Opponent's support, and then to be found out in some petty deception, must destroy Party's credibility both for the negotiation in question and for a long time to come.

The tactic is essential in the type of negotiation which occurs during the course of the contract, and arises out of delays or the failure to meet some specification limit, by either side. The true interests of both sides in these circumstances are to ensure that the work is completed as soon as possible to whatever technical standards are necessarily required to meet the employer's essential needs. Only integrative bargaining can provide the basis upon which those objectives may be achieved.

It is recognized that frank disclosure may be prejudicial to Party's contractual position and that agreement by Opponent to some action may constitute a waiver of his legal rights. But what are the rights of the two sides worth in relation to contract performance? In the nature of events there can be no single answer but the question must be answered by any who advocate, in such circumstances, the maintenance of an arm's-length distributive bargaining position.

It would hurt you more than it would hurt me

A favourite defensive tactic with many negotiators is to seek to demonstrate that, on balance, agreeing to Opponent's demands would hurt Opponent more than it would hurt Party. In a typical example Party might state that if he gives Opponent a discount, this must come out of the margin which means the business is less attractive for Party and less money will be available for investment in research and development. Therefore the facilities which Party can provide for Opponent today will not be available in the future. In the long run therefore Opponent will be the loser.

The argument is often totally genuine, but the tactic can only be effective if the person to whom it is presented is both convinced of the honesty of the other negotiator and willing to take the long view. If not, then Party is wasting his time. Opponent will reply that he will judge what is best in his own interests, and will then ask Party what discount he is willing to offer.

NOTES

1. See also T. C. Schelling, *The Strategy of Conflict* (London: Oxford University Press, 1963), p. 18 ff.

2. The parallel can be drawn between bargaining irrationality in which each side pursues its own selfish interests without regard for moral principle or the interests of the other and the state of nature described by Hobbes in *The Leviathan* (London: Dent). In the same way, as in Hobbes' view, men agree to be bound by laws in order to avoid being harmed by the conflicts that would occur if there were no laws, so negotiators agree tacitly to comply with certain conventions of behaviour to avoid the uncertainty that would otherwise occur.

Further, just as Hobbes foresaw that laws are ineffective without a body responsible for their enforcement and capable of so acting, so negotiating conventions only remain operative if there exist sanctions for their breach which it is known are applied in practice. One such sanction is the threat of reciprocal action; others may be the threat to cease trading, or reference of the matter to a government agency or trade association. It has been remarked that the Soviet Union make prompt payments in international trade because they believe a sequence of kept promises is the way to establish a good credit rating. This belief must carry with it the fear that failure to make prompt payments, ie behaving 'irrationally' when it suited their immediate purposes, would result in the long term in the withdrawal of credit facilities.

3. R. B. Cattell, *The Scientific Analysis of Personality* (Baltimore: Penguin Books, 1965).

4. An individual's personality may be described in terms of traits; a sizothemic personality would be described by R. B. Cattell (see note 3) in terms of being critical, grasping, cool, aloof and suspicious. But these traits may only be characteristic of that person when acting under certain environmental conditions, eg at work as a buyer, and his behaviour may be quite different under domestic conditions. The situation under which the individual is acting influences his traits and may either provide the outlet for their expression or modify them.

5. A *side letter* is the term used to describe a letter written at the time of signing the main contract, and signed by the persons who signed the main contract, which defines the way in which some clause in the contract, is to be interpreted. To the extent that the side letter actually modifies the main contract, its legal validity may be doubtful and will depend on the legal system by which the contract is governed. However, commercially it is normally regarded as binding, and its value as a device is that if the contract document as such has to be

approved by some third party or made public, the side letter can be kept private.

6.   If the reader is not convinced, let him think how often he has been involved in a discussion which has taken a letter written by one side as the agenda and the other side has started off by saying something like: 'We have been through this and we have no problem with points one to four, but five to six do create some difficulty, so I suggest that we concentrate on these two and the others can be taken as agreed'. Four possible 'straw issues' which, following the norm of reciprocity, could have been used to create a sense of obligation to repay the favour have been thrown away and nothing gained in return. One at least of these issues could have been of importance to the letter writer who is now inwardly much relieved at having obtained something for nothing.

7.   It may be suggested that time spent in haggling is normally regarded by the Westerner as a waste, and that his objective is often simply to reduce this time to a minimum. This is understandable in a society in which in domestic matters it is the custom to purchase requirements on standard terms and at fixed prices. As demonstrated in Section 5.1, if the other side has made their offer on the basis of bargaining, or at least a risk of bargaining, then a negotiator is compelled to bargain whether he likes it or not. Given that premise then clearly he should do so in the most efficient manner.

8.   Sir Francis Bacon, 'Cunning', in *Essays of Sir Francis Bacon* (London: Grant Richards, 1902), p. 62.

EPILOGUE

Negotiation has been examined as an exercise in micro-economic analysis and more so as a study of interpersonal human behaviour. Although the need has been stressed for building up long-term business relationships on the foundations of mutual respect for the other's legitimate interests, accusation may still be made for having at times been cynical and distrustful of the existence of honesty in human communications. Contract negotiation is not unique in the demands which it makes on human behaviour; the motives which lead to deception in business do not differ in nature from those which cause men to deceive their wives or politicians the electorate. Man's nature does not change with the centuries, either as buyer or seller, as the following lines from *The Ship of Fools*, written in 1494, testify and serve as a conclusion.[1]

> They try to kill off competition;
> Then, bankrupt take an expedition,
> For, having slashed their prices downward,
> Their best direction's out of townward;
> If one of them won't cut the price
> His brothers won't be overnice,
> For if the customer is tight,
> The goods he gets will serve him right;
> The masters now make shoddy wares:
> If they can sell 'em then who cares?
> But such a business will not keep:
> To buy stuff dear and sell things cheap;
> Some tradesmen underestimate
> A deal, then take the city gate.
> Whoever loves a bargain, he
> Won't get much for a guarantee.
> They makes so much at little cost;
> They sell it quick and nothing's lost;
> They profit from a slick veneer
> Now honest tradesmen disappear.

NOTE
1.   Sebastian Brant, *The Ship of Fools*, translated by William Gillis (London: The Folio Society, 1971).

APPENDIX 1

CHECKLIST OF FACTORS TO BE CONSIDERED IN COMPARING PARTY AND COMPETITORS

Price
Currency in which bidder is willing to accept payment
Willingness to accept payment under barter arrangement
Facilities for reciprocal trading
Ability to make off-set arrangements
Credit terms which can be offered
Availability of Government to Government loan
Delivery including reputation for keeping delivery promises
Risk of territory in which manufacture taking place being subject to
    industrial disputes
Conformity with mandatory specifications
Reliability of product
Quality of product
Ease of maintenance and level of running costs
Standardization with Purchaser's existing plant/system
Ability to comply with performance guarantees
Design and technical merit of product
Capability of plant/system for expansion to meet purchaser's future
    requirements
After-sales service
Availability and price of spares
Willingness to accept purchaser's commercial terms of contract
Reputation on commercial negotiations of being 'hard' or 'soft'
Willingness to employ local labour
Willingness to manufacture locally
Willingness to make local investment
Local political connections
Location of manufacturing plant in development area or area of high
    unemployment
Quality of technical and managerial staff
Customer preference for company or product based on prior contact
    or knowledge

APPENDIX 2

RESOURCES REQUIRED FOR BIDDING AND CONTRACT EXECUTION

BIDDING

Marketing
Staff required for:
1   Customer discussion
2   Market intelligence
3   Bid preparation

Engineering/manufacturing/installation
Staff required for:
4   Analysis of customer specification
5   Design and development
6   Tender specification
7   Site survey
8   Obtaining data on local conditions
9   Fixing of work quantities for estimating
10 Cost estimating
11 Establishment of contract programme

Contracts/legal
Staff required for:
12 Examination of customer's terms and conditions
13 Research into local laws and regulations
14 Establishment of special purchasing/subcontract conditions

Purchasing
Staff required for:
15 Obtaining vendor and subcontract quotations
16 Analysis of quotations received and necessary negotiations
17 Production of material costs for estimating

Finance
Staff required for:
18 Review of terms of payment/currency/exchange regulations
19 Research into local financial regulations
20 Establishment of bonds
21 Obtaining indication of ECGD cover
22 Negotiating credit terms with banks and ECGD.

CONTRACT EXECUTION

Staff and facilities required for:
1   Planning and survey
2   Engineering and design
3   Production of manufacturing drawings and specifications

Production facilities to meet the manufacturing programme including:
4   Jigs, tools, moulds
5   Machine tools, identifying type and capacity to meet required rate of output
6   Skilled labour
7   Inspection facilities and staff
8   Test facilities including special to type test gear

Procurement staff including:
9   Buyers
10   Inspectors skilled in the type of procurement involved
11   Expeditors

Facilities required for:
12   Storage
13   Delivery and packing
14   Special handling

Installation staff and facilities including:
15   Labour by trade involved
16   Skilled supervision
17   Plant
18   Tools and tackle
19   Vehicles
20   Test gear
21   Support facilities, eg temporary accommodation, canteen, etc

Subcontract and contract management including:
22   Project manager at head office
23   Field manager
24   Administrative staff for accounts and personnel
25   Technical supervisory staff
26   Finance needed to execute the contract

APPENDIX 3

CHECKLIST: CONTRACT DISPUTE

SECTION A CONTRACTUAL

1 Has a legally-binding contract been formed? If so by what law is it governed?

2 What are the contract documents? What is the order of precedence?

3 What are the rights given expressly by the contract documents? In answering this question, make sure that *all* the contract documents are looked at as a whole. These may include preliminary correspondence in which representations were made or minutes of meetings post contract in which the parties agreed to variations.

4 To what extent have these rights been supplemented or modified by the general legal system by which the contract is governed?

5 Have the rights available under 3 or 4 been waived either in whole or in part by the conduct of either of the parties?

6 To what extent are the rights available under 3 and 4 exerciseable in practice? This will depend upon:

  (a) Which court or tribunal has jurisdiction.

  (b) Whether such court or tribunal is independent or open to influence.

  (c) The time which such proceedings are likely to take.

  (d) The availability of local lawyers and their freedom to practice in the court or tribunal.

  (e) The costs which are likely to be incurred and the extent to which these may be recovered from Opponent in the event of the proceedings being successful.

7 What is the measure of damages which may be recovered or other legal remedy available?

8 To what extent may any judgement obtained be enforced in practice upon Opponent? This will depend upon 3 factors:

  (a) What are the assets of Opponent situate within the jurisdiction of the court of tribunal. If none, can a judgement be enforced within a territory where Opponent does have assets by registration and without re-examination of the merits of the case?

(b) Is there any immunity of Opponent from process either in theory or practice?

(c) Where Opponent is resident overseas, can any sums awarded against him easily be transferred or can they be blocked under exchange control or taxation legislation?

SECTION B CONTRACTUAL

9   What payments if any are outstanding? When are these payable and how are they secured?

10   Is there a performance bond covering the performance of any contractual obligations? If so under what circumstances can it be encashed and by what procedure?

11   What retention monies are held and when are these due to be released?

12   Are there any goods or plant which may be seized and either held as security or sold?

13   Are there payments due under any other contract between the parties which may be used as offset?

14   On an export contract is there any insurance cover against default by the purchaser in making payments and if so is such cover still valid?

SECTION C COMMERCIAL

Possible action by the purchaser

15   Is there any other tender from the supplier under adjudication which the purchaser may refuse to accept or whose potential acceptance the purchaser may use as a bargaining counter?

16   Is there any future business pending between the parties which the purchaser could threaten to award to another supplier?

17   Are there other contracts in existence between the parties on which it is possible for the purchaser to claim damages or otherwise enforce strictly his contractual rights to the disadvantage of the supplier?

18   Are there reciprocal trading arrangements between the parties which the purchaser could threaten to restrict or suspend?

19   Are there concessions which the purchaser normally allows to the supplier on this and other contracts, eg on inspection and testing, which the purchaser could threaten to withdraw?

20   Could the purchaser blacklist the supplier for future work and, if so, could this extend to associate companies or other firms/ administrations with which the purchaser has contacts?

Possible action by the supplier

21 Could the supplier suspend work even without any contractual right to do so, and would this cause serious difficulty to the purchaser in depriving him of the supplies/services to which the contract relates?

22 Is the supplier in a position to refuse to tender for other of the purchaser's requirements and would this be harmful to the purchaser?

23 Could the supplier bring pressure through his government, trade association or Member of Parliament either directly on the purchaser or indirectly by, for example, persuading his credit insurance bureau to restrict future credit facilities to the purchaser?

APPENDIX 4

STRATEGY CHOICE REASONING

SUPPLIER'S STRATEGY CHOICE WHEN MAKING COMPETITIVE BIDS IN A SITUATION OF UNCERTAINTY AS TO THE PURCHASER'S STRATEGY CHOICE

Axiom
The supplier must always prefer the outcome (HB) (HB) to (QK) (QK) or be indifferent between each.

Proof
The conditional value to the supplier of the outcome (QK) (QK) is the level of his minimum negotiating objective. The conditional value to the supplier of (HB) (HB) is either greater than the level of his minimum negotiating objective, because he has been able to retain a part of his negotiating margin, or equal to the level of his minumum negotiating objective, below which he will not reduce.

The success probability to the supplier of (HB) (HB) should not be less than that of (QK) (QK), since he is willing in the ultimate to drop to the level of his minimum negotiating objective.

Therefore the expected value to the supplier of (HB) (HB) will not be less than that of (OK) (OK).

Axiom
The supplier must always prefer the outcome (HB) (QK) to (QK) (HB) or be indifferent between them.

Proof
The conditional value of outcome (HB) (QK) will always be greater than (QK) (HB) since it contains a negotiating margin which, by definition of the purchaser's strategy as (QK), the supplier must retain. The success probability of (QK) (HB) must always be lower than that of (HB) (QK) since, by definition, the purchaser has chosen to negotiate and the supplier has no negotiating margin included within his price.

Therefore the expected value to the supplier of (HB) (QK) will not be less than that of (QK) (HB).

Assuming an equal probability of the purchaser adopting a QK or a

394

HB strategy, it follows that the expected value to the purchaser of a hold-back strategy must exceed that of quick kill.

EXPLANATION OF THE FIGURES IN THE MATRIX IN FIGURE 5:6

The assumed level of possible bidding and the purchaser's corresponding utility values are as shown in Figure A:1.

Price level	Utility value	Comment
95	10	Lowest price foreseen after allowing maximum discount possible
97.5	9	
100	8	Lowest price foreseen on a straight competitive bid, no negotiation
105	5	Higher competitive bid price.
110	1	Highest price foreseen either on a quick-kill bid or with the inclusion of a negotiating margin

Figure A:1 Bid price and utility values

Party's strategy quick kill		*Value*
All quick kill	One of the bidders will submit an offer at the assumed minimum acceptable level of 100	8
Majority quick kill	Probability that the original quick-kill bidder will still submit a low bid =0.66. Probability that a bid at 105 will now be low = 0.33. Therefore EV= $(8 \times 0.66) + (5 \times 0.33) = 7$.	7
All hold back	The previous low bidder will add a negotiating margin of 10%.	1
Majority hold back	Probability that the previous low bidder has submitted a quick-kill bid = 0.33. Probability that the previous next to low bidder has submitted a quick-kill bid = 0.33 Probability that the original high bidder has submitted a quick-kill bid = 0.33. Therefore EV = $(8 \times 0.33) + (5 \times 0.33) + (1 \times 0.33) = 4.7$ (rounded in Figure 5:6 to 4.5).	4.5

Party's strategy hold back

All quick kill

Probability that the low bidder would grant a 5% discount = 0.1.
Probability that the low bidder would grant a discount of 2½% = 0.25.
Probability that the low bidder will refuse to grant any discount = 0.6. This also allows for the case that the next to lowest bidder would allow a discount sufficient to equate his bid with the lowest bidder. Therefore expected value = $(10 \times 0.15) + (9 \times 0.25) + (8 \times 0.6) =$ 8.8 rounded to   9

Majority quick kill

Probability that the lowest bidder will bid hold back and reduce to his minimum negotiating objective = 0.33.
Probability that the lowest bidder will bid quick kill and behave as in the above case = 0.66.
Therefore EV = $(8 \times 0.33) + (8.8 \times 0.66) = 8.44$ rounded to   8.5

All hold back

It is assumed that the lowest bidder has added a negotiating margin of 10% which is reduced in negotiation to 5%.   5

Majority hold back

Probability that the lowest bidder has bid at quick kill = 0.33 and will not reduce.
Probability that the lowest bidder has bid at hold back and will reduce to a level of 105 as suggested in the previous case = 0.66. Therefore expected value = $(5 \times 0.66) + (8 \times 0.33.) = 5.99$ rounded to   6

APPENDIX 5

ESTIMATING SUCCESS PROBABILITY IN BIDDING, TAKING ACCOUNT OF CUSTOMER'S NON-PRICE BIAS

Party, a substantial manufacturer of electronic equipment was tendering to a public authority for an important development contract. There were two other competitors, Firms X and Y. The authority was insistent that the contract should be placed on a firm price basis and the non-price factors which Party considered were of significance to the authority were:

1 Prior technical experience in that particular field.
2 Total system capability.
3 Willingness to accept the authority's terms on ownership of patent and design rights.

Party's rating of the importance of these factors to authority relative to price was:

Prior technical experience	15%
Total system capability	40%
Patent rights	25%
Price	20%

Party's assessment of himself against his competitors, assuming that he followed his normal commercial practices in relation to patent rights, is shown in Figure A:2.

	Party	Firm X	Firm Y
Prior technical experience	70	60	100
Total system capability	70	70	80
Patent rights	50	80	80

Figure A:2 Production comparison grid

On the basis that the total utility value to the authority of the best offer he was likely to receive was 100, and that of the offer which he would reject was 0, Party estimated that the authority's utility function based on the rating of the importance of the factors involved was as follows:

Price in £'000s	Utility
200	0
190	0.5
180	2
170	7
160	11
150	15
140	18
130	19
120	20

Prior technical experience	*Utility*
Complete over whole field	15
Absent in any one significant area, depending on which area	10–7
Absent in any two significant areas, depending on which areas	4–2
Absent in more than two significant areas	0
Total system capability	
Complete	40
Absent in any one significant area, depending on which area	30–20
Absent in any two significant areas, depending on which areas	15–10
Absent in more than two significant areas	
Patent rights	
Total acceptance of authority's terms	25
Willing to licence background freely on minimum royalty	20
Willing to licence on a restricted basis	10
Not willing to licence background	0

Applying these assumed utility values for the authority to Party's comparison of himself against firms X and Y, it is evident to Party that he can only be successful if X bids >£155 000 and Y bids > £175 000. Party assesses Y's probable price range as:

£'000s	Probability of a bid at that price
120	0.05
120–130	0.1
130–140	0.25
140–150	0.40
150–160	0.15
160	0.05

Therefore, if Party is to stand any chance of being successful he must alter one or more of the non-price factors in his favour. He decides he cannot in the time scale of the bid alter either technical experience or system capability and therefore the only one is the patent and design rights. If he accepts the authority's terms completely this must substantially alter the balance.

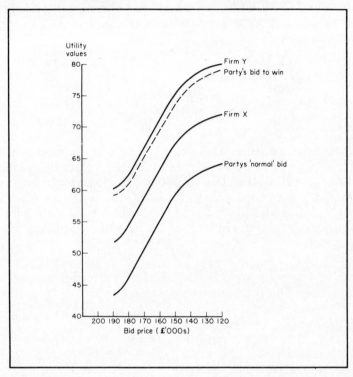

Figure A:3 Utility curves for the authority for each of Party's possible bids

The position is summarized in the graph in Figure A:3 in which the three solid lines represent the authority's utility function relative to each of the possible bid prices based on Party's comparison of himself against his two competitors. Thus, for example, Party's bid at £120 000, with his normal attitude towards patent and design rights, has a total utility value to the authority of 64, made up of the following:

Price	20
Technical experience	9
Systems capability	25
Patent rights	10
	64

In Figure A:3 the dotted line represents the amended worth to the authority of Party's bid if Party accepts completely the authority's patent clause.

Reading across the graph horizontally it can be seen which value of bid possesses for the authority the same value and, therefore, Party can estimate his success probability against firm Y if he uses the amended bid as follows:

Bid in £'000s	Chance of success
120	0.85
130	0.6
140	0.3
150	0.15

Assuming he is willing to accept the authority's patents and design right clause, Party can now estimate the utility values to himself of the bids between £120 000 and £140 000 and decide which one possesses the maximum expected value. If he is not willing to accept the authority's clause then his decision should be no bid, unless he wishes to put in a tender to avoid indicating to the authority a lack of interest in the project.

APPENDIX 6

DATA CHECKLIST

SELLING
1 Budget available to the purchaser for this purchase.
2 Time scale within which the purchaser is committed to:
   (a) Place the order
   (b) Complete the contract
3 Importance to the purchaser of the transaction financially and politically.
4 What are the key factors to the purchaser technically? These may be in terms of:
   (a) Purity of product
   (b) Yield
   (c) Facilities offered
   (d) Reliability
   (e) Standardization
   (f) Interfacing with other parts of the purchaser's system
5 Extent of the competition, with a technical and financial comparison between their offer and yours.
6 Local conditions which may affect operation of the contract:
   (a) Importation and customs regulations
   (b) Taxation
   (c) Labour laws
   (d) Safety requirements
   (e) Weather conditions
   (f) Availability of local facilities, eg servicing, materials.
7 Proposed schedule for the carrying out of the contract identifying customer activities.
8 Procedure for acceptance of the contract works.
9 Data supporting company's prices with indices showing recent changes in labour and material costs.
10 Data supporting the physical programme relating to factory output, suppliers' deliveries and productivity of field operations.
11 Identification of key personalities on the purchaser's side, their personality and allegiance, significant likes and dislikes, and their importance in the negotiations.
12 Credit facilities likely to be requested and extent towhich purchaser is considered credit worthy.

13   Reliability of your local agent.
14   Names and addresses of useful contacts.

PURCHASING
1   Supplier's current work load and future order book relative to his capacity.
2   Extent to which supplier wants to obtain the contract for prestige or other non-economic motives. Is there other business about to be negotiated?
3   How soon supplier wants to obtain the order to meet his internal objectives.
4   What are the areas in which the supplier is non-responsive to the call for bids? Although non-responsive, is his offer still acceptable?
5   What services/facilities doe the supplier demand and can these be provided to the extent and at the time required?
6   Has the supplier made maximum use of our local resources? If not, what additional areas should we propose?
7   Does the supplier's offer look out of balance in any respects? Has he 'loaded' any prices for which the quantity is likely to be increased?
8   How does the supplier's programme compare with that of other comparable works?
9   What is the prior experience of the supplier in terms of performance and reliability?
10   How does the supplier's price compare with other comparable quotations, adjusted as necessary for changes in labour and material costs.
11   How does the supplier's offer on terms and conditions compare with those which are normally obtained?
12   What assurance will there be on the future availability of spares at reasonable prices?
13   Are maintenance or operating personnel required?
14   Personalities in the supplier's team and their significant characteristics.

CONTRACT DISPUTE
1   The legal system by which the contract is governed and the tribunal which would adjudicate.
2   The validity of the contract according to that legal system.
3   The practical enforceability of the contract by legal action.
4   What performance bonds are held by the purchaser and the terms under which they can be encashed?
5   Payments currently outstanding and retention moneys held.
6   Nature of evidence relating to the dispute. Is this verbal and, if so,

standing and reliability of witnesses? If written, in what documents and are these agreed to by the other side?

7 Would an arbitrator/court be likely to hold that the evidence established a breach of contract? If so, does the contract provide any express remedy, eg penalty? If not, what would be the normal measure of damages?

8 What is the present commercial relationship between the parties? Do they contemplate a continuing relationship? If so, what importance is this to them?

9 Are there any other political or commercial pressures which either side might bring to bear?

10 What effect, if any, will non-settlement of the disputes have on the completion of the contract? If the purchaser is contemplating termination does he have any practical alternative?

11 Degree of emotional involvement of key personalities in the dispute and their personal commitment.

INDEX

Amin, Idi 369
Attitudinal tactics 347–8
  later phases 353
    changing opponent's
    assessment of success
    probability 358–62
    changing opponent's utility
    valuation 353–8
  opening phase 348–53
Auden, W.H. 12

Bacon, Sir Francis 273
Bargain conclusion
  ensuring genuineness of
    agreement 342–3
  final concession 340–1
    ensuring reciprocity 342
    magnitude 341–2
    timing 341
  final review 340
  recording bargain 343–4
Bargain identification
  focal point coordination
    334–6
  policy issues and 337–8
  power point coordination
    331–4
  signalling to opponent 328–
    31
  strategy choice and 336–7
Bargaining 38
  bargain forseeable 280–7
  bargain immediately identifi-
    able 279–80
  distributive 3
  level of initial offer relative to
    zone of 166–9

limits of zone of 145–7,
  163–6
no bargain foreseeable 287–
  91
overall bargain 174
pattern 171
process in relation to selection
  of initial demand 149–51
  compared with Cross's
  model 151–3
  See also Competitive bidding
  and Non-competitive
  bidding
Baron, R. A. and Liebert, R.
  M. 154
Bartos, O. J. 162
Bass, B. M. 196
Bayes procedure 107–8
Bid desirability 56, 60, 65, 75
  analysis 61–4
  questionnaire 61–2
Bid/no bid decision 56–61,
  68–9, 75
  analysis example 57
  determination of bid expected
    value and 68–9
  determining 59
  question of export finance
    58–9
Bid strategies
  'hold back' strategy 101,
    102, 173
  in state of uncertainty 105–
    6, 110–12
    as purchaser 109–10
    as supplier 106–9
  quick kill 101, 102

Bid Strategies *continued*
  when dominant as purchaser
    103–4
  when dominant as supplier
    102–3
  when subordinate as
    purchaser   104–5
  when subordinate as supplier
    105
Bid submission   121
Bidding   55–6
  financial resources   74
  guidelines   75
  resource employment   71–4,
    75
  success probability   56, 58,
    60, 64–8, 69–71, 128–34,
    358–62
  See also Competitive bidding
    and Non-competitive
    bidding
Bluffing   328, 330
Brand, G. T.
  *The Industrial Buying
    Decision*   355
Buyer
  considerations for   77–8,
    78–9
  in tender submarket   80

Caggiula, A. R.   162
Cattell, R. B.   375
Chertkoff, J. M. and Conley,
  M.   162
Coddington, A.   38, 151, 298
  on decision rules   26–7
Communication
  between negotiators   328–9
  form specified in negotiating
    brief   257
  need for   246, 247–8
  reasons for minimizing
    246–7, 248
  reporting back   249–50, 257
Competitive bidding   145
  assessment of concession
    factor   156–8

bargaining model in relation
  to initial demand   149–53
bargaining zone   145–7,
  163–9
effect of time on initial offer
  level   147–9
multiple opportunities
  135–7, 171–2
  interdependent   137–41
  pattern bargaining   171
  use of utility scales   141–
    4
numerical example   158–62
selection of optimal demand
  153–5
single opportunity, hold back
  or uncertainty   169–71
single opportunity, quick kill
  121–2
  computation of bid
  expected value   134–5
  conditional utility value of
    bid   122–4
  possible form of bid utility
    value   124–8
  success probability   128–
    34
  utility value of price/time of
    agreement   162–3
Consequential liability   287,
  292
Contract dispute   86, 88, 112–
  13, 177–8
  achieving negotiable objec-
    tive   181–3
  action outside contract
    116–17
  activity/resource schedule
    87
  appraisal of   94
  commercial power and   93–
    4
  determining level of initial
    offer   183–5
  exercise of legal power   90–
    2
  financial power and   92–3

Contract dispute *continued*
  intangible situation 113–16
  legal framework 88–90
  options 112
  resources and competing
    objectives 94–5
  sensitive issues 117–18
  valuation of opponent's
    negotiating objective
    178–81
  when opponents are con-
    sultants 116
Cross, J. G. 1, 5, 38, 120, 148
  bargaining theory 151–3

Decision techniques
  bidding guidelines 75
  choice under risk 15–17
  expected value 17–21
  games theory 26–39
  riskless utility 39–44
Department of Trade 58, 230
Diesing, P. 329, 330
Douglas, Ann 328
Druckmann, D. 196

ECGD 58, 59, 229, 249
Edelman, S. 69

Fairness of trade 2, 355–7
Financial resources
  in relation to contracts 74
First offer
  bidding and procurement
    101–12
  level of 120
    effect of time on 147–9
Fishing 372
  possible reactions to 372–3
Ford Motor Company
  guide to commercial equity
    355
Friedman 88

Games theory 26–39
  decision rules 26–7
  games against nature 38–9
  non-zero-sum games 32–8
  strategy choice 28
  zero-sum games 29–32
General Electric of America
  113
Goffman, I. 330

Haire, M. and Morrison, F.
  208
Harsanyi, J. C. 162
Haywood, O. G. 30

IMF 229
Interpersonal Orientation 212
  table 213–15
IUE 113

Laplace criterion 108
Lee, W. 35
Level of aspiration theory 198
Liebert, R. M., Smith, W. P.,
  Hill, J. H. and Keifer, M.
  13
Lock, D. 21
Luce, R. D. and Raiffa, H. 34,
  35, 355

Macauley, S. 91
Malaysia
  bidding in 58
Managers
  attitude to risk taking 22,
    143–4
  purchasing manager 86
Marsh, P. D. V.
  Business Ethics 58
  *Contracting for Engineering
  and Construction Projects*
  92, 116

Maslow, A. H.   16
  needs classification   191

Nash, J. F.   37, 38
  on fairness of negotiation
    355, 356
Negotiating brief   254
  covering communications and
    reporting   257
  covering minimum acceptable
    terms   256
  covering negotiating objective
    255–6
  naming negotiating team
    257
  settling time period for
    negotiations   256–7
Negotiating environment over-
    seas   225–6
  acquiring detailed knowledge
    of relevant issues   232
  checking business system
    228
  checking financial and fiscal
    system   229
  checking infra-structure and
    logistical system   229–30
  checking legal system   227–
    8
  checking political system
    226–7
  checking religion   227
  checking social system
    228–9
  fitting environmental issues
    into strategic planning
    232–3
  obtaining data   230–1
  selecting appropriate tactics
    and team   233–4
Negotiating objectives
  example of brief on   255–6
  modification   318–20
  on corporate social level   2–
    3
  on personal social level   3

  on structural or economic
    level   2
Negotiating plan
  administrative arrangements
    262–3
  definition of initial strategy
    259–60
    on receipt of offer   260
    on submission of offer
    259–60
  functions of   259
  location of negotiations
    261–2
  supporting arguments   260–
    1
  supporting data   261
Negotiating rehearsal   264
Negotiating tactics, *see* Atti-
    tudinal tactics and Situation
    tactics
Negotiating team
  advisers   237, 238
  character and composition
    235
  names in negotiating brief
    257
  role of agent   240–1
  selection   238–40
  size   235–8
  team leader   241–4, 296,
    368, 369
  visits by senior personnel
    244
Negotiation
  approach   267
  area of contract negotiation
    235
  defined   1
  objective formulation   54
  objectives   2–3, 255–6
  planning   11–14, 52–3,
    196–7, 216
  process of   11
  psychology of   190
  reaching mutually satisfying
    agreement   3–4

Negotiation *continued*
  scope and plan of present
    study 5–6
  stages enumerated 267–8
  time scales 1
  See also Opening negotiations
Negotiation categories
  bargain foreseeable
    example 285–7
    resistance points 283–5
    review of negotiating area
    280–3
  bargain immediately identifi-
    able 279–80
  no bargain foreseeable 287
    breaking off relations
    287–8
    continuing and seeking
    revised authority 288–91
    influencing opponent to
    seek revised authority
    291
Negotiation follow up 296
  influence of time limits
    306–7
    negotiating time frame-
    work 307–8
    strategic 307
  modification of negotiating
    objective 318–20
    choice of strategy 320,
    321
    making next move after
    320, 322–4
  reappraisal of opponent's
    concession factor 296–7
    dealing with irrational
    behaviour 305–6
    decision rules to adopt
    300–1
    if in accord with expecta-
    tions 297–300
    if less and/or slower than
    expected 303–5
    if more and/or faster than
    expected 301–3
  tactical effect of time 314
    extended negotiations
    316–17

    importance of decision and
    314–15
    isolation of negotiator and
    318
    natural breaks 317–18
    shortness of time 315–16
  threat strategy 308–14
Negotiators 238–9
  areas affected by psychology
    of 190
  belief pattern 206–7
    attitude towards opponents
    207–9
    attitude towards subject
    matter of contract 209–
    10
    attitude towards the
    organization 209
  communication and 246–50
  conflict and adjustment in
    motivation 205–6
  effects of need for professional
    fulfilment 203
  effects of need for security
    191–3
  effects of need for self-esteem
    by satisfying oneself
    197–203, 357
  effects of need for self-esteem
    by satisfying others 193–
    7, 333
  effects of need to know and
    understand 204–5
  focal point coordination and
    334–6
  guide to opening negotiations
    275–6
  humiliation and retaliatory
    action 200–2
  management support for
    289
  negotiating motives table
    332
  personality interaction
    between 210
    question of good inter-
    personal relationships
    210

Negotiators *continued*
   question of integrity
     211–12
   question of legitimacy of
     interest 211
   study of interpersonal
     attitudes 212–16
   power point coordination
     and 331–4
   problem of setting too low a
     target 200
   qualities needed 239
   rationalizations of 329
   security and 250–3
   time limits and 314–18
   training for 240
Neuman, J. and Morgenstern, O.
   development of games theory
     28
Non-competitive bidding
   in dominant position 172
   in subordinate position
     172–3
Non-zero-sum games 29, 32–
   3
   collaborative 36–8
   non-collaborative 33–6

Opening negotiations 269
   estimating effect of conces-
     sions 291–4
   exposing negotiating area
     274–6
   guidelines 274
   making verbal proposals only
     273–4
   reviewing 279
   submitting written proposal/
     answer with discussion
     271–2
   submitting written proposal/
     answer without discussion
     269–71
   See also Negotiation
     categories

Performance bonds 92–3
PERT network 261
Peters, E. 155
Planning process 11–14
   effect of psychology of
     negotiation on 216
   steps in 12–13, 52–3
   value of 196–7
   See also Negotiating plan
Prejudices 208–9
Probability assessments 20–1
Procurement 75–7, 173–4
   competing objectives and
     resource requirement/
     availability 84–6
   cost/time evaluation 82,
     83–4
   demand 77–8
   market nature and 76, 77
   negotiation with multiple
     suppliers 177
   negotiation with single
     supplier 174–5
   network for action 81
   overall bargain 174
   supply 78–80
   tender submarket 80
   ultimate use 80–4
Pruitt, D. G. 22
   and Drew, J. L. 147
   and Johnson, D. F. 147
Purchase price analysis (PPA)
   82

Qu'ran 2

Resources employment
   at contract stage 72–4
   on bidding 71–2
Risk
   choice under 15–17
   utility under 21–6
Riskless utility 39–40
   domination and conflict
     43–4